FE 884

Grammar and Writing

AUTHORS AND ADVISERS

Walter Loban
General Adviser
Professor of Education
University of California at Berkeley

Donald C. Freeman
Specialist, Linguistics
Temple University
Philadelphia, Pennsylvania

Robert W. Reising
Specialist, Grammar and
    Composition
Pembroke State University
Pembroke, North Carolina

James Harkness
Specialist, Libraries and
    Information
State University of New York
Albany, New York

Patricia Laurence
Specialist, Composition
The City College, C.U.N.Y.
New York, New York

Vicki Jacobs
Specialist, Vocabulary
Holbrook Public Schools
Holbrook, Massachusetts

Norman Rudnick
Specialist, Argumentation
    and Logic
Miramonte High School
Orinda, California

Robert J. Jones
Specialist, Test Taking
Educational Testing Service
Princeton, New Jersey

Sandra Stotsky
Specialist, Vocabulary
Curry College
Milton, Massachusetts

Norman Unrau
Specialist, Argumentation
    and Logic
Miramonte High School
Orinda, California

CONSULTANTS

Martha Brooks, Abilene Independent School District, Abilene, Texas
Leslie MacIntyre, Homestead High School, Mequon, Wisconsin
Henry F. Mooney, Danvers Public Schools, Danvers, Massachusetts
Norman Rudnick, Miramonte High School, Orinda, California
Milton Schaeffer, Maplewood-South Orange School District, New Jersey
Mary Jo Wagner, Leland High School, San Jose, California

Grammar and Writing

Macmillan Publishing Co., Inc.
New York
Collier Macmillan Publishers
London

WALTER LOBAN, General Adviser, has been active in English education for many years. Among his scholarly publications in the area of language is *Teaching Language and Literature: Grades 7–12*, of which he is co-author. Dr. Loban's landmark study *Language Development: Kindergarten Through Grade 12* (NCTE: 1976) has provided unique and valuable information about the acquisition of syntactic elements by student writers.

DONALD C. FREEMAN, who is special adviser on grammar, is professor of English and chairman of the committee on linguistics at Temple University, Philadelphia. His examination of student writing has made him a leader in error analysis.

ROBERT W. REISING, who is adviser on grammar and composition, is professor of communicative arts at Pembroke State University, Pembroke, North Carolina. He has led workshops in English, most recently at the University of North Carolina at Charlotte.

PATRICIA LAURENCE, who is adviser on composition, teaches basic writing, literature, and linguistics at The City College of the City University of New York.

SANDRA STOTSKY, who developed the vocabulary section, is associated with Curry College, Milton, Massachusetts, and Harvard University. She works extensively with teachers in the Holbrook and Boston public schools.

1983 Printing

Macmillan Publishing Co., Inc.
866 Third Avenue, New York, New York 10022
Collier Macmillan Canada, Inc.

Printed in the United States of America
Student Edition ISBN 0-02-245950-2
Teacher's Edition ISBN 0-02-245960-X
987654

ACKNOWLEDGMENTS

Grateful acknowledgment is given authors and publishers for permission to reprint the following material:

We are indebted to Mary S. Lawrence for significant contributions in the form of ideas and exercises that appear in Section 11 of this text. This material is from *Writing As a Thinking Process* by Mary S. Lawrence, published by the University of Michigan Press, copyright © by The University of Michigan 1972.

The American Heritage Dictionary of the English Language. Copyright © 1979 by Houghton Mifflin Company. Selections reprinted by permission of the publisher.

The Andromeda Strain by Michael Crichton. Copyright © 1969 by Centesis Corporation. Selection reprinted by permission of Alfred A. Knopf, Inc.

Biological Science, Revised Edition, by William H. Gregory and Edward H. Goldman. © Copyright 1971, 1965 by Ginn and Company (Xerox Corporation). Selections reprinted by permission of the publisher.

HM Study Skills Program, Level II. Copyright © 1979, by NASSP, 1904 Association Drive, Reston, Va. 22091. All Rights Reserved. Selections reprinted by permission of the publisher.

Macmillan Dictionary, William D. Halsey, Editorial Director. Copyright © 1977, 1973 by Macmillan Publishing Co., Inc. Selections reprinted by permission of the publisher.

"The Making of Walt Disney World" by Randy Melick. Reprinted by permission of the author.

Of Mice and Men by John Steinbeck. Copyright © 1937, 1965 by John Steinbeck. Reprinted by permission of Viking Press Inc. and by permission of William Heinemann Ltd. and McIntosh and Otis.

"New Generation of Elevators" by Peter J. Schuyten. © 1980 by The New York Times Company. Selection adapted and reprinted by permission of the publisher.

Readers' Guide to Periodical Literature. Copyright © 1979 by The H. W. Wilson Company. Material reproduced by permission of the publisher.

Webster's New Collegiate Dictionary. Copyright © 1980 by G. & C. Merriam Co., Publishers of the Merriam-Webster Dictionaries. Selections on pages 317 and 321 reprinted by permission of the publisher.

Webster's New World Dictionary, Second College Edition. Copyright © 1978 by William Collins + World Publishing Co., Inc. Selections reprinted by permission of the publisher.

Webster's Third New International Dictionary. Copyright © 1976 by G. & C. Merriam Co., Publishers of the Merriam-Webster Dictionaries. Selection on page 316 reprinted by permission of the publisher.

Courtesy acknowledgment is given authors and publishers for the use of passages from the following sources:

Introduction to "Conversations with a Gorilla" by Francis Patterson from *National Geographic*, October, 1978. (Appears on page 11.)

Introductory Foods by Marion Bennon and Osee Hughes, Macmillan Publishing Company, 1975. (Appears on pages 630–631.)

The Pageant of World History by Gerald Leinwald, Allyn and Bacon, Inc., 1977. (Appears on page 632.)

"Vanished Washington and Its 'Capital Losses.' " by James M. Goode from *Smithsonian*, December, 1979. (Appears on page 451.)

CONTENTS

Grammar, Usage, and Sentences

Word Study

Writing Aids

1

PARTS OF SPEECH

Parts of Speech

You can classify, or group, the parts of language in several different ways. You can classify words according to meaning. For instance, you can group together words that refer to what animals do (*bark, growl, meow*) or to the parts of a tree (*leaf, root, bark*). Notice that the word *bark* is included in both of the preceding groups.

Another very useful way of classifying words is by how they are used in a sentence—that is, by their *part of speech*. You should keep in mind, though, that the same word can be two or three different parts of speech, depending upon how it is used in a sentence. The word *bark*, for example, can be used as either a noun or as a verb.

The parts of speech include nouns, verbs, adjectives, pronouns, adverbs, prepositions, conjunctions, and interjections. This section examines what the various parts of speech contribute to the spoken or written sentence. It also examines other words called verbals, which are important in their own right. Then Section 2 shows how the parts of speech work in different parts of the *sentence*.

1.a NOUNS

A **noun** is a word that names a person, place, thing, or idea.

The words *secretary* and *athlete*, for example, are both nouns naming persons. *City* and *sea* are nouns that name places. Some nouns that name things are *antelop* and *spoon*, while *happiness* and *beauty* are nouns that name ideas. As you can see from the following examples, nouns name all kinds of things:

EXAMPLES

PERSON: pioneer, employee, governor, clown, barber
ANIMAL: caterpillar, pet, frog, goose, mammal, salmon
OBJECT: clock, slipper, tulip, meteor, tray, sandal
PLACE: coast, corner, city, forest, nation, edge
GROUP: family, bunch, company, class, crowd, squad
ACTION: a fall, an earthquake, an explosion, a sneeze
TIME: youth, the future, night, moment, infancy, noon
EVENT: meeting, wedding, trial, game, holiday
IDEA OR QUALITY: democracy, fame, heat, softness, calm, disappointment

EXERCISE 1. Match each group of three nouns with one of the lettered categories below.

1. *parade, marathon, meeting*
2. *peanut, vitamin, pin*
3. *kick, journey, movement*
4. *dragon, squirrel, worm*
5. *lace, chair, clock*
6. *turn, jump, walk*
7. *community, herd, committee*
8. *harvest, sermon, funeral*
9. *eternity, midnight, weekend*
10. *romance, wealth, fear*
11. *mother, athlete, musician*
12. *neck, tire, helicopter*
13. *harbor, outdoors, house*
14. *success, beauty, paleness*
15. *duchess, hero, winner*
16. *tiger, mouse, reptile*
17. *past, summer, tomorrow*
18. *election, sale, concert*
19. *library, upstairs, cafeteria*
20. *carrot, finger, door*

a. person
b. animal
c. object
d. place
e. group
f. action
g. time
h. event
i. idea or quality

APPLICATION. Select five groups of nouns from Exercise 1. For each group write one sentence using all three nouns. Be sure that each of the words is used as a noun in your sentence.

EXAMPLE   1. *parade, marathon, meeting*

ANSWER   *During the* **meeting** *I daydreamed about runners in a* **marathon** *colliding with a* **parade.**

1.a.1 Proper nouns and common nouns

There are two kinds of nouns: common nouns and proper nouns. The *general* names for things and people are **common nouns**. They include all the nouns covered so far in this chapter. For example, words like *monument, governor,* and *nation* are common nouns. The names of *specific* things are called **proper nouns**. *Statue of Liberty, Ella Grasso,* and *Egypt* are proper nouns. Your own name refers to you in particular and is a proper noun.

Proper nouns are capitalized. Common nouns are not usually capitalized. (For more information on capitalization of proper nouns, see 7.a.4.)

EXAMPLES

PERSON: Cleopatra, Marilyn Horne, Larry, Kate, Prince Charles

ANIMAL: Black Beauty, Winnie the Pooh, Secretariat

OBJECT: the Bible, Statue of Liberty, *Star Wars,* the Astrodome

PLACE: Mediterranean Sea, Mexico, Milky Way

GROUP: the Beatles, the United Nations, Sierra Club

TIME: Thursday, April, the Middle Ages, Halloween

EVENT: the Boston Marathon, the Rose Bowl, World War I

IDEA OR QUALITY: Judaism, Buddhism

EXERCISE 2. Match the lettered common noun in the right column with its corresponding proper noun in the left column.

1. Rockies	a. automobile
2. Cleopatra	b. religion
3. Lassie	c. queen
4. Michelangelo	d. university
5. Harvard	e. painter
6. Catholicism	f. dog
7. Halloween	g. mountains
8. *Wall Street Journal*	h. holiday
9. Chevrolet	i. newspaper
10. Canada	j. country

1.a.2 Compound nouns

A noun that is made up of more than one word is called a **compound noun**. Three kinds of compound nouns exist: those written as one word (*football*), those written as two or more words (*ice cream*), and those written as two or more words connected by hyphens (president-elect).

EXAMPLES

aircraft	air conditioning	self-defense
headache	shopping center	hand-me-down

EXERCISE 3. For each category below, list four common nouns and one proper noun. You may invent proper nouns if you wish. Try to use several compound nouns.

EXAMPLE nouns that have leaves—for example, *book*
ANSWER common nouns: *magazine, tree, rosebush, table*
proper noun: *Newsweek*

1. nouns you can bake—for example, *bread*
2. nouns you can open—for example, *jar*
3. nouns on which you can write—for example, *chalkboard*
4. nouns you might pack for a trip—for example, *toothbrush*
5. nouns you can hang on the wall—for example, *bulletin board*
6. nouns you can draw with—for example, *chalk*

7. nouns that fly—for example, *seagull*
8. nouns you can wear—for example, *pants*
9. nouns you can eat with a spoon—for example, *cereal*
10. nouns you can climb—for example, *stairs*

APPLICATION. Look again at the four common nouns and one proper noun that you listed for *one* of the items in Exercise 3. Write *one* sentence that uses all five nouns.

> EXAMPLE 10.   stairs, Stratton Mountain, hills, slopes, bunks
>
> ANSWER   *Climbing the **stairs** brought us to the ski lift that led to the top of **Stratton Mountain**; after skiing down many **hills** we left the **slopes** and jumped into our **bunks**, exhausted.*

1.a.3 Singular nouns and plural nouns

Most nouns can take either a singular or plural form. *Singular* means "one"; a **singular noun** names one person, place, thing, or idea. *Plural* means "more than one"; a **plural noun** names more than one person, place, thing, or idea.

EXAMPLES

Singular nouns	Plural nouns
evening	evenings
movie	movies
friend	friends
bus	buses
star	stars

Singular nouns that end in *s* or *es* may look and sound plural. They are singular, however, because they name only one thing.

SINGULAR NOUNS THAT END IN S

comics	mathematics
phonics	rabies

For most nouns, add s.	**For nouns ending in s, x, z, sh, ch, add es.**	**For nouns ending in y preceded by a consonant, change the y to i and add es.**
path, paths squirrel, squirrels fence, fences	gas, gases lynx, lynxes topaz, topazes bush, bushes patch, patches	cranny, crannies puppy, puppies sky, skies

For nouns ending in y preceded by a vowel, add s.	**For most nouns ending in f or fe, add s.**	**For some nouns ending in f or fe, change the f or fe to v and add es.**
toy, toys chimney, chimneys	belief, beliefs fife, fifes	thief, thieves wife, wives

For most nouns ending in o preceded by a consonant, add es.	**For nouns ending in o preceded by a vowel, add s.**	**For some irregular nouns, learn the special plurals.**
potato, potatoes veto, vetoes	trio, trios bamboo, bamboos	ox, **oxen** foot, **feet** tooth, **teeth** mouse, **mice**

For some nouns, the plural form is the same as the singular.	**For compound nouns written as one word, follow the preceding rules. If the compound is hyphenated or written as separate words, make the most important part of the compound plural.**	**For most proper nouns, add s. Add es to proper nouns that end in s, x, z, sh, ch.**

fowl, **fowl**
bison, **bison**
moose, **moose**
haddock, **haddock**
	baseball, baseballs
	box office, box offices
	go-between, go-betweens
	lily of the valley, lilies of
	  the valley
	passer-by, passers-by
		Shelby, Shelbys
		Moss, Mosses
		Essex, Essexes
		Gomez,
		  Gomezes
		Cash, Cashes
		Fitch, Fitches

EXERCISE 4. The italicized words in the following sentences are singular nouns. Rewrite each sentence, giving the plural form of each italicized noun.

> EXAMPLE The *carpenter* must know different woods.
> ANSWER *The **carpenters** must know different woods.*

1. Very hard lumber comes from the *hickory*.
2. Boards from *ash* are too hard to nail when dry.
3. Build your *pantry* from black walnut.
4. The *lumber yard* can season boards either by air drying or by kiln drying.
5. Make sure you have a place for everything in your *workbench*.
6. Keep the *chisel* sharp.
7. Sharpen the *saw* with a file.
8. Sharpen the *knife* on a grindstone.
9. The *adz* would not be useful for chopping firewood.
10. The *jack-of-all-trades* should excel in carpentry.

EXERCISE 5. The italicized words in the following phrases are singular nouns. For each phrase replace the word *one* with *two*. After *two* write the plural form.

> EXAMPLE one elf
> ANSWER *two elves*

1. one *Halloween*
2. one *tomato*
3. one *son-in-law*
4. one *costume party*
5. one *woman*
6. one *witch*
7. one *fortuneteller*
8. one *editor in chief*
9. one *passer-by*
10. one *monkey*
11. one *brick*
12. one *wolf*
13. one *mummy*
14. one *moose*
15. one *shriek*
16. one *goblin*
17. one *clue*
18. one *alibi*
19. one *detective*
20. one *radio*

APPLICATION. Select five nouns from Exercise 5. For each noun write *one* sentence that uses *both* the singular and the plural forms of the noun.

1.a.4 Collective nouns

A **collective noun** names a group of people or things.

EXAMPLES

the class	the fleet (of ships)
the faculty	the range (of mountains)
the team	the swarm (of insects)
the public	the flock (of birds)

You can make collective nouns either singular or plural, depending on the meaning you want. When you talk about a group as a whole, you should consider the collective noun singular.

HINT: Most collective nouns are used as singular nouns. There is a clue you can use to help determine whether a collective noun is singular. Substitute the word *it* for the collective noun in the sentence. If *it* can be substituted, the collective noun is singular.

SINGULAR COLLECTIVE NOUNS

The **cast** included a small chorus.
It included a small chorus.

The **chorus** is a well-trained group.
It is a well-trained group.

When you talk about individual members of a group, you should consider the collective noun plural.

HINT: If you can substitute *they* or *them* for the collective noun in the sentence, the collective noun is plural.

PLURAL COLLECTIVE NOUNS

The **cast** stay at different hotels.
They stay at different hotels.

The **chorus** compete for important roles.
They compete for important roles.

EXERCISE 6. There are ten collective nouns in the following paragraph. Identify each collective noun.

¹At five o'clock in the morning, the population of a small Vermont farmhouse is active. ²Soon after the family wakes up, a batch of breakfast rolls is already in the oven. ³The dairy staff assembles the milking tools. ⁴As her half-grown litter scamper at her heels, the collie runs out to round up the cows. ⁵The herd is restless. ⁶A flock of hens surround the rooster. ⁷A swarm of bees hum softly in the hive, waiting for the sun to dry the dew. ⁸The approaching whine of a truck signals the arrival of the crew who thresh the wheat. ⁹A range of the Green Mountains is pink and gray in the morning light.

1.a.5 The possessive form of nouns

The **possessive form** of a noun can show either possession (ownership) or the relationship between two nouns.

POSSESSIVE USE	ALTERNATE USE
a week's pay	pay received for a week
the accountant's office	the office where the accountant works
Beethoven's *Fifth Symphony*	the *Fifth Symphony* written by Beethoven

See 5.b.6 and 7.k.1 for a summary of the rules for making the possessive forms of nouns.

EXERCISE 7. Each of the following quotations contains an italicized phrase. Rewrite each quotation, changing the italicized phrase to an expression with a possessive noun. Study the example first.

EXAMPLE Sunday is the *seventh day of the week*.

ANSWER *Sunday is the **week's seventh day***.

1. All *the ills of democracy* can be cured by more democracy.—Alfred E. Smith
2. *The history of every country* begins in the heart of a man or a woman.—Willa Cather

3. You can tell *the ideals of a nation* by its advertisements.
—Norman Douglas
4. Beauty is in the *eye of the beholder*.—Margaret Hungerford

---

AVOIDING ERRORS WITH NOUNS

1. Remember to change a singular noun to its plural form when you mean "more than one."

NOT   two ~~thumb~~   many ~~hand~~
BUT   two thumb**s**   many hand**s**

2. Do not confuse the possessive form *'s* with the plural forms *s* and *es*. Do not use an apostrophe with a noun when you mean "more than one."

NOT   February has twenty-nine ~~day's~~ every fourth year.
BUT   February has twenty-nine day**s** every fourth year.

REVIEW EXERCISE A. Identify each of the twenty-five nouns in the following paragraph, and indicate whether each noun is a common noun or a proper noun. Then go back over the list of nouns, and indicate whether each is a singular noun or a plural noun.

During the past decade researchers have successfully taught several chimpanzees to converse with signs. In a project partly funded by the National Geographic Society, Koko is the first gorilla to achieve an impressive vocabulary. After six years of study, she has a working vocabulary of about 375 signs, including *airplane, belly button, lollipop, friend,* and *stethoscope.* Koko responds to and asks questions, tells when she feels happy or sad, refers to past and future events, and has begun to give definitions for objects. She also shows an impish sense of humor.

1.b VERBS

A **verb** is a word that expresses action or that helps to make a statement.

Sentences do not really have meaning without verbs. The two main kinds of verbs are action verbs and linking verbs.

Action verbs tell what someone or something *does*. **Linking verbs** tell that someone or something *is*, not what someone or something *does*.

EXAMPLES

Action verbs	Linking verbs
Carpenters **build** houses.	Carpenters **are** helpful.
Hammers **drive** nails.	Hammers **seem** heavy.

EXERCISE 8. From the parentheses, select the action verb, which completes the sentence.

1. Many foreign plants and animals _____ in Florida. (thrive, lake)

2. Most of these foreign plants and animals _____ in freighters or in someone's luggage. (arrive, article)

3. Fifty varieties of foreign animals _____ in Florida. (response, reside)

4. Siamese walking catfish _____ out of Florida canals. (alligator, crawl)

5. The Asian weed hydrillas _____ Florida waterways. (choke, speech)

6. In southern Florida, Colombian iguanas _____ through Australian pines. (book, scamper)

7. Left over from Tarzan films, rhesus monkeys _____ tourists to Silver Springs. (attract, action)

8. Florida's lakes and canals _____ with some thirty different species of foreign tropical fish. (topic, teem)

9. The fierce South American pirahnas sometimes _____ from tropical fish dealers. (escape, expert)

10. Cuban tree frogs _____ insects harmful to citrus trees. (consume, cobra)

EXERCISE 9. Indicate which of the following words can be action verbs. Remember that an action verb tells what someone or something does.

1. scatter	8. dribble	15. nomad
2. tree	9. amble	16. glue
3. wallop	10. stalk	17. misplace
4. whether	11. her	18. surround
5. awkward	12. weary	19. freedom
6. glide	13. surprise	20. protect
7. graceful	14. hide	

APPLICATION. Select five of the action verbs that you identified in Exercise 9. Use each one in a sentence.

1.b.1 Action verbs: physical and mental

Some action verbs express physical movement.

EXAMPLES
Ballet dancers **pirouette**.
Folk dancers **swing** their partners.
Choreographers **describe** new dances.
Folk dance callers **announce** new steps.

Some action verbs express the actions of the mind.

EXAMPLES
Ballet dancers **desire** fame.
Folk dancers **prefer** fast music.

1.b.2 Transitive and intransitive verbs

A **transitive verb** is an action verb that is followed by a word that answers the question *what?* or *whom?* The word that follows the action verb and that answers the question *what?* or *whom?* is called the direct object (see 2.j).

TRANSITIVE VERBS

Lapidarians **cut** gems. [action verb + word that answers the question *cut what?*]

Jewelers **buy** diamonds. [action verb + word that answers the question *buy what?*]

An **intransitive verb** is an action verb that does not take a direct object. An intransitive verb is not followed by a word that answers the question *what?* or *whom?* If a verb is followed by a word that tells *how* or *where* or *when* an action takes place, it is an intransitive verb.

INTRANSITIVE VERBS

Diamond miners **dig**. [action verb alone]

Diamond miners **dig** in the earth. [action verb + words that tell *where*]

Many action verbs, like *dig* and *split*, can be either transitive verbs or intransitive verbs. Remember that if it takes a direct object, a verb is transitive; if it does *not* take a direct object, a verb is *in*transitive.

EXAMPLES

Lapidarians **split** diamonds. [The verb *split* takes the direct object *diamonds*; therefore, it is transitive.]

Diamonds **split** easily. [The verb *split* has no direct object; therefore, it is intransitive.]

EXERCISE 10. Identify the transitive verb and its direct object in each of the following sentences.

1. In New York City thousands of commuters ride trains.
2. Texas ranchers drive trucks across the plains.
3. Construction companies pave parking lots for cars.
4. Buses in downtown Seattle give free rides to shoppers.
5. Elevators carry miners below ground.
6. In some cities, express buses transport commuters.
7. Tankers carry oil across the sea.
8. Car pools reduce highway traffic at rush hours.
9. Ferries cross San Francisco Bay every morning.
10. Some small airlines operate commuter flights.

EXERCISE 11. Identify the action verb in each of the following sentences. Tell whether each action verb is a transitive verb or an intransitive verb.

1. Shipping containers and telephone poles require huge quantities of lumber.
2. Pulp mills devour tons of softwood trees.
3. Americans consume 30 percent of the world's industrial wood.
4. Of course, residential buildings take much lumber.
5. Fortunately, America possesses vast timber resources.
6. Many timber camps develop in southern Alaska.
7. Many Alaskan loggers live at sea.
8. Redwoods from California travel to Japan and Korea.
9. Western forests produce more wood than eastern forests.
10. People can replace timber supplies, but not oil resources.

1.b.3 *Be:* a linking verb

The most common and familiar linking verb is the verb *be*. Remember that **linking verbs** tell that someone or something *is*, and they are always followed by words that answer the question *what?*, *who?*, or *where?*

The common forms of *be* include *am, is, are, was, were, be, being, been.*

EXAMPLES
A symphony **is** a work for musical instruments.
The plots of operas **are** often curious.
Aaron Copland **was** an American composer.

1.b.4 Other linking verbs

There are a number of other linking verbs besides *be*. Like *be*, they link one word or group of words to another word or group of words that describes the first. Some of these other linking verbs are listed on the next page.

EXAMPLES

LOOK: Opera singers **look** impressive in costumes. [*Impressive* describes *singers*.]

GROW: Opera buffs **grow** enthusiastic about favorite singers. [*Enthusiastic* describes *buffs*.]

FEEL: Soloists **feel** grateful for applause. [*Grateful* describes *soloists*.]

APPEAR: Tenors **appear** sad in many operas. [*Sad* describes *tenors*.]

REMAIN: Audiences **remain** quiet throughout George Gershwin's opera *Porgy and Bess*. [*Quiet* describes *audiences*.]

SEEM: Ballet dancers **seem** energetic during rehearsal. [*Energetic* describes *dancers*.]

SOUND: Sopranos **sound** happy in parts of *Porgy and Bess*. [*Happy* describes *sopranos*.]

STAY: Opera broadcasts **stay** popular on radio. [*Popular* describes *broadcasts*.]

EXERCISE 12. Identify the linking verb in each of the following sentences.

1. Experienced swimmers sometimes grow careless.
2. Only careful swimmers remain safe.
3. Solitary swimmers are not really sensible.
4. Dangerous lakes often look harmless.
5. Some lake waters seem icy and deep.
6. In the hot sun some beach bathers stay under umbrellas.
7. Even strong swimmers become tired.
8. Lifeguards always appear alert.
9. Small ponds are frequently muddy and weedy.
10. Some water plants feel like rubber.

1.b.5 Linking verb or action verb?

All linking verbs except *be* and *seem* can also be used as action verbs. The following pairs of sentences show the same word used first as a linking verb and then as an action verb:

EXAMPLES

LINKING: Many outdoor statues **remain** undamaged for centuries.

ACTION: The huge sculptures of Louise Nevelson **remain** on display all over the country.

LINKING: The portrait paintings by Andrew Wyeth **appear** lifelike.

ACTION: Paintings of the desert by Georgia O'Keeffe occasionally **appear** at auctions.

LINKING: Tape recordings of museum tours **sound** informative.

ACTION: Most museums **sound** a bell at closing time.

EXERCISE 13. Find the verb in each sentence in each pair. Indicate if it is a linking verb or an action verb.

1. a) Many statues look best in an open area.
   b) Art lovers look at statues from all angles.
2. a) Gardeners grow spectacular roses at Longwood Gardens in Pennsylvania.
   b) Museum guards grow impatient with misbehavior.
3. a) Art critics feel skeptical about the authenticity of certain paintings.
   b) Children feel the texture of the famous statue of Alice in Wonderland in New York City.
4. a) Many museums stay open on Sundays.
   b) Traveling exhibits stay at each museum a limited amount of time.

1.b.6 Agreement in number

A verb, action or linking, must **agree in number** with the person or thing that it is talking about (its **subject**).

Except for the verb *be*, agreement in number is an issue only in the present tense and only with a singular third-person subject. You have to add -*s* or -*es* to the basic form of the verb in the present tense with a **singular** third-person subject. With a **plural** third-person subject, do not add -*s* or -*es* to the verb. (See 1.b.13.)

HINT: Here is a way to remember when to add -*s* or -*es* for present-tense verbs: In general, an *s* appears on the noun *or* on the verb—but not on both.

One ostrich move**s**.   Two ostriche**s** move.

EXERCISE 14. Twenty words in the following paragraphs end in *s*. Some are plural nouns (review 1.a.3). Some are present-tense verbs that agree in number with third-person singular nouns or pronouns. Copy the passage. Write *n* above each noun that ends in *s*. Write *v* above each verb that ends in *s*.

¹Styles in fashion go in circles. ²The all-American prep school look often returns to replace less-tailored costumes. ³Tired of crinkled clothes, a woman changes and turns to oxford-cloth shirts and shetland sweaters. ⁴A navy blazer often completes the look.

⁵The blazer appears in male wardrobes too, of course. ⁶A man examines and buys regimental ties to make sure he conveys the classic look. ⁷He wants to appear in vogue and scans newspaper advertisements so that he shops intelligently and economically.

1.b.7 Principal parts of verbs

All verbs have four forms, called **principal parts**. All tenses of verbs and all verb phrases are formed by using these principal parts, either alone or with other words. The principal parts of some common verbs are listed below.

PRINCIPAL PARTS OF VERBS

Basic verb	Present participle	Past tense	Past participle
chew	chewing	chewed	chewed
eat	eating	ate	eaten
smile	smiling	smiled	smiled
be	being	was/were	been
bite	biting	bit	bitten

1.b.8 Regular verbs

The two groups of verbs, regular verbs and irregular verbs, are distinguished by the ways they form their past tense and past participle.

If the past tense and past participle of a verb both end in -ed, it is called a **regular verb**. Most verbs are regular verbs.

1.b.9 Irregular verbs

An **irregular verb** is a verb that does not form its past tense and past participle by adding -ed to the basic verb. The past tense and past participle of irregular verbs are not formed in any regular way. Sometimes the past tense and past participle are the same (won and won), sometimes they are the same as the basic form of the verb (burst and burst), and sometimes the two forms are different (rode and ridden). Since there are no rules for forming irregular verbs, you must memorize the forms to use them correctly.

COMMON IRREGULAR VERBS

Basic verb	Past tense	Past participle
be	was, were	been
beat	beat	beaten or beat
become	became	become
begin	began	begun
bite	bit	bitten
blow	blew	blown
bring	brought	brought
burst	burst	burst
catch	caught	caught
choose	chose	chosen
come	came	come
creep	crept	crept
dive	dived or dove	dived
do	did	done
draw	drew	drawn

Basic verb	Past tense	Past participle
drink	drank	drunk
drive	drove	driven
eat	ate	eaten
fall	fell	fallen
feel	felt	felt
fly	flew	flown
freeze	froze	frozen
get	got	got *or* gotten
give	gave	given
go	went	gone
grow	grew	grown
hang	hanged *or* hung	hanged *or* hung
have	had	had
know	knew	known
lend	lent	lent
lose	lost	lost
put	put	put
ride	rode	ridden
rise	rose	risen
run	ran	run
see	saw	seen
shake	shook	shaken
sing	sang	sung
speak	spoke	spoken
steal	stole	stolen
swim	swam	swum
take	took	taken
tear	tore	torn
think	thought	thought
throw	threw	thrown
wear	wore	worn
win	won	won
write	wrote	written

EXERCISE 15. In order to practice using the principal parts of both regular and irregular verbs, use the appropriate forms of each of the following ten basic verbs in the following sentence:

You are _____ today, and you _____ yesterday,
     present participle   past tense

    but I have _____ for years.
        past participle

EXAMPLE basic verb   = worry

ANSWER   _You are **worrying** today, and you **worried** yesterday, but I have **worried** for years._

1. smile	6. lose
2. drive	7. shake
3. fly	8. think
4. freeze	9. throw
5. grow	10. write

1.b.10 Auxiliary verbs

Auxiliary verbs are used with present participles or past participles of verbs to help form certain verb tenses and to help express continuing action. Auxiliary verbs are also called helping verbs.

An auxiliary verb and a participle together form a **verb phrase**. The only auxiliary, or helping, verbs are the forms of _be_ and _have_. The auxiliary _have_ and the auxiliary _be_ can be used together.

EXAMPLES
I **am** listening.
I **was** listening.
I **have** listened.
I **had** listened.
I **have been** listening.
I **had been** listening.

Remember that the auxiliary _have_ and the auxiliary _be_ must agree in number with the person or thing that you are talking about.

SINGULAR
A child **is** laughing.
My aunt **has** arrived.

PLURAL
The children **are** arguing.
My cousins **have** arrived.

1.b.11 Modals

Modals act like auxiliary verbs. They are used to form questions and to help make an expression negative. Modals also help to show emphasis, possibility, obligation, and condition.

With the exception of *do*, every modal can be used either (1) before a basic verb or (2) before the auxiliary verbs *have* and *be*. The modal, the auxiliary, and the basic verb together form a **verb phrase**.

MODALS

do, does, did

To form a question: **Do** they believe?

To make an expression negative: She **does** not believe.

To show emphasis: He **did** believe.

can, could	He **can** type.
may, might	He **may/might** type his paper.
must	You **must** clear your desk.
will, shall	They **will** leave today.
would	I **would** go if I had the time.
should, ought to	You **should/ought to** do your homework.

EXERCISE 16. Identify the verb phrase in each of the following sentences. Remember that a verb phrase is made up of an auxiliary verb or modal plus a form of an action verb or linking verb. In one sentence the two parts of the verb phrase are separated.

1. You can use just one hand in many electronic games.
2. In some electronic baseball games you are always batting against the computer's pitches.
3. In one baseball game you might stretch a double into a triple.
4. You could turn a single into a tag-out at second base.
5. You probably ought to try several different games at the store.

6. Some electronic football games will play you against the computer.

7. In some games you can change plays even at the line of scrimmage.

8. People with spelling problems should consider an electronic spelling game.

9. This game would entertain you with taped human voices.

10. An electronic word game can challenge two players at once.

APPLICATION. Choose five of the verb phrases that you identified in Exercise 16, and write an original sentence for each.

EXERCISE 17. In the following sentences the two parts of each verb phrase are separated by at least one word. Identify both parts of each verb phrase.

1. According to Hoyle, young card players should immediately adopt card table etiquette.

2. The classic source of card game rules, Hoyle's book should still be useful.

3. According to Hoyle, you should always sit straight and still at the table.

4. A smooth shuffle might indeed require practice.

5. In an expert shuffle the two halves of the deck will thoroughly mesh.

6. You should never look at the bottom card after the cut.

7. Etiquette does not permit conversation at the table.

8. Even experienced card players do sometimes make mistakes.

9. You must never criticize your partner or your opponents.

10. Did you already know the source of the phrase *according to Hoyle*?

1.b.12 Time and tense

The **tenses** of a verb are forms that help to show time.

Verbs not only tell *what* happens, but they can also

tell *when* something happens. Verbs tell us that things happened in the past, are happening now, or will happen in the future.

EXAMPLES

	When	Tense
You **understand**.	now	present
You **understood**.	before now	past

1.b.13 Present time: the present tense

The **present tense** shows that something occurs now: *You understand* (now). The present tense of an action verb tells that something *happens now*. The present tense of a linking verb tells that someone or something *exists now*.

EXAMPLES

Action verb	Linking verb
The wind **howls**.	The wind **is** strong.
The snowflakes **sparkle**.	The snowflakes **are** tiny.

In addition to showing that something happens "right now," the present tense can also express the idea of habitual ("ongoing") truth and of general truth (such as a scientific fact).

EXAMPLES

Menomini children **ride** bareback. [something that happens every time the children ride]

The Menominis **are** a Native American tribe of Wisconsin. [a fact]

Except for *be*, all verbs have two forms in the present tense. One form is used to talk about *I, you*, or more than one (a plural) person or thing. This form is spelled the same way as the basic verb. The other form is used to talk about one (a singular) person or thing. This form is usually made by adding *-s* to the basic verb.

PRESENT TENSE OF VERB

	Singular	Plural
1ST PERSON:	I grin.	We grin.
2ND PERSON:	You grin.	You grin.
3RD PERSON:	He grin**s**.	They grin.
	She grin**s**.	
	The cat grin**s**.	The cats grin.

Be has three forms in the present tense: *am, is,* and *are.* Remember to use the form that agrees in number with the person or thing about which you are talking or writing (see 1.b.6).

PRESENT TENSE OF *BE*

	Singular	Plural
1ST PERSON:	I **am** late.	We **are** late.
2ND PERSON:	You **are** late.	You **are** late.
3RD PERSON:	He **is** late.	They **are** late.
	She **is** late.	
	The train **is** late.	The trains **are** late.

EXERCISE 18. Write the answer to each of the following questions. Begin each of your answers with *yes.*

EXAMPLE Do backpackers hike?

ANSWER *Yes, backpackers hike.*

1. Do backpackers explore the high country of New Mexico around the Pecos River?
2. Is the Rocky Mountain chain near the northern part of the Pecos River?
3. Does the Pecos River flow south into Texas?
4. Do the Pecos Pueblo tribes make ceremonial offerings of cornmeal?
5. Do trails of the Pecos Wilderness Area climb to Santa Fe?
6. Does Lake Katherine nestle just below Santa Fe?
7. Does the trail to Lake Katherine pass Stewart Lake?
8. Does a rider see the sunset over the Rockies?
9. Does the climb to Lake Katherine tax hikers' skills?
10. Do the Spirit Lakes lure trout fishers?

SPELLING PRESENT–TENSE VERBS

1. To form the third-person singular, generally add -s to the basic verb.

   I run.   She run**s**.

2. If the verb ends in *s, o, x, zz, ch,* or *sh*, add -es.

They confess.	She confess**es**.
They do.	She do**es**.
They relax.	She relax**es**.
They buzz.	The bee buzz**es**.
They catch.	She catch**es**.
They fish.	She fish**es**.

3. If the verb ends in a consonant + *y*, change the *y* to *i* and add -es.

   I study.   He stud**ies**.

4. The verb *have* becomes *has*.

   I **have** a dog.   He **has** a dog.

EXERCISE 19. In each of the following sentences, tell which present-tense form of the verb *be* should replace the blank.

1. A publishing company _____ an organization of people who edit and distribute books.
2. I _____ interested in publishing.
3. A book editor _____ a person who edits the writing of an author.
4. You _____ an editor when you correct, rewrite, and reorganize your papers.
5. Typographers _____ people who set a manuscript in type.
6. Proofreaders _____ responsible for correcting errors in grammar and punctuation and in typing.

7. You _____ a proofreader when you correct mistakes in your compositions.
8. Most modern printing presses _____ very fast.
9. A modern book _____ likely to be a paperback.
10. The covers of a hardback book _____ stronger than those of most paperbacks.

1.b.14 Present time: the present progressive

You can use the **present progressive** to emphasize that an action or a state of being is going on "right now." For instance, if you are doing your homework right now, you would probably use the present progressive—*I am doing my homework*—rather than the present tense—*I do my homework.*

Form the present progressive in the following way:

Present tense of *be* + **Present participle of verb**

I am | waxing
you are | polishing
he/she/it is | dusting
we are
you are
they are

EXAMPLES
I **am waxing** the floor.
She **is polishing** the silver.

AVOIDING ERRORS WITH THE PRESENT PROGRESSIVE

Do not use *is* in the present progressive when you should use another form of the verb *be*. Remember: *I am, he* (or *she* or *it*) *is, you are, we are, they are.*

NOT   I i̶s̶ dusting.   They i̶s̶ dusting.
BUT   I **am dusting**.   They **are dusting**.

EXERCISE 20. In each of the following sentences, tell which form of the verb *be* should replace the blank to form the present progressive.

1. Large parks ＿＿＿ getting closer to large cities all the time.
2. Nowadays San Francisco's Golden Gate Recreation Area ＿＿＿ bustling with such activities as hiking, hang gliding, and surfing.
3. San Franciscans ＿＿＿ discovering forest and mountain trails only an hour's ride from the inner city.
4. Urban parks ＿＿＿ bringing the wilderness to the city.
5. Nearly three thousand miles east, another city ＿＿＿ enjoying the Gateway National Recreation Area.
6. This piece of wilderness ＿＿＿ offering New Yorkers a glimpse of a striped bass.
7. Park rangers in New York ＿＿＿ constructing a beach area with picnic and play facilities for the handicapped.
8. Other parts of New York State ＿＿＿ becoming urban recreation centers.
9. Already about nine million New York City dwellers ＿＿＿ braving the wilds of Gateway.
10. The National Park Service ＿＿＿ now establishing urban recreation areas in Atlanta and Los Angeles.

1.b.15 Past time: the past tense

Use the **past tense** to show that an action or a state of being happened or existed in the past.

Except for *be*, all verbs have only one form in the past tense. The past tense of most verbs ends in *-ed*; these verbs are regular verbs (see 1.b.8). A verb with a past tense that does not end in *-ed* is an irregular verb (see 1.b.9).

EXAMPLES

She **painted** with oils. [regular verb in the past tense]
He **threw** the discus. [irregular verb in the past tense]

There are two forms of the past tense of the irregular verb *be*: *was* and *were*. Use the form that agrees in number with the person or thing about which you are talking or writing (see 2.c).

PAST TENSE OF *BE*

	Singular	Plural
1ST PERSON:	I **was** asleep.	We **were** asleep.
2ND PERSON:	You **were** asleep.	You **were** asleep.
3RD PERSON:	He **was** asleep.	They **were** asleep.
	She **was** asleep.	
	It **was** asleep.	
	The hedgehog **was** asleep.	Both hedgehogs **were** asleep.

EXERCISE 21. For each of the following sentences, give the past-tense form of the verb in parentheses.

1. Elizabeth Gray (want) to be a writer.
2. She (finish) her first novel, *Meredith's Ann*, in 1927.
3. In 1933, after only four years of marriage, her husband (pass) away.
4. Elizabeth Gray Vining's extraordinary appointment as tutor to Crown Prince Akihito of Japan (happen) in 1946.
5. The Emperor (wish) his son to have weekly one-hour English conversations with an American.
6. At that time Vining (work) for the American Friends Service Committee.
7. Vining (enjoy) Margaret Landon's novel *Anna and the King of Siam*.
8. After being chosen for the position, Vining (tutor) not only Crown Prince Akihito but also his brothers, his sisters, and his classmates.
9. In 1959 Vining (return) to Japan for the wedding of Crown Prince Akihito and his bride Michiko Shoda.
10. In her book *Windows for the Crown Prince*, Vining (detail) her unforgettable years as a tutor in Japan.

APPLICATION. Select five of the past-tense verbs from Exercise 21. Write an original sentence for each.

EXERCISE 22. For each of the following sentences, give the past tense of the verb or verbs in parentheses. The past-tense forms of the irregular verbs are given in 1.b.9.

1. In the 1930s musical child prodigies (tour) everywhere.
2. Many of these gifted youngsters (vanish) from the concert stages in their teens.
3. One former pianist, who (begin) her career at the age of four, (write) a book about her unhappy childhood.
4. Most famous musicians (start) their rigorous training in early childhood.
5. Mozart (perform) his own compositions in European courts at the age of seven.
6. Haydn (earn) his living as a church singer at five.
7. Yehudi Menuhin (play) in his first violin recital when he (be) ten.
8. André Watts (win) the highest honors when he (enter) his first piano competition at ten.
9. At the age of three, pianist Lorin Hollander (sing) a Haydn composition after hearing it once.
10. Artur Rubinstein (be) not yet three when he (learn) to play the piano by eavesdropping on his older sister's piano lessons.

APPLICATION. Select five of the past-tense verbs from Exercise 22. Write an original sentence for each.

EXERCISE 23. For each of the following sentences, give the past tense of the verb in parentheses. The past-tense forms of the irregular verbs are given in 1.b.9.

1. In Ohio two different families (adopt) identical twin boys shortly after birth.
2. Thirty-nine years later the twins (speak) to each other for the first time.
3. The twins (discover) that each had married a first wife named Linda and a second wife named Betty.
4. Identical twin women, also separated at birth and unknown to each other, (have) daughters named Kristen and (work) as hairdressers.

5. Twin sisters in Staunton, Virginia, (take) standardized tests in opposite corners of a classroom.
6. The results (be) remarkable.
7. Both sisters (choose) the same essay topic and (write) the same kind of story.
8. Two male twins (become) professional basketball players.
9. They (play) for different teams, but they (have) surprisingly similar records.
10. After studying more than fifteen thousand pairs of twins, Professor Luigi Gedda of the Gregor Mendel Institute of Rome (develop) a theory about twins.

APPLICATION. Select five of the past-tense verbs from Exercise 23. Write an original sentence for each.

1.b.16 Past time: the past progressive

Use the **past progressive** to show that an action or condition *continued* for some time in the past. For example, you could use the past progressive to say *She **was gardening** all afternoon* rather than use the past tense to say *She **gardened** all afternoon*.

Form the past progressive in the following way:

Past tense of *be* + **Present participle of verb**
was   weeding
were   fertilizing

EXAMPLES
She **was weeding** the flowers.
They **were fertilizing** the bushes.

If you want to show that some action happened while another action was going on, write a sentence that has one verb in the past tense and another verb in the past progressive.

EXAMPLES
He **was vacuuming** the dining room when they **arrived**.
   past progressive   past

They **were standing** outside when the rain **started**.

    past progressive   past

We **were singing** when the clock **struck** twelve.

    past progressive   past

EXERCISE 24. In each of the following sentences, give the past progressive of the verb in parentheses.

1. The crew of a sailing canoe (retrace) an ancient sea route when they sailed from Hawaii to Tahiti.
2. The replica of a twelfth-century canoe (carry) no navigational instruments when it sailed on May 1, 1976.
3. Navigator Mau Piailug (study) to become a navigator when he was only six.
4. Piailug (travel) an unfamiliar route when he guided the canoe to Tahiti.
5. A large boat (shadow) the canoe when it made the trip.
6. On the fourth day the canoe (sail) smoothly when the crew learned about their exposure to hepatitis.
7. The men (prepare) for inoculations when a U.S. Coast Guard plane parachuted serum to them.
8. Boredom (set) in when the canoe entered the area around the equator.
9. The canoe (drift) off course when the animals got indigestion from eating a sail.
10. Thousands of Tahitians (shout) a welcome when the canoe triumphantly sailed into Papeete Harbor on June 4, 1976.

1.b.17   Past time: the present-perfect tense

Use the **present perfect** to show that an action happened or a condition existed at some time in the past. The word *perfect* is used here with its original meaning of "completed" or "finished." You use the present-perfect tense to tell about something that has been completed or finished. You can also use the present-perfect tense when an action or condition began in the past and has continued up to the present.

Form the present-perfect tense in the following way:

has or **have** + **Past participle of verb**
has   swum
have   dived

EXAMPLES

He **has swum** in the Caribbean. [an action that happened at an indefinite time in the past]

They **have lived** in Arizona for three years. [a condition that began in the past and has continued up to the present]

Form the **present perfect progressive** in the following way:

has been or **have been** + **Present participle of verb**
have been   trapping

EXAMPLES

New Englanders **have been trapping** lobsters for over two hundred years.

The days **have been growing** longer since December 21.

Although the past tense and the present-perfect tense of verbs both express past time, they often indicate slightly different meanings. The past tense usually refers to a state of being or an event that occurred at a specific time in the past: *He **swam** before breakfast* [today]. The present-perfect tense can sometimes refer to past time that is not specific: *He **has swum** before breakfast* [at times].

EXERCISE 25. In each of the following sentences, the verb in parentheses is in the past tense. Rewrite the sentences by changing the verb in parentheses to the present perfect. Also, change the italicized word or phrase in each sentence to the word or phrase given in parentheses at the end of each sentence.

    EXAMPLE   The moving van (came) *today*. (twice this week)

    ANSWER   *The moving van **has come twice this week**.*

1. The apartment next door (was) empty *last week*. (for a month)
2. New neighbors (moved) in *on Monday*. (since then)
3. The new neighbors (changed) the lock *that evening*. (already)
4. The two sons (walked) to school with us *yesterday*. (all week)
5. Their mother (started) her new job *on Thursday*. (already)
6. The superintendent (padded) the freight elevator *yesterday*. (for other new tenants)
7. The neighbors (hung) the parakeet cage *in the front window*. (in a different window every day)
8. Our parents (told) the neighbors *where to find the nearest supermarket*. (many things about our neighborhood)
9. We (took) the boys *to the playground on Sunday*. (on several neighborhood excursions)
10. We (moved) *to this building four years ago*. (twice since I was born)

1.b.18 Past time: the past-perfect tense

Use the **past perfect** to show that one past action ended before another past action began.

Form the past perfect in the following way:

had + **Past participle of verb**
had   glided
had   bowled

EXAMPLES
He **had bowled** six strikes before the game **ended**. [past-perfect tense; past tense]
Until you **bowled** that strike, your team **had trailed** by twenty points. [past tense; past-perfect tense]

Form the **past perfect progressive** in the following way:

had been + **Present participle of verb**
had been   sailing

EXERCISE 26. Read the following paragraphs and answer the following questions using the past-perfect tense of the verb.

Dow Baker had bucked his share of storms before he encountered the 1870 hurricane in the Caribbean. The hurricane eased in like a passing spring shower. Suddenly, a raging twister struck Dow's ship, the *Telegraph*, from all sides. When the storm was over, every part of the ship had suffered damage. Only the skill of Captain Baker and young Griggy Lujan saved the schooner.

Lujan had boarded the *Telegraph* before Captain Baker sailed from Bermuda. When the hurricane had raged for quite a while, Lujan recognized the welcoming bonfires of Jamaica.

After near disaster the storm-battered *Telegraph* found safety in the harbor at Port Antonio. There Lujan introduced Dow to bananas. Before the *Telegraph* sailed for Boston, Dow had loaded his hold (space below the deck of a ship) with the "fruit with a natural wrapper." By noon of the day they reached port, Dow had sold his entire shipment. Before the end of 1871, the banana boom had begun.

1. Who had bucked his share of storms before he encountered the 1870 hurricane in the Caribbean?
2. What part of the ship had suffered damage when the storm was over?
3. Who had boarded the *Telegraph* before Captain Baker sailed from Bermuda?
4. Where had the storm-battered ship found safety after near disaster?
5. What did Lujan see when the hurricane had raged for a while?
6. Where had Lujan introduced Dow to bananas?
7. With what had Dow loaded his hold before sailing for Boston?
8. What had Dow sold by noon of his first day in Boston?
9. As a result of Captain Dow's stopover in Jamaica, what had begun before the end of 1871?
10. What had Lujan described as "fruit with a natural wrapper"?

1.b.19 Future time

You can show future time in these ways:

1. Using *will* or *shall*:
   You **will graduate**.
2. Using *going to*:
   You **are going to graduate**.
3. Using *about to*:
   You are **about to graduate**.
4. Using the present tense or the present progressive with an adverb or a prepositional phrase that shows future time:
   You **graduate** in two years.
   You **are graduating** soon.

Use the **future perfect** to show that a future event will be finished before another future event begins. Form the future perfect in the following way:

will have + **Past participle of the verb**
will have   finished

EXAMPLES
You **will have finished** your exam before the bell signals that time is up.
When the bell rings, **you will have spent** thirty minutes on your exam.

EXERCISE 27. The following sentences are slightly mis-worded quotations by Americans. Correct the sentences by replacing the italicized part of the verb phrase with the word *will* before the verb. Your revised sentences will be the exact words of the famous Americans.

EXAMPLE   I *am going to* be as harsh as truth and as un-compromising as justice.—William Lloyd Garrison

ANSWER   I **will** be as harsh as truth and as uncom-promising as justice.

1. Human nature *is* not *going to* change.—Abraham Lincoln
2. The world *is going to* little note nor long remember what we say here, but it can never forget what they did here. —Abraham Lincoln
3. Eternal truths *are going to* be neither true nor eternal unless they have fresh meaning for every new social situation.—Franklin Delano Roosevelt
4. Together we *are going to* achieve victory.—Dwight David Eisenhower
5. I look forward to a world which *is going to* be safe not only for democracy and diversity but also for personal distinction.—John Fitzgerald Kennedy

1.b.20 Voice: active and passive

The **voice** of a sentence indicates whether someone or something actually performs the action of the verb or is instead acted upon. If the someone or something performs the action, the sentence is in the **active voice**. If the someone or something is acted upon, the sentence is in the **passive voice**.

EXAMPLES
ACTIVE VOICE: The owner painted the house.
PASSIVE VOICE: The house was painted by the owner.

In the first sentence above, the *owner* (who performs the action) is emphasized. In the second sentence the *house* (which is acted upon) is emphasized. In the first sentence the *owner* is the subject (see 2.b). In the second sentence the *owner* is the **agent**.

Form the passive voice of a verb in the following way:

Form of *be* +	Past participle + of verb	Agent (optional)
are being	gathered	by pollsters
will be	lit	by Mother
was being	cooked	by the chef
should have		
been	brought	by my sister

EXAMPLES

The opinions **are being gathered** by pollsters.
The candles **will be lit** by Mother.
The steak **is being cooked** by the chef.

Often you have a choice between using the active voice or the passive voice. In general, you can follow these guidelines:

1. Use the passive if you want to emphasize the receiver of the action.
2. Use the passive if you do not want to emphasize the performer of the action.
3. Use the passive if you do not know the performer.
4. In most other cases use the active.

The active voice, in general, gives writing more vitality.

EXERCISE 28. In each of the following sentences, change the voice of the verb. Make passive verbs active, and make active verbs passive.

EXAMPLE Sometimes, their wives accompanied whaling captains on voyages. [active]

ANSWER *Sometimes, whaling captains were accompanied by their wives on voyages.* [passive]

EXAMPLE Both exotic ports and dangerous seas were known to sailors. [passive]

ANSWER *Sailors knew both exotic ports and dangerous seas.* [active]

1. Boston Harbor was reached by Charlotte Jernegan in 1860.
2. Four years had been spent by Charlotte Jernegan and her husband, Captain Jernegan, aboard his whaling ship.
3. On board the *Niger*, a large pantry was inhabited by Charlotte.
4. Stone weights kept the ship's tables horizontal.
5. Charlotte was left temporarily by her husband in Chile to have their son.
6. Charlotte's sea-going was followed by her daughter Amy.

7. Hobbies were practiced by Amy aboard her husband's ship.
8. Whaling ships were taken by whaling captains to more remote regions every year.
9. Lucy Smith, aboard her husband's ship, the *Nautilus*, heard the sounds of whales off the African coast.
10. Cape Horn was crossed six times by Charity Norton, the wife of Captain John O. Norton.

AVOIDING ERRORS WITH VERBS (GENERAL)

Unless your topic requires it, do not shift from one verb tense to another. Unnecessary shifts will confuse your reader or listener.

NOT The hikers made camp: Kevin ~~pitches~~ the tents, and Martin ~~gathers~~ wood.

BUT The hikers made camp: Kevin **pitched** the tents, and Martin **gathered** wood.

REVIEW EXERCISE B. Give the correct or appropriate form of the italicized verb or verb phrase in each of the following sentences. Make sure if there is more than one verb in a sentence that they go well together. The reference keys in parentheses will help you review material if necessary.

1. The 1970s *seen* many changes in popular music. (1.b.9, 1.b.15)
2. The Beatles *breaked* up. (1.b.9, 1.b.15)
3. Throughout the 1960s and early 1970s the Beatles *had maked* one hit record after another. (1.b.9, 1.b.18)
4. Then, each of the Beatles *beginned* to develop his own distinctive style. (1.b.9, 1.b.15)
5. Their music *were* changing and developing. (1.b.15)
6. After they had begun their career imitating American singers of the 1950s, the Beatles *create* their own style. (1.b.18)
7. Recordings made with Capitol Records and Apple Records *selled* well. (1.b.9, 1.b.15)

8. The Beatles' albums and singles *maked* a great deal of money. (1.b.9, 1.b.15)

9. After their "concept album" *was release*, popular music was changed forever. (1.b.20)

10. The Beatles *is* undoubtedly four of the most creative and innovative musicians of this century. (1.b.13)

1.c ADJECTIVES

An **adjective** is a word that tells more about a noun or a pronoun.

When you add the adjective *scrawny* to the noun *chicken*, you more closely define and describe *chicken*. It is a *scrawny* chicken. Adjectives describe size, shape, color, texture, speed, temperature, and other conditions.

EXAMPLES

Size	Speed
a **gigantic** cookie	a **quick** glance
a **tiny** speck	a **leisurely** pace

Shape	Temperature
a **circular** table	a **feverish** brow
an **oblong** box	an **icy** wind

Color	Degree
a **scarlet** ribbon	a **minor** burn
hazel eyes	a **vivid** memory

Texture	Quality
chewy fudge	a **comfortable** chair

When an adjective tells something about a noun, it is said to *modify* the noun.[1] When you are looking for an adjective to modify a noun, you usually have a wide choice, depending upon what you want to say.

For example, after an evening at a school dance, would you use the adjective *nice* to describe it? Maybe,

---

[1]Adjectives also modify pronouns (a *lucky* someone) and gerunds (*reckless driving*). For the sake of simplicity, we talk only about nouns here.

but *nice* is a bland and imprecise adjective. Would you call it an *enjoyable* dance? A *wonderful* dance? A *terrific* dance? These adjectives would probably better describe your opinion. Depending on what aspect of the dance you wanted to describe, you might also call it an *eventful* dance (if many things had happened) or a *delightful* dance (if you had a good time). Always try to choose adjectives that describe precisely what you mean.

EXERCISE 29. Identify each of the adjectives in the following sentences. The noun that the adjective describes is italicized. Most sentences here have more than one adjective.

1. In recent *years* soybeans have become a major *source* of protein in the world.
2. Growing soybeans presents a serious *problem*, however.
3. Soybeans grow well only in mild *climates*.
4. There is a great *need* for this rich *source* of protein, however, in hot *climates*.
5. In 1976 a popular *vegetable*, the winged bean, began to attract scientific *attention*.
6. This important *crop* could be a powerful *weapon* in the fight against malnutrition.
7. The plant grows in remote *areas* of New Guinea and Asia.
8. The hardy *vine* of the plant can climb on a tall *pole*.
9. Its mass of curly *leaves* is covered with white *flowers* that develop quickly into pods.
10. The pods are the size of an average *arm* of an adult.
11. The plant has "wings" that stick out from the corners of the rectangular *pods*.
12. The raw *plants* can be eaten as a tasty *snack*.
13. When cooked they are a crisp *delicacy*.
14. The valuable *leaves* resemble spinach and contain vitamin A.
15. The juicy *tendrils* look like thin *asparagus*.
16. Even the white *flowers* can be made into a sweet *garnish*.
17. Its root grows to the size of a small *potato* and has a high *level* of protein.

18. The firm *flesh* of the root has a nutty *flavor*.

19. The seed of the plant has the nutritional *value* of a soybean and contains large *amounts* of iron and vitamins.

20. The plant is practically an entire *meal* on a single *stalk*!

EXERCISE 30. For each noun below, list five adjectives that can describe it. Indicate what condition each adjective describes: size, speed, shape, temperature, color, degree, texture, or quality. Include adjectives for at least two different conditions in each group of five adjectives.

> EXAMPLE floor
>
> ANSWER *slippery (texture); triangular (shape); chilly (temperature); narrow (size); wooden (quality)*

1. elephant	11. island
2. harmonica	12. problem
3. statue	13. invention
4. boxer	14. haircut
5. stone	15. sneakers
6. fire	16. wish
7. steak	17. conversation
8. balloon	18. movie
9. task	19. day
10. vacation	20. camera

APPLICATION. Select two nouns from the preceding list. For each noun write five sentences, each of which uses a different one of the adjectives that you listed for it.

EXERCISE 31. Each of the following sentences includes two adjectives in parentheses. Indicate the adjective that makes sense in the sentence. Then supply a synonym or another adjective that would make sense in the sentence.

> EXAMPLE Years ago (handmade, intelligent) saddles were common in the American Southwest.
>
> ANSWER *handmade; valuable*

1. Modern ranchers often use a (soft, fast) truck.

2. In the (old, fluffy) days the rancher's saddle was the best place from which to view the herd.
3. Dwain "Sody" Soderquist is one of the few artists who still make (beautiful, cheerful) saddles by hand.
4. The first step in making a Sody saddle is to choose a (ridiculous, smooth) piece of leather.
5. Sody cuts the hide without a pattern and then molds it to the customer's (salty, personal) measurements.
6. He makes but a few cuts with his (huge, blind) shears.
7. Then Sody's skillful hands form the leather into (graceful, sour) curves.
8. Most modern saddles have (decorative, fat) patterns stamped on by machine.
9. Sody carves his designs with (quick, soapy) movements of his fingers and (plastic, long) sweeps of his arm.
10. For over forty years Sody has been creating (magnificent, reluctant) saddles from his home town in Utah.

APPLICATION. Select five adjectives that you did *not* choose in Exercise 31. Write one original sentence for each of the five adjectives.

1.c.1   Positions of adjectives in sentences

Adjectives can be used in various positions and in various ways in the sentence. Notice that in the first sentence below, the adjective comes before the noun. In the second sentence the adjective appears after the noun and a linking verb.

EXAMPLES
The **empty** wagon rolled away.
The wagon was **empty**.

Here are other circumstances in which adjectives can follow the noun:

EXAMPLES
Tracy considered the wagon **colorful**.
The wagon, **old** and **wobbly**, fell apart.

EXERCISE 32. Write two sentences for each of the following adjectives. In the first sentence use the adjective before a noun. In the second sentence use the adjective after a linking verb.

> EXAMPLE garish
>
> ANSWER *Unfortunately, the lovely evergreen tree was overloaded with* **garish** *decorations.*
> *His suit was conservative and modest, but his tie was* **garish**.

1. insignificant
2. cross
3. courteous
4. flowery
5. customary

1.c.2 Properties of adjectives

Most adjectives can be identified by two important properties.

1. You can use the word *very* before most adjectives.

   EXAMPLES
   How **very bright** that wagon is!
   The **very funny** wagon rattled away.
   This wagon is **very slow**.

2. Most adjectives have comparative and superlative forms (see 1.c.3). For example, the comparative form of the adjective *old* is *older*. The superlative form of *old* is *oldest*.

EXERCISE 33. Rewrite each of the following sentences, replacing each blank with an adjective that makes sense in the sentence. Do not use *a*, *an*, or *the*. If you have trouble, see the Word Bank on the next page for suggestions.

> EXAMPLE _____ shoes are _____.
>
> ANSWERS *Tight* shoes are *painful*.
> *New* shoes are *stiff*.

1. _____ clothes make people look _____.
2. _____ men like to wear _____ pants and _____ shirts.
3. _____ jeans are not _____ at _____ restaurants.
4. _____ women like to wear _____ gowns to _____ events.
5. Some people put on _____ shorts to play tennis.
6. Actors sometimes appear in _____ costumes to play _____ roles.
7. _____ clowns work in _____ wigs, _____ makeup, and _____ clothes.
8. A mechanic's uniform is likely to get _____ and _____ on the job.
9. Kings and queens wear _____ crowns and _____ robes.
10. Santas wear _____ beards, _____ boots, and a _____ suit.

Word Bank

blue	important	loose	acceptable
comic	curly	short	long
tight	velvet	rich	funny
white	red	dirty	baggy
expensive	wide	gold	imaginative
black	greasy	bright	colorful
narrow	dark	thin	

APPLICATION. Write five original sentences, each of which uses one of the adjectives in the above Word Bank.

1.c.3 Forms of adjectives: comparison

Most adjectives have three **degrees**: the regular form, the **comparative**, and the **superlative**. An adjective that shows two things being compared is called comparative. An adjective that shows three or more things being compared is called superlative.

EXAMPLES

The mechanic's hands are **rougher** than the surgeon's. [comparative]

The ballet dancer's legs are **stronger** than the pianist's. [comparative]

That is the **roughest** sandpaper in the batch. [superlative]
The **strongest** code of behavior is always fair play. [superlative]

The regular form of an adjective describes a basic condition or quality. The comparative degree describes "more," and the superlative degree describes "most."

Many adjectives, like *rough* and *strong*, take the endings *-er* and *-est* to show their comparative and superlative forms. Sometimes, however, you must express the comparative and superlative forms in other ways:

1. with *more* and *most*

   The special effects in this film are even **more** imaginative than those in his last film.
   In fact, they are the **most** imaginative special effects I have ever seen.

2. with *as*

   This film is **as** long **as** *2001: A Space Odyssey*.
   The first film in the double feature was just **as** long.

3. with *less* and *least*

   Amanda is **less** timid than Beatrice.
   Amanda is the **least** timid person in the class.

▄▄▄ COMPARATIVE AND SUPERLATIVE FORMS OF ADJECTIVES ▄▄▄

	-er, -est	*more, most*
one-syllable adjectives	**two-syllable adjectives; two-syllables and prefix**	**three-or-more-syllable adjectives**
sweet sweet**er**, sweet**est**	**bitter** bitter**er**, **more** bitter bitter**est**, **most** bitter	**delicious** **more** delicious, **most** delicious
	unhappy unhapp**ier**, **more** unhappy unhapp**iest**, **most** unhappy	**imaginative** **more** imaginative, **most** imaginative

When you add -er and -est to the basic form of the adjective, you sometimes have to make a spelling change. Here is a summary of the rules. See also 5.c.

SPELLING COMPARATIVE AND SUPERLATIVE FORMS OF ADJECTIVES

1. Adjective ends in a consonant + *y*.

   salty
   creamy

   1. Change the *y* to *i*, and add -*er* or -*est*.

      saltier, **saltiest**
      creamier, **creamiest**

2. Adjective ends in silent *e*.

   stale
   vile

   2. Drop the final *e*, and add -*er* or -*est*.

      staler, **stalest**
      viler, **vilest**

3. One-syllable adjective ends in a single vowel + a single consonant.

   fat
   thin

   3. Double the consonant, and add -*er* or -*est*.

      fatter, **fattest**
      thinner, **thinnest**

1.c.4 Irregular adjectives: comparison

The following common adjectives have irregular comparative and superlative forms:

	Comparative form	Superlative form
good	better	(the) best
well (health)	better	(the) best
bad	worse	(the) worst
ill	worse	(the) worst
far (distance)	farther	farthest
far (degree)	further	furthest

EXERCISE 34. Give both the comparative and superlative forms of each of the following adjectives. Five of them will take *more* and *most*, eight adjectives require special spelling changes, and one is irregular.

1. elastic	11. marvelous
2. sleek	12. blue
3. elaborate	13. dim
4. bland	14. slight
5. lumpy	15. insecure
6. stiff	16. bulky
7. flat	17. chunky
8. ill	18. crisp
9. fair	19. deliberate
10. fine	20. lazy

EXERCISE 35. The following paragraph contains ten errors in the comparative or superlative form of adjectives. Rewrite the paragraph to correct these errors. Before you begin, read the "Avoiding Errors" box on page 49.

¹Going to college is a good way to train for some kinds of work but not for all. ²Apprenticeship is probably a more better way to train to be a carpenter, for example. ³Apprentices learn their trade on the job. ⁴As their training progresses, they become handyer at various job skills. ⁵After about four years—more longer for some trades and not so long for others—they become experts. ⁶Then they can receive the most best wages.

⁷In 1977 the construction industry was more crowded with registered apprentices than any field. ⁸There are 450 different occupations that require apprenticeship. ⁹Most people find some attractiver than others. ¹⁰Apprenticeship programs have entrance exams and minimum age and education requirements. ¹¹If you would like to become an apprentice, the intelligentest thing you can do is to find out about the field while you are still in school. ¹²Sometimes you will find that the goodest thing you can do is to finish college first. ¹³A biger percentage of artists and craftspeople are trained in colleges today than formerly. ¹⁴Many people believe, however, that the close relationship between artist and apprentice provides better training than anything.

AVOIDING ERRORS WITH ADJECTIVES FOR COMPARISON

1. Do not make a double comparison. A **double comparison** incorrectly uses both *-er* or *-est* and *more* or *most*.

   NOT Texas is ~~more bigger~~ in area than Oklahoma.
   BUT Texas is **bigger** in area than Oklahoma.

2. Do not make an incomplete comparison. Use *other* or *else* when you compare one member of a group to the other group members.

   NOT Alaska is closer to Russia than ~~any~~ state.
   BUT Alaska is closer to Russia than **any other** state.

   NOT She had more books than ~~everyone~~.
   BUT She had more books than **everyone else**.

1.c.5 Adjective or noun?

Many words that are usually nouns can also be used as adjectives. Very often you cannot be sure what part of speech a word is until you see it in a sentence.

EXAMPLES

Mark has a **new pet**.
adjective   noun

His **pet raccoon** eats **fish** and drinks **pond water**.
adjective noun   noun   adjective noun

There is a **fish pond** behind the **house**.
adjective noun   noun

When a noun and an adjective are often used together to identify something, they are considered a unit. Such a combination is called a **compound noun** (see 1.a.2).

EXAMPLES

Adjective and noun	Compound noun
public session	public school
red hair	red tape
hot oven	hot dog

EXERCISE 36. In each of the following sentences, indicate whether the italicized phrase is a simple adjective and noun combination or a compound noun.

1. *Fairy tales* usually deal with magic or the supernatural.
2. The term is used loosely to cover a wide variety of *traditional tales*.
3. In "The Three Little Pigs" animals behave like *human beings*.
4. In "Cinderella," *supernatural beings* control the events.
5. The folk tale, on the other hand, reflects the *traditional customs* and beliefs of people of a certain culture.

1.c.6 Proper adjectives

Proper adjectives are adjectives formed from proper nouns (see 1.a.1). Proper adjectives are capitalized.

Sometimes both proper nouns and proper adjectives have the same form.

EXAMPLES

Boston is cold in winter.
|
proper noun

Boston baked beans are delicious.
|
proper adjective

Most proper nouns change form when they become proper adjectives.

EXAMPLES

Shakespeare wrote plays and poems.

proper noun

Shakespearean comedies have serious moments.

proper adjective

The proper nouns that name countries and continents form proper adjectives in a number of different ways.

EXERCISE 37. There are ten proper adjectives in the following paragraph. Identify them.

[1]Walter Elias Disney, who was born in Chicago on December 5, 1901, had a long and productive career. [2]"Walt" Disney was the creator of the Mickey Mouse cartoons and the Donald Duck cartoons, among many others. [3]Disney grew up on a Missouri farm. [4]His art training was limited to a few courses at an art academy and at a Kansas City school. [5]During World War I Disney was a Red Cross ambulance driver in the French sector. [6]After the war Disney began producing his Laugh-O-Gram cartoons. [7]In 1928 Disney established his company and soon brought out his first sound film, *Steamboat Willie*. [8]Disney's *Trees and Flowers* was the first Technicolor cartoon. [9]In 1937 Disney began producing feature-length cartoons, such as *Snow White and the Seven Dwarfs*. [10]The Disneyesque style is rich in color and humor. [11]Films like his masterpiece, *Cinderella*, earned Disney American recognition.

EXERCISE 38. Rewrite each of the following phrases by changing the proper noun into a proper adjective and placing it before the common noun.

1. a holiday in Costa Rica
2. a hound from Afghanistan
3. a lullaby from Ireland
4. chocolate from the Netherlands
5. a bank account in Switzerland

REVIEW EXERCISE C. Identify each adjective in each of the following quotations. Indicate if it is the regular, comparative, or superlative form.

1. To stumble twice against the same stone is a proverbial disgrace.—Cicero
2. To err is human, to forgive divine.—Pope
3. Excellent things are rare.—Plato
4. Imitation is the sincerest form of flattery.—Colton
5. All is fair in love and war.—English proverb
6. I can believe anything, provided it is incredible.—Wilde.
7. Round numbers are always false.—Samuel Johnson
8. I awoke . . . and found myself famous.—Byron
9. Fame is the perfume of heroic deeds.—Socrates
10. What a heavy burden is a name that has become too famous.—Voltaire
11. The family is more sacred than the state.—Pope Pius XI
12. Earth and the great weather move me.—Eskimo traditional
13. That men's and women's lives are becoming more alike seems to me to open doors to understanding and affectionate friendship between them.—Elizabeth Janeway
14. Where shall be my house? I am miserable on earth. —Aztec traditional

1.d PRONOUNS

A **pronoun** is a word that takes the place of a noun.

In a sentence, a pronoun is used just like a noun. The English language has about seventy-five pronouns. They may be grouped into five categories:

- personal pronouns, including possessive pronouns and reflexive pronouns
- demonstrative pronouns
- interrogative pronouns
- relative pronouns
- indefinite pronouns

PRONOUNS

PERSONAL PRONOUNS

	nominative case singular	nominative case plural	objective case singular	objective case plural
first person	I	we	me	us
second person	you	you	you	you
third person	he	they	him	them
	she		her	
	it		it	

POSSESSIVE FORMS

	singular	plural	singular	plural
	used as determiners	used alone	used as determiners	used alone
first person	my	mine	our	ours
second person	your	yours	your	yours
third person	his	his	their	theirs
	her	hers		
	its	its		

REFLEXIVE FORMS

Reflexive pronouns have no case.

	singular	plural
first person	myself	ourselves
second person	yourself	yourselves
third person	himself	themselves
	herself	
	itself	

DEMONSTRATIVE PRONOUNS

Demonstrative pronouns have no case or person.

	singular	plural
near	this	these
far	that	those

INTERROGATIVE PRONOUNS

Who is the only interrogative pronoun that has an objective case and a possessive form.

people only	nonpeople	people and nonpeople
who? whom? whose?	what?	which?

Compounds: whoever, whomever, whatever

RELATIVE PRONOUNS

Who is the only relative pronoun that has an objective case and a possessive form.

people only	nonpeople	nonpeople (formal) people (informal)
who whom, whose	which	that

INDEFINITE PRONOUNS

	universal	"some"	"any"	negative
always singular[1]	everybody everyone everything each either	somebody someone something somewhere another	anybody anyone anything anywhere	nobody no one nothing neither nowhere
always plural		both few many several		
singular or plural	all	some enough more most such	any	none

---

[1]By "always singular" we mean that the verb will have a singular form (usually adding -*s* in third-person present tense).

1.d.1 Personal pronouns

Personal pronouns refer to specific persons or things and have one of three functions in a sentence: (1) They identify the *person* speaking (*I*, *we*); (2) they identify the *person* spoken to (*you*); (3) they identify the *person* or *thing* spoken about (*he*, *she*, *it*, *they*).

■ Case

All personal pronouns except *you* and *it* have two different forms, called **cases**. The **subjective** (or **nominative**) **case** is used when the pronoun is the subject of a sentence. The **objective case** is used when the pronoun is the object of a verb or the object of a preposition.

Be sure to use the subjective case of a pronoun in a compound subject made up of a noun and a pronoun.

EXAMPLES
Ann and **I** had made a ping-pong table last winter.
She and Tom bought the net and paddles.

Be sure to use the objective case of a pronoun in a compound object made up of a noun and a pronoun.

EXAMPLES
Tom's serve was challenging for Manuel and **me**.
Manuel teases Ann about the rivalry between Tom and **her**.

In general, use the subjective case of a pronoun after a form of the verb *be*.

EXAMPLES
The best ping-pong player was **he**.
Tom said that it was really **I**.
Ann hoped that it would soon be **she**.

In speaking, people sometimes use *me* instead of *I* after a form of the linking verb *be*: *It is **me***. In writing, however, always use the subjective case after the linking verb *be*: *It is **I***.

EXERCISE 39. In each of the following sentences, choose the personal pronoun or pronouns that correctly complete the sentence.

1. My sister and (I, me) are just learning to play bridge.
2. Mother gave my sister and (I, me) a book about bridge.
3. Counting the honor points is easy for both of (we, us).
4. (Us, We) are already fairly accurate at making the right opening bid.
5. Remembering what cards have already been played is confusing for (she and I, her and me), though.
6. Gin rummy is much easier for my sister and (I, me).
7. Cribbage is the two-handed card game that (I, me) like best.
8. (She, Her) and I call combinations that add up to fifteen.
9. Teaching friends how to play cards is fun for (we and they, us and them).
10. Maybe my sister and (I, me) can win when we play our parents.

■ Number and person

All personal pronouns (except *you*) are either singular or plural; that is, they have **number**. For example, *I* and *she* are singular forms, and *we* and *they* are plural forms. *You* is both a singular and a plural form.

Personal pronouns can also be grouped by **person**:

- **First-person pronouns**, which refer to the person (or persons) doing the speaking or writing, are *I*, *me*, *we*, *us*.

- The **second-person pronoun**, which refers to the person (or persons) being addressed, is *you*.

- **Third-person pronouns**, which refer to the person or persons (and to the thing or things) spoken or written about, are *he*, *him*, *she*, *her*, *it*, *they*, *them*.

■ Gender

Third-person pronouns have three genders:

- Masculine pronouns—*he*, *him*, *his*—refer to males.
- Feminine pronouns—*she*, *her*, *hers*—refer to females.
- Neuter pronouns—*it*, *its*—refer to things that are neither male nor female.

The plural pronouns *they*, *them*, *their*, *theirs*, and *themselves* refer to people or things in the third-person plural, regardless of gender.

■ Pronoun-antecedent agreement

An **antecedent** is the noun (or other word or phrase) to which a pronoun refers. The antecedent may appear in the same sentence as the pronoun that refers to it or in a preceding sentence.

EXAMPLES
When skiers schuss, **they** make a high-speed run straight down the hill. [*They* refers to *skiers*. *Skiers* is the antecedent.]
The skiers schussed straight down the hill. Before reaching the bottom **they** were traveling at a very high speed. [*They* refers to *skiers* in the preceding sentence.]

Often the antecedent is understood from the context.

EXAMPLE
When schussing down a steep hill, **you** ski at high speed. [The second-person pronoun, *you*, refers to the person (or persons) being addressed.]

Although the word *antecedent* means "something that comes before," the pronoun may come before its antecedent.

EXAMPLE
Before **they** reached high speed, the skiers had to bypass several trees. [*They* refers to *skiers*.]

The pronoun's antecedent may be a noun, another pronoun, or an element being used as a noun (such as a gerund, an infinitive, a noun clause, or a prepositional phrase). In all instances, a pronoun must have the same number (singular or plural) and the same gender (masculine, feminine, or neuter) as its antecedent.

EXAMPLES

Feminine antecedent and pronoun

Emily Brontë published **her** first novel, *Wuthering Heights*, in 1847. [singular, feminine pronoun]

Emily, Charlotte, and Anne Brontë published **their** collected poems in 1845. [plural pronoun]

Masculine antecedent and pronoun

Henry James published **his** first novel, *The American*, in 1877. [singular, masculine pronoun]

Henry James and his brother William are highly respected for **their** writing. [plural pronoun]

Neuter antecedent and pronoun

The spruce, because of **its** soft wood, is used to make paper. [singular, neuter pronoun]

Spruce and aspen are economical to raise because of **their** rapid growth. [plural pronoun]

Traditionally, a masculine pronoun is used when the gender of the antecedent is not known or may be either masculine or feminine.

EXAMPLE

A skier must keep **his** legs strong and limber.

If you do not wish to use a masculine pronoun when the antecedent may be feminine, you can frequently reword the sentence so that the pronoun is plural or eliminated entirely.

EXAMPLES

Skiers must keep **their** legs strong and limber.
Skiers must have strong, limber legs.

(Agreement between personal pronouns and antecedents that are indefinite pronouns is discussed in 1.d.7.)

AVOIDING ERRORS WITH
PERSONAL PRONOUNS

1. Be sure to use the objective case of a personal pronoun after a preposition.

   NOT The race was a tie between you and ~~he~~.
   BUT The race was a tie between you and **him**.

2. Do not use a personal pronoun that could possibly refer to more than one antecedent. Either reword the sentence to make the antecedent clear, or eliminate the pronoun.

   NOT When the apples fell among the leaves, ~~they~~ were hidden. [What was hidden?]
   BUT The apples were hidden when they fell among the leaves.
   OR   The fallen apples were hidden by the leaves.

3. Be careful to use the appropriate case of the pronoun after *than* or *as*.

   NOT You answered the phone faster than ~~him~~. [Did you answer him?]
   BUT You answered the phone faster than **he**. [You answered faster than *he* answered.]

   Notice the difference in meaning between the two sentences that follow.

   You wrote me more often than **him**. [You wrote to me more often than you wrote to him.]
   You wrote me more often than **he**. [You wrote to me more often than he wrote to me.]

EXERCISE 40. In each of the following sentences, indicate which of the pronouns in the parentheses makes the sentence correct.

1. You arrived at the swimming pool earlier than (I, me).
2. Diving from the high board was as difficult for me as it was for (he, him).
3. He made a much bigger splash than (she, her).
4. The cold water made me shiver as much as it made (she, her) shiver.
5. The coach dove much more quietly than (we, us).
6. You practiced diving from the low board as many times as (he, him).
7. You climbed to the high board by the same steps as (she, her).
8. She dove off more quickly than (he, him).
9. I watched you just as closely as I watched (he, him).
10. During the next dive you will be less afraid than (I, me).

1.d.2 Personal pronouns: possessive forms

Each personal pronoun except *it* and *he* has two possessive forms. The possessive forms are listed in the chart on page 53. One possessive form can be used as a determiner before a noun (see 1.e). The second form is used alone, like a noun.

POSSESSIVE FORMS USED AS DETERMINERS
I rode **your** bike yesterday.
Dolores lent you **her** bike last week.
Tony bought **his** bike secondhand.

POSSESSIVE FORMS USED ALONE
I rode **yours** yesterday.
Dolores lent you **hers** last week.
Tony bought **his** secondhand.

EXERCISE 41. In each of the following sentences, identify the antecedent to which the italicized possessive pronoun refers. The antecedent may be a noun or pronoun.

1. Animated cartoons can reproduce anything that we can imagine in *our* minds.

2. An animated cartoon achieves *its* effects through a simple technique.
3. Cartoon artists draw *their* pictures on a large board.
4. In each picture the figure changes *its* position slightly.
5. A figure who flutters *her* eyelashes would be drawn in the first picture with her eyes open.
6. In the next picture of the woman, *her* eyes would be half closed.
7. In the following picture of the woman, *her* eyes would be completely closed.
8. The camera operator films these individual pictures repeatedly in *their* proper sequence.
9. When the individual frames are run through a projector, *their* rapid projection creates the illusion of movement.
10. As you view the animated cartoon, *your* eyes seem to see the figure's eyelashes flutter.

EXERCISE 42. In the following sentences, indicate which possessive pronoun should replace the blank.

1. The *Natchez Trace Parkway* wends _____ way from Natchez, Mississippi, to Nashville, Tennessee.
2. *Mrs. Roane Fleming Byrnes* spent _____ years as president of the Natchez Trace Association promoting the parkway.
3. In the early 1800s *Samuel Mason* and _____ robber band had a hide-out in the Natchez Trace.
4. *Little Harpe*, Mason's friend, had a price on _____ head in Kentucky.
5. When caught, *Mason and Little Harpe* admitted that _____ assistant was named Anthony Glass.
6. _____ job was to inform the bandits when rich travelers passed through town.
7. *Samuel Mason* was betrayed by two of _____ own men.
8. _____ fate was to be caught and sentenced.
9. The trace ends at *Andrew Jackson*'s Hermitage, which he built for _____ wife, Rachel.
10. *Rachel Jackson* died before _____ husband moved to the White House in 1829.

1.d.3 Personal pronouns: reflexive forms

Reflexive pronouns are used to refer back to a preceding noun or pronoun in the same sentence. They are also used to emphasize a word that came before. Each personal pronoun except *you* has only one reflexive form. *You* has two reflexive forms: the singular *yourself* and the plural *yourselves*.

EXAMPLES

I built **myself** a new workbench.

Al and Robert bought new jeans for **themselves**.

We **ourselves** discovered the stolen bicycles.

EXERCISE 43. Identify the reflexive and possessive pronoun forms in the following sentences.

1. I taught myself how to skate.
2. My first pair of skates no longer fitted my brother.
3. In our town a green flag is hoisted near the pond when the ice is thick enough for safe skating.
4. The police themselves are often the first on the ice.
5. The hockey players clear the ice themselves before practicing.
6. The players built their own cages.
7. We all bought our own hockey sticks.
8. I myself have an extra stick.
9. My sister said that hers was too short.
10. If the hockey team wins the playoffs again this year, the trophy is ours to keep.

EXERCISE 44. In the following paragraphs, identify the antecedent of each italicized personal pronoun.

Sandpiper, our labrador retriever, had *her* nine puppies on November 23. Five of *them* are black, and four are white. We set *ourselves* the task of naming the puppies after different birds. Our neighbors loaned us *their* copy of a bird encyclopedia. They *themselves* own the father of Sandpiper's litter. *He* has won many prizes in hunting dog field trials. His name is Whippoorwill.

Whippoorwill's owners chose the biggest black pup. *Theirs* is named Dabchick. Sandpiper has taught all of *her* puppies to eat from a pan by *themselves*. They are five weeks old today. You can take *yours* home when it is eight weeks old.

1.d.4 Demonstrative pronouns

Demonstrative pronouns are used to point out a certain person, place, thing, or idea. The two demonstrative pronouns are *this* and *that*, which have the plural forms *these* and *those*. They can be used either as determiners in front of a noun or in place of a noun. Demonstrative pronouns used as determiners are sometimes called **demonstrative adjectives**.

DEMONSTRATIVE PRONOUNS USED AS DETERMINERS
This pair of gloves is two years old.
These coat cuffs are too short.
That pair of gloves I saw downtown is fur-lined.
Those fur trimmings will keep my wrists warm.

DEMONSTRATIVE PRONOUNS USED ALONE
This is where I saw the gloves.
These are the most colorful windows on the street.
That was where I found the sailboat model.
Those were mostly models of gliders.

AVOIDING ERRORS WITH DEMONSTRATIVE PRONOUNS

1. Do not use *this* when you simply mean *a* or *an*.

   NOT I learned ~~this~~ new game.
   BUT I learned **a** new game.

2. Do not use *here* or *there* after a demonstrative pronoun.

   NOT This ~~here~~ game is called Monopoly.
   BUT **This** game is called Monopoly.

3. Do not use *them* when you mean *those*.

   NOT You could easily learn ~~them~~ lines.
   BUT You could easily learn **those** lines.

1.d.5 Interrogative pronouns

Interrogative pronouns are used to ask questions. The three basic interrogative pronouns are *who, which,* and *what*. The objective case of *who* is *whom*, and the possessive form of *who* is *whose*.

EXAMPLES

Who reached the theater first?
Whom did you bring with you?
Whose ticket was dropped on the sidewalk?
In **which** pocket did you carry them?
What is playing at the theater tonight?

Some people do not use *whom* in everyday speech. In writing, always use *whom* when the pronoun is the object of a verb or the object of a preposition.

EXERCISE 45. In each of the following sentences, correct the error in the use of a demonstrative or interrogative pronoun.

1. For who is Hermit's Peak named?
2. The sign gives facts about this hermit who lived on the mountain.
3. This here hermit, named Juan Agostini, was born in Italy in 1800.
4. When the hermit came to the United States, he lived in this cave in Hermit's Peak.
5. By the time he reached that there mountain, the hermit was over sixty years old.
6. Who was the hermit trying to avoid?
7. The hermit joined this exploring party that was heading west along the Santa Fe Trail.
8. During them long days on the journey, the leader of the exploring party and the hermit became friends.
9. By who was the hermit's cabin built?
10. If you want to learn more about that there hermit, read *Treasure of the Sangre de Cristos* by Arthur L. Campa.

EXERCISE 46. The following statements are possible answers to questions. For each statement, write the question that the statement answers. Your question should ask for the information given in the italicized words of each statement.

EXAMPLE   Ethel Waters was born *in the year 1900*.
ANSWER   *In what year was Ethel Waters born?*

1. *Ethel Waters* was the first black woman to star in a dramatic play on Broadway.
2. The name of the play was *Mamba's Daughters*.
3. The play was directed *by Guthrie McClintic*.
4. *DuBose Heyward* is the author of the novel on which the play is based.
5. The date of the opening of the play was *January 3, 1939*.
6. The play was staged *at the Empire Theater* in New York City.
7. *Brooks Atkinson's* review of the play was unenthusiastic.
8. Ethel Waters' age at the time of the opening was *thirty-eight*.
9. *Ethel Waters* received seventeen curtain calls.
10. Ethel Waters made her comeback in 1950 at the Empire Theater in *The Member of the Wedding*.

1.d.6 Relative pronouns

Relative pronouns are used at the beginning of subordinate clauses (see 2.o) to relate the subordinate clause to the main clause. There are three basic relative pronouns: *who, which,* and *that. Whom* is the objective case of *who,* and *whose* is the possessive form of *who.*

■ *who*

When referring to people, always use *who* and its related forms. Always use the objective form *whom* if the pronoun is the object of a verb or the object of a preposition.

EXAMPLES

The young woman **who** married James Madison was Dorothea Payne.

Dorothea Payne, **who** married James Madison, was nicknamed Dolley.

The young woman **whom** James Madison married was named Dorothea Payne. [*Whom* is the object of the verb *married.*]

Dolley Madison knew Thomas Jefferson, for **whom** she acted as hostess in the White House. [*Whom* is the object of the preposition *for.*]

Dolley Madison, **whose** vivacity, wit, and intelligence earned her popularity, was a gracious hostess in the White House.

▌ which, that

In writing, use *which* and *that* to refer to things, not to people. (You may hear *that* used in referring to people, but always write *who* to refer to people.)

EXAMPLES

Dolley Madison rescued a portrait of George Washington from the White House, **which** was burned in 1814.

The first personal message **that** was sent over Morse's telegraph was from Dolley Madison.

EXERCISE 47. Identify each relative pronoun in the following sentences. One of the sentences contains two relative pronouns.

1. Carpets that are vacuumed regularly rarely need professional cleaning.
2. Rooms in which the traffic is heavy should have flooring that is easy to keep clean.
3. Coffee and mustard, both of which will stain a carpet, should be wiped up with mild detergent.
4. People look for the stain removers that work best for removing chewing gum.
5. The process that removes chewing gum is a sequence of cleaning fluid, detergent, ammonia, and white vinegar.
6. If chair legs on the carpet leave dents that do not disappear with brushing, hold a steaming iron over the marks.
7. If you spill paint on a floor that is porous, clean it up immediately.

8. Anyone who has dropped a lipstick knows it makes marks.

9. Lipstick can be removed with liquid cleaning wax, which is used for cleaning enamel.

10. A kitchen chopping block, which usually gets much use, should be wiped regularly with mineral oil.

AVOIDING ERRORS WITH RELATIVE PRONOUNS

1. In writing, do not use *that* to refer to people.

   NOT Abigail Smith was the young woman ~~that~~ John Adams married.

   BUT Abigail Smith was the young woman **whom** John Adams married.

2. Do not use *which* unless the antecedent is clear.

   NOT In 1765 Harvard Hall burned, ~~which~~ started from an overheated fireplace. [What started from an overheated fireplace? A fire started, but *fire* does not appear in the sentence.]

   BUT In 1765 a fire, **which** started from an over-heated fireplace, ruined Harvard Hall.

1.d.7 Indefinite pronouns

Indefinite pronouns are called "indefinite" because you often do not know the nouns to which they refer.

EXAMPLES

Everything is exciting just before the holidays in December.

There is a new book that I should like to give to **somebody** this year.

Anything you buy these days costs a lot of money.

Nobody expects to have every gift wish come true.

■ Subject-verb agreement with indefinite pronouns

The form of the present-tense verb that you use with an indefinite pronoun depends on whether the indefinite pronoun is considered singular or plural.

ALWAYS SINGULAR
Everything in our house *looks* festive during the holidays.
Each of the doorways *has* a holly wreath.

ALWAYS PLURAL
Few of the children really *believe* in Santa Claus.
Many of the neighbors *have* candles in their windows.

SINGULAR OR PLURAL
All *is* on the table for an early dinner by four o'clock. [*All* refers to *food*, which is singular.]
All *are* at the table fifteen minutes later. [*All* refers to *people*, which is plural.]

■ Pronoun-antecedent agreement with indefinite pronouns

You must make a personal pronoun agree in number and in gender with an indefinite pronoun that is its antecedent.

EXAMPLES
Each of the men on our block makes **his** own holly wreath for the front door.
Each of the women lights **her** candles one by one.
All of the children get **their** exercise by running.

Writers traditionally use a masculine pronoun—*he, him, his*—when the antecedent might be either male or female. If you do not want to use a masculine pronoun when the indefinite pronoun may be female, try rewording your sentence. Make the indefinite pronoun plural, or rephrase the sentence to eliminate the personal pronoun entirely. You may also use two pronouns (*he or she, him or her, his or her*).

EXAMPLES

Each of the children opened **his** gifts before breakfast.
All of the children opened **their** gifts before breakfast.
All of the children's gifts were opened before breakfast.
Each of the children opened **his or her** gifts before
breakfast.

EXERCISE 48. In each of the following sentences, identify
the indefinite pronoun and indicate whether it is singular or plural. Then select the proper verb from the
parentheses.

1. Everybody (thinks/think) that Alaskan Eskimos used to
   live in igloos.
2. No one (seems/seem) to know that only Canadian Eskimos
   lived in igloos.
3. Anyone visiting Barrow, Alaska's biggest Eskimo town,
   (finds/find) homes heated by natural gas.
4. Few of the Barrow Eskimos (has/have) television sets.
5. In summer many of the Eskimos (puts/put) wheels on their
   sleds.
6. Most of the teen-agers in Barrow (prefers/prefer) modern
   American dances to traditional Eskimo dances.
7. In winter some of the citizens of Barrow (drives/drive)
   snowmobiles.
8. Some of the gold rush spirit (is/are) still alive among aging
   prospectors, but gold mines are now rare.
9. Most of Alaska's mineral wealth (lies/lie) in oil.
10. Some of the canned salmon and crab that you eat
    (comes/come) from Alaskan canneries.

EXERCISE 49. Supply the missing possessive personal
pronoun in each of the following sentences.

1. In Shakespeare's time all of the female characters, regardless of _____ age or importance, were portrayed by men.
2. Each of the main female characters in Shakespeare's
   Twelfth Night finds _____ true love in the last act.
3. Everything in the plot takes _____ humor from Viola's mas-
   querade as a man.

4. Many of the funniest lines in *Twelfth Night* adopt _____ puns from the gender mix-up.

5. Any of today's actresses would probably choose the character of Viola for _____ role.

6. Both of the male leads in *Twelfth Night* proclaim _____ love for the character Olivia.

7. Neither of the male leads achieves _____ meeting with Olivia until the play is nearly over.

8. Most of one character's lines owe _____ humor to his pompous language.

9. Some of the scenes have Olivia's garden as _____ setting.

10. All of the play has as _____ setting a city in Illyria, a region north of Greece.

REVIEW EXERCISE D. Rewrite each of the following sentences to eliminate pronouns that have unclear antecedents and to correct any other mistakes in the use of pronouns. There is one error in each sentence.

1. South Carolina's Low Country has earned this nickname of "the barefoot paradise."

2. You and me could catch enough flounder for several delicious dinners.

3. Anyone that likes crab can catch many along the beach.

4. Everyone will appreciate them massive statues by Anna Hyatt Huntington in the Brookgreen Gardens.

5. In the wildlife preserve the deer run free, which is fascinating to watch.

1.e DETERMINERS

A **determiner** is a word other than an adjective (or a participle used as an adjective) that can be used before a noun to identify the noun.

Determiners differ from adjectives in that they always appear *before* a noun or an adjective-and-noun combination. Most adjectives, on the other hand, can occupy many different positions in a sentence.

1.e.1 Articles

Articles are the words *a*, *an*, and *the*. The **indefinite articles** are *a* and *an*. They are used to indicate a noun that has not been mentioned before or to indicate something in general. *The* is the **definite article**. It identifies a definite or specific noun. For example, **The** *cat jumped into my lap* means something different from **A** *cat jumped into my lap*.

Use *a* before all words beginning with a consonant *sound*, even if the first letter is a vowel: **a** *useful object*, **a** *European country*. Use *an* before all words beginning with a vowel *sound*, even if the first letter is a consonant: **an** *hour*. Follow the same rules for abbreviations: *a UFO*, *an FCC decision*.

1.e.2 Indefinite pronouns as determiners

Indefinite pronouns (see 1.d.7) can be used before a noun to tell "how many." Such words as *no*, *every*, and *other* are also used as determiners, even though they are not pronouns.

EXAMPLES
Several musicians found work. [The indefinite pronoun *several* is used as a determiner before *musicians*, which is the subject of the sentence. Notice that this is different from *Several of the musicians found work*. In that sentence *several* is not a determiner; it is the subject.]
All musicians found work.
Few musicians found work.
No musicians found work.
Every musician found work.

1.e.3 Possessive pronouns as determiners

The possessive pronouns *my*, *your*, *his*, *her*, *it*, *our*, and *their* are used as determiners. The possessive forms of some indefinite pronouns are also used as determiners.

EXAMPLES

Our apartment overlooks the river.
My eyeglasses are too loose.
Conserving energy is **everyone's** concern.

1.e.4 Demonstrative pronouns as determiners

The demonstrative pronouns *this* and *that* are used as determiners before singular nouns. The plural forms *these* and *those* are used as determiners before plural nouns.

EXAMPLES

This sailor swims.
That sailor is seasick.
These sailors cannot swim.
Those sailors dance the hornpipe.

1.e.5 Numbers and numerals as determiners

Numbers and numerals can also be determiners. Numbers and numerals are sometimes considered adjectives, but they are used in the same way that indefinite pronouns are used as determiners: ***Three** tires needed air*. Numbers and numerals can also be used with other determiners: ***These three** tires need air, but **the fourth** tire is filled*.

EXERCISE 50. Identify the determiners in each of the following sentences. The number of determiners in the sentence is shown in parentheses after each sentence.

1. In 1979 Bryan Allen flew an unusual aircraft across the English Channel. (2)
2. The flight from the southeast coast of England to the French coast was 22.5 miles. (4)

3. Allen was part of a team of twenty-two people who worked on this project. (3)

4. Their aircraft, named *Gossamer Albatross*, weighed seventy-five pounds and was powered by two legs! (3)

5. The span of that craft's one wing was about ninety-four feet. (4)

6. Its pilot pedaled a propeller that was thirteen feet across. (3)

7. To maintain a minimum speed of twelve miles per hour, Allen would have to pedal at eighty revolutions per minute. (3)

8. The constant air turbulence forced Allen to make many adjustments to keep his altitude at ten feet. (4)

9. "As I begin to sweat from exertion, moisture forms on the transparent cockpit walls, obscuring my view," Allen recalls. (2)

10. The radio transmitter failed, probably from a dose of his perspiration. (3)

11. After pedaling for two hours, Allen had to battle winds of up to six miles per hour. (2)

12. With several miles still to go, Allen got a cramp in his leg. (3)

13. The exhausted pilot had no choice but to keep pedaling and to ignore his pain. (3)

14. Some instinct warned him just in time to pull up his craft when it dipped to inches above the water. (3)

15. In those last moments before reaching the beach, Allen felt a surge of power in his limbs. (4)

16. Many people gathered below the landing point, waving their arms and running around. (3)

17. Everyone's attention was riveted on this amazing aircraft and its daring captain. (3)

18. The weary Allen stopped pedaling, but his craft stayed aloft on its own for some seconds. (4)

19. Finally touching ground, Allen broke his way through the taped door, and fans cheered their hero. (3)

20. The achievement earned Allen and his co-workers world fame and a prize of $220,000. (3)

1.f ADVERBS

An **adverb** is a word that tells more about a verb, an adjective, or another adverb.

Adverbs tell *when, where, how,* or *to what degree.* The adverbs in the sentence below are shown in bold type. The words in red type indicate what the adverb tells about the word that it modifies. The arrows indicate what words the adverbs modify.

EXAMPLE

to what
degree   when   how   where

Extremely old people **sometimes** move **slowly upstairs**.

1.f.1 Kinds of adverbs

The five basic kinds of adverbs are adverbs of time, adverbs of place, adverbs of degree, adverbs of manner, and sentence adverbs.

■ Adverbs of time

Adverbs of time tell *when.* Some adverbs of time tell "at what time" (*simultaneously, eventually*), some tell "how long" (*briefly, eternally*), and some tell "how often" (*rarely, often*).

EXAMPLES

Melba arrives **today**.   She **seldom** visits us.
You will see her **soon**.

COMMON ADVERBS OF TIME

afterward	forever	sometimes
again	immediately	tomorrow
always	late	usually
before	never	weekly
finally	now	yearly
first	once	yesterday

▩ Adverbs of place

Adverbs of place tell *where*. Some adverbs of place tell about position (*locally*), some tell about direction (*right, downward*), and most can tell about either position or direction (*here, elsewhere*).

EXAMPLES
Robert ate **nearby**.   He ate **downtown**.
He did not go **far**.

COMMON ADVERBS OF PLACE

above	downward	out
anywhere	east	over
away	everywhere	off
back	forward	past
backward	here	sideways
below	left	straight
beside	near	through
by	nowhere	upstairs

▩ Adverbs of degree

Adverbs of degree tell *to what degree or extent*. When you use adverbs of degree with adjectives or other adverbs, you can call them **intensifiers**.

EXAMPLES
Wheat germ tastes **very** good with yogurt.
I tasted it **quite** reluctantly.

Following are other common adverbs of degree (in bold type).

COMMON ADVERBS OF DEGREE

absolutely idiotic	**otherwise** careful
almost perfect	**partly** cloudy
certainly beautiful	**rather** lazy
greatly aged	**scarcely** used
hardly damaged	**so** important
successful **indeed**	**somewhat** interesting
only once	**too** frilly

■ Adverbs of manner

Adverbs of manner tell *how* an action is done (*walked* **awkwardly**) or *the means by which* an action is done (*steered* **manually**). Adverbs of manner can also give information about adjectives (**hilariously** *funny*).

EXAMPLES

"How"	"By what means"
chopped **finely**	chopped **manually**
carved **skillfully**	carved **mechanically**
complained **angrily**	complained **officially**

Most adverbs of manner end in -*ly* and are formed from adjectives. For example, adding -*ly* to the adjectives *crisp* and *square* forms the adverbs *crisply* and *squarely*. Not all adverbs of manner end in -*ly* (for example, the adverb of manner *together* in *They ate* **together**). Furthermore, some words that end in -*ly* are adjectives (*friendly, lovely*).

■ Sentence adverbs

Sentence adverbs tell about an entire sentence rather than about one word in the sentence.

EXAMPLES
Luckily, the avalanche missed us.
It came uncomfortably close, **actually**.
It was caused, **apparently**, by melting snow.

EXERCISE 51. Identify the adverb in each of the following sentences. Tell what each modifies.

1. Diamonds are very valuable stones.
2. They have always been prized as gems.
3. Diamonds are used for practical purposes here.
4. Actually, an American spacecraft was equipped with a diamond window.
5. Diamond is the transparent material that could easily stand the extremes of temperature and pressure.

6. Eye surgeons can now remove cataracts with diamond knives.
7. Diamonds often are associated with romance and superstition.
8. The beautifully cut Hope Diamond is reputed to have brought disaster to its owners.
9. A diamond ring is usually given for engagements and weddings as a symbol of everlasting love.
10. This mysterious and highly prized gem is crystallized carbon.

APPLICATION. Select five of the adverbs that you identified for Exercise 51. Write one original sentence for each adverb.

EXERCISE 52. Identify each italicized adverb in the following sentences as: a) an adverb of time, b) an adverb of place, c) an adverb of degree, d) an adverb of manner, or e) a sentence adverb.

1. *Very* intense heat and pressure crystallize carbon into diamonds *underground*.
2. Diamonds vary *rather widely* in value.
3. Experts *usually* determine diamond value *quite simply* by evaluating carat, cut, clarity, and color.
4. A high weight in carats *definitely* raises a diamond's value.
5. The carat weight of a rough diamond may be *greatly* reduced when it is cut.
6. If a diamond is polished and shaped *expertly*, it is more valuable than a rough diamond weighing the same.
7. Fifty-eight facets sparkle *brilliantly* from the most popular diamond cut.
8. Well-cut diamonds are *breathtakingly* beautiful.
9. Diamonds that are flawed *heavily almost always* cost less than flawless stones.
10. *Generally*, colorless diamonds are the most highly valued.

APPLICATION. Select five of the adverbs that you identified for Exercise 52. Write one original sentence for each adverb.

1.f.2 Negative words as adverbs

Adverbs include the word *not* and the contraction *-n't*. Here are other negative words that also serve as adverbs:

EXAMPLES
The runner was **not** very fast.
He **never** won a race.
He was **nowhere** near the front of the line.
He **hardly** managed to finish at all.
He ran **only** to keep in shape.

1.f.3 Forms of adverbs: comparison

Most adverbs have three degrees—the regular form, the **comparative**, and the **superlative**.

The comparative degree compares two people or things (*faster, more cheerfully*). The superlative degree compares more than two people or things (*fastest, most cheerfully*). You can express a comparison with adverbs in several ways:

1. by using *-er* and *-est* or *more* and *most* (In general, use *-er* and *-est* for all except *-ly* adverbs.)
2. by using *as*
3. by using *less* and *least*

1.f.4 Irregular adverbs: comparison

Some adverbs have special forms.

	COMPARATIVE ADVERB	SUPERLATIVE ADVERB
badly	worse	(the) worst
well	better	(the) best
little	less	(the) least
far (distance)	farther	(the) farthest,
far (degree)	further	(the) furthest

EXERCISE 53. There are two blanks in each item below. Fill in the first blank with the appropriate comparative form of the adverb in bold type. Fill in the second blank with the superlative form.

> EXAMPLE Olympic athletes swim **quickly**.
> a) Some swim *more quickly* than others. (comparative)
> b) Those who swim *most quickly* win medals. (superlative)

1. Olympic medals are **highly** prized by athletes.
   a) The silver medal is _____ prized than the bronze medal. (comparative)
   b) The gold medal is the _____ prized of the three medals. (superlative)
2. Some athletes throw the javelin **far**.
   a) The competitors try to throw it _____ than their rivals. (comparative)
   b) The gold-medal winner is the one who throws the javelin the _____. (superlative)
3. Gymnasts perform **gracefully**.
   a) Those gymnasts who perform _____ receive a higher score. (comparative)
   b) The gymnasts who perform the _____ sometimes receive a score of ten. (superlative)
4. The popularity of gymnastics has grown **rapidly** in America.
   a) The popularity of gymnastics has grown even _____ among girls than among boys. (comparative)
   b) It has grown _____ among young children. (superlative)
5. The walking race in the Olympics is not known **well**.
   a) People who have seen the walking race appreciate it _____. (comparative)
   b) Its participants like it the _____. (superlative)

1.f.5 Adjective or adverb?

Certain words can be either adjectives or adverbs, depending on how you use them in a sentence. To decide whether a word is an adjective or an adverb, look at the word it tells about, or modifies. Adjectives tell more about nouns (see 1.c). Adverbs tell more about verbs, adjectives, and other adverbs.

EXAMPLES

Hilda likes **hard** candy. [The adjective *hard* describes the noun *candy*.]

Hilda bit **hard** on the candy. [The adverb *hard* tells *how* Hilda bit on the candy.]

Other words that can be either adverbs or adjectives include *well, early, long, late*, and *low*.

1.f.6 *Good* vs. *well*; *bad* vs. *badly*

Good and *bad* are always adjectives. *Badly* is always an adverb. *Well* can be an adverb of manner: *He drove* ***well*** (meaning "skillfully"). *Well* can also be an adjective: *He is* ***well*** (meaning "in good health"). The following chart shows the different uses of each word.

GOOD VS. WELL; BAD VS. BADLY

	good	well
adjective (after linking verb)	I feel **good**. [in good health; happy] I look **good** in that. [well dressed]	I feel **well**. [in good health; satisfactory]
adverb (after action verb)	DO NOT USE WITH ACTION VERB.	I play **well**. [how I play]

	bad	badly
adjective (after linking verb)	I feel **bad**. [in poor health; sad] I look **bad**. [in poor health]	DO NOT USE WITH LINKING VERB.
adverb (after action verb)	DO NOT USE WITH ACTION VERB.	It hurts **badly**. [how it hurts]

EXERCISE 54. Tell whether the italicized word in each sentence is an adjective or adverb. Refer to 1.f.4 and 1.f.6 for help with *good, bad*, and *well*.

1. On October 15, 1973, Peter Jenkins began a *long* hike from a small town in New York.
2. He was a *better* walker than most people.
3. When Jenkins reached his goal, he had traveled *far* in both distance and experience.
4. His best experience came *midway* in his journey, at the New Orleans Baptist Theological Seminary.
5. Jenkins arranged to stay with a seminary student *there*.
6. Having traveled two thousand miles, Jenkins felt *good* as he entered New Orleans.
7. A few of his experiences had made him feel *bad*; for instance, he saw his dog killed by a car.
8. That was the *worst* experience, however, and most days had gone *well* for Jenkins.
9. Now he needed some time to consider what would happen *next*.
10. He also needed money and was willing to work *hard* to earn it.
11. Then a woman came *along*.
12. *Actually*, Jenkins passed the mansion where female students lived.
13. The front door flew *open*, and a student ran out, laughing.
14. Curiosity drew the young man inside the *open* door.
15. A girl stepped *forward* and gleefully poured a jug of water over him.
16. It did not take *long* for Jenkins to return Barbara Pennel's favor by thoroughly dousing her.
17. As they laughed and dried themselves, Barbara agreed to show him *around*.
18. They fell in love *immediately*.
19. After much *hard* thinking the couple decided to marry and finish the trip *together*.
20. They had many adventures—*good* and *bad*— before they reached the Oregon coast over two years later.

1.f.7 Noun or adverb?

Some words can be either nouns or adverbs of time or place, depending on how you use them in a sentence. Words like *yesterday, today*, and *tomorrow* can function as nouns or as adverbs of time. Words that can be both nouns and adverbs of place include *home, uptown, downstairs*, and *outdoors*.

EXAMPLES

noun	adverb
Yesterday was eventful.	We were busy **yesterday**. [adverb of time]
Today is a holiday.	We will celebrate **today**. [adverb of time]
The great **outdoors** is beautiful.	Children love to play **outdoors**. [adverb of place]

AVOIDING ERRORS WITH ADVERBS

1. Ordinarily, do not use two negative words (a **double negative**) in the same clause. Use only one negative word to express a negative idea.

   NOT I ~~never~~ ate ~~none~~ of that fudge.
   BUT I **never** ate **any** of that fudge.

   NOT They do ~~not~~ have ~~no~~ brownies.
   BUT They do **not** have **any** brownies.

2. Place adverbs of degree as close as possible to the words they modify. Misplaced adverbs make a sentence confusing.

   NOT He has ~~almost~~ completed all his chores. [Has he not completely finished any of them?]
   BUT He has completed **almost** all his chores. [He has finished most of them.]

REVIEW EXERCISE E. Identify the fifty italicized words in the paragraph below as (a) nouns, (b) adjectives, (c) adverbs of time, (d) adverbs of place, (e) adverbs of degree, (f) adverbs of manner, (g) sentence adverbs, or (h) negative words used as adverbs.

1   It was a perfect night for Halloween. A *full* moon hung
2 *low* on the horizon. A leafless tree cast *long* shadows on the
3 face of the deserted manor. Georgia was waiting for Clar-
4 ence *outside*. He had asked her *yesterday* to meet him
5 *there*. Clarence was *always* developing *unusual* ideas.
6 Sometimes they were *good*, but *often* they were *not so*
7 good. Georgia had arrived *early*, even though she knew
8 that Clarence was *usually late*. *Strange* sounds, like
9 moans, floated down from an *open* attic window. To keep
10 her spirits *high* Georgia began singing softly. This did *not*
11 make her feel *better*, however. Georgia did not sing *well*.
12 Her voice sometimes shook *badly*. Listening to her own
13 singing *only* compounded Georgia's uneasy feelings.
14   The hours passed *slowly*. It was *early morning*. *Yester-*
15 *day* seemed a *long* time ago. Would Clarence *never* arrive?
16 When Georgia sat down, the *hard* steps made her feel even
17 *worse*. She would be *very* angry with Clarence when she
18 saw him *next*.
19   *Suddenly*, the front door flew *open*. As she whirled
20 *around*, a *dark* figure loomed *forward*. Georgia jumped
21 back, terrified, and let out a loud shriek. She was bolting
22 *away* when the "ghost" laughed and stepped into the
23 moonlight.
24   Clarence could *hardly* speak because he was laughing *so*
25 *hard*. "My plan worked *perfectly*," he gasped. "I promised
26 you a Halloween that you would *never* forget."
27   Georgia sat down again, smiling weakly. *Actually*, Clar-
28 ence had treated her *badly*, but it was *good* to see a
29 *friendly* face after gazing at the moon *so long*.

1.g PREPOSITIONS

A **preposition** is a word that shows the relationship of a noun or pronoun to some other word in the sentence.

Prepositions are always used in a phrase. They are never used alone. Prepositions show space, time, and other relationships.

SPACE
The drugstore is **on** the street corner.
The candy counter is **near** the drugstore.
The pharmacist is **behind** the counter.

TIME
The drugstore stays open **until** midnight.
The students stop for sodas **after** school.
The waiter is extremely busy **during** lunch hour.

OTHER
The drugstore has a service **for** developing films.
It has three racks **of** paperback books.
The paperbacks are arranged alphabetically **by** author.

COMMON PREPOSITIONS

about	by	over
above	concerning	past
across	despite	pending
after	down	regarding
against	during	respecting
along	except	since
amid	excepting	through
among	for	throughout
around	from	to
as	in	toward
at	inside	under
before	into	underneath
behind	like	until
below	of	unto
beneath	off	up
beside	on	upon
besides	onto	with
between	out	within
beyond	outside	without

Some prepositions are called **compound prepositions** because they are made up of more than one word.

COMMON COMPOUND PREPOSITIONS

according to	in spite of
apart from	instead of
aside from	on account of
as to	on top of
because of	out of
by way of	owing to
in addition to	

EXERCISE 55. Identify each of the prepositions in the following sentences. The number of prepositions in the sentence is shown in parentheses after each sentence.

1. For short-range forecasts, private citizens can be more accurate at times than the weather bureau. (2)
2. Records of weather prediction date back to 4000 B.C. (2)
3. The actions of birds were linked to approaching storms. (2)
4. Swallows fly higher in fair weather than they do before a storm. (2)
5. If New England lobster trappers see gulls and wild geese fly to the sea in the morning, they follow. (2)
6. You can even tell the correct temperature by the number of chirps of a cricket. (3)
7. If you add thirty-seven to the number of times a cricket chirps in fifteen seconds, you will know the correct temperature in degrees Fahrenheit. (4)
8. Bees return to their hives before a storm and remain inside it until the end of the storm. (5)
9. The sky at sunset is another indication of the next day's weather. (2)
10. Yellows and greens in the sky at dusk usually mean that there will be dry weather during the next twenty-four hours. (3)

EXERCISE 56. Identify the compound prepositions in each of the following sentences.

1. According to Nelson Algren, the Federal Writers' Project helped Richard Wright to become known.
2. In addition to novels Richard Wright wrote short stories.

3. The success of the novel *Native Son* was assured because of the author's talent.
4. Aside from his other achievements, Wright won a prize for his piece called "Portrait of Harlem."
5. In addition to his other prizes, Richard Wright won a Guggenheim Fellowship.

1.g.1 Prepositional phrases; objects of prepositions

A **prepositional phrase** is a group of words that begins with a preposition and usually ends with a noun or pronoun.

The **object of a preposition** is usually a noun or pronoun that follows the preposition.

Objects of prepositions can be nouns, proper nouns, pronouns, gerunds, other prepositional phrases, or noun clauses.

EXAMPLES

The elevator goes **to the basement**. [noun as object of preposition]

Many early elevators were manufactured **by the Otis Elevator Company**. [proper noun as object]

Elevators are familiar **to us**. [pronoun as object]

Some people stay fit **by walking**. [gerund as object]

A noise came **from under the elevator**. [prepositional phrase as object]

Whether or not you take the elevator may depend **on where you live**. [clause as object]

Adjectives or determiners can be placed between the preposition and its object.

EXAMPLES

The elevator goes all the way **to** the cool, dark **basement**.

Many early elevators were manufactured **by** the inventive and highly successful **Otis Elevator Company**.

EXERCISE 57. Identify the preposition and its object (or objects) in each of the following sentences.

1. Concerned Omaha business leaders formed a civic group in 1895.
2. Ak-Sar-Ben, the name of Omaha's civic group, is *Nebraska* spelled backward.
3. Omaha's Ak-Sar-Ben has encouraged the citizens' sense of pride and accomplishment.
4. Among the Ak-Sar-Ben's many civic projects are an annual rodeo and many scholarship programs.
5. Omaha now prospers because of many new industries.
6. Many people are involved in the huge meat-packing organizations.
7. In addition to numerous insurance companies, there are food processing and construction firms.
8. Downtown Omaha has skyscrapers and hotels, connected by walkways.
9. Ak-Sar-Ben is a model for civic groups.
10. Omaha's Ak-Sar-Ben is very proud of what the city has achieved.

1.g.2 Preposition or adverb?

Certain words can be prepositions or adverbs, depending upon the way you use them in a sentence. The list of prepositions on page 85 includes many words that can also act as adverbs. There is a major difference between them: Prepositions always take objects. Adverbs never take objects. Notice the difference, for example, between *outside* as a preposition and *outside* as an adverb.

EXAMPLES
Why did you wait **outside**? [adverb]
Why did you wait **outside the terminal**? [preposition and object]

EXERCISE 58. In each of the following sentences, identify the preposition and its object.

1. Elizabeth Blackwell was the first woman who earned a medical degree in America.
2. Blackwell originally worked as a schoolteacher.
3. Students objected, but the Geneva College medical school rejected Blackwell's application in spite of them.
4. The student council, however, voted unanimously for Elizabeth Blackwell's acceptance.
5. Philadelphia's Blackley Almshouse gave a junior resident's job to her.
6. Elizabeth Blackwell's courageous conduct during a typhus epidemic won everyone's respect.
7. Blackwell received her medical diploma with the other 1849 graduates.
8. Elizabeth Blackwell's marks were well above the average.
9. Dr. Blackwell founded a woman's hospital in New York City.
10. In addition to Florence Nightingale, Elizabeth Blackwell had many other famous friends.

EXERCISE 59. Identify the italicized words in the following sentences as prepositions or adverbs.

1. You may have heard the phrase "little goody two shoes" *before*.
2. Few people know that there is a book by that same name *around*.
3. People *around* the publishing industry recognize the name of the man who published the book: John Newbery.
4. *Besides* children's books, Newbery published books *for* adults.
5. No one had published children's books successfully *before*.
6. Newbery's children's books were handsomely illustrated *throughout* by talented engravers.
7. Newbery captured the children's literature market *through* modern advertising techniques.
8. He published books that have *since* become classics.
9. *After* whom is the annual award for the best children's book by an American named?
10. The Newbery Medal for children's literature was around *before* your birth.

AVOIDING ERRORS WITH PREPOSITIONS

Use prepositions consistently in a series.

NOT   The train stopped at Boston, New York City, and at Philadelphia. [Two items in the series have prepositions; one does not.]

BUT   The train stopped at Boston, New York City, and Philadelphia. [one preposition for the entire series]

OR   The train stopped **at** Boston, **at** New York City, and **at** Philadelphia. [a preposition for each item in the series]

1.h CONJUNCTIONS

A **conjunction** is a word that joins other words or groups of words.

Conjunctions can link two or more nouns, pronouns, adjectives, verbs, adverbs, prepositions, other conjunctions, phrases, or clauses. Remember that *conjunctions connect.*

1.h.1 Coordinating conjunctions

Coordinating conjunctions connect parts of a sentence that are of equal, or coordinate, value. Coordinating conjunctions link words, phrases, or clauses. The three most common coordinating conjunctions are *and, but,* and *or. For* and *nor* are sometimes used as coordinating conjunctions.

EXERCISE 60. Identify the coordinating conjunction in each of the following sentences. One sentence contains two coordinating conjunctions.

1. Airline dispatchers are responsible for the safety of planes and of millions of passengers.
2. The pilot and the dispatcher are two of the authorities who can cancel or delay a flight.
3. Dispatchers control hundreds of lives at one time, and so they are trained thoroughly.
4. Dispatchers must be twenty-three, but few are so young.
5. A college education is essential, and courses in meteorology are valuable.
6. Many have had experience as pilots or radio operators.
7. The dispatchers' day is a long one, for they must discuss flight conditions with the next person on duty.
8. Before permitting a plane to take off, the dispatcher checks the plane's fuel capacity and weight.
9. There are no hasty decisions in the work of an airline dispatcher, nor are there irreversible orders.
10. Flight conditions may change, and so the dispatcher must constantly keep track of many variables.

AVOIDING ERRORS WITH COORDINATING CONJUNCTIONS

1. Do not forget to use a coordinating conjunction between two main clauses (see 2.n). If you forget the conjunction, you will have a **run-on sentence**.

   NOT There is a cassette sale at the store I bought three blank tapes.

   BUT There is a cassette sale at the store, **and** I bought three blank tapes.

2. Do not use *so* as a coordinating conjunction in writing. Use *and so*, or reword your sentence.

   NOT I use my cassette deck frequently, so I clean the heads twice a week.

   BUT I use my cassette deck frequently, **and so** I clean the heads twice a week.

COMMAS WITH COORDINATING CONJUNCTIONS

1. Use a comma before a coordinating conjunction that links two main clauses (see 2.n).

   I wanted to ski**,** **but** I did not know how.

2. Do not use a comma before the coordinating conjunction that links the two parts of a compound verb.

   NOT   We showered̸and changed after skiing.
   BUT   We showered and changed after skiing.

EXERCISE 61. Identify the coordinating conjunction in each of the following sentences. Indicate the words, phrases, or clauses that are linked by the conjunction.

1. Atop Mount Washington, wind velocity has been measured at 231 miles per hour, and temperature has been recorded at minus 47° Fahrenheit.

2. Station WMTW-TV maintains transmitting facilities on Mount Washington, for the high altitude increases transmitting range.

3. The U.S. Weather Bureau has a year-round station on the summit, and meteorologists spend the winter there.

4. The weather station meteorologists and the television technicians say that they have sensed an invisible presence on Mount Washington.

5. These people are not superstitious, nor do they believe in ghosts.

6. The Kennebec-Abnaki tribe considered Mount Washington the home of "the great spirit," and so they named it Agiocochook.

7. Three men spent the winter on Mount Washington, but S. A. Nelson was the first to weather a summit gale alone.

8. In May of 1871 Nelson wrote in his journal that a dead calm followed the winds and that he felt that he was not alone.

9. Al Oxton of the Mount Washington Observatory watched a curtain being lifted off its hooks and dropped around his neck.
10. Do you think that there is a ghost or a great spirit on Mount Washington?

1.h.2 Correlative conjunctions

Correlative conjunctions are pairs of words.

both . . . and	neither . . . nor
either . . . or	not only . . . but also
just as . . . so	whether . . . or

EXAMPLES

Coordinating conjunctions	Correlative conjunctions
Men **and** women wear sneakers.	**Both** men **and** women wear sneakers.
A man **or** a woman will win the election.	**Either** a man **or** a woman will win the election.

EXERCISE 62. Identify both parts of the correlative conjunction in each of the following sentences.

1. In 1979, the International Year of the Child, children's art appeared on both U.S. postage stamps and holiday seals.
2. The 1979 holiday seals showed children's paintings not only from the fifty states but also from Puerto Rico, the Virgin Islands, and Guam.
3. Both traditional holiday scenes and abstract art were selected.
4. The themes for the seals were chosen neither by the American Lung Association nor by the design sponsors.
5. Each school decided whether to tell the child what to draw or just to suggest a holiday theme.
6. Just as the 1979 holiday seals celebrated children's art, so did postage stamps from many other countries.
7. Either art by children or art for children was chosen to decorate 1979 postage stamps.

8. Colorful stamps of Walt Disney's cartoon characters were issued by both Grenada and Dominica.
9. Neither Ireland nor Mexico neglected to issue special stamps.
10. Famous paintings of children chosen for commemorative stamps included works by both Goya and Titian.

1.h.3 Conjunctive adverbs

Conjunctive adverbs are used as conjunctions to link closely related main clauses in a compound sentence (see 2.n). They are stronger than coordinating conjunctions because they more precisely explain the relationship of the two clauses. A conjunctive adverb is always preceded by a semicolon and often followed by a comma.

EXAMPLES
Airplanes are much faster than trains, **but** they are more often delayed by bad weather. [coordinating conjunction]
Airplanes are much faster than trains; **however**, they are more often delayed by bad weather. [conjunctive adverb]

Buses are comfortable for short trips, **and** bus trips are relatively inexpensive. [coordinating conjunction]
Buses are comfortable for short trips; **moreover**, bus trips are relatively inexpensive. [conjunctive adverb]

Conjunctive adverbs have these uses:

1. to replace *and* or to reinforce: *also, besides, furthermore, moreover*
2. to replace *but*: *however, nevertheless, still, though, yet*
3. to state a result: *consequently, therefore, thus*
4. to state equality: *equally, likewise, similarly*

EXERCISE 63. In each of the following sentences, the italicized word is a coordinating conjunction that links two clauses. Replace the coordinating conjunction with a conjunctive adverb that makes sense in the sentence.

1. The wheel was among the most influential of the ancient technological inventions, *and* it is vital to today's civilization.
2. Modern transportation depends upon wheels, *and* most everyday appliances use the principle of rotation.
3. Sharp-edged tools were undoubtedly found in nature, *but* there are no examples of wheels in nature.
4. Most ancient inventions were made simultaneously by several different peoples, *but* the wheel was invented only once.
5. The wheel was invented in the Middle East around 4000 B.C., *but* it was never used in ancient Africa.
6. Early wheels were solid wooden disks, *and* the axle rotated with each pair of wheels.
7. Later, an ingenious person made a hole in the center of each wheel, *and* the wheels could revolve around a fixed axle.
8. The wheel is necessary to most moving devices, *and* it is vital to modern vehicles.
9. The potter's wheel revolutionized pottery production, *and* it allowed for symmetry.
10. Many ancient peoples used the potter's wheel, *but* some of these never used the wheel for transportation.

1.h.4 Subordinating conjunctions

Subordinating conjunctions join subordinate clauses to main clauses in sentences (see 2.o). A subordinating conjunction shows the relationship of the main clause and the subordinate clause.

EXAMPLES
He bought a new stereo **because** the old speakers broke. [The subordinating conjunction explains the relationship between the main and the subordinate clauses by telling *why*.]

He bought a new stereo **after** the old speakers broke. [The subordinating conjunction explains the relationship by telling *when*.]

COMMON SUBORDINATING CONJUNCTIONS

after	since	whenever
although	than	where
as	though	whereas
because	unless	wherever
before	until	while
if	when	

Notice that some words that are used as subordinating conjunctions can also be used as other parts of speech. For example, *after, before, since,* and *until* can be prepositions, and *after, before,* and *since* can be adverbs.

Compound subordinating conjunctions are made up of more than one word.

COMPOUND SUBORDINATING CONJUNCTIONS

as far as	for fear (that)	seeing (that)
as long as	inasmuch as	so long as
as soon as	in order that	so that
as though	in the hope that	supposing that
considering (that)	provided (that)	to the end that

COMMAS WITH SUBORDINATING CONJUNCTIONS

If a subordinating conjunction (followed by a subordinate clause) begins the sentence, use a comma after the subordinate clause.

As soon as the electricity goes off, all the electric clocks stop.

Unless they are powered, electric clocks will not show the right time.

EXERCISE 64. Identify the subordinating conjunction in each of the following sentences. Remember that compound subordinating conjunctions are made up of more than one word.

1. Considering that he was totally blind by his eighth birthday, Harold Krents's achievements are extraordinary.
2. Life is not easy when you are visually handicapped.
3. When he was in high school, Harold became president of the school.
4. Because Krents was brilliant, he was accepted at Harvard.
5. Before he went to Harvard, Krents spent the summer as a music and dramatics counselor at a camp.
6. Inasmuch as he could find his way among the tents in the dark, Krents easily kept the campers quiet after taps.
7. As soon as he had graduated *cum laude* from Harvard College, Krents was accepted at Harvard Law School.
8. Harold Krents became acquainted with his future wife while she was reading for blind law students.
9. Harold Krents was very surprised when his draft board mistakenly classified him 1-A.
10. After he had heard Krents's story, Leonard Gershe wrote a Broadway hit about a blind man.

REVIEW EXERCISE F. Identify the conjunction in each of the following sentences as (a) a coordinating conjunction, (b) a correlative conjunction, (c) a conjunctive adverb, or (d) a subordinating conjunction.

1. Because people are still searching for it, you may have heard Atlantis called "the lost island continent."
2. While many tales of rediscovered islands seem unlikely, the "lost" island of Bouvet was indeed rediscovered.
3. Bouvet Island was first seen in 1739 by sailors when they were seeking a southern polar continent.
4. Either the sea was too rough for the sailors to land, or the coast was too rocky.
5. In 1772 Captain James Cook twice tried to find Bouvet Island and failed.
6. As far as the world was concerned, an island that Captain Cook could not find did not exist.
7. In 1808 Captain James Lindsay not only saw Bouvet Island but also sailed his ship around it.

8. People did not believe Captain Lindsay, for Captain Cook could not fail.

·9. An American seal hunter claimed that he had landed on Bouvet Island; however, he was known to be a boastful liar.

10. On December 1, 1927, a Norwegian whaler rediscovered Bouvet Island; furthermore, he hoisted the Norwegian flag there.

REVIEW EXERCISE G. Replace the blank in each of the following sentences with a conjunction that makes sense. The kind of conjunction to use is stated in parentheses after each sentence. Use commas and semicolons correctly.

1. The Flathead River lies mostly in the United States; _____ its headwaters are in Canada. (conjunctive adverb)

2. The lands drained by the Flathead River are forest, _____ they are populated by about two thirds of the remaining grizzly bears. (coordinating conjunction)

3. _____ the threatened grizzly _____ the Rocky Mountain wolf inhabit the Flathead wilderness. (correlative conjunction)

4. The North Fork of the Flathead River is eventually joined by _____ the Middle Fork _____ the South Fork. (correlative conjunction)

5. _____ you visit the North Fork valley, you may meet Mary McFarland, a retired veterinarian. (subordinating conjunction)

6. From Mary McFarland's window you can see mountains _____ you turn. (subordinating conjunction)

7. Luckily, _____ a Dolly Varden trout _____ a rare cutthroat trout is a likely catch along the Flathead River. (correlative conjunction: Pay attention to the form of the linking verb.)

8. Otters play along the Flathead River _____ bald eagles soar overhead. (subordinating conjunction)

9. _____ it leaves the wild country, the Flathead River meanders through rich farmlands into Lake Flathead, which is just west of the Mississippi. (subordinating conjunction)

10. _____ the Flathead emerges from the lake, it turns west to join the mighty Columbia River. (subordinating conjunction)

1.i INTERJECTIONS

An **interjection** is a word or phrase that expresses emotion or exclamation. An interjection has no grammatical connection to any other words.

An interjection can either be part of a sentence or stand alone.

EXAMPLES
Oh, I cannot remember that.
Well, she said so.
My gosh!
Ha! I told you so!
Ouch, that hurts!

1.j VERBALS

Verbals are formed from verbs and, therefore, carry the idea of action.

Verbals are used as nouns, adjectives, and adverbs. They resemble verbs in some ways, but they also resemble other parts of speech.

There are three kinds of verbals:

1. participles (used as adjectives)
2. gerunds (used as nouns)
3. infinitives (used as nouns, adjectives, or adverbs)

1.k PARTICIPLES AS ADJECTIVES

The present-participle form and the past-participle form of a verb can be used as adjectives.

EXAMPLES

Verb	Present participle	Past participle
freeze	freezing	frozen
heat	heating	heated
lose	losing	lost

The **freezing** rain slowly turned to hail.
Frozen switches delayed all the trains.
A **heated** argument occurred among the **losing** players.

Present participles always end in *-ing*. Past participles often end in *-ed*, but they can also take other forms, as in *frozen* or *lost*. (See 1.b.7.)

1.I PARTICIPIAL PHRASES

A **participial phrase** contains a participle and other words that describe, or modify, the participle.

A participial phrase can be formed with a present participle or a past participle. Participial phrases can be used in various positions in a sentence.

EXAMPLES
We saw John McEnroe **playing tennis**. [a present participle plus its object]
Disappointed with his first serve, McEnroe then served a winner. [a past participle plus a prepositional phrase]
You rarely see fans **sitting quietly** when John McEnroe plays. [a present participle plus an adverb]
Graciously accepting the trophy from the sponsor, McEnroe grinned at the crowd. [an adverb plus a present participle plus an object plus a prepositional phrase.]

EXERCISE 65. Identify the participial phrase in each of the following sentences.

1. American women, dressing in various styles, often adopt the clothes of other countries.
2. The demand for clothing and jewelry imported from other lands is great.
3. Chinese textile mills export silk decorated by hand.
4. A wool scarf woven in Ecuador is warm and colorful.
5. Brides wear lace veils made by French nuns.
6. Thin bracelets, shining with gold and glass beads, come from India.

7. East European cloths, delicately embroidered, make beautiful head scarves.

8. Freshwater pearls imported from Japan become necklaces and earrings.

9. Czechoslovakian garnets glittering in a gold ring will flatter your fingers.

10. Italy exports gold hoops for ears pierced for the latest look.

COMMAS WITH PARTICIPLES AND PARTICIPIAL PHRASES

1. Use commas to set off participles or participial phrases that are not essential to a sentence. If the sentence makes sense without the participle or participial phrase, commas are usually necessary.

> The young tennis player, **defeated in the first game,** went on to beat the champion.
> The champion, **playing an aggressive game,** ran to net at every opportunity.

2. Do not use commas to set off a participle or participial phrase that is essential to the meaning of the sentence.

> The man **playing tennis in the near court** is Jimmy Connors.
> A ball **served by Connors** is often a winner.

3. Always use a comma after a participial phrase that begins a sentence.

> **Played at Flushing Meadow in New York,** the U.S. Open is a major American tennis competition.
> **Remodeled recently,** the Louis Armstrong Stadium is the site of the U.S. Open.

AVOIDING ERRORS WITH PARTICIPLES AND PARTICIPIAL PHRASES

1. Do not make a participle or participial phrase refer to an idea that is in your head but not in your sentence. This error is called a **dangling modifier** or **dangling participial phrase**.

NOT Wandering off without permission, a ~~search party~~ found her the next day.

BUT Wandering off without permission, **the girl** was found by a search party the next day.

NOT Hiking in unfamiliar country, an ~~unusual plant~~ lured her off the trail.

BUT Hiking in unfamiliar country, **the girl** was lured off the trail by an unusual plant.

In the first example, *wandering off without permission* seems to refer to *search party*. Actually, it refers to *the girl*, a term that is not in the sentence. In the second example, *hiking in unfamiliar country* seems to refer to *plant*. It refers to *the girl*, a term not in the sentence.

2. Do not make a participle or participial phrase modify the wrong noun or pronoun in the sentence. This error is called a **misplaced modifier**.

NOT The search party found her ~~using binoculars that could spot her a mile away~~. [Who used the binoculars?]

BUT **Using binoculars that could spot her a mile away, the search party** found her.

NOT The girl hiked in unfamiliar territory ~~leaving her compass in the camp~~. [Did the territory leave the compass in the camp?]

BUT The **girl, leaving her compass in the camp**, hiked in unfamiliar territory.

EXERCISE 66. Reword the following sentences to correct the dangling or misplaced participles or phrases.

1. Elected to her first term, the Eighty-ninth Congress received Patricia Takemoto Mink as its eighth congresswoman.
2. Interested in politics at an early age, her high school elected Mink president of the student body.
3. Obtaining her law degree from the University of Chicago in 1952, law firms were not interested in hiring a woman.
4. The lawyer opened a one-person law firm undaunted by her situation.
5. Learning to organize young politicians, her efforts began to pay off in 1954.
6. Ringing doorbells and handing out leaflets, the 1954 campaign introduced Patricia Mink into politics.
7. Running successfully for a position in the Hawaiian House of Representatives, encouragement was given to her by her husband.
8. Well qualified for the Congress in Washington, four years in the Hawaiian Congress were Patricia Mink's credentials.
9. Recognized as a champion of women's rights, an early equal rights bill was sponsored by Mink.
10. Advising young female politicians to develop a specialty, expertise in politics was encouraged by Mink.

1.m GERUNDS

A **gerund** is a verb form that ends in *-ing* and that is used in the same ways a noun is used.

The difference between a present participle and a gerund is that a present participle is used as an adjective and a gerund is used as a noun.

EXAMPLES

Gerunds	Nouns
I enjoy **eating**.	I enjoy **dinner**.
Snacking adds calories.	**Chocolate** adds calories.
Cooking requires talent.	**Ballet** requires talent.

1.n GERUND PHRASES

A **gerund phrase** contains a gerund and other words that describe, or modify, the gerund.

A gerund phrase can vary in length, depending upon how you expand the gerund.

EXAMPLES
Making a success of your career requires maturity. [a gerund plus an object plus a prepositional phrase]
More diligent studying is required in college than in high school. [a comparative adjective modifying a gerund]
Success in any field depends on **planning well** and on **taking necessary risks**. [two gerund phrases]

EXERCISE 67. Identify the gerunds and gerund phrases in the following sentences. The number of gerunds or gerund phrases is given in parentheses at the end of each sentence.

1. Studying abroad has alway been popular with American students. (1)
2. Planning is important so that you can obtain a proper program of study. (1)
3. Many young people mistakenly think that relaxing and sightseeing will take up most of their time. (2)
4. Attending classes and studying take at least as much time and effort abroad as in America. (2)
5. In many foreign countries learning the language is the American student's first problem. (1)
6. Understanding foreign customs is often difficult. (1)
7. Methods of teaching are sometimes very different abroad. (1)
8. Lecturing is more common than conducting seminars. (2)
9. Counseling students or initiating class discussion is not considered the professor's responsibility. (2)
10. Students are held entirely responsible for mastering the subject. (1)

APPLICATION. Select five of the gerunds that you identified in Exercise 67, and write one original sentence for each. Make sure that you use the -*ing* word as a gerund, not as a present participle.

EXERCISE 68. Identify the gerund phrases in each of the following sentences.

1. Finding a part-time or temporary job is sometimes difficult for young people.
2. Training temporary employees is not always profitable for employers.
3. Getting a temporary or part-time job in Europe is even more difficult for young Americans.
4. Living and working in Europe means learning to speak another language fluently.
5. Getting the work permit that most foreign countries require is often very difficult.

1.0 INFINITIVES

An **infinitive** is a verb form, usually preceded by the word *to*, that is used as a noun, an adjective, or an adverb.

When you use the word *to* before a verb, the *to* is not a preposition.

Infinitives can be used in the same ways that you use nouns, adjectives, and adverbs.

EXAMPLES

Infinitives	**Nouns**
To sleep is relaxing.	**Travel** is relaxing.
Everyone needs **to sleep**.	Everyone needs **food**.

Infinitives	**Adjectives**
I had a tendency **to drowse**.	**It was a constant** tendency.

Infinitives	**Adverbs**
He was eager **to read**.	He was **immediately** eager.

1.p INFINITIVE PHRASES

An **infinitive phrase** contains an infinitive and other words that describe, or modify, the infinitive.

EXAMPLES
They wanted **to eat quickly**. [an infinitive followed by an adverb]

It was fun **to tell her the news**. [an infinitive followed by an indirect object and a direct object]

My baby sister loves **to nap holding her toy bear**. [an infinitive followed by a participial phrase]

We decided **to hurry to arrive early for the party**. [Adding another infinitive to the first infinitive creates an infinitive phrase.]

In general, do not split an infinitive. A **split infinitive** has an adverb between the *to* and the basic verb. It is almost always better to place the adverb elsewhere in the sentence.

NOT   Frank wished to ~~quickly~~ end the argument.
BUT   Frank wished to end the argument quickly.

EXERCISE 69. Identify the infinitive phrase in each of the following sentences. One sentence has two infinitive phrases.

1. One of the most remarkable figures to join the American labor movement was Mary Harris Jones.
2. In 1880, at age fifty, Jones decided to change her life.
3. After abandoning her work as a teacher and dressmaker, she went on to become a union organizer.
4. It was her habit to travel about the country in a black gown and bonnet.
5. She worked in the cotton mills of the South to gather evidence for her campaign against child labor.
6. Later, she worked in New York City to support the garment workers' and streetcar workers' strikes.
7. While in Pittsburgh to support a steel mill strike, Jones was asked who had issued her a permit to speak publicly.

8. Jones, quick to reply, said, "Patrick Henry, Thomas Jefferson, John Adams!"

9. The last great struggle Mary Jones was to engage in actively was the 1919 steel strike.

10. Jones remained dedicated throughout her life, and she was able to make a vigorous labor speech on her one hundredth birthday.

REVIEW EXERCISE H. Identify each of the verbal phrases in the following sentences. Tell whether it is a participial phrase, a gerund phrase, or an infinitive phrase.

1. Searching for gold has always been a favorite activity of treasure seekers.

2. The story behind the Lost Dutchman Mine in Arizona's Superstition Mountains is unusual, fascinating to many listeners.

3. The story began in 1887 with Jacob Walz, who used gold nuggets to pay a bill in Phoenix, Arizona.

4. Jacob Walz, claiming he had found a gold mine, intended to keep the location a secret.

5. Most people, assuming he had stolen his gold nuggets, did not believe the man.

6. Miners began to follow him everywhere but without success.

7. Jacob Walz died in 1891, predicting that no one would ever find his mine.

8. Proved right so far, Walz must have covered his tracks well.

9. Each summer, however, treasure hunters explore the Superstition Mountains, leaving no stone unturned.

10. To find the lost gold is quite a goal.

SECTION REVIEW EXERCISE I. This exercise will ask you to work with forty items in the following passage from President Truman's *Memoirs*.

I never allowed myself to forget that the final authority was mine. I would ask the Cabinet to share their counsel with me, even encouraging disagreement and argument to sharpen up different points of view. On

major issues I would frequently ask them to vote, and I   5
expected the Cabinet officers to be frank and candid in
expressing their opinions to me. At the same time, I
insisted that they keep me informed of the major activities of their departments. . . .

1. Identify the fifteen personal pronouns in the passage.
2. Rewrite the passage, changing the ten first-person singular personal pronouns to first-person plural. (For example,
   change *I* to *we*.)
3. Identify the thirteen nouns in the passage.
4. Identify the eight adjectives (including the one proper adjective), and indicate which noun or pronoun each adjective tells more about.
5. Identify four of the five infinitives.

SECTION REVIEW EXERCISE II. This exercise will ask
you to work with thirty items in the following passage.
The passage is from a campaign speech by Adlai E.
Stevenson, given when he ran for President in 1952.

The federal government made the Louisiana Pur-
chase, and on that land a nation grew to greatness. No
private corporation would have built Grand Coulee
Dam; yet in the Grand Coulee country people are building their homes and are establishing their private busi-   5
nesses, and farmers are converting desert into garden....
We take our stand upon the fundamental principle
that the role of government is . . . just this: To remove
the roadblocks put in the way of the people by nature
and by greedy men; to release the energies of the people   10
so that free men may work the miracles of the future as
they have worked the miracles of the past.

1. Identify the ten verbs and verb phrases in the passage. You
   will find both action verbs and linking verbs. Make sure
   that you select only real verbs, not verbals.
2. Identify the seven conjunctions in the passage. You will
   find coordinating conjunctions, a conjunctive adverb, and
   subordinating conjunctions.
3. Identify the thirteen prepositions in the passage. Remember that *to* is not always a preposition.

2

PARTS OF A SENTENCE

2 Parts of a Sentence

You can use most of the parts of speech described in Section 1 in different positions in a sentence. For example, you can use the noun *science* in several different positions in a sentence.

EXAMPLES
Science is one important subject.
My favorite subject is **science**.
The laws of **science** are universal.

In the sentences above, the word *science* has the same meaning. *Science* is a noun in each sentence. Notice, however, that the noun *science* has a different function, or purpose, in each sentence. In the first sentence *science* is the subject (see 2.b). In the second sentence *science* is the predicate nominative (see 2.1.1). In the third sentence *science* is the object of the preposition *of* (see 2.h).

2.a THE SENTENCE

A **sentence** is a group of words that expresses a complete thought.

To express a complete thought in itself, every sentence must have a subject and a predicate. Each of the following sentences expresses a complete thought and contains a subject and a predicate.

EXAMPLES

Ostriches flee.
The cooks make lunch.
Most cities are exciting.
Stories entertain people.

2.b SUBJECT AND PREDICATE

Every sentence can be divided into two parts: the **subject** and the **predicate**. The subject is the part about which you are speaking or writing. The predicate is the part that discusses the subject.

In the example below, *ostriches* is the subject, and *flee* is the predicate.

SUBJECT	PREDICATE
Ostriches	flee.

The subject answers the question *who?* or *what?* about the predicate. (See 2.b.3 for details about the *simple subject.*) The subject can be a single word or a group of words. In the following examples, notice that different parts of speech can be used as the subject:

SUBJECTS	PREDICATES
Ostriches	flee.
Frightened ostriches	flee.
Ostriches in trouble	flee.
They	flee.

In a command sentence, the subject is omitted but "understood." See 2.c.3 for a discussion of command sentences.

EXAMPLES

Flee!
Help the cooks make lunch.
Visit cities during your vacation.
Entertain people with stories.

The predicate tells what the subject does or is. The predicate must include either an action verb or a linking verb. The predicate can be a verb alone or a verb plus other words. The verb alone is called the **simple predicate**. The **complete predicate** consists of the verb plus other words.

A predicate must always have a *verb*, not simply a participle or an infinitive. Each of the following predicates has a verb. Some also include other words.

SUBJECTS	PREDICATES
Ostriches	**flee.**
Ostriches	**flee immediately.**
Ostriches	**flee immediately across the plain.**
Ostriches	**cannot fly.**
Ostriches	**are birds.**
Ostriches	**are large.**
Ostriches	**lay large eggs.**

If a group of words begins with a capital letter and finishes with an end mark but does not have *both* a subject and a predicate, it is a **sentence fragment**. Sentence fragments can be confusing to your reader. Avoid sentence fragments in your writing. (Professional writers, however, sometimes use them for special effects.)

AVOIDING ERRORS WITH SENTENCE FRAGMENTS

One way to avoid writing sentence fragments is to be sure that you write sentences with an action verb or a linking verb, not with just an infinitive or a participle.

NOT Ostriches fleeing.
BUT Ostriches **are fleeing**.

NOT Ostriches to run.
BUT Ostriches **like to run**.

EXERCISE 1. Indicate whether each of the following numbered items is a complete sentence or a sentence fragment.

1. Consumers in America are protected from dishonest selling practices.
2. Before 1977, poorly made products, no warranties, and angry customers.
3. A warranty states that a product is guaranteed to last a certain length of time.
4. The Magnuson-Moss Warranty Act of 1977 gave consumers more rights.
5. Not only expensive products but items as inexpensive as fifteen dollars.
6. Even without a written warranty, consumers protected.
7. A product broken upon arrival can be returned for a full refund.
8. All companies behind their products.
9. Satisfaction for all customers.
10. The new act also gives consumers more power in court.

APPLICATION. Rewrite each item that you labeled *fragment* so that it is a complete sentence.

2.b.1 Finding the subject and the predicate

You usually can find the subject of a sentence by first identifying the predicate. A predicate always has either an action verb or a linking verb. Therefore, you can find the predicate by finding the verb. Then ask *who?* or *what?* before the verb. The answer to that question is the subject.

Consider the following example:

| SUBJECT | PREDICATE |
| Frightened ostriches | flee from lions. |

First, find the predicate by finding the verb. The action verb is *flee*; the predicate is *flee from lions*. Second, ask *who?* or *what?* before the verb. *What* flees? *Frightened ostriches* flee. *Frightened ostriches* is the subject.

The subject of a sentence, as shown below, is not always first in the sentence. Sometimes the subject follows the predicate. In the first example below, the action verb is *hide*. *What* hides? The answer, *ostriches*, is the subject. The second example has the linking verb *are*. *What* are? *Two frightened ostriches* are. Therefore, *two frightened ostriches* is the subject.

PREDICATES	SUBJECTS
On the plain hide	ostriches.
On the plain are	two frightened ostriches.

In question sentences, as shown below, the subject is often between two parts of the predicate (see also 2.c.3). In the first example below, *can fly* is the verb phrase. *What* can fly? The answer, *ostriches*, is the subject. In the second example the verb phrase is *do live*. *Ostriches* is the subject because it answers the question *what?*

PREDICATES	SUBJECTS	PREDICATES
Can	ostriches	fly?
Where do	ostriches	live?

EXERCISE 2. Indicate where the subject ends and the predicate begins in each of the following sentences.

1. Babies learn language in several stages.
2. Their first sounds are gurgles.
3. Babies of different nationalities make similar sounds at first.
4. "Baby talk" is universal.
5. A baby practices speech through cries.
6. Babies learn language from the people around them.
7. A nine-month-old baby imitates the sounds of others.
8. The first word comes at about one year of age.

9. Babies usually form sentences after age two.
10. A three-year-old child can use about nine hundred words in sentences.

APPLICATION. Compose a new predicate to go with each subject in Exercise 2.

EXERCISE 3. Identify the complete predicate in each of the following sentences. Remember that sometimes the predicate or part of the predicate can come before the subject.

1. Butterflies are beautiful insects.
2. Most butterfly wings are strikingly colorful and eye-catching.
3. The wings are made up of tiny scales.
4. Have you held a butterfly?
5. Did you notice the colored powder on your fingers?
6. The colored powder is made up of thousands of tiny scales.
7. These kinds of wings distinguish butterflies and moths from all other insects.
8. Entomologists examine insects under a microscope.
9. Have you examined an insect's wing under a microscope?
10. Iridescent are the tiny scales on butterfly wings.

2.b.2 Finding the subject in sentences beginning with *there* and *it*

Many sentences begin with the expletives *there* and *it*. An **expletive** is a word with no real meaning of its own. Expletives are often used to begin a sentence. When an expletive begins a sentence, the subject always follows the predicate. Notice that in the following examples the predicate comes before the subject.

PREDICATES	SUBJECTS
There are	stories about ostriches.
It is interesting	to watch ostriches.

EXERCISE 4. Identify the subject and the predicate in each of the following sentences. Remember that the subject usually follows the verb in a sentence that begins with an expletive.

1. There is little beauty in worn furniture.
2. It is easy to renew the beauty of old furniture.
3. There are many ways to refinish an old wooden table or chest.
4. It is important to clean the piece of furniture first.
5. It is best to sand the piece next.
6. It is necessary to remove old stain and wax.
7. There are many colors of stain: mahogany, cherry, pine, walnut.
8. There are glossy finishes and flat finishes.
9. It is easier simply to paint the piece of furniture.
10. It is best to spread a cloth before cleaning or staining.

2.b.3 The simple subject

The **simple subject** is the principal word or words in the subject.

The subject of a sentence can be a single word or a group of words. A subject made up of a group of words is called the **complete subject**. The complete subject always includes one key term. That important term is called the **simple subject**. Of course, a simple subject can occur by itself. The simple subject can be a common noun, a proper noun, a compound noun, a pronoun, a gerund, or an infinitive. The following examples show how a simple subject can be included within the complete subject.

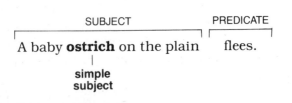

SUBJECT   PREDICATE

A baby **ostrich** on the plain   flees.

simple
subject

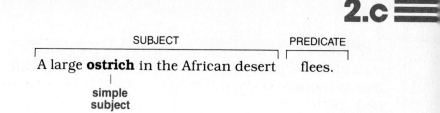

Both of the complete subjects in the above examples contain prepositional phrases: *on the plain* and *in the African desert*. The simple subject of a sentence never appears within a prepositional phrase. A prepositional phrase often contains a noun (such as *plain* or *desert*), but that noun cannot be the subject of the sentence. (See 1.g and 2.h for further discussion of prepositional phrases.)

HINT: Cross out all prepositional phrases when you are looking for the simple subject.

2.c SUBJECT–VERB AGREEMENT

You must be able to identify the simple subject in your sentence so that you can make it agree in number with the action verb or linking verb. For example, if the simple subject is third-person singular (such as *he, she, Tony, Janet, it*), you must use one form of the verb. If the simple subject is third-person plural (such as *they, Tony and Janet*), you must use another form of the verb.

EXAMPLES
The bird sings.
The birds sing.

The ostrich flees.
The ostriches flee.

Study the following chart carefully. It contains examples of the different kinds of words that can be simple subjects. By learning to identify different kinds of simple subjects, you will be able to make your simple subjects and verbs agree in number.

KINDS OF SIMPLE SUBJECTS

	SUBJECT	PREDICATE
COMMON NOUNS		
3rd-person singular	An ostrich on the plain	flee**s**.
3rd-person plural	Ostrich**es** on the plain	flee.
PROPER NOUNS		
3rd-person singular	Tony down the street	dance**s**.
3rd-person plural	The Yang**s** upstairs	dance.
COMPOUND NOUNS		
3rd-person singular	The guidance counselor	help**s**.
3rd-person plural	The guidance counselor**s**	help.
PERSONAL PRONOUNS		
3rd-person singular	He	work**s**.
	She	work**s**.
3rd-person plural	They	fall.
INDEFINITE PRONOUNS		
Singular	Anybody in the street	hope**s**.
	Anything in the boxes	remain**s**.
	Each of the books	remain**s**.
	Either of the girls	hope**s**.
	Everybody in study hall	hope**s**.
	Everything on the mantel	remain**s**.
	Neither of the dictionaries	remain**s**.
	Nobody in the family	hope**s**.
	Nothing in the garage	remain**s**.
	One of the doctors	hope**s**.
	Somebody in the library	hope**s**.
	Something on the desk	remain**s**.
Plural	Both of the classes	remain.
	Few of the students	hope.
	Many of the sophomores	hope.
	Several of the teachers	hope.

INDEFINITE PRONOUNS

Singular or plural

The following indefinite pronouns can be considered singular or plural, depending on the noun to which they refer:

	SUBJECT	PREDICATE
all	S: All of the air	escapes.
	P: All of the ostriches	flee.
any	S: Any of the air	escapes.
	P: Any of the ostriches	flee.
more	S: More of the air	escapes.
	P: More of the ostriches	flee.
most	S: Most of the air	escapes.
	P: Most of the ostriches	flee.
none	S: None of the air	escapes.
	P: None of the ostriches	flee.
some	S: Some of the air	escapes.
	P: Some of the ostriches	flee.

INFINITIVES AND GERUNDS

Singular	To flee	**is** necessary.
	Fleeing	**is** necessary.

AVOIDING ERRORS WITH SUBJECTS AND PREPOSITIONAL PHRASES

Remember that the simple subject of a sentence can never be within a prepositional phrase. Therefore, you must make sure that the action verb or linking verb agrees in number with the simple subject, *not* with the object of a preposition.

NOT   The **egg** of the ostriches remain.
BUT   The **egg** of the ostriches **remains**. [The simple subject, *egg*, is singular.]
NOT   The **eggs** in the nest remains.
BUT   The **eggs** in the nest **remain**. [The simple subject, *eggs*, is plural.]

EXERCISE 5. In each of the following sentences, identify first the complete subject and then the simple subject.

> EXAMPLE Sailing across the ocean is leisurely.
>
> ANSWER complete subject: *Sailing across the ocean*
> simple subject: *Sailing*

1. Pleasure trips on steamships were very popular in the last century.
2. World travelers in the past needed ships to cross the oceans.
3. A sea voyage from England to the United States was once a slow and relaxing vacation.
4. Wealthy passengers on large ships enjoyed luxurious cabins.
5. The pleasures of steamship travel included an abundance of rich foods.
6. Some of the passengers on steamships rarely left the dining room.
7. Conversation with fellow passengers was an interesting way to pass the time.
8. Dancing to a live band was the entertainment at night.
9. Everybody on a steamship played shuffleboard.
10. The ocean liners of today have tennis courts, nightclubs, and swimming pools.

APPLICATION. Compose a new subject for each of the ten sentences in Exercise 5.

> EXAMPLE *Explorations of this continent* were very popular in the last century.

EXERCISE 6. For each of the following sentences, select the verb or verb phrase in parentheses that agrees in number with the simple subject. Remember that the simple subject cannot be within a prepositional phrase.

1. The rules for good health (is/are) simple.
2. One of the basic rules (is/are) to eat properly.
3. The important food groups (includes/include) dairy products, meats, grains, and vegetables.

4. Usually, foods from each group (is eaten/are eaten) every day.
5. To stay healthy (requires/require) exercise and sleep.
6. Everyone (needs/need) exercise.
7. Those in school (dances/dance) in special classes.
8. People of all professions (enjoys/enjoy) strenuous sports, such as tennis and football.
9. Watching football games or tennis matches on television (is/are) not considered exercise.
10. Touching your toes (pays/pay) off eventually.

2.c.1 Subject-verb agreement in sentences beginning with *there* or adverbs

In many sentences beginning with the word *there* or *here*, the verb comes before the subject. Therefore, you must look ahead or think ahead to find the simple subject. Then, you can decide which form of the verb you need to make it agree with the subject.

EXAMPLES

There **is** an ostrich at the zoo. [The simple subject, *ostrich*, is singular; the linking verb agrees.]

There **are** ostriches at the zoo. [The simple subject, *ostriches*, is plural; the linking verb agrees.]

Here **comes** the ostrich. [The simple subject *ostrich*, is singular; the action verb agrees.]

Here **come** the ostriches. [The simple subject, *ostriches*, is plural; the action verb agrees.]

EXERCISE 7. For each of the following sentences, select the verb in parentheses that agrees in number with the simple subject. Remember to identify the simple subject before selecting the verb.

1. There (is/are) mistaken beliefs among many people.
2. There (is/are) a need to check facts.
3. There (exists/exist) in the library many reference books.

4. Here (is/are) two fascinating references: *The Dictionary of Misinformation* and *Adventures in Error*.
5. There (is/are) entries from A to Z.
6. Here (follows/follow) examples of popular misinformation.
7. There (is/are) no truth to the belief that hot water freezes faster than cold water.
8. There (exists/exist) no goat capable of eating tin cans.
9. There (is/are) no ostriches that bury their heads in sand.
10. Here (is/are) a fact: The moon is not made of green cheese.

2.c.2 Subject-verb agreement with special subjects

Some subjects require special attention when you select the form of the action or linking verb that agrees with them. Certain subjects can be either singular or plural, depending on their meaning in the sentence. The following chart lists the most important examples.

━━━━ SUBJECT–VERB AGREEMENT ━━━━

collective nouns

A collective noun that refers to a group as a whole has a singular meaning. A collective noun that refers to individual members of a group has a plural meaning. (See 1.a.4 for additional examples of collective nouns.)

	SUBJECT	PREDICATE
singular	The committee	**votes** by secret ballot.
	The Chicago Symphony	**is** an excellent orchestra.
plural	The committee	**vote** by raising their hands.
	The Chicago Symphony	**are** all fine musicians.

special nouns

Some nouns that end in *s* or *es* may look plural, but they are singular because they refer to only one thing.

	SUBJECT	PREDICATE
singular	Acoustics	**is** the science of sound.
	Measles	**is** a disease.

nouns of amount

The noun of amount is singular when it refers to only one unit. The noun of amount is plural when it refers to a number of separate units.

	SUBJECT	PREDICATE
singular	Five days	**is** too long to wait.
	Six dollars	**is** the fee.
plural	Five days	**are** spent in school.
	Six dollars	**are** lying on the desk.

titles

The title of a book, magazine, newspaper, film, or work of art is always considered singular. Many titles include plural nouns, but the title as a whole is singular.

	SUBJECT	PREDICATE
singular	The *Los Angeles Times*	**is** published daily
	Star Wars	**is** a science-fiction film.

the number, a number

	SUBJECT	PREDICATE
singular	The number of students	**is** large.
plural	A number of students	**are** absent.

EXERCISE 8.
Select the appropriate form of the action verb or linking verb in parentheses in each of the following sentences.

1. Party-goers (is/are) happy people.
2. *Parties and More Parties* (is/are) a book that all party planners can use.
3. Students in Jackson, Michigan, (has/have) a big party every year.
4. A number of planners (oversees/oversee) preparations for the parties.
5. Four weeks (is needed/are needed) for planning each party.
6. The number of tasks to be completed (is/are) overwhelming.

7. Nonetheless, the planners (motivates/motivate) the students.
8. Economics (is/are) an important aspect of the planning.
9. Two hundred dollars (is/are) the cost of each party.
10. The *Jackson High News and Views* (prints/print) photographs taken at the party.

2.c.3 Subject-verb agreement in commands and questions

A **statement sentence**, or **declarative sentence**, always has a subject and an action verb or linking verb. The subject usually comes before the verb.

STATEMENT SENTENCES

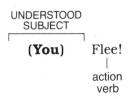

Another kind of sentence is the **command sentence**, or **imperative sentence**. The subject of a command sentence is "understood" to be the pronoun *you*. You use the same form of the verb whether you are talking to one subject or to more than one.

COMMAND SENTENCE

```
UNDERSTOOD
SUBJECT
┌──────────┐
  (You)      Flee!
              │
            action
             verb
```

The **question sentence**, or **interrogative sentence**, asks a question. The subject of a question sentence usually follows a linking verb, an auxiliary, or a modal (see

1.b). The linking verb, the auxiliary *be* or *have*, or the modal *do* must agree in number with the subject.

QUESTION SENTENCES

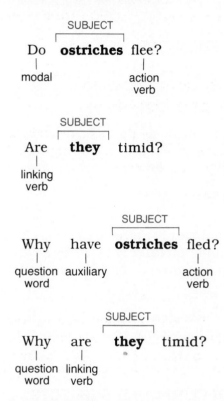

EXERCISE 9. Select the appropriate form of the auxiliary, modal, or linking verb in parentheses in each of the following sentences.

1. How many planets (is/are) in the solar system?
2. (Is/Are) there nine planets or ten?
3. (Does/Do) astronomers consider the sun a planet?
4. Which planet (is/are) closer to Earth—Mars or Venus?
5. How many planets (has/have) rings?
6. (Does/Do) the moon orbit the sun?
7. Which (is/are) the largest planets?

8. (Isn't/Aren't) Pluto the farthest from Earth?
9. (Has/Have) we learned about life on any other planet except Earth?
10. (Is/Are) there any other galaxies besides the Milky Way?

2.d COMPOUND SUBJECTS

A **compound subject** is made up of two or more subjects that are joined by a conjunction and that have the same verb.

```
    COMPOUND SUBJECT      PREDICATE
  ┌────────────────┐    ┌──────────┐
  Cooks   and   waiters    work.
    │      │        │         │
  noun  coordinating noun    verb
        conjunction
```

The parts of the compound subject are usually joined by a coordinating conjunction (*and* or *or*) or by a correlative conjunction, such as, *either . . . or* or *neither . . . nor*.

EXAMPLES
Either the **cooks** or the **waiters** work late.
Neither the **cooks** nor the **waiters** work on Sundays.

COMMAS WITH COMPOUND SUBJECTS

With compound subjects of three or more items in a series, use a comma after each item except the last.

Cooks, waiters, and cashiers work together.

Do not use a comma after the last item in the series. Also, do not use commas if you use *and* or *or* between each part of the compound subject.

Cooks and waiters and cashiers work together.

EXERCISE 10. Identify the compound subject in each of the following sentences. The subject may be made up of nouns, gerunds, or infinitives.

> EXAMPLE Reading and writing are essential skills.
>
> ANSWER *reading (and) writing*

1. American schools and homes in the early nineteenth century contained mainly British books.
2. Only British names and places were mentioned in early textbooks used in America.
3. The Bible and British spelling books were Noah Webster's first reading materials.
4. American spelling and American vocabulary were not used in these books.
5. British names and the events of English history were foreign to Webster.
6. To write American schoolbooks and to publish them became Webster's goal.
7. A spelling book, a grammar book, and a reader were the first books Webster published.
8. Researching and writing an American dictionary took Webster twenty years.
9. The authority and the precision of Webster's dictionary have been recognized for over 150 years.
10. Scholars, writers, and students depend upon Webster's and others' dictionaries.

2.e SUBJECT–VERB AGREEMENT WITH COMPOUND SUBJECTS

You know that the action verb or the linking verb of a sentence must agree in number with the subject. Not all compound subjects are plural, even though they have more than one part. To make the verb agree with a compound subject, you must pay attention to the conjunction joining the parts of the subject as well as to the meaning of the subject.

and

When the conjunction *and* joins the parts of a compound subject, the subject is generally considered plural. A compound subject is considered singular, however, when its parts together make up one unit or when the parts refer to the same person or thing.

	SUBJECT	PREDICATE
plural	The cook **and** the waiter	**work**.
	Chopping **and** slicing	**are** time-consuming.
singular	Ham **and** eggs	**is** the special.

       [Ham and eggs together make up one dish.]

       Her teacher **and** counselor   **gives** advice.

       [One person is both the teacher and the counselor.]

or, nor

When the conjunction *or* or *nor* joins the parts of a compound subject, always look at the part of the subject that is closest to the verb. The verb must agree in number with that part of the compound subject.

	SUBJECT	PREDICATE
plural	The cook **or** the waiters	**work**.
	Neither the cooks **nor** the waiters	**work**.
singular	The cook **or** the waiter	**works**.
	The cooks **or** the waiter	**works**.
	Neither the cooks **nor** the waiter	**works**.

EXERCISE 11. Select the appropriate form of the action verb or linking verb (or verb phrase) in parentheses in each of the following sentences.

1. The acronym, or shortened form, *laser* (comes/come) from the expression "*l*ight *a*mplification by *s*timulated *e*mission of *r*adiation."
2. Both radio waves and light waves (is/are) forms of energy.
3. Neither weak radio waves nor weak light waves (affects/affect) us.

4. Producing and transmitting intense light (is/are) the basic purpose of a laser.

5. Either a rare metal or a rare gas (is used/are used) to intensify light waves.

6. Chromium and helium (is/are) two elements that were used in early lasers.

7. Various kinds of lamps or the sun (produces/produce) the light that a laser intensifies.

8. Electrons and light waves (interacts/interact) to make the light extremely intense.

9. To focus and to direct light beams (is/are) the abilities of the laser.

10. Neither space flights nor new kinds of intricate eye surgery (is/are) possible without lasers.

2.f SUBJECT–VERB AGREEMENT WITH INTERVENING EXPRESSIONS

Sometimes a subject is connected to another word by an expression like the ones listed below. When words are linked by such "intervening" expressions, the subject is still singular. Intervening expressions are considered interrupters; therefore, they do not create compound subjects.

EXPRESSIONS NOT AFFECTING NUMBER OF SUBJECT

accompanied by	in addition to
along with	plus
as well as	together with

EXAMPLES

One **plus** two *makes* three.

[The intervening expression *plus* does not affect the number of the singular subject *one*.]

The cook **as well as** the waiter *works* hard.

[The intervening expression *as well as* does not affect the number of the singular subject *cook*.]

A compound subject is considered singular when it follows the expressions *many a* or *every*.

EXAMPLES
Many a cook and waiter *works* late.
Every student, teacher, and parent *wants* an effective school system.

EXERCISE 12. Choose the appropriate form of the action verb or linking verb in parentheses in each of the following sentences.

1. Every chef and gourmet (knows/know) that the proper kitchen tool makes any job easier.
2. Preparing food as well as serving the meal often (depends/depend) on having the correct utensils.
3. Many an inexperienced cook and homemaker (is/are) surprised by how many utensils are needed.
4. A food processor accompanied by several different attachments (makes/make) everything from juices to garnishes.
5. For carving meat, a fork and a sharp knife (is/are) essential.
6. A kitchen scale together with measuring cups (helps/help) cooks to measure ingredients.
7. A slotted spoon and tongs (makes/make) hot or greasy food easy to handle.
8. A strainer plus colanders of various sizes (is used/are used) to sift flour or to shake water from foods.
9. Many a lover of fudge or boiled eggs (finds/find) a timer or a stopwatch useful.
10. A grater and a blender (is/are) useful for making soups and sauces.

APPLICATION. Rewrite each sentence in Exercise 12, using the same subject and verb but adding a new ending.

EXAMPLES   Every chef and gourmet knows *how to make chocolate mousse.*

Preparing food as well as serving the meal often depends *on the weather.*

2.g COMPOUND VERBS

A **compound verb** is made up of two or more verbs that are joined by a conjunction and that have the same subject.

SUBJECT   PREDICATE

Cooks   **chop**   and   **slice.**

noun   verb   coordinating   verb
               conjunction

compound verb

A compound verb can be made up of two or more action verbs.

EXAMPLES
Athletes **practice** and **exercise**.
Athletes **eat** and **sleep** in moderation.
Athletes **train**, **develop**, and **watch** their bodies.

A compound verb can also be made up of two or more linking verbs.

EXAMPLES
The Olympics **are** and probably always **will be** the greatest test for nonprofessional athletes.
Athletes **were**, **are**, and always **will be** proud to compete in the Olympics.

EXERCISE 13. Identify the compound verb in each of the following sentences.

1. Baseball umpires have been and still are necessary to the sport.
2. Disgruntled players criticize, challenge, and sometimes irritate the umpire.
3. Fans cheer or boo decisions of the umpire.
4. Umpires evaluate and call plays quickly.
5. Umpires sometimes disagree and argue with each other.

6. Umpires were, still are, and always will be the final judge of a disputed play.

7. Jobs for baseball umpires in the major leagues are and will remain scarce.

8. In 1979 the major leagues hired and employed only fifty-two umpires.

9. Major-league umpires travel and work for six months out of the year.

10. Good umpires want and deserve appreciation.

EXERCISE 14. In each of the following sentences, indicate whether the subject is *compound* or *not compound* and whether the verb is *compound* or *not compound*. Three of the sentences do not have compounds.

1. Sky diving and hang gliding are two thrilling pastimes.

2. Sky divers ride in and then parachute from an airplane.

3. Hang gliders descend in a mechanism resembling a bicycle frame with wings.

4. A sky diver or hang glider needs and demonstrates unusual courage.

5. Air currents along with air pressure greatly affect the smoothness of the ride.

6. Falling or gliding through space is and always will be a rare experience.

7. Dipping, turning, and soaring in midair create feelings of weightlessness and freedom.

8. Both the excitement of being airborne and the danger of falling make these sports thrilling.

9. The dangers plus the thrills make air sports attractive to many people.

10. Sky diving and hang gliding require a great deal of skill.

2.h PREPOSITIONAL PHRASES

A **prepositional phrase** is a group of words that begins with a preposition and usually ends with a noun or pronoun.

Prepositional phrases can be used anywhere in a sentence. Sometimes a prepositional phrase is part of the subject, and sometimes it is part of the predicate. It is even possible for a prepositional phrase itself to be the subject of a sentence. The subject of a sentence, however, can never occur *within* a prepositional phrase. The following examples show that prepositional phrases can be part of the subject or part of the predicate:

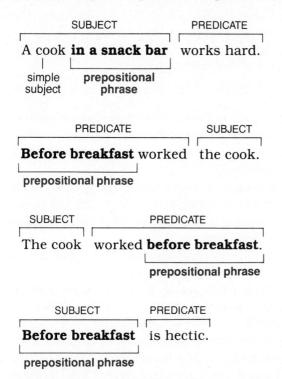

Notice that in the first example above, the prepositional phrase *in a snack bar* is used like an adjective to tell you more about the simple subject, *cook*. In the second and third examples the prepositional phrase *before breakfast* is part of the predicate: Like an adverb, it tells you *when* the action takes place. In the last example the prepositional phrase *before breakfast* is the subject of the sentence.

REVIEW EXERCISE A. Follow the directions or answer the question in parentheses at the end of each of the following items.

1. Astrology, the study of the sun signs in the zodiac. (How can you make the sentence fragment a complete sentence? Write the complete sentence.)

2. The constellations in the sky (provides/provide) the names in the zodiac. (Select the appropriate form of the verb.)

3. The word *zodiac* (means/mean) "circle of animals." (Select the appropriate form of the verb.)

4. Most of the constellations (is/are) animals. (Select the appropriate form of the linking verb.)

5. Everyone (has/have) a sun sign. (Select the appropriate form of *have*.)

6. It is interesting to think about your own astrological sign. (What is the complete subject of the sentence?)

7. Have you plotted your astrological chart? (What is the subject of the sentence?)

8. Linda Goodman's *Sun Signs* (is/are) a popular book on astrology. (Select the appropriate form of the linking verb.)

9. The number of signs (is/are) twelve. (Select the appropriate form of the linking verb.)

10. There (is/are) four different kinds of signs. (Select the appropriate form of the linking verb.)

11. Air signs in the zodiac are Aquarius, Gemini, and Libra. (What is the complete subject of the sentence? What is the simple subject?)

12. Talking with an Aquarius (provides/provide) pleasure. (Select the appropriate form of the action verb.)

13. Both Pisces and Scorpio are water signs. (What is the compound subject of the sentence?)

14. Strength as well as stubbornness (is/are) noticeable in the earth signs. (Select the appropriate form of the linking verb.)

15. Every Aries, Sagittarius, and Leo (is/are) exciting and admirable. (Select the appropriate form of the linking verb.)

16. At the beginning of the zodiac is Aries the Ram. (Identify the complete predicate of the sentence.)

17. An Aries has been and always will be argumentative. (Identify the compound verb of the sentence.)
18. A Taurus in an argument is unbeatable. (Identify the prepositional phrase in the sentence.)
19. A Pisces politely smiles and escapes arguments. (Identify the compound verb in the sentence.)
20. Will you reveal your sun sign? (Identify the subject of the sentence.)

2.i OTHER PARTS OF THE PREDICATE

You know that a sentence must have a subject (sometimes "understood") and a predicate. You also know that a predicate always includes an action verb or a linking verb. You probably have noticed, however, that some predicates in the examples have had more than just a simple verb or a compound verb. The following items (2.j–2.l) discuss the additional parts of a sentence that may be included in the predicate.

2.j DIRECT OBJECTS

The **direct object** answers the question *what?* or *whom?* after a subject and an action verb.

```
     SUBJECT        PREDICATE
    ┌────────┐  ┌──────────────────┐
     Cities      attract tourists.
                    │        │
                 action    noun
                  verb       │
                          direct
                          object
```

In the above example the noun *cities* is the subject and *attract* is the action verb. Cities attract *whom?* The answer, *tourists*, is the direct object. In the following examples, notice that the direct objects all answer the question *what?* or *whom?* after the subject and the action verb. Direct objects, of course, can be modified by adjectives, determiners, and prepositional phrases.

Cities have protected **people**.
|
noun

Cities frequently like **to advertise**.
|
infinitive

Cities encourage **sightseeing** and **shopping**.
| |
gerund   gerund

Cities attract **whoever likes show business**.
|
clause

direct objects

Notice the example that has two direct objects: the gerunds *sightseeing* and *shopping*. This is a **compound direct object**. Just as a compound subject or a compound verb has two or more elements, a compound direct object contains two or more elements.

EXERCISE 15. Identify the direct object in each of the following sentences. Remember that the direct object can be a compound.

1. Thomas Jefferson showed many talents.
2. Jefferson as a young man studied Latin, ancient Greek, and French.
3. Jefferson attended college in Virginia.
4. He was practicing law by the age of twenty-three.
5. The idealistic Jefferson encouraged states' rights.
6. In 1775 Jefferson attended the Second Continental Congress.
7. In that same year he drafted the Declaration of Independence.

8. The Declaration of Independence revolutionized American thought.

9. Jefferson served the country as its third President.

10. Thomas Jefferson embodied the beliefs and ideals of a free society.

EXERCISE 16. Look again at Review Exercise A following 2.h. Eight of the sentences have a direct object. Identify each one.

2.k INDIRECT OBJECTS

An **indirect object** answers the question *to whom?* or *for whom?* or *to what?* or *for what?* after an action verb.

```
  SUBJECT              PREDICATE
┌────────┐  ┌──────────────────────────────┐
  Cities     offer  residents  services.
    │          │        │          │
  noun       action   noun       noun
             verb       │          │
                     indirect    direct
                      object     object
```

In the above example the noun *cities* is the subject, and the noun *services* is the direct object of the action verb *offer*. The noun *residents* is the indirect object because it tells *to whom* cities offer services. An indirect object can be a noun, a pronoun, a gerund, or a clause.

The labels *direct object* and *indirect object* indicate whether the person, place, thing, or idea is affected directly or indirectly by the action of the verb. In the above example it is the services that are offered directly, but it is the residents who are affected indirectly by the offering of the services.

A sentence can have an indirect object only if it has a direct object as well. The above example would not make sense without the direct object: *Cities offer their residents*. Cities offer their residents *what?* A direct object is needed to answer this question and complete the sentence. Notice in the following examples that the indirect object always appears *before* the direct object:

Cities give **tourists**   a thrill.
|
noun

Cities give **everyone**   an exciting time.
|
pronoun

Cities give **whoever visits** discounts.
|
clause

└──────────────────┘
indirect objects

An indirect object of more than one element is called a **compound indirect object**.

Cities give **students** and **senior citizens** discounts.

An indirect object never occurs after the prepositions *to* or *for*. If a word follows one of these prepositions, it is the object of the preposition, not an indirect object. For instance, the noun *tourists* is *not* an indirect object in the sentence *Cities give a thrill to tourists*. (See 1.g and 2.h for further discussion of prepositional phrases.)

EXERCISE 17. Identify the direct objects and indirect objects in each of the following sentences. Remember that a direct object or an indirect object can be a compound. Two of the sentences do not have an indirect object.

1. The United States government offers its citizens many publications.
2. The Bureau of Mines, for example, will send you a booklet about first aid.
3. The Department of Agriculture sends farmers and consumers free information about food products.
4. Several government agencies offer consumers advice about saving money.

5. The Federal Deposit Insurance Corporation has a booklet called "Your Savings Account."
6. The Department of Agriculture can send your family pamphlets and booklets about budgeting.
7. The U.S. Postal Service offers the public a booklet called "Fraud."
8. The Department of State will send advice and information about passports.
9. The U.S. Forest Service gives campers and tourists free information about our national parks.
10. Whatever your questions are, the government can offer you advice, information, and answers.

2.1 SUBJECT COMPLEMENTS

A **subject complement**, or completer, follows a subject and a linking verb and identifies or describes the subject.

A linking verb is almost always followed by one or more words in the predicate. After all, the linking verb *links* the subject to something else.

The following items describe the three kinds of subject complements: predicate nominatives (2.1.1), predicate adjectives (2.1.2), and predicate adverbs (2.1.3).

2.1.1 Predicate nominatives

A **predicate nominative** is a noun or pronoun that follows a linking verb and that points back to the subject and further identifies it.

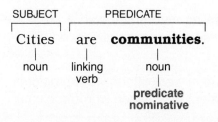

In the above example the noun *cities* is the subject, and *are* is the linking verb. The noun *communities* is the predicate nominative: It further identifies the subject, *cities*.

A predicate nominative can be a noun, pronoun, gerund, infinitive, or clause. The arrows below show how the predicate nominatives point back to the subjects.

EXAMPLES

City Hall is a new **structure**.

The mayor is **she**.

Voting is **taking responsibility**.

To be a citizen is **to vote**.

The winner will be **whoever campaigns hardest**.

Most predicate nominatives occur in sentences that use some form of the linking verb *be*. In addition, such linking verbs as *become, seem, appear, remain*, and *look* can be followed by a predicate nominative.

EXAMPLES

Cities are **communities**.

Washington became the **capital** of the United States.

The painting seems a **masterpiece**.

Nashville remains an exciting **city** and **center** of music.

AVOIDING ERRORS WITH PREDICATE NOMINATIVES

1. Do *not* make a linking verb agree with a predicate nominative. The linking verb must always agree with its *subject*.

   NOT The assignment were fifteen word problems.
   BUT The assignment **was** fifteen word problems.

Continued

2. Do *not* use the objective case (such as *me, us, him, her, them*) for a pronoun that is a predicate nominative. A predicate pronoun is usually in the nominative case (such as *I, we, he, she, they*). If your sentence sounds awkward to you, rewrite it.

NOT The caller was ~~her~~.
BUT The caller was **she**.

NOT I am ~~him~~.
BUT I am **he**.

In speaking, some people use *me* after forms of *be* and other linking verbs. In writing, however, *I* is preferred: *It was I*.

EXERCISE 18. Identify the predicate nominative in each of the following sentences. Remember that a predicate nominative can be a compound.

1. In 1959 Hawaii became the fiftieth state of the United States.
2. Hawaii is a group of 132 islands in the Pacific Ocean.
3. The main islands of Hawaii are Oahu, Lanai, Maui, Molokai, Kauai, Niihau, and Kahoolawe.
4. Oahu is the site of Pearl Harbor.
5. Hawaii's capital is Honolulu.
6. The first settlers of Hawaii were Polynesians.
7. Tourism and sugar and pineapple production have become Hawaii's main sources of income.
8. Other important industries are fishing and mining.
9. Hawaii has long been an attractive spot for vacationers.
10. Hawaii will always remain a unique and fascinating state.

APPLICATION. Use each predicate nominative from Exercise 18 as the *subject* in a sentence of your own.

2.1.2 Predicate adjectives

A **predicate adjective** follows a linking verb and points back to the subject and further describes it.

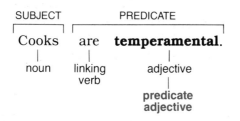

SUBJECT   PREDICATE

Cooks   are   **temperamental**.

noun   linking   adjective
       verb

predicate
adjective

In the above example the noun *cooks* is the subject, and *are* is the linking verb. The adjective *temperamental* is the predicate adjective: It describes *cooks*.

Notice that either adjectives or participles can function as predicate adjectives.

EXAMPLES
The cook is **careful**.
The cook is **busy**.
The cook is **educated**.
The cook is **amusing**.

Like predicate nominatives, predicate adjectives can follow other linking verbs besides forms of *be*.

The cook became very **excited**.
Hang gliding appears **dangerous**.
The class remained **seated**.
The audience grew **restless** and **inattentive**.

EXERCISE 19. Identify the predicate adjective in each of the following sentences. Remember that a predicate adjective can be a compound. Four of the sentences have more than one predicate adjective.

1. American artist Georgia O'Keeffe has become famous for her paintings of natural objects.
2. O'Keeffe's canvases are stunning and vibrant.
3. Her painted objects become huge and overwhelming.

4. O'Keeffe's enlarged flowers and stones seem unique.
5. Her paintings are generally realistic.
6. Most of them look abstract, however.
7. O'Keeffe's colors are bold and startling.
8. A patch of blue and green on a field of white is stark.
9. Most of O'Keeffe's paintings remain popular with art lovers.
10. The art of O'Keeffe is intense, realistic, and unique.

2.1.3 Predicate adverbs: adverbs of place as subject complements

A **predicate adverb** follows a linking verb and points back to the subject and states its condition.

SUBJECT	PREDICATE	
Cooks	are	**everywhere**.
noun	linking verb	adverb of place
		predicate adverb

In the above example the noun *cooks* is the subject, and *are* is the linking verb. The adverb *everywhere* is the predicate adverb: It tells where cooks are. Notice that a predicate adverb may be one word or a compound.

EXAMPLES
The cooks are **here**.
The cooks are **here**, **there**, and **everywhere**.

EXERCISE 20. Identify the predicate adverb in each of the following sentences.

1. National parks are everywhere in the United States.
2. Whether you vacation in Maine or in Florida, parks are there for your pleasure.

3. Parks have always been there, as long as naturalists can remember.
4. Parks are here in California, too.
5. Campers are everywhere in the parks.

REVIEW EXERCISE B. Identify the subject complement in each of the following sentences. Then indicate whether it is (a) a predicate nominative, (b) a predicate adjective, or (c) a predicate adverb.

1. For centuries, North America remained a little-known continent.
2. The earliest visitors to North America remain mysterious.
3. Presumably, the first explorer of this continent was Leif Ericsson.
4. The year of Ericsson's supposed visit was A.D.1002.
5. Ericsson's tales of "Vinland" became more believable.
6. By the fifteenth century, exploring North America became common.
7. The interest in exploring was strong.
8. Many early explorers were Portuguese and Spanish.
9. Columbus' supporter, Queen Isabella of Spain, remained interested.
10. Columbus' plan was simple but bold.
11. His idea was to reach the Far East by sailing west.
12. That route to the Far East was wrong.
13. Westward was a "new world."
14. The three ships Columbus led from Spain in 1492 were the *Niña*, the *Pinta*, and the *Santa María*.
15. Soon after, European explorers were everywhere.
16. The first Europeans to settle North America were the English, the French, and the Portuguese.
17. The Native Americans, however, were there before anyone else.
18. They were America's first inhabitants.
19. Interest in exploration grew stronger.
20. The Lewis and Clark expedition of the nineteenth century was one of the major efforts to explore America.

REVIEW EXERCISE C. Each of the following sentences has more than a verb in its predicate. Identify each additional element as (a) a direct object, (b) an indirect object, (c) a predicate nominative, (d) a predicate adjective, or (e) a predicate adverb. Some sentences have more than one of those elements. Remember, too, that any of those elements may be compound.

1. The Sierra Club is a conservationist organization.
2. The club offers a catalogue of its outings.
3. The catalogue groups the outings by place and by activity.
4. For example, vegetarians can take a backpack trip to the Sequoia High Country.
5. The club will show bicyclists Maui and horseback riders Kenya.
6. A walking tour of Crete is available.
7. A camel caravan in the Sahara may be more exciting, perhaps.
8. Another unusual Sierra Club adventure is Christmas in Nepal.
9. Obviously, Sierra Club members are everywhere.
10. The club is famous and has become a favorite organization for many adventurers.

REVIEW EXERCISE D. Look again at Exercise 2, page 114. For each sentence, indicate if it has (a) a direct object, (b) a predicate nominative, or (c) a predicate adjective. If a sentence has none, write *None*.

2.m THE CLAUSE

A **clause** is a group of words that has a subject and a predicate and that is used as part of a sentence.

The difference between a sentence, which also has a subject and predicate, and a clause is that a clause can function as *part* of a sentence. When a sentence has more than one subject-and-predicate combination, each combination is called a clause. The following example is a sentence that has two clauses:

| SUBJECT | PREDICATE | | SUBJECT | PREDICATE |

Stories entertain, and people listen.

CLAUSE 1   CLAUSE 2

There are two kinds of clauses:

1. *main clauses*, also called independent clauses
2. *subordinate clauses*, also called dependent clauses

A **main clause** can stand alone as a sentence. It is independent and makes sense all by itself. Every sentence must have at least one main clause. A sentence can also have more than one main clause. Both of the clauses in the above example are main clauses because they both make sense on their own.

Notice that a clause can be a main clause even when it includes a coordinating conjunction (*and, but, or, nor, for*). Both of the clauses above make sense by themselves: *Stories entertain. And people listen.*

A **subordinate clause** cannot stand alone. It is dependent on the rest of the sentence because it does not make sense all by itself. A subordinate clause needs a main clause to complete its meaning.

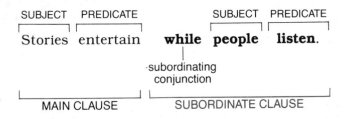

The first clause in the above example can stand on its own as a sentence: *Stories entertain.* The second clause, however, cannot stand on its own because it is incomplete: *while people listen.* The word *while* together

with *people listen* makes a subordinate clause. Because of the word *while, people listen* is dependent grammatically on the main clause, *Stories entertain.*

Without the word *while, people listen* is a main clause. It is also a main clause when the coordinating conjunction *and* is used. It becomes a subordinate clause when *while* is added to it.

EXERCISE 21. In each of the following sentences, the first clause appears in italics. Indicate whether that clause is a main clause or a subordinate clause.

1. *Although furs and frozen food may seem an odd combination,* one American made his fortune from both.
2. *When he was only ten years old,* Clarence Birdseye was selling muskrats to an English firm.
3. *Muskrat trading must have been profitable,* since it paid for the boy's college education.
4. *After he graduated from college,* Birdseye worked for the Department of Agriculture.
5. *He became a full-time fur trader* when he saw the growing demand for furs.
6. *He borrowed money to start his own company* because he thought he had found his life's work.
7. *He traded furs for five years in Canada* before he made an important discovery.
8. *While he was fishing through the ice one day,* Birdseye noticed that the fish froze instantly upon reaching the air.
9. *When the fish were thawed and cooked,* they tasted fresh.
10. *That discovery changed Clarence Birdseye's life* because it led him to pioneer the frozen-food industry.

2.n MAIN CLAUSES: SIMPLE SENTENCES, COMPOUND SENTENCES

A main clause can stand alone as a sentence because it has a subject and a predicate. You know that a sentence can have a compound subject or a compound verb. The subject and the predicate can be expanded in many other ways with adjectives, adverbs, infinitives, participles, and prepositional phrases. As long as the sentence has only one main clause, however, it is called a **simple sentence**. The following examples are simple sentences because they contain only one main clause (one subject and one predicate).

EXAMPLES
Stories entertain. [simple sentence]
Stories and riddles entertain. [simple sentence with compound subject]
Stories entertain and amuse. [simple sentence with compound verb]
Stories about the Old West entertain adults and children alike. [simple sentence expanded]

When a sentence has two or more main clauses, it is a **compound sentence**. As the following examples show, each main clause of a compound sentence has its own subject and predicate. Notice that the main clauses of a compound sentence are usually joined by a comma and a coordinating conjunction (*and, but, or,* or *for*).

COMPOUND SENTENCES

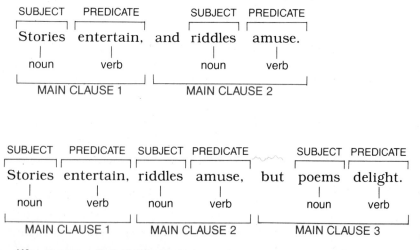

PUNCTUATION: COMPOUND SENTENCES

1. If a compound sentence has two main clauses joined by a coordinating conjunction, use a comma before the coordinating conjunction.

   Edgar Allan Poe's stories are thrilling, **but** Agatha Christie's mysteries are more realistic.

   You may also use a semicolon without a coordinating conjunction between the main clauses.

   Edgar Allan Poe's stories are thrilling; Agatha Christie's mysteries are more realistic.

2. If a compound sentence has three or more main clauses, use a comma after each clause except the last.

   Horror stories are thrilling, **but** mystery stories are more realistic, **and** people love both.

AVOIDING ERRORS: RUN-ON SENTENCES

In a sentence with two main clauses, do not use *only* a comma to separate the clauses. You must also use a coordinating conjunction. If you use only a comma, you will have a **run-on sentence.**

NOT Horror stories are thrilling, most people enjoy them.

BUT Horror stories are thrilling, **and** most people enjoy them.

You can also use (1) a semicolon without a coordinating conjunction or (2) a period to create two sentences.

   Horror stories are thrilling; most people enjoy them.

   Horror stories are thrilling. Most people enjoy them.

EXERCISE 22. Indicate whether each of the following sentences contains one or two main clauses. Remember that a single main clause can have a compound subject or a compound verb.

1. Nineteenth-century American scenes and customs were recorded and preserved by the firm of Currier & Ives.
2. Nathaniel Currier was a printer, and James Ives was a business executive.
3. The two men produced "engravings for the people."
4. Currier favored current events; he produced drawings of ships, battles, and other news events.
5. Ives had broader interests and favored scenes from country life.
6. Together the two men published color engravings depicting every facet of American life.
7. Currier & Ives produced thousands of engravings, and each print was rich in color and detail.
8. Many drawings showed city life, but most drawings depicted life in the country.
9. A century ago most Americans lived in the country, and many events happened outdoors.
10. Currier & Ives's engravings show how Americans worked and relaxed at the turn of the century.

2.o SUBORDINATE CLAUSES

You know that a subordinate clause cannot stand alone as a sentence, even though it contains a subject and a predicate. A subordinate clause is dependent on the main clause of the sentence.

A subordinate clause begins with a word called a subordinator. A **subordinator** is also called an *introductory word*. A subordinator, or introductory word, reduces the subject-and-predicate combination to a nonsentence.

A subordinator can be a subordinating conjunction (for example, *when* or *because*) or a relative pronoun (for example, *who* or *that*). (See 2.q for an extensive list of subordinators.) Sometimes a subordinator appears before the subject and predicate, as in the following examples:

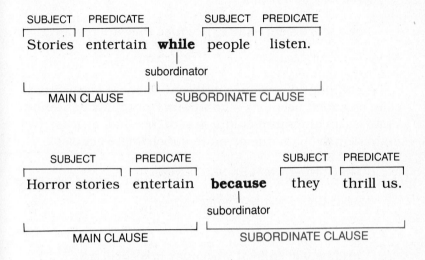

Subordinators do not always appear before the subject and predicate. Sometimes a subordinator is the subject of the subordinate clause itself. Following is an example of a subordinator (a relative pronoun) that is also the subject of a subordinate clause:

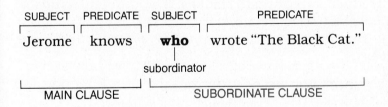

2.p COMPLEX SENTENCES; COMPOUND–COMPLEX SENTENCES

A simple sentence with one or more subordinate clauses added becomes a **complex sentence**. That is, a complex sentence has a main clause plus one or more subordinate clauses:

COMPLEX SENTENCE

Poe's stories entertain   because they are thrilling.

MAIN CLAUSE	SUBORDINATE CLAUSE

A compound sentence with one or more subordinate clauses added becomes a **compound-complex sentence**. That is, a compound-complex sentence has at least two main clauses plus one or more subordinate clauses.

COMPOUND–COMPLEX SENTENCE

Mary Shelley wrote *Frankenstein*,

MAIN CLAUSE

and people enjoy it   because it is thrilling.

MAIN CLAUSE	SUBORDINATE CLAUSE

2.q   SUBORDINATORS

Following is a list of subordinators that can be used to introduce subordinate clauses. The different kinds of subordinate clauses are discussed in 2.r–2.t. There you will find *adverb clauses*, *adjective clauses*, and *noun clauses*.

SUBORDINATING CONJUNCTIONS

after	even though	unless
although	how	until
as	if	when
as if	in order that	whenever
as long as	provided (that)	where
as soon as	since	whereas
as though	so that	wherever
because	than	whether
before	though	while

RELATIVE PRONOUNS
that
what, whatever
which, whichever (in which, for which, of which, by which)
who, whoever
whom, whomever (in whom, for whom, of whom, by whom)
whose (in whose)

AVOIDING ERRORS WITH SENTENCE FRAGMENTS

Be careful not to confuse main clauses and subordinate clauses. Remember that a subordinate clause cannot stand on its own. You must make it into a main clause or add a main clause to it.

NOT   ~~When favorite stories are told~~.
BUT   **I listen** when favorite stories are told.

In writing, do not treat a subordinate clause as if it were a sentence. A subordinate clause treated like a sentence creates a **sentence fragment**. No matter how long and complicated it may be, a subordinate clause is never a sentence.

NOT   ~~When Frankenstein comes to life, slowly opening his eyes and then breaking the chains that bind him.~~
BUT   **We are amazed** when Frankenstein comes to life, slowly opening his eyes and then breaking the chains that bind him.

EXERCISE 23. Identify the subordinate clause in each of the following sentences.

1. Although only 10 percent of American businesses are corporations, corporations control a large percent of the market.

2. Corporations arose because private business owners needed money to expand their operations.

3. A corporation in a sense borrows money from people when the people buy stock.

4. The investors, or stockholders, own a part of the business when they buy stock in it.

5. Investors study the corporation carefully before they buy stock.

6. People invest money in a corporation because they expect to earn a profit.

7. When the corporation earns profits, it repays the investors.

8. Investors earn a profit when their shares of stock increase in value.

9. Investors are sometimes not repaid if the corporation goes out of business.

10. Because private owners often cannot take all the risks of doing business today, they form corporations.

APPLICATION. Rewrite each of the preceding sentences, reversing the order of the clauses. If the subordinate clause came first, put it last. If the subordinate clause came last, put it first. Then indicate which version you prefer, and try to explain why.

EXERCISE 24. Identify the subordinate clause in each of the following sentences. Indicate whether each sentence is a *complex* sentence or a *compound-complex* sentence.

1. Although everyone talks about the weather, no one can affect it.

2. When some people talk about the weather, they mean only the temperature.

3. People need to understand temperature, air pressure, and wind, since all these factors make up the weather.

4. Unless people learn more about these factors, they can report the weather, but they cannot predict it.

5. Because communications, industry, farming, and space technology depend on the weather, everyone must learn more.

6. People need to know when weather conditions are dangerous; then they can avoid disasters.
7. If weather instruments could accurately predict a hurricane, people could be warned, and lives might be saved.
8. When the weather changes, people's moods often change.
9. Some people are sluggish whenever it is raining.
10. As soon as the sun shines, many people feel happy, and they go outdoors.

2.r ADVERB CLAUSES

An **adverb clause** is a subordinate clause that tells more about a verb, an adjective, or an adverb. It tells *when, where, how, why*, or *under what conditions.*

EXAMPLES
I study hard. [main clause with action verb]
Wherever it is quiet, I study hard
Because I want a good job, I study hard.
I study hard **in order that I may go to college**.

I was calm. [main clause with linking verb]
Although you got angry, I was calm.
I was calm **until you arrived**.
As long as you were there, I was calm.

The subordinators that can be used to introduce adverb clauses are grouped according to meaning:

SUBORDINATORS FOR ADVERB CLAUSES
SUBORDINATORS THAT TELL <u>WHEN</u>: after, as, as long as, as soon as, before, since, until, when, whenever, while
SUBORDINATORS THAT TELL <u>WHERE</u>: where, wherever
SUBORDINATORS THAT TELL <u>HOW</u>: as if, as though, than
SUBORDINATORS THAT TELL <u>WHY</u>: as, because, in order that, since, so that
SUBORDINATORS THAT STATE <u>CONDITIONS</u>: although, as long as, even though, if, provided (that), though, unless, whereas, whether, while

Some of the preceding subordinators are included in more than one category. These subordinators can mean different things, depending on how they are used in a sentence. In the following sentences, for example, the subordinator *since* is used in two different ways.

We have been celebrating **since** the game ended. [*Since* tells "when."]

We celebrated, **since** the game ended in victory. [*Since* tells "why."]

An adverb clause can come either before the main clause or after it. Notice that the following sentences have the same meaning even though their adverb clauses are in different places.

Because the game ended in victory, we celebrated.
We celebrated **because the game ended in victory**.

COMMAS AND ADVERB CLAUSES

Always use a comma after an introductory adverb clause, even a very short one.

When the team came on the field, the fans roared.
After the team won, we had a party.

In general, do not use a comma before an adverb clause that ends a sentence.

The fans roared when the team came on the field.
We had a party after the team won.

See 7.g.10 for more details on commas before adverb clauses in final position.

An **elliptical adverb clause** is an adverb clause that is incomplete because some words have been left out. The omitted words can easily be supplied, however, because they are understood, or implied.

This tastes better **than that** [tastes].
He works harder **than you** [work].
I am busier today **than** [I was] **yesterday**.

Sometimes you have to recognize an elliptical adverb clause and be able to supply the missing words in order to know which case of a pronoun to use in a sentence. Use the case of the pronoun that you would use if the clause were complete. (See also page 59.)

EXAMPLES

George likes Molly better *than **she***. [The elliptical clause is *than **she*** because the complete clause would be *than **she** likes Molly*.]

George likes Molly better *than **her***. [The elliptical clause is *than **her*** because the complete clause would be *than he likes **her***.]

EXERCISE 25. Identify the adverb clauses in the following sentences. Some sentences have more than one adverb clause.

1. Wherever he went, Henry David Thoreau made an impression.
2. Although Thoreau died in 1862, his writings still excite readers.
3. Thoreau earned his place in history because he believed in the power of the individual.
4. As Thoreau saw it, life would be richer if everyone were more self-reliant.
5. Thoreau did not favor selfishness, however, since he believed in harmonious cooperation among people.
6. If someone needed help, Thoreau gave it because that was the moral thing to do.
7. He sympathized when anyone, even an animal, was hurt or suffering.
8. Although Thoreau believed in human cooperation, he lived alone during an important part of his life.
9. Thoreau wrote essays while he was living alone at Walden Pond.

10. Whenever Thoreau was at Walden Pond, he was happy.
11. If he had not lived at Walden Pond, Thoreau might not have written *Walden, or Life in the Woods.*
12. After he left his cottage by Walden Pond, Thoreau published his book about it.
13. Because his friends might benefit from the experience, Thoreau advised them to attempt a completely self-sufficient life.
14. "Possessions are like leg irons," he wrote, as his friends had become increasingly materialistic.
15. Thoreau pursued a quiet, thoughtful life wherever he lived.
16. After he left Walden Pond, Thoreau worked at editing his journals because he had not long to live.
17. Many people today try to "return to the land" because they find urban life too complicated.
18. When Thoreau went to live in the woods, he hoped to discover the ideas important to him.
19. His message of keeping life as simple as possible will be relevant as long as people seek a satisfying life.
20. Thoreau is famous because he was idealistic, humane, and talented.

EXERCISE 26. Choose the appropriate form of the pronoun to complete each of the following sentences. Indicate what the complete adverb clause would be.

EXAMPLE We are better than (they/them.)
ANSWER *they   than they are*

1. Before the debate our adviser looked at our competitors and asked us whether we were as well prepared as (they/them).
2. Until this year our team captain was not as confident as (we/us).
3. Our team has lost more debates than (they/them).
4. Judges have usually decided that the team from Rivervale was more knowledgeable than (we/us).
5. Judges scoring the two teams always gave Rivervale more points than (we/us).

6. This year, however, more debates were won by us than (they/them).

7. Our team also spent more time researching than (they/them).

8. Our experience and preparation made us as quick and knowledgeable as (they/them).

9. We were sure the judges would score them lower than (we/us).

10. By winning the debate we surprised our team captain as much as (they/them).

2.s ADJECTIVE CLAUSES

An **adjective clause** is a subordinate clause that, like an adjective, gives more information about a noun, a pronoun, or a gerund.

An adjective clause can appear in various positions within a sentence. In the following examples, arrows point to the words that the adjective clauses are describing.

EXAMPLES

The horror story **that is my favorite** is "The Black Cat" by Edgar Allan Poe.

The writer **whom I like best** is Edgar Allan Poe.

I like any writer **who interests me**.

SUBORDINATORS FOR ADJECTIVE CLAUSES

who[1]
whom (in whom, for whom, of whom, by whom)
whose (in whose)
that

which (in which, for which, of which, by which)
where
when

[1]In adjective clauses *who*, *whom*, *whose*, *which*, and *that* are often referred to as *relative pronouns* (see 1.d.6).

An adjective clause is sometimes essential to the sentence; that is, it is needed to make the meaning of the sentence clear. This kind of adjective clause is called a **restrictive clause**, or an **essential clause**. Without the essential adjective clause, the sentence would not make sense.

EXAMPLES

Edgar Allan Poe is the only American writer **who always surprises me**.

"The Black Cat" is the story **that I like best**.

The above examples would not make sense without their essential adjective clauses. Edgar Allan Poe is certainly not the only American writer; the adjective clause, *who always surprises me*, is needed to complete the meaning of the sentence. In the second example the essential adjective clause, *that I like best*, is needed because the sentence makes no sense without it.

An adjective clause that is *not* needed to make the meaning of the sentence clear is called a **nonrestrictive clause**, or a **nonessential clause**. It can also be called an **extra clause**. An extra adjective clause may add information to the sentence, but the sentence would be perfectly logical without the clause.

EXAMPLES

Edgar Allan Poe, **who is my favorite author**, wrote "The Black Cat."

"The Black Cat," **which was written by Edgar Allan Poe**, is my favorite short story.

The sentences above would still make sense without their extra adjective clauses. The clauses are not essential to the meaning of the sentences.

You can use either *that* or *which* to introduce an essential clause. You must always use *which* before an extra clause. Never use *that* before an extra clause. (It helps to remember never to use *that* after a comma.)

"The Black Cat**,**" **which** I like best, is thrilling.
[nonessential (nonrestrictive), or extra, clause]
I like a story **that** thrills me. [essential (restrictive) clause]

COMMAS AND ADJECTIVE CLAUSES

1. With an extra (nonessential, or nonrestrictive) adjective clause, use extra commas. If the extra clause appears at the end of a sentence, put a comma before it. If the extra clause appears within the sentence, use a comma before and after it. The important word to remember is *extra*: A clause containing *extra* information requires *extra* commas.

> Edgar Allan Poe wrote "The Raven**,**" **which is a mysterious poem.**
> "The Raven**,**" **which is a mysterious poem,** was written by Edgar Allan Poe.
> Edgar Allan Poe**,** **who wrote "The Raven,"** also wrote "The Black Cat."

2. With an essential (restrictive) adjective clause, do *not* use commas. The information in an essential clause is needed for the sentence to make sense. Information in an essential adjective clause is *not* extra information and does *not* take extra commas.

> "The Raven" is the poem **that I love to read aloud.**
> The poem **that I love to read aloud** is "The Raven."
> The man **who wrote that poem** is most famous for his contributions to the short story art form.

HINT: If an adjective clause *describes*, it is probably an extra clause. If an adjective clause *identifies*, it is essential.

EXERCISE 27. Identify the adjective clause in each of the following sentences.

1. William Sydney Porter wrote stories under a pseudonym, which is another word for pen name.
2. Porter, who lived from 1862 to 1910, used the pseudonym O. Henry.
3. Porter contributed articles to a humor magazine, which he had founded in Texas in 1894.
4. He wrote a daily column that was humorous and witty.
5. As O. Henry, Porter published many short stories that were sympathetic and touching.
6. He created unusual plots that ended in surprise.
7. *The Four Million*, which is a collection of O. Henry's stories, was published in 1906.
8. "The Gift of the Magi" is a story that many people enjoy.
9. Another story that is popular is "The Third Ingredient."
10. Readers who enjoy the unusual and the humorous will delight in O. Henry's stories.

EXERCISE 28. Following are five pairs of sentences. For each pair, indicate which sentence has an essential (or restrictive) adjective clause and which sentence has an nonessential (or nonrestrictive or extra) adjective clause.

1. a. Space flights, which excite our imagination, are always important news.
   b. Space vehicles that land on other planets are always newsworthy.
2. a. John Glenn, who was an American astronaut, orbited the earth.
   b. John Glenn was the first American astronaut who orbited the earth.
3. a. In 1969 the Americans Neil Armstrong and Edwin Aldrin, Jr., were the first people who walked on the moon.
   b. In 1969 Neil Armstrong and Edwin Aldrin, Jr., who were Americans, first walked on the moon.
4. a. People who watched on television were thrilled.
   b. It was a major achievement for Americans, who have incredibly sophisticated space technology.

5. a. Intergalactic voyages, which are impossible now, may someday be common.
   b. Voyages to galaxies that are beyond the Milky Way may someday be common.

2.t NOUN CLAUSES

A **noun clause** is a subordinate clause used as a noun.

You can use a noun clause as a subject, a direct object, an object of a preposition, or a predicate nominative.

SUBJECT

Farmers eat home-grown food.
|
noun

Whoever lives on a farm eats home-grown food.
|
noun clause

The weather affects **crops**.
|
noun

The weather affects **whatever grows in the ground**.
|
noun clause
direct object

Crops are fed with **fertilizer**.
|
noun

Crops are fed with **what will make them grow**.
|
noun clause
object of preposition

Farmers are hard **workers**.
|
noun

Farmers are **what this country needs**.
|
noun clause
|_____|
predicate nominatives

Some of the subordinators that can be used to introduce noun clauses are listed below.

SUBORDINATORS FOR NOUN CLAUSES

how	whichever
that	who
what	whoever
whatever	whom (in whom, for whom, by whom)
when	whose
where	why
which	

Here are additional examples of noun clauses with some of the above subordinators.

EXAMPLES
Do you know **why farmers are hard workers**?
Whatever is grown for food needs much care.
Farmers grow **what is nourishing and tasty**.
Whoever eats fruits, grains, and vegetables is dependent upon farmers.
Eggs, milk, and beef are **what other farmers produce**.
Spring is **when most farmers plant their crops**.

EXERCISE 29. Identify the noun clause in each of the following sentences. Three of the sentences have two noun clauses each.

1. Whoever is interested in mountain climbing should read *Mountaineering* by Alan Blackshaw.
2. That mountain climbing requires strength and courage is well known.

3. What makes mountain climbing exciting is that it is dangerous and demanding, yet satisfying.
4. Whatever happens during the climb can endanger the climber.
5. Until a climb is finished, no one knows how it will end.
6. Why someone would want to climb a mountain is easy to understand.
7. What many mountain climbers say is "I climb a mountain because it is there."
8. Whoever questions such an answer would never be found on the side of a mountain.
9. What challenges climbers is whatever seems dangerous yet immensely rewarding.
10. Where no one has been is where daring people want to go.

REVIEW EXERCISE E. Identify each subordinate clause in the following sentences. Tell whether the subordinate clause is (a) an adverb clause, (b) an adjective clause, or (c) a noun clause. Each sentence has only one subordinate clause.

1. Books on how you should rear children are very popular.
2. *The Common Sense Book of Baby and Child Care*, which was written by Dr. Benjamin Spock, revolutionized child care.
3. This book has sold over thirty million copies since it was published in 1946.
4. What accounts for Dr. Spock's success is a combination of events.
5. There were few guides to child rearing before Dr. Spock wrote his book.
6. Most parents previously used a book that had been published in 1894.
7. Although this book was useful, it advised a rather harsh approach to rearing children.
8. A factor that made Dr. Spock's book popular was the rising interest in child psychology.
9. Why children behaved as they did became very important both to psychologists and to parents.

10. Psychological studies, which were becoming more common, raised many questions about discipline and encouragement for children.
11. Parents began to wonder about how they were rearing their children.
12. Parents were uncertain about when they should discipline or reward their children.
13. In the midst of this confusion, Dr. Spock offered advice that parents could understand.
14. Whereas earlier books advised parents not to spoil a child, Dr. Spock approved of tenderness and love.
15. Spock advised parents to trust themselves whenever they faced a problem with their children.
16. He also suggested that parents should not take the advice of neighbors.
17. The most important idea that Dr. Spock encouraged in parents was self-confidence.
18. When Dr. Spock spoke, parents listened.
19. Dr. Spock's book became essential to couples who had children after World War II.
20. Whoever was reared according to Dr. Spock's advice was treated with loving care and attention.

2.u *WHO* VS. *WHOM* IN SUBORDINATE CLAUSES

The case, or form, of the subordinator depends on how it is used within the subordinate clause.

When you have to decide between *who* and *whom* for a subordinate clause, use the following guidelines:

1. Look only at the subordinate clause. Do not pay attention to any other words in the sentence outside of the subordinate clause.
2. Decide if the subordinator is also the subject of the subordinate clause or the predicate nominative of the subordinate clause. If it is, use the nominative, or subjective, case: *who* or *whoever*.

3. Decide if the subordinator is also a direct object *within* the subordinate clause or the object of a preposition *within* the subordinate clause. If it is, use the objective case: *whom* or *whomever*.

Study the following solutions:

EXAMPLES

The farmers (who/whom) sow their seeds reap their harvest.

1. The subordinate clause is *who/whom sow their seeds*.
2. The subordinator is the subject of the verb *sow* in the subordinate clause. Therefore, the subordinator should be in the nominative, or subjective, case: *who*.

The 4-H Club gave its award to (whoever/whomever) raised the best calf.

1. The subordinate clause is *whoever/whomever raised the best calf*. The preposition *to* is outside the subordinate clause and should, therefore, be ignored.
2. The subordinator should be the subject of the verb *raised*. Therefore, the subordinator should be in the nominative, or subjective, case: *whoever*.

The farmers (who/whom) you respect know their land.

1. The subordinate clause is *who/whom you respect*.
2. The subordinator cannot be the subject of the subordinate clause; *you* is the subject. The subordinator cannot be the predicate nominative because the subordinate clause does not include a linking verb.
3. The subordinator is the direct object of the verb *respect*. Therefore, the subordinator should be in the objective case: *whom*.

EXERCISE 30. Select the appropriate subordinator.

1. Clothes are not always important to actresses and models (who/whom) have become famous.
2. Mariel Hemingway, (who/whom) is an actress, likes fancy fashions but also likes outdoor exercise.

3. Ali McGraw gives her attention to (whoever/whomever) designs beautiful fabrics.
4. McGraw, to (who/whom) fabric is important, will not be a slave to clothes, however.
5. Like Hemingway, McGraw is an actress (who/whom) works out daily.
6. Cheryl Tiegs, (who/whom) models fancy clothes, prefers jeans and T-shirts during the day.
7. Tiegs, (who/whom) photographers love to work with, insists that good health is most important.
8. The three women (who/whom) this exercise describes are all concerned about physical fitness.
9. (Whoever/Whomever) puts all her trust in clothes is short-sighted.
10. Obviously, clothes alone do not make the woman (who/whom) is successful today.

2.v A REVIEW OF SENTENCES: SIMPLE, COMPOUND, COMPLEX, COMPOUND–COMPLEX

The four kinds of sentences are summarized below.

1. **Simple sentence:** A simple sentence has only one main clause and no subordinate clauses. Therefore, a simple sentence has one subject (singular or compound) and one predicate (a single or compound verb plus any additional elements).

EXAMPLES
Ostriches flee.
Cooks and waiters work hard and have long hours.

2. **Compound sentence:** A compound sentence has two or more main clauses but no subordinate clauses. Each of the main clauses has a subject and a predicate. Therefore, each main clause in a compound sentence can stand alone as a simple sentence, described above.

EXAMPLES

Cooks prepare food, and waiters take orders.

Cities are exciting places, and many people enjoy their cultural activities and restaurants.

Ostriches flee, but the myth about their burying their heads in the sand is not quite true.

Some people like to read horror stories, but other people prefer to watch horror movies, for they enjoy the special effects.

3. **Complex sentence:** A simple sentence to which at least one subordinate clause has been added becomes a complex sentence. Therefore, a complex sentence has one main clause and one or more subordinate clauses.

EXAMPLES

Many people are thrilled when they visit a city.

Although horror stories are frightening, some of them have a comic ending.

Whenever they are frightened, ostriches flee on foot, since they cannot fly.

American cooks, who are always adventurous people, have been experimenting more and more often with cuisines that come from faraway places.

4. **Compound-complex sentence:** A compound sentence to which at least one subordinate clause has been added becomes a compound-complex sentence. Therefore, a compound-complex sentence has at least two main clauses and at least one subordinate clause.

EXAMPLES

Ostriches are frightened easily, but they must flee on foot because they cannot fly.

Whenever I visit a city, I buy a map, and I see as many of the attractions as I can.

The American public seemed to like a series of made-for-television films that were based on famous American short stories, and the stories themselves became popular again in classrooms around the country.

DIAGRAMING SENTENCES

Diagraming is a method of showing the relationship of various words and parts of a sentence to the sentence as a whole. You can check your understanding of how subjects, predicates, phrases, and clauses work together by using diagrams. On the following pages you will see how a simple two-part diagram grows as you add more parts to a sentence and, therefore, more lines to the diagram. In this book the new element on each diagram will always be in red.

You begin a sentence diagram by drawing a horizontal line and then dividing it into two parts, one for the subject and one for the verb, as shown in Diagram 1.

Diagram 1: Subject, verb

Divide the horizontal line into two parts, one for the subject, one for the verb. Make sure the vertical appears above and below the horizontal. This is the major division of a diagram.

SENTENCE: *Carpenters build.*

Diagram 2: Understood subject

Place *you* in parentheses on the subject line.

SENTENCE: *Build.*

Diagram 3: Sentence beginning with expletive *there* or *it*

Place *there* or *it* on a separate line.

SENTENCE: *There are carpenters.*

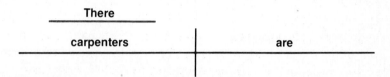

Diagram 4: Compound subject, compound verb

Place the parts of a compound element on a "fork." Then place them at the appropriate point on the diagram. Notice how to write in a conjunction.

SENTENCE: *Carpenters and mechanics both plan and build.*

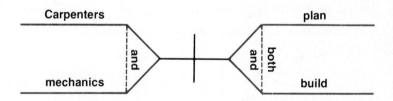

Diagram 5: Adjectives, adverbs, determiners

Place all modifiers on slanted lines below the noun or verb that they modify.

SENTENCE: *The successful carpenters build quickly and expertly.*

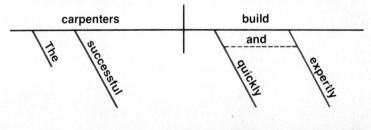

Diagram 6: Adverbs that modify adjectives or adverbs

You can place an adverb on one slanted line that grows out of another.

SENTENCE: *Extremely successful carpenters build very accurately.*

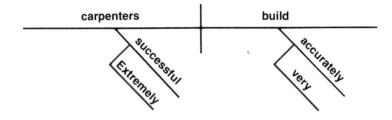

Diagram 7: Predicate nominatives

Place a predicate nominative along the horizontal line of the predicate. Separate it from the linking verb by using a slanted line.

SENTENCE: *Carpenters are careful planners.*

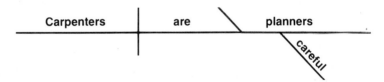

Diagram 8: Predicate adjectives

Place a predicate adjective the same way that you place a predicate nominative. Notice the "fork" for a compound element.

SENTENCE: *Expert carpenters are careful and accurate.*

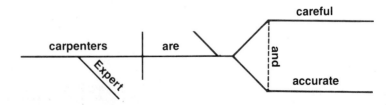

Diagram 9: Direct objects

Place a direct object along the horizontal line of the predicate. Separate it from the action verb by using a vertical line (which does *not* cut through the horizontal).

SENTENCE: *Carpenters saw wood.*

| Carpenters | saw | wood |

Diagram 10: Indirect objects

Draw a slanted line below the verb and then a horizontal line off the slanted line.

SENTENCE: *Carpenters give people service.*

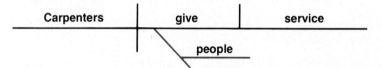

Diagram 11: Compound direct objects and indirect objects

Notice the "forks."

SENTENCE: *Carpenters give customers and apprentices explanations and advice.*

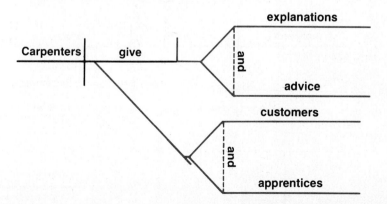

Diagram 12: Prepositional phrases

Place the preposition on a slanted line that comes down from the word modified by the prepositional phrase. Then draw a horizontal line off the slanted line. Place the object of the preposition on the horizontal.

SENTENCE: *Carpenters of today use tools with electric power in their work.*

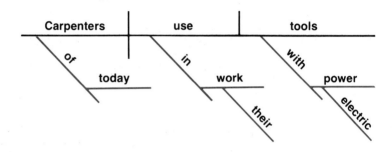

Diagram 13: Participles and participial phrases

Curve the participle as shown below.

SENTENCE: *Pounding nails, the carpenter bruised his thumb.*

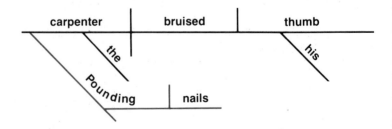

Diagram 14: Gerunds and gerund phrases

Place the gerund on a step as shown below. The phrase in the subject position is placed on a "stilt" so that it will fit.

SENTENCE: *Using an electric saw is a quick way of cutting wood.*

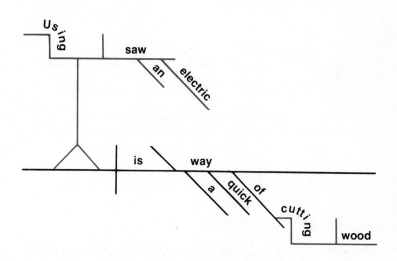

Diagram 15: Infinitives and infinitive phrases

These infinitives are diagramed like prepositional phrases (see Diagram 12).

SENTENCE: *Carpenters strive to build carefully.*

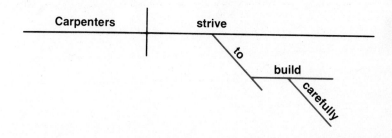

Diagram 16: Infinitives and infinitive phrases as nouns

Here, you have to use stilts again.

SENTENCE: *To love work is to know satisfaction.*

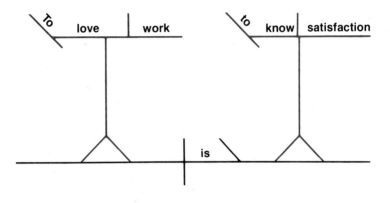

Diagram 17: Appositives

Place the appositive in parentheses.

SENTENCE: *The teacher, a professional carpenter, empha-sizes design, an important skill.*

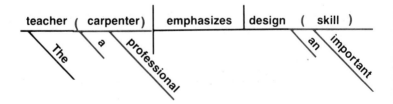

Diagram 18: Compound sentences

Place each main clause on a diagram of its own. If the main clauses are connected by a semicolon, use a dotted line to connect the verbs of each main clause. If the main clauses are connected by a conjunction, place it on a solid horizontal line.

SENTENCE: *Mechanics like to fix objects, but carpenters must learn to build.*

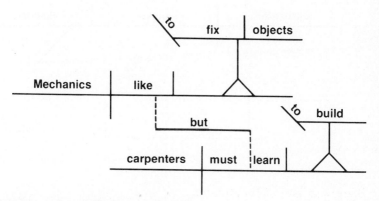

Diagram 19: Adjective clauses

Place the main clause in one diagram and the subordinate clause in another diagram. Use a dotted line to connect the subordinator of the subordinate clause to the word it modifies.

SENTENCE: *The carpenter whom you hired fixed shelves that were uneven.*

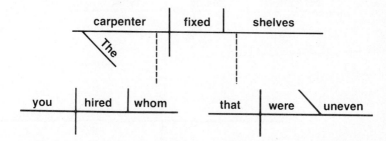

Diagram 20: Adverb clauses

Place the main clause in one diagram and the subordinate clause in another diagram. Place the subordinating conjunction on a dotted line connecting the verb of each clause.

SENTENCE: *Before they cut the wood, carpenters make a design.*

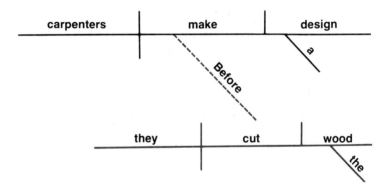

Diagram 21: Noun clauses as subject

Use a stilt growing out of the subject position for the noun clause. Place the subordinator as subject, object, or predicate nominative of the noun clause itself.

SENTENCE: *What the carpenter builds is sturdy.*

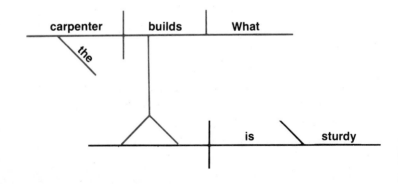

Diagram 22: Noun clauses as object

Use a stilt growing out of the object position. If the subordinator merely introduces the noun clause, simply place it on a line of its own.

SENTENCE: *We know that the mechanic fixes machines.*

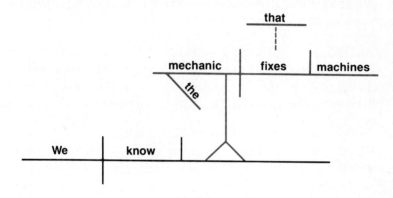

EXERCISE 31. Using Diagrams 1-5 as models, diagram the following sentences.

1. Cook!
2. Clay cooks well.
3. There are good clays.
4. Europeans and Americans cook and compare.
5. The clay cooks and moistens effectively.

EXERCISE 32. Using Diagrams 1-5 and Diagram 12 (prepositional phrases) as models, diagram the following sentences.

1. The clay soaks before use.
2. The moisture blends with natural juices of the food.
3. The moisture blends during preparation in the oven.
4. Each pot comes with a brief manual.
5. Eat food from these casseroles.

EXERCISE 33. Using Diagram 9 (direct objects) as a model, diagram the ten sentences in Exercise 15, page 136.

EXERCISE 34. Using Diagrams 7–9 as models, diagram the ten sentences in Exercise 2, page 114. *(You will find direct objects, predicate adjectives, and predicate nominatives in the exercise.)*

EXERCISE 35. Using Diagrams 7–9 as models, diagram the ten sentences in Exercise 13, page 131. *(You will find direct objects, predicate adjectives, and predicate nominatives. Review, also, the diagram for compound verbs.)*

EXERCISE 36. Using Diagram 10 (indirect objects) as a model, diagram the first four sentences of Exercise 17, page 138.

EXERCISE 37. Diagram Sentences 1–5 in Review Exercise C, page 145. *(This exercise will serve as a review of how to diagram direct objects, indirect objects, predicate adjectives, and predicate nominatives.)*

EXERCISE 38. Diagram Sentences 2, 4, 7, 8, and 9 in Exercise 22, page 150. Use Diagram 18 as a model of how to diagram compound sentences.

EXERCISE 39. Using Diagram 19 as a model for how to diagram adjective clauses, diagram Sentences 1–5 in Exercise 27, page 162.

EXERCISE 40. Using Diagram 20 as a model for how to diagram adverb clauses, diagram Sentences 1–5 in Exercise 25, page 157. (Ignore the word *however* in Sentence 5.)

EXERCISE 41. Using Diagrams 21 and 22 as models of how to diagram noun clauses, diagram Sentences 1 and 5 in Exercise 29 on page 164.

WRITING SENTENCES

Writing Sentences

One of the things that makes good writing pleasurable to read is the variety of sentence structures used. The reader does not become bored, because the rhythm and flow of the sentences change.

Being able to vary your sentences is a skill that you can learn. This section will show you that even using only one subject and one verb, you can make your sentences fresh and interesting. You will also learn how to combine clauses into more complex sentences.

Once you are familiar with the different kinds of sentences, you will find that you can use these sentence structures naturally in your writing. The job of putting varied sentences together into paragraphs and compositions will then be one that you can approach with confidence.

WRITING SIMPLE SENTENCES

3.a SIMPLE SENTENCES

A **simple sentence** has only one subject (single or compound) and one predicate.

There is actually quite a variety possible when you write simple sentences. Here you will consider nine kinds of simple sentences. They will all have the same subject. The differences between them, then, will be in the predicates.

You do not have to memorize the nine basic kinds of simple sentences listed here. Remember, though, that these are the kinds of sentences that can be expanded and varied even more when you write a paragraph, a composition, a letter, or anything else. It is variety, after all, that helps to make writing interesting.

■ Kinds of simple sentences

1. Trains **move**.
   subject + action verb
2. Trains **move people**.
   subject + action verb + direct object
3. Trains **save people money**.
   subject + action verb + indirect object + direct object
4. Trains **are transporters**.
   subject + linking verb + predicate nominative
5. Trains **are important**.
   subject + linking verb + predicate adjective
6. Trains **are everywhere**.
   subject + linking verb + predicate adverb
7. Trains **seem to save time**.
   subject + linking verb + infinitive phrase
8. Trains **are appreciated again**.
   passive-voice sentence
9. There **are trains**.
   subject + linking verb (in inverted order)

3.a.1 Expanding simple sentences

The nine basic simple sentences listed above have two things in common. They each have a subject, and they each have a verb (an action verb or a linking verb). You may not be able to communicate your message fully, though, if you limit yourself to subjects and verbs. You may want to tell more about subjects and more about verbs. You may, in other words, want to *expand* your simple sentences.

Consider the following basic simple sentence and then the two expanded versions. Obviously, the added words paint different pictures.

EXAMPLE

Basic simple sentence
Trains move.

Expanded sentence (version 1)
Old trains move slowly.

Expanded sentence (version 2)
European trains move majestically.

The following sentences illustrate ways of building up, or expanding, one of the nine basic simple sentences:

■ To tell more about nouns

BASIC SIMPLE SENTENCE
Trains move people.

ADD ADJECTIVE
Suburban trains move people.
Trains move **busy** people.
Suburban trains move **busy** people.

ADD PARTICIPLE (OR PARTICIPIAL PHRASE) AS ADJECTIVE
Trains move **working** people.
Overcrowded trains move people.
Traveling night and day, trains move people.

ADD POSSESSIVE
Today's trains move people.
Trains move **America's** people.

ADD PREPOSITIONAL PHRASE AS ADJECTIVE
Trains **along the coast** move people.

ADD INFINITIVE (OR INFINITIVE PHRASE) AS ADJECTIVE
Trains **to carry passengers** move people.

■ To tell more about verbs

BASIC SIMPLE SENTENCE
Trains move people.

ADD ADVERB OF MANNER
Trains move people **conveniently**.

ADD ADVERB OF PLACE
Trains move people **everywhere**.

ADD ADVERB OF TIME
Trains **often** move people.

ADD PREPOSITIONAL PHRASE AS ADVERB
Trains move people **in comfortable surroundings**.

ADD INFINITIVE (OR INFINITIVE PHRASE) AS ADVERB
To save energy, trains move people.

Exercises 1-9 and Review Exercises A and B will give you practice in writing sentences that have expanded subjects or predicates.

EXERCISE 1: Expanding sentences with all structures. Rewrite each of the following basic simple sentences twice. First add Item *a* to the original sentence, creating a new sentence. Then add Item *b* to the original sentence, creating another new sentence. You will have to decide where in the sentence to put the new items; sometimes you will have a choice.

1. Henry Ward Beecher was a minister.
   a. outspoken
   b. in the nineteenth century
2. His sermons were famous.
   a. against slavery
   b. throughout the nation
3. Guest speakers shared his pulpit.
   a. from time to time
   b. invited by Beecher

4. Many celebrities visited his church.
   a. to hear his sermons
   b. of the day
5. The church still stands in Brooklyn, New York.
   a. on Orange Street
   b. famed
6. Plaques and paintings cover the walls.
   a. to honor celebrated visitors
   b. historical
7. One painting is of Harriet Beecher Stowe.
   a. in the church
   b. celebrated
8. The writer was Henry Ward Beecher's sister.
   a. of *Uncle Tom's Cabin*
   b. well-known
9. *Uncle Tom's Cabin* described slavery.
   a. as a social evil
   b. clearly
10. The book's purpose was to end slavery.
    a. in the United States
    b. primary

EXERCISE 2: Using adjectives. Expand each of the five simple sentences below by placing the most appropriate word from the Word Bank before the italicized word. Use each Word Bank item only once.

1. Congress sets aside *holidays*.
2. Each state proclaims its own *holidays*.
3. Some holidays originated as *events*.
4. Several *states* observe the birthday of Robert E. Lee.
5. April Fools' Day is a *holiday*.

WORD BANK
unofficial
federal
special
southern
sacred

EXERCISE 3: Using participles as adjectives. Expand each of the five simple sentences below by placing the appropriate participle from the Word Bank in front of the italicized word. Use each Word Bank item only once.

1. Almost every month has a *tradition*.
2. February has a special day for *couples*.
3. March is known for its *weather*.
4. July is the time for *parades*.
5. November is welcomed by *citizens*.

WORD BANK
voting
flag-waving
dating
changing
time-honored

EXERCISE 4: Using participial phrases as adjectives. Expand each of the five simple sentences below by placing a participial phrase from the Word Bank after the italicized word. Use commas to set off the phrases. Use each Word Bank item only once.

1. *Memorial Day* is at the end of May.
2. *Flag Day* is in June.
3. *Labor Day* is the first Monday in September.
4. January 13 is the birthday of *Martin Luther King, Jr.*
5. October's Halloween is a treat for young *folk*.

WORD BANK
masked to disguise themselves
appreciated by workers
honoring those killed in battle
celebrated by patriots
respected by people concerned with civil rights

EXERCISE 5: Using prepositional phrases as adjectives. Expand each of the following simple sentences by adding one of the prepositional phrases from the Word Bank below. The phrase will modify the italicized word. Use each Word Bank item only once.

1. April Fools' Day can be *fun*.
2. *Valentines* are popular again.
3. *Fireworks* light the sky on the Fourth of July.
4. Thanksgiving brings *relatives* together.
5. *Saint Patrick's Day* is the first green of spring.

WORD BANK
in March
for pranksters
of lace
from across the country
in dramatic patterns

EXERCISE 6: Using infinitive phrases as adjectives.

Expand each of the simple sentences below by placing the appropriate phrase from the Word Bank after the italicized word. Use each Word Bank item only once.

1. Ancient *festivals* took place in the fall.
2. One fall *holiday* is Halloween.
3. Youngsters wear *costumes*.
4. The English and the Irish carve *beets, potatoes, and turnips*.
5. Fortunetelling and bobbing for apples are two Halloween *traditions*.

WORD BANK
to amuse party-goers
to disguise themselves
to use as lanterns
to delight children today
to celebrate the harvest

EXERCISE 7: Using adverbs.

Expand each of the following five simple sentences by placing the appropriate word from the Word Bank in the sentence. The Word Bank item will modify the italicized word. Use each Word Bank item only once.

1. True loves *appear* on Valentine's Day, according to custom.
2. The custom of sending romantic messages *replaced* giving gifts.
3. Some valentines *are decorated* with ribbons, flowers, and lace.
4. On Groundhog Day people *wait* for the woodchuck's forecast.
5. Scientists *study* the groundhog to no avail.

WORD BANK
expectantly
gradually
supposedly
exquisitely
repeatedly

EXERCISE 8: Using prepositional phrases as adverbs.

Expand each of the following simple sentences by adding one of the prepositional phrases from the Word Bank below. Use each Word Bank item only once. Let the question words in the parentheses guide you.

1. Soldiers and sailors march. *(when?)*
2. Special services are held. *(where?)*
3. The holiday started as Armistice Day. *(when?)*
4. Veterans speak. *(how?)*
5. Flags are displayed. *(how?)*

WORD BANK
at the Tomb of the Unknown Soldier
on Veterans Day
after World War I
in emotional tones
with pride

EXERCISE 9: Using infinitive phrases as adverbs. Expand each of the simple sentences below by placing the most appropriate phrase from the Word Bank within the sentence. The phrase will modify the italicized word. Use each Word Bank item only once.

1. Since ancient times people have *celebrated*.
2. On January 1 ancient Romans *looked* back.
3. Ancient Romans *gave* New Year's gifts to their senators.
4. English people *cleaned* their chimneys on New Year's Day.
5. Modern Americans *watch* their televisions.

WORD BANK
to win political favors
to bring good luck to their homes
to remember the old year
to mark the coming of a new year
to see a lighted ball drop from a building

REVIEW EXERCISE A: Expanding sentences in a variety of ways. Rewrite each of the following sentences by adding words or phrases from the Word Bank on the facing page. The italicized letters at the end of each sentence indicate which lettered list in the Word Bank contains the appropriate word or phrase.

EXAMPLE Dogs are pets. *A, E*
ANSWER   *Dogs are **popular** pets **in America.***
                       A   **E**

1. Have you had a pet? *D, E*
2. Pet stores are booming. *B, D*
3. Pets include fish and birds. *A, C*
4. Parrots imitate human speech. *A, D*
5. Cats are adorable. *A, B*
6. Some people buy boa constrictors. *B, E*
7. A pet owner has some problems. *D, C*
8. Doghouses and litter boxes burden owners. *C, E*
9. Dog food companies sell customers meat. *B, E*
10. The food varies. *A, C*

WORD BANK

A. Adjectives
proper
cuddly
common
~~popular~~
tropical

B. Participial phrases
washing the car
selling animals of all kinds
trying to be different
toying with balls of string
flooding supermarket shelves

C. Infinitives or infinitive phrases as adjectives
to combat
to give your pet
to clean
to buy

D. Adverbs
instinctively
ever
everywhere
upward
naturally

E. Prepositional phrases
at home
~~in America~~
in the doghouse
with daily chores
in moist or dry varieties
for thirty dollars

REVIEW EXERCISE B. Rewrite each of the following sentences twice by making each of the specified additions. When the instructions call for an added *phrase*, add words as necessary to complete the phrase. There is more than one possible answer to each item.

EXAMPLE   Both children and adults seem to like tops.
          Use a form of *spin*
          a. as a participle before a noun
          b. in a participial phrase after a noun

ANSWERS a. *Both children and adults seem to like* **spinning** *tops.*
        b. *Both children and adults seem to like tops,* **spinning in a dizzying way***.*

1. Tops have long been popular.
   Use a form of *universe*
   a. as an adverb
   b. in a prepositional phrase as an adverb

2. Some tops amuse babies.
   Use a form of *music*
   a. as an adjective
   b. in a prepositional phrase as an adverb

3. Scientists use gyroscopic tops to control boats.
   Use a form of *rock*
   a. as a participle before a noun
   b. in a participial phrase after a noun
4. People in China and Japan admire top spinning.
   Use a form of *profession*
   a. as an adjective
   b. in a prepositional phrase
5. Tops were some of the earliest toys in the United States.
   Use a form of *patent*
   a. as a participle used as an adjective
   b. within an infinitive phrase used as an adjective

3.a.2 Varying the position of modifiers

When you expand a basic simple sentence, you sometimes have choices about where you will place the adjectives, adverbs, and phrases. One way to decide where to place the modifiers is to consider the preceding sentences in your paragraph. You usually do not want too many sentences to start the same way or to end the same way. Variety, again, is important.

EXAMPLES

BASIC SIMPLE SENTENCE: Trains move people.

EXPANDED WITH ADVERB: Trains move people **conveniently**.

ADVERB IN ANOTHER PLACE: Trains **conveniently** move people.

ADVERB IN ANOTHER PLACE: **Conveniently**, trains move people.

BASIC SIMPLE SENTENCE: Trains move people.

EXPANDED WITH INFINITIVE PHRASE: **To save energy**, trains move people.

INFINITIVE PHRASE IN ANOTHER PLACE: Trains, **to save energy**, move people.

INFINITIVE PHRASE IN ANOTHER PLACE: Trains move people **to save energy**.

Always make sure, however, that your modifiers are placed so that they clearly refer to the part of your sentence that you intended. Misplaced modifiers, especially participial phrases and adverbs of degree, are a common error.

EXERCISE 10. Go back to the sentences that you wrote for Exercises 7, 8, and 9. See how many of the sentences you can rewrite by changing the position of the adverb or the phrase.

EXERCISE 11. Go back to the sentences that you wrote for Review Exercise A. See how many of the sentences you can rewrite by changing the position of an adjective, adverb, infinitive, or phrase.

WRITING COMPOUND SENTENCES

3.b JOINING MAIN CLAUSES

A **compound sentence** consists of two or more main clauses.

No matter how much you expand your simple sentences, you must learn to write other kinds of sentences as well. Compound sentences make it easier for you to show the relationship between two or more ideas. Therefore, it is important to learn to write them effectively.

3.b.1 Joining main clauses with coordinating conjunctions

One way that you can show the relationship between two or more ideas is to join them with coordinating conjunctions. The coordinating conjunctions that you will use most frequently to join main clauses are *and, but, or,* and *for.*

COMMAS BETWEEN MAIN CLAUSES

Use a comma before the coordinating conjunction in compound sentences. The comma is necessary to avoid possible confusion. Notice how Sentence 2 is clearer than Sentence 1.

1. The farmer waved at the traiñand the horse neighed.

2. The farmer waved at the train‚ and the horse neighed.

A reader might mistakenly read Sentence 1 as *The farmer waved at the train and the horse.*

▪ The coordinating conjunctions and their uses

AND
1. Long-distance trains move people comfortably, and families can travel together.
2. The train was late in departing, and the travelers became impatient.

You can use *and* to balance two main clauses that are equally important (as in Sentence 1). You can also use *and* between two main clauses to show a time sequence or a cause and an effect (as in Sentence 2): First this happened, and then that happened.

BUT
3. Long-distance trains move people comfortably, **but** some commuters still prefer their cars.

You can use *but* to join ideas that contrast with each other or that are opposite in some other way. If you had used *and* instead of *but* in Sentence 3, your readers would not have fully understood your meaning.

OR

4. Long-distance trains move people comfortably, **or** people complain.

You can use *or* to state an alternative or to mean "otherwise" (as in Sentence 4).

FOR

5. Long-distance trains move people comfortably, **for** they are equipped with sleepers and diners.

You can use *for* to join two clauses when the second clause gives a reason for the statement in the first clause (as in Sentence 5).

EXERCISE 12. Rewrite the following sentences, adding the appropriate conjunctions (*and, but, or,* and *for*). Use two different conjunctions for each pair.

1. a. The United States Navy, a branch of the armed forces, protects the seas, _____ it also carries out errands of mercy during disasters.
   b. The United States Navy, a branch of the armed forces, protects the seas, _____ it fights an enemy if necessary.

2. a. The Navy has many kinds of ships at sea, _____ each has its admirers.
   b. The Navy has many kinds of ships at sea, _____ the ships depend on onshore services for supplies.

3. a. Do people join the Navy to see the world, _____ do they see the Navy as a way to learn a trade?
   b. Do people join the Navy to see the world, _____ do they realize their dreams?

4. a. "Anchors Aweigh" is the Navy's marching song, _____ blue and gold are its official colors.
   b. "Anchors Aweigh" is the Navy's marching song, _____ the anchor must be raised ("weighed") for a ship to sail.

5. a. Most crew members stand four-hour watches, _____ each member has a battle station for emergencies.
   b. Most crew members stand four-hour watches, _____ some exceptions are always necessary.

EXERCISE 13. Rewrite the following sentences, adding the appropriate conjunctions (*and, but, or,* and *for*). Use two different conjunctions for each pair.

1. a. The Marine Corps, a branch of the armed forces, stages amphibious assaults, _____ Marines have been the first to fight in every major war of the United States.
   b. The Marine Corps, a branch of the armed forces, stages amphibious assaults, _____ Marines also guard embassies and perform other "land" functions.

2. a. Marines are often called "leathernecks,"_____ in the early days the collars of their uniforms had leather linings.
   b. Marines are often called "leathernecks," _____ today the nickname has no real application.

3. a. Marine training has always been rigorous, _____ now the exercise routine is more scientific.
   b. Marine training has always been rigorous, _____ Marines must be physically fit at all times.

4. a. Does the Marine motto, *Semper Fidelis*, mean "Always Faithful," _____ does it mean "The President's Own"?
   b. Does the Marine motto, *Semper Fidelis*, mean "Always Faithful," _____ how did it become their motto?

5. a. Most people have heard of the Marine boot camp in Parris Island, South Carolina, _____ recruits are also trained in San Diego, California.
   b. Most people have heard of the Marine boot camp in Parris Island, South Carolina, _____ most people know the words of the "Marine Hymn."

EXERCISE 14. Compose a main clause to go with the given clause and coordinating conjunction in each of the following sentence frames.

1. Trips to the moon were once science fiction, but _____ .

2. _____ , for American astronauts set foot on the moon in July 1969.

3. _____ , or they saw the moon walk on television.

4. _____ , and it was called "one giant step for mankind."

5. Space exploration had made the impossible possible, and _____ .

6. The United States has since launched several sky laboratories, and _____ .

7. The Apollo-Soyuz Test Project was the first manned international space flight, for _____ .

8. Some people criticize space exploration, for _____ .

9. _____ , and our tax dollars have more pressing claims down here on earth.

10. You may agree with these critics, or _____ .

3.b.2 Joining main clauses with conjunctive adverbs

A semicolon is a more formal mark of punctuation than a comma for joining main clauses. With a comma you must use a coordinating conjunction (*and, but, or,* or *for*). With the more formal semicolon you often use a conjunctive adverb (see 1.h.3) or an expression such as *in addition, as a result,* and *for example.* Conjunctive adverbs and expressions with similar meanings are grouped together in the following list.

CONJUNCTIVE ADVERBS
instead, however, nevertheless, still, yet
also, besides, furthermore, in addition, moreover, similarly
as a result, consequently, therefore, hence, thus
for example, for instance, that is

The sentences in each of the following pairs are the same except that the first uses a coordinating conjunction (and a comma) whereas the second uses a conjunctive adverb (and a semicolon). Notice that the second sentence in each pair sounds more formal.

EXAMPLES
Each subway station in Montreal is unique**, and** each offers fascinating shops and restaurants.
Each subway station in Montreal is unique**; moreover**, each offers fascinating shops and restaurants.

Subways in Tokyo are much cleaner than New York's, **but** rush-hour crowds are much worse.

Subways in Tokyo are much cleaner than New York's; **however**, rush-hour crowds are much worse.

PUNCTUATION WITH CONJUNCTIVE ADVERBS

You must use a semicolon before a clause that begins with a conjunctive adverb. Usually, you should use a comma after the conjunctive adverb.

Rush-hour passengers cannot push themselves into overcrowded Japanese subways; **therefore,** people are hired to push passengers into the cars.

Japanese passengers line up to get on subways; **as a result,** there are few arguments.

EXERCISE 15: Compose a main clause that will logically complete the sentence in each of the items. If you need ideas, check the Idea Bank following the exercise items for topics to use in the main clauses.

1. Comparative shopping will save you money; hence, ——— .
2. Comparative shopping will save you money; besides, ——— .
3. Check the price per unit for similar products; that is, ——— .
4. Check the price per unit for similar products; also, ——— .
5. Store brands are often cheaper than national brands; thus, ——— .
6. Store brands are often cheaper than national brands; nevertheless, ——— .

7. Some stores may offer weekly "specials" at lower prices; therefore, _____ .

8. Some stores may offer weekly "specials" at lower prices; furthermore, _____ .

9. Newspaper and magazine coupons can save your pennies; consequently, _____ .

10. Newspaper and magazine coupons can save your pennies; still, _____ .

IDEA BANK
clip coupons
try store brands
buy produce in season
even with discount, other products may cost less
look at prices per ounce, etc.
pays to shop around
discount stores' prices often even lower
check newspaper ads
with today's costs, no other way to shop
some still prefer particular brands

AVOIDING ERRORS WHEN JOINING MAIN CLAUSES

Do not join two main clauses with just a comma. If you do, you will create a comma splice (a run-on sentence).

Use either (1) a coordinating conjunction and a comma or (2) a semicolon and a conjunctive adverb. One other choice is to begin a new sentence.

NOT The Boston subway system was the first in the New World it is still transporting Bostonians.

BUT The Boston subway system was the first in the New World**, and** it is still transporting Bostonians.

OR The Boston subway system was the first in the New World**; moreover,** it is still transporting Bostonians.

WRITING COMPLEX SENTENCES

A **complex sentence** has one main clause and one or more subordinate clauses.

If you use only main clauses in your writing, it will begin to sound monotonous. Instead of using coordinating conjunctions and conjunctive adverbs to show relationships between ideas, you can use subordinate clauses.

When you combine a main clause with a subordinate clause, you immediately show how two ideas relate to one another, and your writing takes on a new rhythm.

EXAMPLE

Main clauses only

Americans flying to London can step off their planes and within a few minutes be on a subway to the city. Americans board a train for South Kensington or Russell Square. They notice how small and plush the subway cars are. They will sit comfortably for the short trip. They can read about the London Underground.

London's subways are full of history. For example, London introduced the world's first automatic train doors in 1923. They were regarded with suspicion at first. London also introduced the first underground escalator. It moved people to and from the very deep subways. Most interesting, the Covent Garden station is said to be haunted. According to some people, the ghost of an actor can be seen hurrying down the platform. The actor had been stabbed nearby in 1897.

Main clauses and subordinate clauses

Americans flying to London can step off their planes and within a few minutes be on a subway to the city. **As they board a train for South Kensington or Russell Square**, they notice how small and plush the subway cars are. **While they sit comfortably for the short trip**, they can read about the London Underground.

London's subways are full of history. For example, London introduced the world's first automatic train doors in 1923, **although they were regarded with suspicion at**

first. London also introduced the first underground escalator, **which moved people to and from the very deep subways**. Most interesting, the Covent Garden station is said to be haunted. According to some people, the ghost of an actor, **who had been stabbed nearby in 1897**, can be seen hurrying down the platform.

3.c WRITING SENTENCES WITH ADVERB CLAUSES

An adverb clause, like all subordinate clauses, cannot stand alone. It must be added to a main clause to make sense. An adverb clause can tell *when, where, how* or *why* or can state conditions.

The following examples show how you can use adverb clauses. Notice that each adverb clause is made up of a subordinating conjunction, a subject, and a predicate.

EXAMPLES

TELLING "WHEN": **After the London subways opened in 1863**, well-to-do people traveled on them.

TELLING "WHERE": **Wherever you are in Paris**, you can find a convenient "Métro" station.

TELLING "HOW": People in Stockholm speak of their subway stations **as if they were art galleries**.

TELLING "WHY": Advertisements in Stockholm subways are effective **because there are no commercials on Swedish television**.

STATING CONDITIONS: You can travel on BART **if you visit San Francisco**.

As shown in the preceding examples and as you will see on the following pages, adverb clauses can come before or after a main clause.

3.c.1 Writing adverb clauses that tell "when"

Any of the following subordinating conjunctions can be used to begin an adverb clause that tells "when."

SUBORDINATORS THAT TELL "WHEN"

after	before	when
as	since	whenever
as long as	until	while
as soon as		

Notice that an adverb clause that tells "when" can come before or after a main clause.

EXAMPLES

When you see the beautiful old subway stations of Vienna, you will be impressed.

You will be impressed **when you see the beautiful old subway stations of Vienna**.

EXERCISE 16. Compose five sentences. Match each main clause in Column I with the appropriate clause in Column II. You must use each clause from each column.

Column I

1. Duke Snider was finally elected to the Baseball Hall of Fame in 1980
2. A woman shaved a second off the woman's mile time
3. The Steelers won their fourth Super Bowl
4. A balloon team tried crossing the United States
5. In 1980 the Chinese competed in their first Olympics

Column II

a. after they had faced a tough fourth quarter against the Rams.
b. until weather forced a landing.
c. since the games started.
d. after some of his fans had lost hope.
e. when she ran in Australia in early 1980.

EXERCISE 17. Complete the following sentences. To each main clause add an adverb clause that tells "when." Remember that each adverb clause must have a subject and a predicate.

1. Physical training should begin at an early age before _____ .

2. More and more people are engaging in sports since
   ———— .
3. When ———— , exercise should not stop.
4. When ———— , people are more productive.
5. People can eat more but not gain weight after ———— .

EXERCISE 18: Sentence Combining. Combine each of the following pairs of sentences into one complex sentence. Move the expression in parentheses to the front of the sentence on that line, as the example shows.

> EXAMPLE   Frank McGuire was basketball coach at the University of South Carolina.
> He retired at the age of sixty-six. (**UNTIL**)
>
> ANSWER   *Frank McGuire was basketball coach at the University of South Carolina until he retired at the age of sixty-six.*

1. His final season wound down. (**AS**)
   McGuire had the second highest victory total of any active college coach.
2. He had coached thirty seasons. (**AFTER**)
   McGuire had 545 wins and 230 losses.
3. He made plans to retire. (**AS**)
   People began calling him The Legend.
4. McGuire himself played in Brooklyn.
   He made the Carolinas "basketball country." (**BEFORE**)
5. Wilt Chamberlain played for the losing team.
   North Carolina won the national championship. (**WHEN**)
6. McGuire has seen many changes in college basketball.
   He started with South Carolina in the 1960s. (**SINCE**)
7. He saw the checks from the N.C.A.A. (**WHEN**)
   He knew college basketball had become big business.
8. McGuire is healthy. (**AS LONG AS**)
   He will continue to be active in basketball.
9. McGuire likes getting attention.
   He is alive and well. (**WHILE**)
10. Some athletes and coaches do not receive honors.
    They die. (**UNTIL**)

EXERCISE 19: Sentence Combining. Combine each of the following pairs of sentences into one complex sentence. Move the expression in parentheses to the front of the sentence on that line, as the example shows.

> EXAMPLE She was twenty years old. (**WHEN**)
> Sydney Jacobs broke her back.
>
> ANSWER *When she was twenty years old, Sydney Jacobs broke her back.*

1. She had been mountain-climbing for two years. (**AFTER**)
   She experienced a catastrophic fall in 1974.
2. Tourists visited Washington State in 1979. (**WHEN**)
   Syd, in a wheelchair, led them on nature walks.
3. Sydney suffered the fall. (**AFTER**)
   She made demands on her family.
4. A year had passed. (**AS SOON AS**)
   She was back at the University of Washington.
5. A job opened up with the National Park Service. (**WHEN**)
   Syd knew it was a good opportunity.
6. She was "able-bodied." (**WHILE**)
   She loved competitive sports.
7. She was hurt. (**BEFORE**)
   She could not imagine life in a wheelchair.
8. She has been kayaking, swimming, and playing basketball in a wheelchair.
   She realized how important athletics are. (**SINCE**)
9. She feels too admired. (**WHENEVER**)
   Syd simply says, "I just get around in a different way."
10. She worked in the park. (**AS**)
    She studied how people in wheelchairs can get around.

EXERCISE 20: Sentence Combining. Combine each of the following pairs of sentences into one complex sentence. First select a subordinator that tells "when" from the list in 3.c.1. Begin each complex sentence by placing the subordinator at the beginning of the simple sentence on the top line, as the example shows. Try to use as many different subordinators as you can.

EXAMPLE   People started talking.
           They have probably complained about weather.
ANSWER   *Since people started talking, they have proba-*
           bly complained about weather.

1. There has been no rain for months.
   Farmers and gardeners complain.

2. The storms roll in.
   People on vacation grumble.

3. Students have had no time off for a while.
   They wonder why it has not snowed.

4. The snows snarl traffic.
   Commuters lose their tempers.

5. The summer arrives.
   People long for sun and surf.

6. The first heat wave strikes.
   People count the days until fall.

7. People see their fuel bills.
   They have romantic ideas about wintry days.

8. They remember smog.
   Easterners envy southern Californians.

9. They remember eastern winters.
   Californians may be jealous of eastern foliage.

10. People complain.
    They should think of the alternatives.

3.c.2 Writing adverb clauses that tell "where"

There are two important subordinators that begin adverb clauses that tell "where": *where* and *wherever.* You
will probably most often write an adverb clause that tells
"where" after a main clause. It is possible, however, to
have a "where" clause come first.

EXAMPLES
You will find subways **wherever you travel in Europe.**
Wherever you travel in Europe, you will find subways.

EXERCISE 21. Compose five sentences. Match each main clause in Column I with a suitable clause in Column II. Begin each sentence with the main clause. Use each clause from each column.

Column I	Column II
1. Northampton, Massachusetts, appears charming	a. where Dr. Sylvester Graham lived in the 1900s.
2. Louisa May Alcott rested	b. wherever you look.
3. Sophia Smith of North-ampton founded Smith College	c. where she performed in Northampton.
4. Creedo's Coffeehouse in Northampton serves graham crackers	d. where once there was no school for women.
5. The ghost of Jenny Lind, the singer, still walks	e. where the famous Northampton spa offered peace.

3.c.3 Writing adverb clauses that tell "how"

You can begin an adverb clause that tells "how" with the following subordinators: *as, as if,* and *as though.*

EXAMPLES
The Moscow subway looked exactly **as Tania described it**.
The Arbatskaya station looked **as if it were a palace.**
The Soviets always speak of their subways **as though they are the grandest in the world.**

EXERCISE 22. Complete the following sentences. To each of the numbered items add an adverb clause that tells "how."

1. Some people take to water as if _____ .
2. Some people can ride horses as if _____ .
3. As though _____ , some people play piano by ear.
4. A jazz drummer plays as _____ .
5. Many people today work computers as if _____ .

EXERCISE 23. Compose five sentences. Match each main clause in Column I with a suitable clause from Column II. Begin each sentence with the main clause. Use each clause from each column.

Column I

1. A speed skater comes out of a turn
2. Figure skaters perform
3. A good ice hockey team works
4. Bobsledders must get into their sled
5. Ski jumpers must move

Column II

a. as if they were one person.
b. as if they were going to sit on eggs.
c. as if he were an airplane wing.
d. as though they were dancers.
e. as if they were shot from a cannon.

EXERCISE 24: Sentence Combining. Combine each of the following pairs of sentences into a complex sentence. Move the expression in parentheses to the front of the sentence on that line, as the example shows.

EXAMPLE The man had been looking forward to his vacation.
A child anticipates a treat (**AS**).

ANSWER *The man had been looking forward to his vacation as a child anticipates a treat.*

1. The man was taking a vacation.
The fishing was supposed to be good. (**WHERE**)

2. The fishing school in Scotland was well known.
Anglers exchange stories about such places. (**WHEREVER**)

3. Anglers are famous for exaggerating.
Telling white lies is almost required. (**AS IF**)

4. The man found attaching the fly difficult.
He had two left hands. (**AS IF**)

5. He was proud after his first catch.
He had no humility. (**AS THOUGH**)

6. He fished the rest of the week. (**WHEREVER**)
   He did not have any more luck.
7. He waited patiently.
   He thought the salmon would run. (**WHERE**)
8. He cast. (**WHEREVER**)
   The fish went elsewhere.
9. Philosophy would help. (**AS THOUGH**)
   He tried to be rational.
10. He is now planning this year's fishing trip.
    He has never known defeat. (**AS IF**)

3.c.4 Writing adverb clauses that tell "why"

You can begin an adverb clause that tells "why" with one of the following subordinators: *as, because, since, in order that,* and *so that.* An adverb clause that begins with one of those expressions helps to explain why the action of the main clause takes place.

EXAMPLES
The underground level must be used **because the ground level is too crowded**.
Some countries build subways **so that they will be considered modern**.

EXERCISE 25. Compose five sentences. Match each main clause in Column I with a suitable clause that tells "why" from Column II. Begin each sentence with the main clause. Use each clause from each column.

Column I
1. Everyone needs sleep
2. Rest is necessary
3. You must figure out your own sleep needs
4. A mind shuts off
5. Drink warm milk

Column II
a. so that you will fall asleep.
b. so that you will face a new day refreshed.
c. since everyone is different.
d. because the body and the mind must rest.
e. because it is overtired.

3.c.5 Writing adverb clauses that state conditions

You can use one of the following subordinating conjunctions to begin an adverb clause that states the conditions under which the main clause is true:

SUBORDINATORS THAT STATE CONDITIONS

although	(even) if	whereas
as long as	(even) though	whether (or not)
	unless	while

EXAMPLES

A large modern city cannot survive **unless it has a good transportation system**.

Although subways are important, good bus systems must be developed also.

COMMAS AND ADVERB CLAUSES

1. Use a comma after an adverb clause (even a very short one) that comes *before* a main clause.

   If you visit London, ride on the Underground.

2. In general, do not use a comma before an adverb clause that comes *after* a main clause.

   Ride on the Underground when you visit London.

   EXCEPTIONS: Use a comma if the clause begins with (1) *although* or *though*, (2) *while* meaning "whereas," or (3) *as* or *since* meaning "because."

   The Paris subway is efficient, although it is no longer charming.

   Some people prefer public transportation, while others would rather travel by car.

   More people take trains now, since gasoline has become so expensive.

EXERCISE 26. Compose five sentences. Match each main clause in Column I with a suitable adverb clause in Column II. Begin each sentence with the main clause. Use each clause from each column.

Column I
1. You can fly a plane
2. You can run a marathon
3. You cannot win a scholarship
4. You can enjoy the ocean
5. Anyone can roller-skate

Column II
a. although having a sense of balance helps.
b. if you take flying lessons.
c. if you run many miles each day.
d. unless you study.
e. whether you swim or not.

EXERCISE 27: Sentence Combining. Combine each of the following pairs of sentences into a complex sentence by adding a subordinator that tells "why" or a subordinator that states a condition. Choose from the following: *as, because, since, in order that, so that, although, if, even if, even though, as long as, though, unless, whereas, whether or not, while.* Decide whether the adverb clause should come first or last.

EXAMPLE   Skiing used to require a snowy winter. Today real snow is not necessary.

ANSWER A *Skiing used to require a snowy winter, whereas today real snow is not necessary.*

ANSWER B *Although skiing used to require a snowy winter, today real snow is not necessary.*

1. People use snow machines.
   There is no snow.
2. Machine-made snow is denser.
   A foot of machine snow equals about four feet of real snow.
3. There is real snow.
   Some skiers prefer the firm artificial snow.
4. Artificial snow is obviously important.
   Competitions can proceed on schedule.

5. Purists disapprove of artificial snowflakes.
   They are all identical, unlike real snowflakes.
6. Ski resorts have existed for a long time.
   Snow machines are a recent innovation.
7. It snows during a winter.
   Resorts with snow machines can stay open.
8. Regions of New York and New England may be snowless.
   Resorts in the Alps never seem to have trouble.
9. People go north anyway.
   The snow is not what it used to be.
10. The fresh air and the social atmosphere are fun.
    Skis may not get much wear.

REVIEW EXERCISE C: Sentence Combining. Combine each of the following pairs of sentences into a complex sentence. Move the expression in parentheses to the front of the sentence on that line.

EXAMPLE   You want to express your individuality. (**IF**).
          You can buy a personalized license plate.

ANSWER   *If you want to express your individuality, you can buy a personalized license plate.*

1. License plates have become interesting.
   "Vanity" plates have become popular. (**SINCE**)
2. People use vanity plates.
   They can communicate with other drivers. (**SO THAT**)
3. You travel these days. (**WHEREVER**)
   You are bound to see a startling plate.
4. They cost extra. (**ALTHOUGH**)
   People continue to request special plates.
5. A new Californian has plates with BYBYNY.
   People will know his ex-hometown. (**SO THAT**)
6. You miss New York. (**IF**)
   Your plate might say IMNXNYR.
7. People with vanity plates enjoy them. (**ALTHOUGH**)
   Other people find them silly.
8. You see an interesting plate. (**WHEN**)
   The boredom of driving on highways is relieved.

9. One man in New Jersey has EIEIO.
   He is a farmer. (**BECAUSE**)
10. One man on Long Island is a French teacher. (**BECAUSE**)
    His plates read LE PROF.
11. Some people buy vanity plates.
    They were going out of style. (**AS THOUGH**)
12. Some people advertise their products.
    Other people just have letters and numerals. (**WHERE**)
13. One roadside vendor has more sales.
    He bought plates that say HOT DOGS. (**SINCE**)
14. You can see a car with YOGURT parked.
    A New Jersey yogurt factory stands. (**WHERE**)
15. Connecticut was the first state to have special plates.
    One man asked for YO YO. (**WHEN**)

3.d WRITING ADJECTIVE CLAUSES

You know that you can add an adjective to a sentence to tell more about a noun. Similarly, you can add an adjective clause to a sentence to tell more about a noun.

EXAMPLES

Main clause

Helicopters can act like taxis.

Main clause with adjective

Helicopters can act like modern taxis.

Main clause with adjective clause

Helicopters can act like taxis, which carry passengers.

Main clause

Many people are intrigued by the helicopter.

Main clause with adjective

Many people are intrigued by the practical helicopter.

Main clause with adjective clause

Many people are intrigued by the helicopter, which is so practical.

There are a few things to remember about adjective clauses:

1. You will usually begin an adjective clause with a subordinator, but sometimes you can omit the subordinator.

EXAMPLE

There is the helicopter that I flew.
There is the helicopter I flew.

2. Sometimes the subordinator is also the subject of the adjective clause.

EXAMPLE

I rode in that helicopter, which has a single rotor.

subordinator;   verb
subject

3. You must remember to use a verb in every adjective clause.

You can use the following subordinators to begin an adjective clause. The first five are sometimes called relative pronouns. *Whom, whose,* and *which* are often preceded by a preposition.

SUBORDINATORS

THAT: There is the helicopter **that** I flew.
WHO: Leonardo da Vinci is the first man **who** drew sketches of a helicopter.
WHOM: He is an inventor **whom** I admire.
WHOSE: He is an inventor **whose** ideas later became reality.
WHICH: The helicopter, **which** was really first developed successfully in the 1930s, has many uses.
WHERE: I visited the heliport, **where** tourists can take short flights.
WHEN: I remember the time **when** I saw the city from a helicopter.

COMMAS WITH ADJECTIVE CLAUSES

Remember that there are two kinds of adjective clauses: (1) essential, or restrictive, and (2) nonessential, or nonrestrictive (also called extra clauses).

You should not use commas to set off an essential clause. After all, if the information in the clause is essential, you do not want to separate it from the noun to which it refers.

The helicopter is the one aircraft that I have flown.

You should use *extra* commas to set off an *extra* clause.

The helicopter, which I have flown, is quite practical.

EXERCISE 28. Compose five complex sentences with an adjective clause beginning with *that, who, whom, whose,* or *which.* Match each subordinate clause in Column II with the appropriate main clause in Column I. You must use each clause from each column.

Column I
1. Users of pay phones now deal with computers
2. The recorded voice belongs to Jane Barbe
3. Her voice was recorded and divided into small segments
4. Some people prefer human operators
5. A computer, though, does not know

Column II
a. whom you call.
b. who is an actress from Atlanta.
c. that have female voices.
d. whose voices vary a great deal.
e. which were then stored in a computer

EXERCISE 29. Compose five complex sentences. Match the subordinate clauses in Column II with the appropriate main clause in Column I. You must use each clause from each column.

Column I	Column II
1. Each decade has a personality	a. in which people waited during the Depression.
2. The Roaring Twenties was a period	b. in which contemporary music has many roots.
3. The thirties are remembered for breadlines	c. during which dancing was very popular.
4. The forties brought a war	d. for which it is remembered.
5. The fifties brought rock and roll	e. in which millions died.

EXERCISE 30. Complete each of the following sentences. To each main clause add an adjective clause that tells more about a noun.

1. London is a city where _____ .
2. Paris is a city where _____ .
3. The eighteenth century was a time when _____ .
4. The twenty-first century will be a time when _____ .
5. Mars is a planet where _____ .
6. December is a month when _____ .
7. Museums are places where _____ .
8. Restaurants are places where _____ .
9. Anniversaries are times when _____ .
10. Births, weddings, and confirmations are occasions when _____ .

EXERCISE 31: Sentence Combining. Combine each of the following pairs of simple sentences into one complex sentence. Replace the underlined words with the word in parentheses. The word in parentheses then becomes the first word (subordinator) in the new subordinate clause.

EXAMPLE The safety pin was invented by a debtor.
The debtor sold the model for $400. (**WHO**).

ANSWER *The safety pin was invented by a debtor who sold the model for $400.*

1. In 1909 Henry Ford introduced a car.
   The car was known as the Model T. (**THAT**)
2. On January 25, 1915, Alexander Graham Bell made a call.
   The call was the first transcontinental phone call. (**THAT**)
3. In 1922 two British men discovered the tomb.
   Tutankhamen's mummy was found in the tomb. (**WHERE**)
4. In 1938 nylon was invented by an American.
   The American may not have realized its worth. (**WHO**)
5. In 1946 the first electronic computer was built.
   The computer operated on radio tubes. (**THAT**)
6. Edwin H. Land's daughter inspired the instant camera.
   The instant camera was developed in 1947. (**THAT**)
7. In 1832 John Matthews invented a fountain.
   Soda could be automatically dispensed from the fountain.
   (**FROM WHICH**)
8. In 1892 a Connecticut dentist designed a tube.
   Dental cream could be stored in the tube. (**WHERE**)
9. In 1858 Hyman Lipman patented a pencil.
   An eraser was attached to the pencil. (**TO WHICH**)
10. The year was 1821.
    Emma Willard opened the first girls' high school then.
    (**WHEN**)

EXERCISE 32: Sentence Combining. Combine each of the
following pairs of simple sentences into one complex sentence. Replace the underlined words with the word in
parentheses. The word in parentheses then becomes the
first word of the new subordinate clause. Notice that all of
the subordinate clauses are nonessential (extra) and so
must be set off with extra commas.

> EXAMPLE   California suffers frequent earthquakes.
> California lies on a major fault line. (**WHICH**)
> ANSWER   *California, which lies on a major fault line,*
> *suffers frequent earthquakes.*

1. The volcano on Krakatau erupted in 1883.
   Krakatau is an island in the Dutch East Indies. (**WHICH**)
2. Texans heard the explosion.
   The Texans lived thousands of miles away. (**WHO**)

3. Galveston, Texas, was hit by a huge tidal wave in 1900.
   <u>In Galveston</u> the highest ground is five feet above sea level.
   (**WHERE**)

4. The townspeople rebuilt Galveston.
   <u>The townspeople</u> refused to give in. (**WHO**)

5. San Francisco was the scene of a major earthquake in 1906.
   <u>San Francisco</u> was California's largest city. (**WHICH**)

6. The East Coast hurricane of 1938 was not forecast.
   Lighthouses, homes, and boats crumbled <u>then</u>. (**WHEN**)

7. Hurricane Camille also caused terrible damage.
   <u>Hurricane Camille</u> raged along the Gulf Coast. (**WHICH**)

8. Patrick and Catherine O'Leary are associated with the Chicago Fire of 1871.
   <u>Patrick and Catherine O'Leary</u> had a cow. (**WHO**)

9. The *Hindenburg* crashed in flames in 1937.
   <u>The *Hindenburg*</u> was a zeppelin. (**WHICH**)

10. The *Titanic* sank in 1912.
    <u>The *Titanic*</u> was called unsinkable. (**WHICH**)

3.e WRITING SENTENCES WITH APPOSITIVES

An **appositive** is a noun or pronoun (sometimes with modifiers) that is placed next to another noun or pronoun to identify it or to give additional information about it.

Instead of using adjective clauses, you can sometimes use appositives. An appositive is like an adjective clause: Both tell more about a noun or pronoun. There is a major difference, though. An adjective clause has both a subject and a verb; an appositive does not.

EXAMPLES

ADJECTIVE CLAUSE: People ride hydrofoils across the English Channel, **which is the body of water between England and France**.

APPOSITIVE: People ride hydrofoils across the English Channel, **the body of water between England and France**.

ADJECTIVE CLAUSE: A hydrofoil, **which is a vessel with winglike structures**, can travel faster than an ordinary boat.

APPOSITIVE: A hydrofoil, **a vessel with winglike structures**, can travel faster than an ordinary boat.

EXERCISE 33: Sentence Combining. Combine the following pairs of sentences by forming an appositive phrase out of the second sentence in each pair. Remove all unnecessary or repeated words in the second sentence. Remember to set off the appositive phrase with commas.

EXAMPLE   Margaret Mead wrote *Blackberry Winter*.
                   Margaret Mead was a famous anthropologist.

ANSWER   *Margaret Mead, a famous anthropologist, wrote* Blackberry Winter.

1. Margaret Bourke-White worked for *Life* magazine.
   Margaret Bourke-White was a news photographer.
2. Dorothea Lange worked during the Depression.
   Dorothea Lange was a photographer of rural poverty.
3. Willa Cather wrote many short stories.
   Willa Cather was a southerner.
4. Eleanor Roosevelt was a leader in her own right.
   Eleanor Roosevelt was the wife of a President.
5. Victoria Woodhull had been a publisher.
   Victoria Woodhull was the first woman to run for President.

EXERCISE 34: Sentence Combining. Combine the following pairs of sentences by forming an appositive phrase out of the second sentence in each pair. Remove all unnecessary or repeated words in the second sentence. Remember to set off the appositive phrase with a comma.

EXAMPLE   The first woman doctor in the United States was Elizabeth Blackwell.
                   Elizabeth Blackwell was a determined woman.

ANSWER   *The first woman doctor in the United States was Elizabeth Blackwell, a determined woman.*

1. A pioneer newspaperwoman was Nellie Bly.
   Nellie Bly was a young woman from Pittsburgh.
2. Mary Harris was a labor organizer.
   The labor organizer was an unselfish woman nicknamed "Mother Jones."
3. Pocahontas was a young princess.
   The princess was the wife of an English settler.
4. One heroine of the West was Belle Starr.
   Belle Starr was a friend of Jesse James's.
5. One woman who ran for Vice President was Mary L. Stowe.
   Mary L. Stowe was Victoria Woodhull's running mate.

EXERCISE 35. Each of the following sentences has one adjective clause. Rewrite each sentence, changing the adjective clause to an appositive phrase.

1. Sweden, which is a country that borders Norway and Finland, was formed by the Ice Age glaciers.
2. Switzerland, which is a landlocked country, is neutral.
3. Syria, which is a Middle Eastern country, has a very long history.
4. Tanzania, which is a land of contrasts, contains Mount Kilimanjaro.
5. Thailand, which is a Buddhist country, was formerly Siam.
6. The site of ancient Carthage is in Tunisia, which is a country in northern Africa.
7. Angel Falls is found in Venezuela, which is a country in South America.
8. Argentina is proud of Buenos Aires, which is its capital.
9. Voting is compulsory in Australia, which is a member of the Commonwealth of Nations.
10. Vienna is the capital of Austria, which is a country with many heroes.

3.f WRITING NOUN CLAUSES

You can often make your writing more concise and mature sounding if you use noun clauses. A noun clause can be used in all the ways that a noun or pronoun can be used. Compare the following versions:

EXAMPLES

Ideas expressed in simple sentences
Hydrofoils provide a smoother ride than boats.
That fact is well known.

Ideas expressed with noun clause
That hydrofoils provide a smoother ride than boats is well known.

Ideas expressed in simple sentences
You suggest a gift for her.
We will take it.

Ideas expressed with noun clause
We will take **whatever you suggest**.

You can use the following subordinators to begin noun clauses:

SUBORDINATORS

that	whoever
what	whom
whatever	whomever
who	

EXERCISE 36: Sentence Combining. Combine the following pairs of sentences to create a sentence with a noun clause as subject. Move the word in parentheses to the beginning of the sentence on that line, replacing the underlined word. Then substitute the newly formed noun clause for the SOMEONE or SOMETHING in the first sentence.

EXAMPLE   SOMEONE likes treasure hunts.
                  <u>Someone</u> likes mysteries. (**WHOEVER**)
ANSWER   *Whoever likes mysteries likes treasure hunts.*

1. SOMEONE must have a metal detector.
    <u>Someone</u> takes treasure hunts seriously. (**WHOEVER**)

2. SOMEONE knows about Jim Bowie's "lost silver mine."
   Someone knows about buried treasures. (**WHOEVER**)
3. SOMEONE must search old records for clues.
   Someone is serious about finding treasures. (**WHOEVER**)
4. SOMEONE usually owns what is buried there.
   Someone owns a piece of property. (**WHOEVER**)
5. SOMETHING might belong to the owner of the property.
   Something is found on private property. (**WHATEVER**)

EXERCISE 37: Sentence Combining.

Combine the following pairs of sentences to create a sentence with a noun clause as object. Move the word in parentheses to the beginning of the sentence on that line. Eliminate any underlined word in that sentence. Then substitute the newly formed noun clause for the SOMETHING or SOMEONE in the first sentence.

EXAMPLE   Most people know SOMETHING.
             Montezuma was the last Aztec emperor. (**THAT**)
ANSWER   *Most people know that Montezuma was the last Aztec emperor.*

1. Montezuma buried SOMETHING.
   Something was to be kept from the Spanish. (**WHATEVER**)
2. No one has yet found SOMETHING.
   Montezuma hid something. (**WHAT**)
3. Some people think SOMETHING.
   The treasure is near Taos, New Mexico. (**THAT**)
4. Other people believe SOMETHING.
   The gold and jewels are in Kanab, Utah. (**THAT**)
5. The treasure may make SOMEONE rich.
   Someone finds it. (**WHOEVER**)

EXERCISE 38: Sentence Combining.

Combine the following pairs of sentences to create a sentence with a noun clause as subject or as direct object. Move the word in parentheses to the beginning of the sentence on that line. Eliminate any underlined word in that sentence. Then substitute the newly formed noun clause for the SOMETHING or SOMEONE in the first sentence.

EXAMPLE   In 1865 a revolution in Mexico drove out
              SOMEONE.
              <u>Someone</u> had supported Maximilian.
              (**WHOEVER**)

ANSWER   *In 1865 a revolution in Mexico drove out*
              whoever had supported Maximilian.

1. SOMETHING is a mystery.
   <u>Something</u> happened to Maximilian's millions. (**WHAT**)
2. Maximilian's men carried SOMETHING from Mexico to Texas.
   <u>Something</u> fit in forty-five flour barrels. (**WHATEVER**)
3. The flour barrels held SOMETHING.
   <u>Something</u> is estimated as $5 million in gold. (**WHAT**)
4. SOMEONE was trustworthy.
   <u>Someone</u> worked for Maximilian. (**WHOEVER**)
5. Once in Texas the soldiers found SOMETHING.
   The bandits were dangerous. (**THAT**)
6. The soldiers hired SOMEONE.
   <u>Someone</u> offered to protect them. (**WHOEVER**)
7. The hired guard suspected SOMETHING.
   <u>Something</u> was in the flour barrels. (**WHAT**)
8. He and his associates stole SOMETHING.
   They could carry <u>something</u>. (**WHATEVER**)
9. SOMETHING was buried near Cattle Gap.
   They could not carry <u>something</u>. (**WHATEVER**)
10. SOMEONE never returned.
    <u>Someone</u> knew the position of the gold. (**WHOEVER**)

WRITING COMPOUND-COMPLEX SENTENCES

A **compound-complex sentence** consists of two or more main clauses and one or more subordinate clauses.

You can add subordinate clauses to compound sentences in the same way that you can add subordinate clauses to simple sentences. Adding one or more sub-

ordinate clauses to a compound sentence creates a compound-complex sentence.

3.g ADDING SUBORDINATE CLAUSES TO COMPOUND SENTENCES

A compound-complex sentence allows you to communicate a great deal of information in one sentence. Do not overuse compound-complex sentences, though, because they are quite long and can become monotonous.

EXAMPLES

Compound sentence

Cities have become less crowded, and people have had to design new transportation systems.

Compound-complex sentences

As families have become smaller, cities have become less crowded, and people **who are involved in urban planning** have had to design new transportation systems. [one adverb clause and one adjective clause added]

Cities have become less crowded, and people have had to design new transportation systems **that will use energy efficiently** and help **whoever needs help**. [one adjective clause and one noun clause]

EXERCISE 39. Expand each of the following compound sentences into a compound-complex sentence by adding a subordinate clause where you see the caret (∧). Begin the subordinate clause with the word given in parentheses at the end of the compound sentence.

> EXAMPLE Scrabble ∧ is fun, but players must have patience. (**WHICH**)
>
> ANSWER *Scrabble, **which is a word game,** is fun, but players must have patience.*

1. Monopoly ∧ is only a game, but some people take it seriously. (**WHICH**)

2. Chinese checkers is a good game to play ∧ , and it is easy to learn. (**WHEN**)

3. Backgammon is popular ∧ , but it requires much concentration. (**WHEREVER**)

4. Checkers ∧ is a favorite of all ages, and it is the first board game some people learn. (**WHICH**)

5. Chess is an ancient game ∧ , and it will probably stay popular. (**THAT**)

6. Some families ∧ enjoy the mystery game called Clue, for it has an element of suspense. (**WHO**)

7. Some people like Parcheesi, but other people like Boggle ∧ . (**BECAUSE**)

8. Jigsaw puzzles enslave some people, but other people can walk away from those puzzles ∧ . (**AFTER**)

9. Candyland is a game for children, but many adults remember it fondly ∧ . (**ALTHOUGH**)

10. Professional bridge players compete in international tournaments, but bridge also attracts many amateurs∧. (**WHO**)

WRITING SENTENCES WITH PARTICIPIAL PHRASES

3.h SENTENCES WITH PARTICIPIAL PHRASES

A **participial phrase** is a group of words that contains a participle and other words that describe or relate to the participle. You can use a participial phrase in many of the same ways that you can use a clause.

SENTENCE WITH SUBORDINATE CLAUSE	SENTENCE WITH PARTICIPIAL PHRASE
When hydrofoils went into service, they drew many fans.	**Going into service**, hydrofoils drew many fans.
People were amazed by hydrofoils, **which were known as flying ships**.	People were amazed by hydrofoils, **known as flying ships**.

You have seen that using subordinate clauses can help give variety to your writing. If you overuse subordinate clauses, though, your writing will lack variety. You should learn to use participial phrases as well.

AVOIDING ERRORS WITH PARTICIPIAL PHRASES

A participial phrase must clearly relate to the proper noun or pronoun elsewhere in the sentence. If it does not, you have a **misplaced modifier**. If the participial phrase does not belong with any noun or pronoun in the sentence, you have a **dangling modifier**.

NOT Buzzing overhead, we recognized a helicopter.
BUT We recognized a helicopter buzzing overhead.
OR   Buzzing overhead, the helicopter that we recognized flew by.

EXERCISE 40: Sentence Combining and Reducing. Combine each of the following pairs of sentences into one new sentence by making the first sentence of each pair into a participial phrase. As the example shows, in each sentence you will have several choices of where to place the participial phrase.

EXAMPLE Beans provide essential protein.
Beans are an important food.

ANSWER A *Providing essential protein, beans are an important food.*

ANSWER B *Beans are an important food, providing essential protein.*

1. Brazilians are fond of beans.
Brazilians put them in the national dish.

2. Mexicans work wonders with beans.
Mexicans have made them famous.

3. Many people think about baked beans.
   Many people picture Boston.
4. Beans are inexpensive.
   Beans become staples during hard times.
5. Senate navy bean soup was created in the U.S. Senate kitchen.
   Senate navy bean soup is a famous dish.
6. Black-eyed peas come from the South.
   Black-eyed peas are an ingredient of hoppin john, a regional specialty.
7. Lima beans were introduced from Peru.
   Lima beans are used here in succotash.
8. The soybean has gained in popularity.
   The soybean is an important source of protein.
9. Chickpeas are used in Italian, Israeli, and Arab cooking.
   Chickpeas flavor soups, stews, and salads.
10. Beans go back a long way.
    Beans were used by Aztecs, Egyptians, and other ancient people.

REVIEW EXERCISE D: Expanding sentences in a variety of ways. The following list reviews the structures you have used in this section to add information to sentences.

METHODS OF EXPANDING SENTENCES
1. adjectives or participles used as adjectives
2. adverbs
3. infinitive phrases
4. prepositional phrases
5. adverb clauses
6. adjective clauses
7. noun clauses
8. appositives
9. participial phrases

Here you will find pairs of sentences. The information in both sentences must be combined into one sentence.

Use any of the methods listed on the previous page to create a new sentence.

1. Jeremy decided to see America.
   He wanted to learn about the people and the places.
2. He had been born in the United States.
   He had been raised in England.
3. He began his trip by flying to New York.
   He landed at Kennedy Airport.
4. He traveled north through New England.
   He compared the old and the new.
5. He returned to New York.
   He headed south.
6. There was something in particular he wanted to see.
   That something was Disney World.
7. Then he went west.
   He had family in Oklahoma.
8. He moved on to Santa Fe.
   His grandmother had often gone there.
9. What did he look forward to most?
   He wanted to see all of California.
10. He returned to the East by the northern route.
    He stopped in several national parks.

MAKING SENTENCES CLEARER

The preceding pages have been concerned with adding variety to your sentences. Remember, however, that your sentences must also be clear. Here are three suggestions for writing clear sentences:

1. Make the subject of the sentence as obvious as possible.
2. Make sure that every word you use is important. Do not use unnecessary words.
3. Use the active voice unless you have a good reason to use the passive voice.

3.i CLEAR SUBJECTS

In general, it is not necessary or advisable to begin a sentence with words such as *I think, It is my opinion,* or *It is the opinion of the author.* The holder of the opinion or the thinker of the thoughts will be obvious from the rest of the paragraph. Get to the point rather than bogging down the sentence with those expressions.

Compare the following pairs of sentences. The second sentence in each pair starts off with the person or thing being discussed. That is, it begins with the subject rather than burying it.

EXAMPLES

It is the opinion of the writer that exercise helps.
Exercise helps, according to the writer.

I feel that flying a helicopter will be a memorable experience.
Flying a helicopter will be a memorable experience.

Of course, there are times when you will want to include a reference to yourself in the sentence. You will want to say *I feel* or *I believe.* Remember, though, that your sentences will drag if too many of them begin that way.

3.j CONCISE SENTENCES

Do not say the same thing over and over in a sentence. Read each of the following pairs of sentences. Notice how much briefer the second sentence in each pair is.

EXAMPLES

The experimental hydrofoil *Denison* was designed in an experiment to see how useful the hydrofoil could be for transporting passengers between two points over rough water.
The experimental hydrofoil *Denison* was designed to test its usefulness in transporting passengers over rough water.

Commercial hydrofoils regularly carry passengers and cargo on schedule over water on lakes, rivers, and harbor routes.

Commercial hydrofoils regularly carry passengers and cargo over lakes, rivers, and harbor routes.

Reread your sentences to make sure that you do not repeat yourself in different words. In addition, consider whether you can find one word that will take the place of a whole group of words.

EXERCISE 41. Rewrite each of the following sentences, eliminating all unnecessary words. Each rewritten sentence must have a clear subject and be as concise as possible. (There will usually be more than one possible way to improve the sentence.)

EXAMPLE   In my judgment the problem of nutrition still continues to remain a serious problem for many Americans in the United States even in spite of the plentiful abundance of food that is available to them.

ANSWER   *Nutrition remains a serious problem for many Americans in spite of the abundance of food available to them.*

1. It is the opinion of some writers who write about food that we eat that we need a variety or mix in our diet of foods.

2. I believe that the writer who suggests a variety is right, and she makes sense because a variety allows you to choose chicken, beef, fish, pork, and beans as the source for your protein.

3. Consumers should watch the amount of sugar they consume when they eat not only the obvious snacks that of course contain sugar (like candies, ice cream, and baked desserts, for example) but also prepackaged soups, sauces, cold breakfast cereals, vegetable juices, salad dressings, crackers, and bread.

4. If you eat herring, many olives, or other salted food on one day of the week, you should stay away from salt for the rest of the week that is left.

5. Balancing your diet between too much and too little of anything is a rule that is good to follow and obey if you are in general a healthy person.

3.k THE ACTIVE VOICE VS. THE PASSIVE VOICE

Reread your compositions to make sure that you do not overuse the passive voice. There is nothing wrong with using the passive voice occasionally, especially when you do not know who performed the action or when the performer is not important. In most cases, though, you probably should state the performer and use the active voice.

EXAMPLES

PASSIVE: Helicopters were designed on paper by many people before a real one was built. [The designers are not as important as the helicopters in this sentence.]

ACTIVE: Leonardo designed a helicopter on paper centuries ago. [Here, emphasis is given to a designer, and he is made the subject of the sentence.]

PASSIVE: Space shuttles have been planned for a long time. [The planners are not important in this sentence.]

ACTIVE: Vacationers will travel on space shuttles in the twenty-first century. [Here, there is no need to use a passive sentence.]

EXERCISE 42. Rewrite each of the following sentences, changing the verb from the passive voice to the active voice.

EXAMPLE A simple style of life was advocated by Henry Thoreau.

ANSWER *Henry Thoreau advocated a simple style of life.*

1. Mount Everest was first climbed by Sir Edmund Hillary.
2. Radium was discovered by Madame Curie.
3. Parties were given in the White House by Dolley Madison.
4. Tightropes are walked by Philippe Petit.
5. Chimpanzees were studied in the wild by Jane Goodall.

4

VOCABULARY

4 Vocabulary

When you write, you want to express your thoughts in such a way that your readers will understand exactly what you mean. Furthermore, you want them to be interested in what you have to say. Your most basic task as a writer is to choose words that will achieve these two goals.

If you write "The horse ran across the field," for example, your readers might picture a scene quite different from the one you intended to describe. The choice of words makes the sentence both vague and dull. If, however, you write "The stallion streaked across the prairie," you will create a specific and vivid image in your readers' minds. The choice of precise words (*stallion, streaked, prairie*) makes the difference.

You will find it easy to make your writing clear and interesting if you practice learning new words and using them. The more words you know, the more precision and variety you can bring to your writing (and your speaking). Here are some ways to expand your vocabulary:

- You can keep a list of words that you hear or read and that you want to learn and use.
- You can learn the meanings of unfamiliar words from their context, or relation to other words in the sentence (see 4.c).
- You can learn to use words that you already know in figures of speech (see 4.d).
- You can learn to add word elements to words that you already know to create new words.

4.a THE VARIED ORIGINS OF ENGLISH WORDS

Adding to your personal vocabulary is especially important because the English language has the largest vocabulary of any of the world's languages. English is particularly rich in synonyms, words that have almost the same meaning. If you want to express the idea of "happy," for example, you can convey many different shades of meaning by choosing among such synonyms as *glad, joyful, exultant, pleased, ecstatic, gleeful*, and *blissful*.

Where did all these words come from? The English language originated as Anglo-Saxon, the language of the Germanic tribes who invaded England in the early Middle Ages. Anglo-Saxon, or Old English, is the source of a large number of the most common, everyday English words. For example, the word *dog* comes from the Anglo-Saxon *docga*.

About three fourths of all present-day English words came into the language from languages other than Anglo-Saxon, however. Among the languages that English has borrowed from most heavily are Latin, French, and Greek. *Indicate*, for example, comes from the Latin *indicatus*. *Autograph* is derived from the Greek roots *auto* ("self") and *graphos* ("written").

Many words have gone through a long series of changes before reaching their present English form. *Music*, for example, began as the Ancient Greek *mousikè*. It then became, in turn, the Latin *musica* and the Old French *musique*. It then entered Old English as *musike* and finally emerged as the Modern English *music*.

Many other languages have contributed words to the English vocabulary. Here are some examples:

FRENCH: rouge, menu, bureau, deluxe, mystique
SPANISH: corral, patio, plaza, ranch
ITALIAN: balcony, fiasco, opera, umbrella
ALGONQUIAN: moccasin
ARABIC: algebra, alcohol
RUSSIAN: parka
DUTCH: cookie

In addition to single words, English has borrowed many expressions and phrases from other languages, especially French and Latin. These include, for example, *tête-à-tête* (French), meaning "a private conversation between two people"; *déjà vu* (French), meaning "a feeling of having experienced a certain situation previously"; and *status quo* (Latin), meaning "the existing state of affairs." By using such expressions instead of their longer English equivalents, you can make your writing more concise and more interesting.

EXERCISE 1. The words and expressions in the following Word Bank have been borrowed from other languages. Use the dictionary to find the meaning of any words or expressions that you do not know. Then rewrite each of the numbered sentences by replacing the italicized words with the appropriate item from the Word Bank. In some cases you will have to put the new word or expression in a different position in the sentence.

WORD BANK

ad nauseam	coup d'état
à la carte ✓	fait accompli
avant garde	libretto ✓
bona fide ✓	terra cotta ✓
carte blanche	totem ✓

1. People should not waste time trying to change a *situation that is already completed and probably irreversible.*
2. A restaurant where each item is *priced separately* is often more expensive than one offering complete meals of several courses at a fixed price.
3. Few architects are given *freedom to do whatever they wish* in designing a building.
4. The archaeologists unearthed several small vases and *reddish-brown baked clay* pots.
5. Realtors often have to separate offers *made in good faith* from those that are not serious.
6. She bragged *to a sickening extreme* about her famous ancestors.

7. In many Latin American countries political power has often changed hands by a *sudden overthrow of the government*.

8. Native American tribes or families were often represented by a *natural object that was considered to be related to them*.

9. The *advanced and unconventional* style of the Impressionist painters was not well accepted by their contemporaries.

10. People often find it easier to follow an opera by consulting a *book that contains the words of the opera*.

EXERCISE 2. Write ten sentences, each of which uses a different item from the Word Bank in Exercise 1.

EXERCISE 3. The words and expressions in the following Word Bank have been borrowed from other languages. Use the dictionary to find the meaning of any words or expressions that you do not know. Then rewrite each of the numbered sentences by replacing the italicized words with the appropriate item from the Word Bank. In some cases you will have to place the new word or expression in a different position in the sentence.

WORD BANK

ad infinitum	ex post facto
cause célebre	faux pas
coup de grâce	intelligentsia
détente	non sequitur
en masse	savoir faire

1. The Sacco and Vanzetti case was a *famous controversy* of the 1920s.

2. The Constitution forbids Congress to enact laws *with a retroactive effect*.

3. The novels of Turgenev depict the Russian *people regarded as the educated and intellectual class* of the late nineteenth century.

4. *The knowledge of what to do or say in every situation* is a basic qualification for a successful diplomat.

5. The Russo-Japanese War seriously undermined the position of the czar, and the disastrous Russian failures in World War I delivered the *finishing blow*.

6. She avoided embarrassment by turning her *tactless act or remark* into a joke.

7. His ignorance of the subject was obvious from his *remark that was unrelated to what had just been said*.

8. President Richard Nixon initiated a policy of *a lessening of tension or hostility* between the United States and the Soviet Union.

9. The list of English words derived from Latin could be extended almost *endlessly*.

10. The committee resigned *as a group* to protest the rejection of its recommendation.

EXERCISE 4. Write ten sentences, each of which uses a different item from the Word Bank in Exercise 3.

4.b NEW WORDS

Other languages are not the only source of new English words. Technological, social, and cultural changes produce new words within the language itself as names are given to new inventions, trends, and ideas. In the twentieth century, for example, science has produced *automobile, radio,* and *television*. From social and cultural developments of recent years have come *disco* and *Sunbelt*. If new words represent only temporary fads or trends, they may pass out of the language as quickly as they entered it. Other new words, however, become part of the permanent vocabulary of standard English.

New words in English are formed in various ways. Many new scientific terms, such as *automobile* and *television*, are combinations of Greek and Latin roots, sometimes with existing English words. For example, medical technology recently introduced the term *autotransfusion*, which refers to a procedure in which a person's own blood is recirculated after being cleaned. This word combines the Greek prefix *auto-* ("self") and the English word *transfusion* (itself a combination of two Latin roots). Other new words combine parts of two English words; examples include *newscast* (from "news broadcast") and *pianotron* (from "electronic piano").

Acronyms are new words formed from the first letters of a series of words. Familiar acronyms are *radar* ("radio detecting and ranging") and *laser* ("light amplification by stimulated emission of radiation").

Changes in the vocabulary of English also occur through changes in the meaning of existing words. Meanings may become either broader or more restricted. At one time, for example, *scenario* referred only to the plot of a play. Now it can mean an intended course of action in any setting, not just in the theater. *Meat*, on the other hand, once meant food in general. Today, of course, it refers only to a specific kind of food.

By being aware of changes in language and by adding new words to your own vocabulary, you can keep your writing up to date and interesting. Be careful, however. Not every new word that you hear or even read is appropriate in formal written English. If you are not sure, check a dictionary to see if the new word is acceptable. Furthermore, remember that when you use a new word your readers must be able to tell what you mean. If they are unfamiliar with the word, you must define it when you introduce it.

4.c CONTEXT AND MEANING

The **context** of a word is the situation in which the word appears. Because many English words have more than one meaning, you often depend on a word's context to make its meaning clear. For instance, if you write "A bank pays interest quarterly," your readers will know from the other words in the sentence that you mean the *bank* where money is kept. No one will think of the bank, or sloping side, of a river. Here is another example:

He was late for work because of a traffic **jam**.
Toast tastes good with butter and homemade **jam**.

The appropriate meaning of *jam* becomes clear within the context of each sentence.

Context can also help expand your vocabulary because it helps you determine the meanings of words that you do not know. Often the other words in a sentence make the meaning of an unfamiliar word apparent. Suppose, for instance, that you are unfamiliar with the word *parsimonious*. In the context of the following sentence, the word's meaning becomes clear:

It is wise to be careful about spending money, but it is not necessary to become **parsimonious**.

From the sentence you can tell that *parsimonious* is nearly synonymous with *stingy*.

EXERCISE 5. Each of the italicized words in the following sentences has more than one meaning. Choose the appropriate meaning for each word from the Word Bank that follows the sentences.

1. Pets are forbidden in the *terms* of some apartment leases.
2. Students often take on part-time jobs between school *terms*.
3. An unexpected *ring* of the doorbell always triggers a sense of anticipation.
4. Fans cheer when boxers enter the *ring*.
5. Some people claim that the lines of their *palm* reveal their past and future.
6. A *palm* in a desert oasis provides relief from the sun.
7. A special drill is usually necessary to *bore* through a brick wall.
8. Comedians with stale jokes *bore* their audiences.
9. A teacher often learns from the questions that students *pose*.

10. Models who *pose* for paintings must remain motionless for long periods of time.

WORD BANK

to pierce or drill
a division of a school year
to make weary by being dull
to ask
a tropical tree

the conditions of an agreement
a vibrating or echoing sound
to maintain a posture
a part of the human hand
an enclosed area for a sports event

EXERCISE 6. Look up each of the following words in the dictionary, and write its meaning. Then write a sentence in which the meaning of the word is clear from its context.

EXAMPLE esoteric

ANSWER *The **esoteric** book, which covered a specialized area of Roman wall painting, was of interest only to a handful of scholars.*

1. edible   3. lucrative   5. amplify
2. empathize   4. adept

EXERCISE 7. For each of the following sentences, use context clues to choose the correct definition for the italicized word from the Word Bank. Write each word and its definition.

1. *Quixotic* people believe in a society where people always think of others before themselves.
2. Ancient and medieval castles were often situated atop an *escarpment* that was impossible to scale.
3. A person with a broken *femur* has to wear a leg cast until the fracture heals.
4. A *surfeit* of tomatoes will cause the market price to drop; a poor harvest will force the price up.
5. The Sears Tower in Chicago is the tallest *edifice* in the world.

6. Providing enough food for the world's population has become a *perpetual* problem that shows no sign of improvement.

7. *Officious* people often interfere in affairs that do not concern them.

8. Eric Blair wrote novels and essays using the *pseudonym* George Orwell.

9. The odor of garlic used in cooking can *permeate* a whole house.

10. It would take an *audacious* sailor to attempt a solo voyage across the Atlantic.

WORD BANK

the thighbone
a building
a steep slope
meddlesome or
    overbearing
to spread through

bold and adventurous
extravagantly idealistic
a fictitious or pen name
continuous
an excess or
    overabundance

4.d FIGURATIVE LANGUAGE

In trying to make your writing clear and interesting, one of your most effective tools can be figurative language, or figures of speech. A **figure of speech**, broadly defined, is a way of saying something in other than literal, or actual, terms. You probably use some figurative language every day in phrases such as "She is as steady as a rock" and "That test was a monster." Clearly, a woman is not a rock, nor is a test a living, breathing monster.

As a writer, you will find that you can often express something more vividly and forcefully by using figures of speech than by saying it directly. If you describe someone as having "a mind like a razor," for example, you are comparing mental keenness to the physical sharpness of a razor. Although the two qualities are, of course, quite different, your figure of speech makes the abstract quality seem vivid and concrete.

■ Simile

A **simile** is a figure of speech that compares two things that are essentially unlike. The comparison is always directly stated with a word such as *like* or *as*.

EXAMPLES

Grandmother had a firm handshake, although she looked as fragile **as** an antique teacup.
The snow sparkled **like** diamonds in the sunlight.
His voice echoed **like** thunder in the small room.

■ Metaphor

A **metaphor**, like a simile, is a figure of speech that compares two essentially unlike things. In a metaphor, however, the comparison is never directly stated, and the words *like* or *as* are *not* used.

EXAMPLES

Her eyes blazed with fire. [The intensity of her expression and feeling is compared to a flame.]
A blanket of gloom descended on the stands as the home team fell further behind. [The concrete physical image of a blanket covering something is used to describe an emotional atmosphere.]
The owl's shrill call pierced the silence. [The sharpness of a sound is compared to the sharpness of an arrow.]

■ Personification

A **personification** is a figure of speech in which human qualities are given to an animal or an object. For example, in the sentence "The spring flowers shouted their colors across the eager meadow," both the flowers and the meadow are given human qualities.

EXAMPLES

The old house moaned and sighed in the wind.
We headed home under an angrily protesting sky.
The plants bowed their heads toward the sun.

■ Clichés

Imaginative figures of speech can make your writing interesting and forceful. In the same way, however, figurative language that is unimaginative can make your writing dull. Some figures of speech, called *clichés*, have been used so much that they have lost any freshness and interest they may once have had. Examples of clichés include *as cold as ice*, *as busy as a bee*, *like a bull in a china shop*, *like a fish out of water*. In your own writing, try to make your figures of speech original by avoiding clichés.

EXERCISE 8. Complete each of the following similes with an original comparison.

> EXAMPLE The trees swayed in the wind like ———.
> ANSWER   *The trees swayed in the wind* **like dancers gracefully moving their arms to the music**.

1. The driving rain against the windows sounded like ———.
2. The winning contestant was as happy as ———.
3. When the starting gun sounded, the runners took off like ———.
4. The setting sun glowed like ———.
5. Her laugh sounded like ———.
6. White houses dotted the mountainside like ———.
7. The silence was as refreshing as ———.
8. The room was as quiet as ———.
9. Bright lights sparkled like ———.
10. The crowd rushed through the doors like ———.

EXERCISE 9. For each of the following qualities, write a sentence in which an object is given that human quality.

> EXAMPLE generosity
> ANSWER   *The fountain gladly gave of its cooling freshness to the happily playing children.*

1. gracefulness
2. contentment
3. drowsiness
4. fright
5. gentleness

EXPANDING YOUR VOCABULARY: WORD BUILDING

Despite its huge size, the vocabulary of the English language is based to a great extent on just a few kinds of word elements. If you learn the meanings of a relatively small number of word roots (see 4.e), prefixes (see 4.f), and suffixes (see 4.g), you will be able to determine the definitions of many words that you have not even encountered yet. For example, by breaking down the word *incredible* into the prefix *in-* (meaning "not") the word root *-cred-* (meaning "believe") and the suffix *-ible* (meaning "able to be acted upon"), you can tell that the word means "not able to be believed."

In the following pages you will learn some of the most common English word roots, their meanings, and examples of words formed from them. In addition, you will learn some of the most common prefixes and suffixes that can be added to words. Finally, you will learn some common patterns by which words take suffixes.

4.e WORD ROOTS AND BASE WORDS

A **word root** is the main part of a word, but it is not a complete word in itself.

Word roots (or, simply, *roots*) are parts of Latin and Greek words. In English they do not stand on their own as independent words; they are always preceded or followed (or both) by another word element. For example, the root *-port-*, meaning "carry," is the basis of **ex**port, **porta-ble**, and **re**port**able**.

A **base word** is an element that can be used to build words but that is also a complete word in itself.

For example, the base words *historic* and *adult* can stand on their own, but they can also have word elements added to them, as in **pre**historic and adult**hood**.

Here are other examples of roots, base words, and added elements:

EXAMPLES

Root	With other elements
-**frag**-. -**frac**- ("break")	fragment, infraction
-**don**- ("give")	donor, donation
-**ped**- ("foot")	pedal, impediment
-**sol**- ("alone")	solo, solitary

Base word

act	actor, action
kind	unkind, kindness
employ	employer, unemployment
inherit	disinherit, inheritance

The elements that are added to word roots and base words are *prefixes* and *suffixes*. In Sections 4.f and 4.g you will see how you can use prefixes and suffixes to increase your writing vocabulary.

As you read through the following list of common word roots, remember that the spelling of the root may change slightly when it is used in an English word.

WORD ROOTS

Root	Meaning	Examples in English Words
-*am*-	love	amiable, amity
-*audi*-	hear	audience, auditory
-*ben*-	good, well	benefactor, benign
-*brev*-	short	brief, abbreviation
-*cap*-	head	capitol, decapitate
-*cogn*-	know	recognize, cognitive
-*corp*-	body	corporal, incorporate
-*domin*-	lord	predominant
-*duc*-	lead	reduce, deduction
-*fac*-, -*fec*-	do, make	factory, effect
-*fin*-	end	final, infinite
-*fus*-	pour	effusive, profuse
-*jac*-, -*ject*-	throw	projection, reject
-*junc*-, -*jug*-	join	juncture, injunction

Root	Meaning	Examples in English Words
-juven-	young	juvenile, rejuvenate
-leg-	law	illegal, legislature
-loqu-	speak	colloquium, loquacious
-magn-	great	magnitude, magnify
-mal-	bad	malice, malignant
-man-	hand	manuscript
-mit-, -miss-	send	transmit, missionary
-mor-	die	immortal, mortician
-nat-	born	native, natal
-prim-	first	prime, primary
-rupt-	break	disrupt, interruption
-sci-	know	omniscient, science
-scrib-, -script-	write	scribe, prescription
-sequ-	follow	consequence, sequel
-son-	sound	consonant, sonorous
-tract-	draw, pull	traction, retract
-ven-, -vent-	come	convene, invention
-verb-	word	verbose, proverb
-vert-, -vers-	turn	convert, perverse
-vid-, -vis-	see	evident, invisible
-vit-	life	revitalize, vitality

EXERCISE 10. Column I is a list of words made up of word roots with prefixes or suffixes. Match each word in Column I with its meaning in Column II. Use the meaning of the word root to help you figure out the meaning of the entire word.

Column I
1. infusion
2. prenatal
3. dissonance
4. extract
5. cognition
6. obsequious
7. juvenilia
8. avert
9. corporeal
10. emit

Column II
a. turn away
b. following slavishly
c. an inpouring
d. send out
e. draw out
f. bodily
g. before birth
h. process of knowing
i. youthful writings
j. clashing sounds

4.f PREFIXES

Prefixes are word elements that are attached to the beginnings of roots and base words.

EXAMPLES

Prefix	Base word	New word
dis-	honest	**dis**honest
co-	worker	**co**worker
sub-	cellar	**sub**cellar
mis-	behave	**mis**behave

Prefixed words are useful additions to your vocabulary because they help to make your writing more concise. In the following pairs of sentences, notice how the substitution of a prefixed word for a longer expression makes the second sentence smoother and more direct.

EXAMPLES

Groups **opposed to slavery** helped many slaves escape from the South before the Civil War.

Antislavery groups helped many slaves escape from the South before the Civil War.

Homes in coastal areas often have an appliance to **take the humidity out of** the air.

Homes in coastal areas often have an appliance to **dehumidify** the air.

Prefixes can be grouped according to their meanings. On the following pages you will find six groups of prefixes. The exercise following each group will show you how to use the prefixes to make your writing more concise.

The spelling of a base word never changes when a prefix is added (see 5.b.3). In some cases, however, a hyphen is used between a prefix and a base word. For example, a hyphen is always required after the prefix *ex-* and before a base word that is a proper noun or proper adjective. If you are unsure about whether to use a hyphen in a prefixed word, consult your dictionary.

PREFIXES WITH NEGATIVE MEANINGS

Prefix	Meaning	Can be used with
a-	without; not; lacking in	moral, social, symmetrical
dis-	not; opposite of	courteous, similar, approval, belief, satisfaction
in-	not; without; lack of	capable, credible, accurate, efficient
il-	variant of *in-*	legal, literate, legible
im-	variant of *in-*	movable, balance, passable, measurable
ir-	variant of *in-*	relevant, rational, regular, revocable
non-	not	competitive, productive, poisonous, existent
un-	not; opposite of	deserved, flattering, forgivable, involved
mal-	bad; wrongful; ill	function, nourished, nutrition
mis-	wrongly; astray	use, treated, spelled, quote, trust

EXERCISE 11. Revise each of the following sentences by combining the prefix given in parentheses with a word in the italicized phrase or clause. Make sure your prefixed word is placed so that your revision reads smoothly.

EXAMPLE Because the human brain is not fully developed at birth, the human infant is *not capable* of surviving alone. (in-)

ANSWER *Because the human brain is not fully developed at birth, the human infant is **incapable** of surviving alone.*

1. In Shakespeare's day the common people often demonstrated their *lack of approval* of a poor performance by throwing rotten vegetables. (dis-)

2. The Society for the Prevention of Cruelty to Animals was formed to protect animals from being *treated badly*. (mis-)

3. Red Cross workers are often permitted complete freedom of movement in war zones because they are *not involved* in the fighting. (un-)

4. A snake *that is not poisonous* has round eye pupils and lacks a heat-sensing pit. (non-)

5. Although faith and hope are *not measurable*, they are very powerful forces. (im-)

6. A good writer is careful to footnote a quoted source and not to *quote incorrectly*. (mis-)

7. A person who does not hold a door open for someone else is usually considered *not courteous*. (dis-)

8. Many magazines allow a subscriber *who is not satisfied* to cancel the subscription and receive a refund. (dis-)

9. Although windmills harness power cheaply in rural areas, they are *not efficient* in urban areas. (in-)

10. A word that is *spelled incorrectly* should be corrected as you edit your writing. (mis-)

PREFIXES THAT REVERSE ACTIONS

Prefix	Meaning	Can be used with
de-	to reverse an action; to deprive of; to remove	personalize, certify, vitalize, activate, populate
dis-	to reverse an action; to take away; to remove	credit, locate, organize, entangle
un-	to reverse an action; to deprive of	cover, load, ravel, roll, tie

EXERCISE 12. Revise each of the following sentences by replacing the italicized phrase with a verb containing the prefix in parentheses.

EXAMPLE   Floods often *drive the population from* an entire valley. (de-)

ANSWER   Floods often ***depopulate*** *an entire valley.*

1. Many feared that the use of television in the classroom would *diminish personal* relationships in teaching. (de-)
2. A good cook knows not to *remove the cover from* rice while it is cooking. (un-)
3. State supervisors may *withdraw certification from* a day care center if the number of children enrolled exceeds legal limits. (de-)
4. Lawyers often try to *take credit away from* witnesses who are damaging to their case. (dis-)
5. Because it is difficult to *remove entangled* branches from electrical wiring, trees are often cut or pruned before wire is strung. (dis-)

PREFIXES THAT SHOW TIME OR ORDER

Prefix	Meaning	Can be used with
ex-[1]	previous; former	President, convict, soldier, husband
post-	after	game, impressionist, natal, diagnostic
pre-	before	existence, season, destined, mixed
re-	again; back	activate, explore, schedule, consider, constructed, establish

EXERCISE 13. Revise each of the following sentences by combining the prefix given in parentheses with a word in the italicized phrase or clause. Make sure your prefixed word is placed so that your revised sentence reads smoothly.

EXAMPLE   Infants with certain digestive problems must eat some foods *that are "digested beforehand"* by a special process. (pre-)

ANSWER   *Infants with certain digestive problems must eat some "**predigested**" foods.*

---

[1] Always hyphenate *ex-* before the base word.

1. Because of heavy bombing, parts of many European cities had to be *constructed again* after World War II. (re-)
2. Under the "G.I. Bill," *former soldiers* were entitled to such benefits as college tuition. (ex-)
3. When new evidence is submitted during a criminal trial, witnesses often must be *examined again.* (re-)
4. The Florida Wintergarden is the scene of practice *before the season* for such baseball teams as the Boston Red Sox. (pre-)
5. Reading programs *designed after diagnostic testing* focus on the student's areas of weakness. (post-)
6. Coaches are often *former athletes* in their respective sports. (ex-)
7. Snowstorms often force schools to *schedule* athletic events *again.* (re-)
8. After the Civil War *former slaves* usually found decent work and respect harder to gain than their freedom had been. (ex-)
9. Medicines *that are mixed before sale* provide the consumer with the correct dosage. (pre-)
10. Because of the energy crisis the government is *again exploring* alternative sources such as solar and wind energy. (re-)

PREFIXES THAT SHOW LOCATION

Prefix	Meaning	Can be used with
circum-	around	navigate, lunar, gyrate, solar
inter-	between; among	state, relationship, tribal, departmental
intra-	within	state, muscular, cellular
mid-	in the middle of	section, week, morning, Atlantic
sub-	under; beneath	cellar, basement, conscious
trans-	across	oceanic, polar, Siberian

EXERCISE 14. From the Word Bank below, select a prefixed word that can replace the italicized phrase in each of the following sentences. Then revise each sentence, placing the prefixed word before the noun.

> EXAMPLE The nucleus is the center of activities *within a cell.*
>
> ANSWER *The nucleus is the center of* **intracellular** *activities.*

1. The first orbit *around the moon* by American astronauts was made in December 1968.
2. Mountain climbers and backpackers who attempt hikes *across the poles* are usually airlifted after reaching their destinations.
3. Most air raid shelters are structures *built under basements.*
4. Many health-conscious office workers use their coffee break *in the middle of the morning* for jogging.
5. Laws *made between states* cannot violate federal laws.

WORD BANK
subbasement
circumlunar
interstate
midmorning
~~intracellular~~
transpolar

PREFIXES THAT SHOW DEGREE

Prefix	Meaning	Can be used with
out-	going beyond; more than; better than	number, scores, run, weigh, do
over-	excessive; too much	anxious, crowded, eat, confident
sub-	lower in status than; less than	station, normal, committee
under-	insufficient; too little; not enough	developed, dressed, sized, estimate

EXERCISE 15. Revise each of the following sentences by combining the prefix given in parentheses with a word in the italicized phrase. Make sure the prefixed word is placed so that your revised sentence reads smoothly.

EXAMPLE Some restaurants will not seat men without jackets because they are considered *insufficiently dressed.* (under-)

ANSWER *Some restaurants will not seat men without jackets because they are considered* **underdressed**.

1. A track meet is won by the school that *scores more than* all others when the individual events are tallied. (out-)

2. Because an *excessively crowded* room is a fire hazard, every public auditorium has a legal limit on the number of people it can accommodate. (over-)

3. Every member of Congress belongs to several committees and several *committees under the standing committees.* (sub-)

4. The bald eagle is now an endangered species because it *does not breed enough.* (under-)

5. The student *who is too confident* will not do any better on a test than the student *who is too anxious.* (over-)

PREFIXES THAT SHOW SUPPORT OR OPPOSITION

Prefix	Meaning	Can be used with
anti-	against; opposite; to protect against	secrecy, aircraft, political, liberal, intellectual
co-	together with; joint	author, editor, defendants
counter-	returning an action against someone or something; parallel but opposite	evidence, challenge, proposal, force
pro-	on the side of; in favor of; in support of	European, conservation, military, union

EXERCISE 16. Revise each of the following sentences by combining the prefix given in parentheses with a word in the italicized phrase or clause. Be sure the prefixed word is placed so that your revised sentence reads smoothly.

> EXAMPLE   If a plan does not suit a member of a group, he or she is likely to suggest a *parallel but opposite proposal*. (counter-)
>
> ANSWER   *If a plan does not suit a member of a group, he or she is likely to suggest a* **counterproposal**.

1. During a trial a jury must carefully weigh the *opposing evidence* of the defendant's counsel against the evidence of the prosecution. (counter-)
2. Richard Rodgers and Oscar Hammerstein were *joint authors* of many popular songs. (co-)
3. In times of steadily increasing prices, measures must be taken *against inflation*. (anti-)
4. Laws *to support conservation* have been passed in many states. (pro-)
5. A devil's advocate will always have a *parallel but opposite argument* to offer in a discussion. (counter-)

4.g DERIVATIONAL SUFFIXES

A **derivational suffix** is a meaningful group of letters that can be added at the end of a base word or a word root to form (derive) a new word with a different but related meaning.

The addition of a derivational suffix often changes the part of speech of the original word.

EXAMPLES

Word	Part of speech	Derivational suffix	New word	Part of speech
class	noun	**-ify**	class**ify**	verb
real	adjective	**-ist**	real**ist**	noun
create	verb	**-ive**	creat**ive**	adjective

Derivational suffixes can be grouped according to whether they derive nouns, adjectives, verbs, or adverbs. The main adverb-forming suffix is *-ly*. The suffix *-ly* can be added to many adjectives to form adverbs of manner (see 1.f.1).

By adding derivational suffixes to words that you already know, you can increase your vocabulary and also make your writing more concise. In the following pairs of sentences, notice how the use of a suffixed word makes the second sentence smoother and more direct.

EXAMPLES

Voting is a right and a responsibility of **the condition of being a citizen**.
Voting is a right and responsibility of **citizenship**.

The fire had **turned** the walls **black**.
The fire had **blackened** the walls.

In the following pages you will find lists of common suffixes grouped according to whether they form nouns, adjectives, or verbs. As you read over the lists, notice that a spelling change is often required when a derivational suffix is added to a base word. For example, when the suffix *-less* is added to *penny*, the *y* is changed to *i*: *penniless*. For a discussion of the most common patterns of spelling changes in suffixed words, see 5.b.4.

SUFFIXES THAT FORM NOUNS

Suffix	Meaning	Base word or word with root	New noun
-acy	state, condition	conspire intimate	conspiracy intimacy
-age	result of action	marry drain	marriage drainage
-al	action	deny portray	denial portrayal

Suffix	Meaning	Base word or word with root	New noun
-ance; *-ence*	state, quality	defy comply prefer insist	defiance compliance preference insistence
-ant; *-ent*	performer of action	occupy complain depend superintend	occupant complainant dependent superintendent
-ation	action, state, result	expect transform	expectation transformation
-dom	domain, condition	king bore	kingdom boredom
-ee	receiver of an action	train employ	trainee employee
-eer	one in an activity	auction mountain	auctioneer mountaineer
-er; *-or*	performer of an action	run read invent compress	runner reader inventor compressor
-ful	amount	mouth cup	mouthful cupful
-hood	state, condition	widow child	widowhood childhood
-ion	action, state, result	perfect aggress	perfection aggression
-ism	system	imperial symbol	imperialism symbolism
-ist	follower, doer	organ national	organist nationalist
-ity	state, quality	real absurd	reality absurdity

Suffix	Meaning	Base word or word with root	New noun
-ment	action or its result	govern astonish	government astonishment
-ness	quality, state	deaf stubborn	deafness stubbornness
-ship	state, condition	hard leader	hardship leadership
-tude	quality, state	grateful certain	gratitude certitude
-ure	act, result, means	expose please	exposure pleasure
-y	quality, condition, action	jealous inquire	jealousy inquiry

SUFFIXES THAT FORM ADJECTIVES

Suffix	Meaning	Base word or word with root	New adjective
-able; -ible	able to be acted upon	break redeem admit divide	breakable redeemable admissible divisible
-al; -ial	character- istic of	region comic face office	regional comical facial official
-ary	related to	supplement planet	supplementary planetary
-en	made of, like	wood gold	wooden golden
-ful	full of, having	fancy hope	fanciful hopeful

Suffix	Meaning	Base word or word with root	New adjective
-ic	having the nature of	metal history	metallic historic
-ish	like, characteristic of	pig green	piggish greenish
-ive	tending to	recede express	recessive expressive
-less	without, lacking	joy humor	joyless humorless
-like	similar to	dog child	doglike childlike
-ly	like, characteristic of	friend heaven	friendly heavenly
-ous	full of, having the nature of	glory murder	glorious murderous
-some	tending to	tire quarrel	tiresome quarrelsome
-y	like, showing	dirt health	dirty healthy

SUFFIXES THAT FORM NOUNS AND ADJECTIVES

Suffix	Meaning	Base word or word with root	New noun or adjective
-an; -ian	belonging to, related to	America republic reptile Castile	American republican reptilian Castilian
-ese	of a style or place	journal Vienna	journalese Viennese

SUFFIXES THAT FORM VERBS

Suffix	Meaning	Base word or word with root	New verb
-ate	become, cause to become	captive active	captivate activate
-en	become, cause to become	quick weak	quicken weaken
-fy; -ify	cause to become	pure liquid	purify liquefy
-ize	become, cause to become	crystal modern	crystallize modernize

4.h DERIVATIONAL PATTERNS

You probably already realize that certain kinds of words follow definite patterns in the suffixes they take. For example, just as *receive* can become *receptive* and *reception*, so *deceive* can become *deceptive* and *deception*. By learning these patterns you can add greatly to your writing vocabulary because you will be able to predict derived forms of words that you already know.

You will find nine patterns of derivational suffixes on the following pages. The words in each pattern take the same derivational suffixes to form two or three related words. Each pattern is followed by an exercise that will give you practice in using the various forms of words in that pattern. Although in your own writing you would probably not use several related forms in the same sentence, the exercises will show you how the words are related in meaning.

The verbs in Patterns 1-5 can be transformed into two different kinds of nouns.

PATTERN 1: -ment, -er

Verb	Noun	Noun
achieve	achievement	achiever
adjust	adjustment	adjuster
announce	announcement	announcer
appoint	appointment	appointer
encourage	encouragement	encourager
enforce	enforcement	enforcer
develop	development	developer
punish	punishment	punisher
rearrange	rearrangement	rearranger
reinforce	reinforcement	reinforcer

EXERCISE 17. Substitute the word in parentheses or one of its derived forms for each blank. (The derived forms will end in -er or -ment.)

EXAMPLE Most people learn more easily with a little _____. A good teacher is always an _____ of students. (encourage)

ANSWER *Most people learn more easily with a little **encouragement**. A good teacher is always an **encourager** of students.*

1. An insurance company sends an _____ to _____ an accident claim submitted by a client. Often the _____ is less than the client's estimate. (adjust)

2. B. F. Skinner, a well-known psychologist, believes that behavior can be changed by _____. For example, to _____ the pecking response of a bird, he would award food as the _____. (reinforce)

3. When a _____ such as an ice cube is floated in a container of water, the water level will rise. The _____ is caused by the volume of the cube. (displace)

4. Although the President has the power to _____ the members of his Cabinet, Congress must approve each _____. (appoint)

5. The _____ over the public address system was difficult to understand because the _____ was speaking too quickly. (announce)

PATTERN 2: *-ify, -ification, -ifier*

Verb	Noun	Noun
amplify	amplification	amplifier
beautify	beautification	beautifier
clarify	clarification	clarifier
classify	classification	classifier
codify	codification	codifier
fortify	fortification	fortifier
justify	justification	justifier
modify	modification	modifier
nullify	nullification	nullifier
pacify	pacification	pacifier
simplify	simplification	simplifier

NOTE: *Satisfy* becomes *satisfaction*.

EXERCISE 18. Substitute the word in parentheses or one of its derived forms for each blank. The derived forms will end in *-ification* or *-ifier*.

EXAMPLE The _____ is the central part of a stereo system. Larger speakers permit greater _____ of the sound. (amplify)

ANSWER *The **amplifier** is the central part of a stereo system. Larger speakers permit greater **amplification** of the sound.*

1. An adjective is a _____ of nouns whereas an adverb is a _____ of verbs, adjectives, and other adverbs. A good writer uses the techniques of _____ to add description. (modify)

2. Biologists _____ plants and animals by genus and species. Species are the most basic units in biological _____. (classify)

3. A summons is a _____ for a person to appear in court. The _____ is said to "serve" the summons. (notify)

4. Police often ask an assault victim to try to _____ the attacker in a lineup. Positive _____ may lead to the arrest of a suspect, although the _____ may fear revenge. (identify)

5. Some people think that "the end will _____ the means," meaning that the worth of a goal is a _____ of the means for reaching that goal. (justify)

PATTERN 3: *-ize, -ization, -izer*

Verb	Noun	Noun
authorize	authorization	authorizer
centralize	centralization	centralizer
colonize	colonization	colonizer
modernize	modernization	modernizer
nationalize	nationalization	nationalizer
organize	organization	organizer
popularize	popularization	popularizer
tranquilize	tranquilization	tranquilizer
vaporize	vaporization	vaporizer

EXERCISE 19. Substitute the word in parentheses or one of its derived forms for each blank. (The derived forms will end in *-ization* or *-izer*.)

EXAMPLE ———— allows a veterinarian to examine a badly injured animal. To ———— a large animal, a veterinarian usually administers a ———— by injection. (tranquilize)

ANSWER **Tranquilization** *allows a veterinarian to examine a badly injured animal. To* **tranquilize** *a large animal, a veterinarian usually administers a* **tranquilizer** *by injection.*

1. ———— preserves milk and cheese by delaying or preventing fermentation. A ———— heats the milk to high temperatures in order to kill bacteria. (pasteurize)

2. Martha Graham was a leading ———— of modern dance in the United States. Her ———— of the form helped to make it an American specialty. (popularize)

3. Before a major order can be processed by a company, a high official must ———— it. An order is usually not honored if the necessary ———— is missing. (authorize)

4. Some states are educating the public to ———— lesser-known seafood such as squid or dogfish. ———— of such fish is also being promoted in Europe. (utilize)

5. England has been an active ———— throughout the world. English ———— of America began in the seventeenth century. (colonize)

PATTERN 4: *-ate, -ation, -ator*

Verb	Noun	Noun
arbitrate	arbitration	arbitrator
calculate	calculation	calculator
educate	education	educator
indicate	indication	indicator
legislate	legislation	legislator
navigate	navigation	navigator
violate	violation	violator

NOTE: Both *-er* and *-or* have the same meaning: "one who does." The suffix *-or* is used to form a noun from verbs that end in *-ate*.

EXERCISE 20. Substitute the word in parentheses or one of its derived forms for each blank. (The derived forms will end in *-ation* or *-ator*.)

EXAMPLE Litmus paper is a chemical _____. If a piece of litmus paper turns red when it is put into a fluid, the color change is an _____ that the fluid is acidic. (indicate)

ANSWER *Litmus paper is a chemical* **indicator**. *If a piece of litmus paper turns red when it is put into a fluid, the color change is an* **indication** *that the fluid is acidic.*

1. Laws now require that public buildings _____ the handicapped. An _____ for those in wheelchairs is the installation of access ramps. (accommodate)

2. Today's farmer is typically a skilled _____ of the land. He has learned scientific techniques of _____ in an agricultural college. (cultivate)

3. Many people do not consider double parking to be a serious _____ of law; however, the _____ blocks moving traffic as well as parked vehicles. (violate)

4. An experienced _____ is often called in to _____ a labor dispute. The task of _____ requires a great deal of patience. (arbitrate)

5. To _____ a cake takes training and artistic skill. Schools exist to train a _____ in the various techniques used in cake _____. (decorate)

PATTERN 5: -ation, -er

Verb	Noun	Noun
admire	admiration	admirer
explore	exploration	explorer
export	exportation	exporter
observe	observation	observer
preserve	preservation	preserver
reform	reformation	reformer
tempt	temptation	tempter
transform	transformation	transformer

EXERCISE 21. Substitute the word in parentheses or one of its derived forms for each blank. (The derived forms will end in *-ation* or *-er*.)

EXAMPLE   The United States is a major _____ of oil. Because this dependence on _____ is unwise, the government is encouraging conservation programs. (import)

ANSWER   *The United States is a major **importer** of oil. Because this dependence on **importation** is unwise, the government is encouraging conservation programs.*

1. Lifeguards are trained to use equipment such as a life _____. They are also trained to administer artificial respiration and other techniques for life _____. (preserve)

2. The famous _____ David Livingstone was the first European to _____ much of Africa. He combined _____ with a career as a medical missionary. (explore)

3. Carpetbaggers were northerners who came to the South to _____ the unsettled conditions after the Civil War. _____ by the carpetbaggers hindered the Reconstruction efforts in the South. (exploit)

4. The French aristocrat Alexis de Tocqueville was an acute _____ of American democracy. His _____ about the future development of America and Russia is particularly famous. (observe)

5. Books about looking for a job often _____ that you obtain a letter of _____ from your supervisor before leaving a job. (recommend)

The verbs in Patterns 6–8 can be transformed into nouns *and* adjectives.

PATTERN 6: *-ion, -ive*

Verb	Noun	Adjective
aggress	aggression	aggressive
connect	connection	connective
exhaust	exhaustion	exhaustive
express	expression	expressive
instruct	instruction	instructive
invent	invention	inventive
oppress	oppression	oppressive
prevent	prevention	preventive
restrict	restriction	restrictive

EXERCISE 22. Substitute the word in parentheses or one of its derived forms for each blank. (The derived forms will end in *-ion* or *-ive*.)

EXAMPLE   Old sayings tell us that people are as _____ as they feel and that _____ is often in the eye of the viewer. (attract)

ANSWER   *Old sayings tell us that people are as **attractive** as they feel and that **attraction** is often in the eye of the viewer.*

1. Debate fosters _____ speech. Careful _____ can influence an audience, and the person who can _____ opinions clearly often wins an argument. (express)

2. Noise can easily _____ people from their studies. Music is a _____ for others. (distract)

3. Most high schools allows students to _____ certain courses. An _____ course usually supplements the required program. (elect)

4. An _____ action by one country often provokes _____ by others. (aggress)

5. Some people _____ severely to bee stings. One common allergic _____ is severe difficulty in breathing. Such _____ effects are usually noted in a person's medical history. (react)

PATTERN 7: *-ion, -ive*

The verbs in Pattern 7 undergo almost the same kinds of changes as those in Pattern 6. In this pattern, however, there is an additional spelling change when the derivational suffixes are added.

Verb	Noun	Adjective
adhere	adhesion	adhesive
compel	compulsion	compulsive
comprehend	comprehension	comprehensive
conclude	conclusion	conclusive
deceive	deception	deceptive
evade	evasion	evasive
explode	explosion	explosive
extend	extension	extensive
permit	permission	permissive
persuade	persuasion	persuasive
receive	reception	receptive
repel	repulsion	repulsive

EXERCISE 23. Substitute the word in parentheses or one of its derived forms for each blank. (The derived forms will end in *-ion* or *-ive*.)

EXAMPLE A person who has illegally tried to _____ payment of income tax may be charged with the crime of tax _____. (evade)

ANSWER *A person who has illegally tried to* **evade** *payment of income tax may be charged with the crime of tax* **evasion***.*

1. Before an election, campaigners try to _____ the public to vote for their candidate by using friendly _____. _____ measures can include the distribution of pamphlets, buttons, and stickers. (persuade)

2. _____ evidence caused the Surgeon General to warn that cigarette smoking is hazardous to health. Because of that _____, many smokers have quit the habit. (conclude)

3. Often trucks are not allowed to carry _____ chemicals through heavily populated areas. If the chemicals were to _____, the _____ could cause heavy fatalities and extensive damage. (explode)

4. A person with perfect pitch can _____ when a musical note is even a quarter tone off. Music teachers wonder if such _____ can be trained, for a _____ ear is invaluable to a developing musician. (perceive)

5. A child with an _____ to vegetables may try to _____ parental attention by hiding the food under a napkin. (avert)

PATTERN 8: -ence, -ent

Verb	Noun	Adjective
depend	dependence	dependent
differ	difference	different
diverge	divergence	divergent
emerge	emergence	emergent
insist	insistence	insistent
recur	recurrence	recurrent
reside	residence	resident
revere	reverence	reverent

EXERCISE 24. Substitute the word in parentheses or one of its derived forms for each blank. (The derived forms will end in -ence or -ent.)

EXAMPLE _____ is often an admirable quality. Sometimes, however, a _____ person is merely being obstinate. (persist)

ANSWER ***Persistence*** *is often an admirable quality. Sometimes, however, a **persistent** person is merely being obstinate.*

1. Many people have _____ dreams. Psychoanalysts try to discover what subconscious feelings cause the _____ of images in dreams. (recur)

2. Because there are tax advantages to _____ in certain countries, a rich person may become a legal _____ of a country in which he does not actually _____ most of the time. (reside)

3. Many writers and thinkers whom later generations _____ were not treated with _____ or even respect in their own lifetimes. (revere)

4. Insects _____ in such huge numbers and great diversity that the _____ of new species is constantly being discovered. (exist)

5. Although the United States is _____, in part, on foreign oil for fuel, many other countries _____ on American grain for food. This mutual economic _____ is characteristic of the modern world. (depend)

The adjectives and nouns in Pattern 9 can be transformed into other adjectives and nouns.

PATTERN 9: *-ist, -ism, -istic*

Adjective or noun	Noun	Adjective
fatal	fatalist, fatalism	fatalistic
legal	legalist, legalism	legalistic
material	materialist, materialism	materialistic
moral	moralist, moralism	moralistic
national	nationalist, nationalism	nationalistic
plural	pluralist, pluralism	pluralistic
rational	rationalist, rationalism	rationalistic
real	realist, realism	realistic
ritual	ritualist, ritualism	ritualistic

EXERCISE 25. Substitute the word in parentheses or one of its derived forms for each blank. (The derived forms will end in *-ist, -ism,* or *-istic*.)

EXAMPLE   In newspapers characterized by _____, a _____ headline does not guarantee that the news in the story is really _____. (sensational)

ANSWER   *In newspapers characterized by **sensationalism**, a **sensationalistic** headline does not guarantee that the news in the story is really **sensational**.*

1. Each of us is a kind of ____ in the morning. Our ____ tendencies are expressed in the ____ of washing, dressing, and eating. (ritual)
2. Aesop was a ____ who explicitly expressed his ____ at the end of his fables. (moral)
3. The French philosopher Descartes was a ____. His influence made ____, the belief in the power of human reason, a hallmark of French philosophy and thought. (rational)
4. The ____ is often quite different from what is predicted in ____ drawings and writings. (future)
5. ____ is the architectural principle of making a building ____, or designing its structure on the basis of its function. Frank Lloyd Wright was a pioneering ____. (functional)

WORD LIST FOR WRITERS

The words in the following list will be useful to you in your writing. They are words that have been used by good writers in highly respected magazine articles and television news broadcasts. Thus, these words have already proved their usefulness to professional writers.

Most of the words on the list are given in several different related forms so that you can explore all of the possible meanings and uses of one basic word.

Keep the following points in mind as you study the list:

1. As many as six forms of a single word can be found on the list: verb, noun, adjective, present participle used as adjective, past participle used as adjective, and adverb of manner. Only those forms that are commonly used in writing are listed, although other forms may exist. Sometimes, if more than one noun or adjective exists for a word, both are given.
2. To show how participles can be used as adjectives before a noun, each participle is followed by a noun.

You should do more than merely recognize these words and know what they mean. Indeed, you should feel confident both about using them in your sentences and about spelling them correctly.

Do not try to learn this list all at one time. Try learning a few words at a time, and begin with the most familiar form of the word (the form that is defined). Write a sentence using that form of the word. Then write other sentences using other forms of the word as they appear on the list.

WRITER'S WORD LIST

VERB	NOUN	▲ ADJECTIVE ● PARTICIPLES ■ ADVERB
abide (1) *put up* *with* (2) *continue;* *stay*	————	▲ ——— ● abiding (faith) *lasting* ■ ———

Jim has an *abiding* belief in wildlife conservation.

VERB	NOUN	
abstain *do without*	abstention abstinence	▲ abstinent ● abstaining (voters) ■ abstinently

Patients are sometimes required to *abstain* from eating before an operation.

VERB	NOUN	
abstract *summarize*	abstraction (1) *a general idea* (2) *absent-* *mindedness;* *preoccupation*	▲ abstract *not concrete* ● abstracted (look) *absent-minded;* *preoccupied* ■ abstractedly *absent-mindedly*

VERB	NOUN	
accede *yield*	accedence	▲ ——— ● ——— ■ ———

One debater *acceded* to the other's point of view.

VERB	NOUN	▲ ADJECTIVE ● PARTICIPLES ■ ADVERB
admonish (1) *reprimand* *mildly* (2) *warn*	admonition	▲ ——— ● admonished (son) ● admonishing (father) ■ admonishingly

"Don't count your chickens before they're hatched" is a familiar *admonition*.

afflict	affliction *suffering;* *distress*	▲ ——— ● afflicted (patient) ■ ———

afford (1) *stand the* *expense of* (2) *give;* *supply*	———	▲ affordable ● ——— ■ ———

(1) We cannot *afford* a piano.
(2) A piano would *afford* her pleasure.

———	aggregate *total*	▲ aggregate ● ——— ■ ———

The *aggregate* number attending the games increases each week.

analogize *indicate* *similarities* *between two* *things*	analogy *explanation of one* *thing by* *comparison with* *another thing*	▲ analogous *similar in certain* *respects* ● ——— ■ analogously

An *analogy* between a storm and rage is often drawn.

articulate (1) *pronounce* *clearly* (2) *express* *clearly*	articulation	▲ articulate ● articulated (sounds) ● articulating (speaker) ■ articulately

The *articulate* speaker persuaded most of his audience.

assent *agree*	assent	▲ ——— ● assenting (answer) ■ ———

VERB	NOUN	▲ ADJECTIVE ● PARTICIPLES ■ ADVERB

attribute
*think of as
  belonging to*
	attribute
	*characteristic;
	  quality*
		▲ attributable
		  assignable to
		● ———
		■ ———

Jack was angry that the cruel remark had been *attributed* to him.

benefit	benefit	▲ beneficial *advantageous* ● ——— ■ beneficially
———	benignity *kindliness*	▲ benign *kindly; favorable* ● ——— ■ benignly
———	ceremonial *ritual*	▲ ceremonial ● ——— ■ ceremonially
———	clique *small, exclusive group*	▲ cliquish ● ——— ■ cliquishly

A *clique* soon formed around the new folk singer.

commit
(1) *give in
  charge*
(2) *pledge;
  bind*
	commitment
	a promise to do
		▲ ———
		● committed (follower)
		■ ———

congest *clog*	congestion	▲ ——— ● congested (streets) ● congesting (traffic) ■ ———

Cars *congested* the routes surrounding the baseball stadium.

deplore
*regard as
  unfortunate*
	———	▲ deplorable
		  wretched
		● deplored (crime)
		■ deplorably

VERB	NOUN	▲ ADJECTIVE ● PARTICIPLES ■ ADVERB
disengage *release;* *loosen;* *detach*	disengagement	▲ ——— ● disengaged (gear) ■ ———
It took some time to *disengage* the tangled typewriter keys.		
encrust *cover;* *decorate*	encrustation	▲ ——— ● encrusted (jewels) ■ ———
The rocks were *encrusted* with barnacles.		
evidence *show*	evidence *proof;* *ground for belief*	▲ evident *obvious; plain* ● ——— ■ evidently
———	exuberance *high spirits*	▲ exuberant *high-spirited* ● ——— ■ exuberantly
The *exuberant* campers began climbing the mountain.		
formulate *express sys-* *tematically*	formulation *systematic* *expression*	▲ ——— ● formulated (explanation) ■ ———
The students had to *formulate* a theory for the popularity of science fiction.		
homogenize	homogeneity	▲ homogeneous *uniform throughout* ● homogenized (milk) ■ homogeneously
The milk and eggs had been beaten to a *homogeneous* texture.		
identify *show to be a* *certain* *person or* *thing*	identification	▲ identifiable *recognizable* ● identified (person) ● identifying (card) ■ identifiably

VERB	NOUN	▲ ADJECTIVE ● PARTICIPLES ■ ADVERB
impede *obstruct*	impediment	▲ ——— ● impeded (street) ■ ———

The heavy fog *impeded* the movements of the boats.

———	indisputability	▲ indisputable *unquestionable* ● ——— ■ indisputably

Her right to the prize was *indisputable*.

invalidate *make null and void*	(1) invalidity *state of having no force* (2) invalidation *act of making null and void*	▲ invalid *having no force; null and void* ● invalidated (passport) ■ invalidly

irritate (1) *cause to be inflamed* (2) *annoy*	irritation	▲ irritant ● irritated (customer) ● irritating (noise) ■ irritatingly

loathe *hate*	loathness	▲ loath *reluctant* ▲ loathsome ● loathed (memory) ■ ———

After breaking her ankle, Janet was *loath* to skate again.

———	margin (1) *blank space around a written page* (2) *amount or degree of difference*	▲ marginal (1) *of the blank space around a written page* (2) *barely adequate or desirable* ● ——— ■ ———

(2) The reading ability of many Americans is still *marginal*.

VERB	NOUN	▲ ADJECTIVE ● PARTICIPLES ■ ADVERB
orchestrate *combine har- moniously*	orchestration	▲ ——— ● orchestrated (song) ■ ———

The director had *orchestrated* the actors into a smooth ensemble.

parallel	parallel	▲ parallel *beside and equidistant from one another* ● ——— ■ parallel

You will find Howard in the aisle *parallel* to this one.

pertain	pertinence	▲ pertinent *relevant* ● ——— ■ pertinently

A good reporter seeks all information *pertinent* to a story.

portend *be a warning, sign, or indication of*	portent *omen*	▲ portentous *ominous; threatening* ● ——— ■ portentously

The dry, cold air was a *portent* of snow.

———	remnant *remainder*	▲ remnant ● ——— ■ ———

———	routine *regular, habitual procedure*	▲ routine (life) ● ——— ■ routinely

scruple *hesitate from doubt or uneasiness*	scruple *hesitation or doubt in deciding what is right* scrupulousness *carefulness*	▲ scrupulous (1) *precise* (2) *honest* ● ——— ● ——— ■ scrupulously

(1) A photographer must have a *scrupulous* sense of lighting.

VERB	NOUN	▲ ADJECTIVE ● PARTICIPLES ■ ADVERB
signify *be a sign of*	significance *meaning*	▲ significant *meaningful* ● ——— ■ significantly
———	singularity *peculiar feature or characteristic*	▲ singular (1) *unique; individual* (2) *exceptional* ● ——— ■ singularly

(1) Greta Garbo's *singular* acting style is apparent in the movie *Camille*.

VERB	NOUN	▲ ADJECTIVE ● PARTICIPLES ■ ADVERB
strive	strife *contention*	▲ ——— ● striving (runner) ■ ———

Strife between environmentalists and land developers was frequent in the 1970s.

VERB	NOUN	▲ ADJECTIVE ● PARTICIPLES ■ ADVERB
tolerate *allow*	tolerance	▲ tolerant ● tolerated (custom) ■ tolerantly
total *add up*	totality	▲ total *entire* ● ——— ■ totally
———	traditionalist *one who adheres to custom*	▲ traditionalistic ● ——— ■ ———
understate *play down*	understatement	▲ ——— ● understated (speech) ■ ———

The police officer *understated* the victim's injuries to his family.

VERB	NOUN	▲ ADJECTIVE ● PARTICIPLES ■ ADVERB
———	uniqueness	▲ unique *one and only* ● ——— ■ uniquely

The following list of words has been divided into nouns, verbs, and adjectives. From each of these groups, select five words at a time. Then for each word write a sentence using the word. Look up words that cause you trouble, and keep a special list of them.

VERBS

allay	engulf	override
assuage	enmesh	
	enrage	reappear
compel	ensue	reconcile
couch	entail	rely
	entwine	resolve
deem	exceed	respond
delve		riddle
detect	harry	
disgruntle		salvage
distinguish	impart	savor
dote	imperil	shackle
	infest	
emerge	invoke	underscore
encase		
engross	menace	wrest
	mull	

NOUNS

adjunct	bereavement	columnist
aftermath	berth	commentary
amenities	buffer	confluence
anarchist		crucible
aplomb	chagrin	
aura	clairvoyance	devastation
avant-garde	claque	diversity

elite
entrant
entrenchment

fanfare
fervor
festoon

grandeur

impermissibility
implement
impresario

mentor
morass
myth

nomad

onset

penalty
pointedness
populace
preconception
prelude

proponent

realm
reputation

solitude
surveillance

tendency
texture
trend

watershed
weaponry

ADJECTIVES

aggressive
anonymous

bombastic

canny
causative
caustic
curative

egoistic

faceless
flexible
fruitful

gallant
grandiose

honorific

imminent
immodest
impenetrable
impromptu
indiscriminate
indistinguishable
infantile
infectious
influential
insuperable
insurmountable

merciful

orthodox
overwrought

paramount
peevish
puritan

ruinous
rustic

simplistic

tense

uncontrollable
underlying
unimpressed
uninhibited
unrelated
unreliable
unremarkable
unspeakable
unthinkable

vengeful
vested
vintage
virtual

5

SPELLING

5 Spelling

In a world of instant communication by computer, telephone, and television, why is it important to learn how to spell? While much modern communication does not involve writing, the fact is that you will be required to write—and hence to spell well—in many situations that are important to you. These situations include writing for school purposes, writing job applications, and writing reports on the job, to name only a few. Each time that you write, your reader will respond to your message partly by the way you spell or, rather, by the way you misspell. When you spell correctly, you are only doing what your reader expects of you.

Learning to improve your spelling is not difficult because there are so many avenues to success. You can use pronunciation as a guide, especially being aware of when mispronunciation can mislead you. You can learn rules that will help you to spell many hundreds of words. You can become alert to words that are commonly confused. You can study lists of frequently misspelled words. All of these methods are discussed in this section.

The general suggestions below will also help you improve your spelling.

1. Tackle one spelling weakness at a time. Concentrate on this problem until you have overcome it.
2. Make lists of your problem words, and consult them frequently. Write these words often enough so that you can spell them almost without thinking.

3. Develop the habit of forming mental pictures of problem words. Many good spellers can tell whether a word "looks right" to them.

4. Use a dictionary when you are not sure of the spelling of a word. Keep a dictionary handy whenever you have a writing task.

5. Proofread your work to catch careless errors that you may have made. This is also a good time to use your dictionary to check words about which you are unsure.

5.a PRONUNCIATION AND SPELLING

Paying attention to the relationship between the way a word is spelled and the way it is pronounced is probably the most basic spelling skill. Most words are spelled the way they sound. That is, there are regular patterns of spelling that follow regular patterns of speech. Many spelling errors, therefore, are simply the result of mispronunciation. If you can train yourself to pronounce the words carefully (*athlete*, not *athalete*, and *library*, not *libary*), the correct spelling will follow naturally.

Even more important, however, is paying attention to words that are *not* spelled the way they are pronounced and to sounds that are spelled in various ways in different words. These are the words that make English spelling such a difficult system to learn. Even these words, however, often fall into patterns that you can learn to recognize. On the following pages you will find a discussion of some of the most common patterns in pronunciation.

5.a.1 Mispronunciation and misspelling

Several kinds of mispronunciation can lead to misspellings. Study each kind and the examples on the chart on the next page. Learn to pronounce the word carefully; then be sure to spell it right.

PRONUNCIATION PITFALLS THAT CAUSE MISSPELLINGS

1. adding extra vowel sounds

correct spelling	incorrect spelling
athlete	athalete
disastrous	disasterous
laundry	laundery
partner	partener
similar	similiar
umbrella	umberella

2. dropping vowel sounds

correct spelling	incorrect spelling
accidentally	accidently
family	famly
literally	litrally
mathematics[1]	mathmatics
miniature	minature
parliament[1]	parlament

3. dropping consonant sounds

correct spelling	incorrect spelling
attempt	attemt
contract	contrac
environment	enviroment
February	Febuary
recognize	reconize
told	tole

4. confusing consonants

correct spelling	incorrect spelling
ask	aks
cattle	cadle
lives	lifes
modern	modren
petal	pedal[2]
president	presidend

EXERCISE 1. Write the following phrases and sentences, choosing the correctly spelled word in parentheses.

1. work with a (partener/partner)
2. a herd of (cadle/cattle)
3. a large load of (laundery/laundry)
4. a (minature/miniature) rose
5. the school's best (athalete/athlete)
6. Don't you (recognize/reconize) me?
7. (similar/similiar) interests
8. a signed (contrac/contract)

---

[1]Although you may sometimes pronounce these words as /math·ma·tics/ or /par·lə·ment/, in writing you must remember to include each syllable.
[2]Notice that *pedal* is the correct spelling of another word.

9. the (family/famly) tree

10. (Aks/Ask) questions if you do not understand.

EXERCISE 2. Write the following phrases and sentences, correcting any misspelled words.

1. presidend of the firm
2. a disasterous idea
3. Febuary fourteenth
4. Take an umberella.
5. a calm enviroment

6. It was a good attemt.
7. tole the truth
8. mathmatics professors
9. elected to parlament
10. A cat has nine lifes.

5.a.2 Variant spellings of some consonant sounds

Some consonant sounds in English cause spelling problems because they can be spelled in more than one way. Fortunately, the various spellings usually follow regular patterns. Studying the following patterns for the sounds /f/, /j/, and /k/ will help you avoid mistakes.

━━━━━━━━━━ **SPELLING SOUNDS** ━━━━━━━━━━

1. The /f/ sound: _f_, _ff_, _gh_, or _ph_?

In general, use _ff_ at the end of a one-syllable word or at the end of a syllable with a short vowel sound.

af·**fect**	pu**ff**
dif·**fer**	sti**ff**

Use _gh_ after _au_ or _ou_ at the end of a word or a syllable.

lau**gh**	cou**gh**
lau**gh**·ter	e·nou**gh**

Use _ph_ in a few words that have come into English from Greek.

phrase	autogra**ph**
em**ph**asize	**ph**ysician

Use _f_ in all other cases.

full	a**f**raid
free	dri**f**t

2. The /j/ sound: *j*, *g*, *ge*, or *dge*?

Initial /j/ sound
In general, use *j* at the beginning of a word or a syllable.

jab	en·**j**oy
join	un·**j**ust

Use *g* for the initial /j/ sound only before *e* or *i*.

gem	**g**inger
genial	**g**igantic

NOTE: Not every word that begins with a /j/ sound followed by *e* or *i* starts with *g*.

jest	**j**eans
jeer	**j**ilt

Final /j/ sound
Use *dge* after a short vowel sound.

bri**dge**	ba**dge**
e**dge**	lo**dge**

Use *ge* after a long vowel sound. (*College* is an exception.)

ca**ge**	obli**ge**
gau**ge**	delu**ge**

3. The /k/ sound: *c*, *k*, or *ck*?

Initial /k/ sound
Use *k* before *i* or *e*.

kick	**k**eep
kind	**k**ettle

Use *c* before *a*, *o*, or *u*.

calm	**cu**rious
cold	

Final /k/ sound
Use *ck* at the end of a one-syllable word with a short vowel sound and at the end of a stressed syllable.

lu**ck**	cra**ck**'er
pe**ck**	sti**ck**'y

Use *c* at the end of a word with an unstressed final syllable.

ep'**ic**	pic'n**ic**
top'**ic**	his·tor'**ic**

EXERCISE 3. Write each of the following words with the correct spelling of the sound shown.

1. chie/f/
2. o/f/er
3. /j/est
4. /j/erm
5. tou/f/

6. /j/eans
7. /j/enes
8. co/f/ee
9. cou/f/
10. colle/j/e

EXERCISE 4. Write each of the following words with the correct spelling of the /k/ sound.

1. topi ___
2. un ___ ind
3. plasti ___
4. ba ___ pa ___
5. clo ___ wor ___

6. ___ anoe
7. qui ___
8. dar ___ en
9. arithmeti ___
10. ___ ondu ___ t

5.a.3 Spelling words with silent consonants

Many English words are spelled with consonants that are silent: for example, the *p* in *pneumonia* and the *gh* in *daughter*. Most of these words have come into English from other languages in which the consonants were pronounced. Although the pronunciation of the words changed in English, their spelling did not.

Such words cause spelling problems because the silent consonants can easily be overlooked. One way to avoid misspelling words with silent consonants is to *visualize* the correct spelling. Then write each troublesome word several times until you can spell it automatically. You might find it helpful to sound the silent consonant to yourself as you write the word. Study the following list of words with silent consonants (dark type).

WORDS WITH SILENT CONSONANTS

SILENT b: bom**b**, com**b**, clim**b**, de**b**t, dou**b**t, dum**b**, plum**b**er, su**b**tle, succum**b**, thum**b**, tom**b**

SILENT g: forei**g**n, **g**narl, **g**nash, **g**nat, **g**naw, campai**g**n, rei**g**n, si**g**n, sovorei**g**n

SILENT gh: bou**gh**t, dau**gh**ter, ei**gh**t, fi**gh**t, hei**gh**t, li**gh**t, throu**gh**

SILENT h: **c**hristen, ex**h**aust, ex**h**ibit, **g**host, **g**hastly, **h**onest, r**h**etoric, r**h**yme, r**h**ythm, sil**h**ouette, ve**h**ement, ve**h**icle

SILENT INITIAL k: **k**nack, **k**napsack, **k**nead, **k**nee, **k**nickknack, **k**nife, **k**night, **k**nit, **k**nob, **k**nock, **k**nowledge

SILENT n: autum**n**, colum**n**, condem**n**, hym**n**, solem**n**

SILENT p: **p**neumonia, **p**salm, **p**seudonym, **p**sychology, **p**sychiatrist, ras**p**berry

SILENT t: bris**t**le, chris**t**en, Chris**t**mas, glis**t**en, has**t**en, hus**t**le, mois**t**en, of**t**en, sof**t**en, wres**t**le

SILENT w: ans**w**er, s**w**ord, t**w**o, **w**reath, **w**rench, **w**restle, **w**retch, **w**iggle, **w**rinkle, **w**rist, **w**rite, **w**rong, **w**ry

OTHER SILENT LETTERS: **sc**ene, sa**l**mon, ya**ch**t

EXERCISE 5. Write each of the following words, supplying the missing silent consonant or consonants.

1. hi ___
2. throu ___
3. ex ___ ibit
4. colum ___
5. ___ sychology
6. ___ reck
7. g ___ ost
8. de ___ t
9. ___ night (in armor)
10. ___ naw
11. plum ___ er
12. ___ salm
13. sa ___ mon
14. hym ___
15. ras ___ berry
16. su ___ tle
17. ya ___ t
18. ___ restle
19. com ___ (for the hair)
20. lis ___ en

EXERCISE 6. For each of the following phrases, write the word with silent consonants that is left uncompleted. The meaning of the word is given in parentheses.

1. a forei ___ visitor (from another country)
2. a heavy ___ apsack (bag)
3. danced to a waltz ___ ythm (beat)
4. moi ___ ened the stamp (made damp)
5. bou ___ a bunch of flowers (purchased)

6. examined by a __chologist (specialist in the science of the mind)
7. saw her o __en (frequently)
8. sprained his __ist (hand joint)
9. succu __ed to a fever (gave in)
10. jumped from a great hei __ (altitude)
11. enjoyed ra __berry sherbet (a flavor)
12. the si __ouette of the tree against the sun (outline)
13. the brilliant leaves of autu __ (a season)
14. a jerk of his thu __ (a finger)
15. ei __ couples (one more than seven)
16. wrote under a __eudonym (false name)
17. visited Grant's To __ (burial place)
18. gli __ened in the sunlight (shone)
19. a rei __ing queen (in power)
20. a front-wheel-drive ve __icle (car)

5.a.4 The schwa: spelling words in unstressed syllables

The most common vowel sound in English is the "uh" sound in syllables that are not stressed (pronounced with emphasis). This sound, called the **schwa**, is written with the symbol ə. The schwa sound occurs quite frequently because English pronunciation tends to emphasize one syllable of a word heavily and to give much less stress to the others. For example, pronounce the following words: pitch′er, sul′fur, pen′cil, a·fraid′, con·nect′. Notice that each word has two syllables, one stressed and the other unstressed. Although each of the unstressed syllables is spelled with a different vowel, each unstressed vowel is pronounced as the schwa sound.

Because the schwa sound may be spelled in so many different ways, it causes many spelling problems. There are no rules that you can apply to spell words with the schwa sound. Your best approach is to study lists, such as those following, that contain words with the sound. For particularly troublesome words, try to make up a mnemonic device, or memory aid. For example, remember that the last syllable of *calendar* starts like *days*, which are what make up a calendar.

COMMON SPELLINGS OF THE SCHWA SOUND

a: **a**fraid, alt**a**r, **a**lone, calend**a**r, cell**a**r, equ**a**l, gramm**a**r, leg**a**l, particul**a**r, par**a**llel, parti**a**l, priv**a**cy, roy**a**l, sep**a**rate, sug**a**r, vineg**a**r

e: alt**e**r, ben**e**fit, bord**e**r, el**e**gant, **e**stablish, del**e**gate, mann**e**r, rip**e**n, writ**e**r

i: defin**i**te, im**i**tate, infin**i**te, med**i**cine, or**i**gin, per**i**l

o: act**o**r, c**o**mplain, c**o**rrect, edit**o**r, govern**o**r, janit**o**r, juni**o**r, mem**o**ry, **o**ccur

u: hopef**u**l, lux**u**ry, murm**u**r, p**u**rsue, s**u**burban, sulph**u**r, vult**u**re

EXERCISE 7. Write each of the following words, filling the blank with *a, e, i, o,* or *u.*

1. rip __ n
2. c __ mplain
3. cell __ r
4. gramm __ r
5. leg __ l
6. __ stablish
7. sug __ r
8. murm __ r
9. calend __ r
10. ben __ fit
11. im __ tate
12. juni __ r
13. del __ gate
14. or __ gin
15. p __ rsue
16. def __ nite
17. __ lone
18. sep __ rate
19. priv __ cy
20. act __ r

5.b SPELLING RULES

Spelling rules are somewhat like directions that you might be given for going from your house to a friend's house in a neighboring town. Even if you found that you had to make several detours because of road construction, you would probably still find the directions helpful. There are exceptions to almost every spelling rule, but by following them you can spell correctly hundreds of common English words. Study the rules below, paying close attention to the exceptions.

5.b.1 *IE* or *EI*?

The following is a very useful rule.

Write *i* before *e*
except after *c*
or when sounded like *a*
as in *neighbor* and *weigh*.

EXAMPLES

i before *e*	except after *c*	or when sounded like *a* as in *neighbor* and *weigh*
achieve	ceiling	eight
belief	conceit	freight
field	deceive	neighbor
niece	receipt	reign
thief	receive	weigh

EXCEPTIONS

either	leisure	seize
financier	neither	weird
foreign	protein	
height	science	

EXERCISE 8. Write each of the following phrases, replacing the blank with *ie* or *ei*.

1. a sh __ld of brass
2. __ther you or I
3. at your l __sure
4. a w __rd shr __k
5. a fr __ndly gesture
6. a high y __ld of corn
7. extent of his conc __t
8. financ __rs' bel __f
9. bes __ge the p __r
10. dec __ve a th __f
11. perc __ve his dec __t
12. n __ghbor's sl __gh

13. cash __ r's rec __ pts
14. a b __ ge v __ l
15. a for __ gn br __ fcase
16. n __ ce's ach __ vements

17. a pr __ st and a rabbi
18. s __ ze the r __ ns
19. w __ gh the fr __ ght
20. an __ ght-foot c __ ling

5.b.2 -CEDE, -CEED, or -SEDE?

The rules for making a choice among these three word endings are not difficult:

> Only one word ends in *sede*: super**sede**
> Only three words end in *ceed*: ex**ceed**, pro**ceed**, suc**ceed**
> Use *cede* in all other cases: ac**cede**, **cede**, con**cede**,
> pre**cede**, se**cede**

EXERCISE 9. Write each of the following phrases, replacing the blank with *-sede*, *-ceed*, or *-cede*.

1. pro _____ with caution
2. ac _____ to the treaty
3. se _____ from the Union
4. super _____ the old law
5. suc _____ in business

6. re _____ from view
7. pre _____ the verb
8. inter _____ for her
9. ex _____ my goals
10. con _____ the election

5.b.3 Adding prefixes

The spelling of a word remains the same when a prefix is added to it.

A prefix is a group of letters that can be placed before a word to form another word with a related meaning. For example, the word *unnatural* contains the prefix *un-*, which means "not," and the word *natural. Unnatural*, therefore, means "not natural." Adding a prefix to a word does not change the spelling of the original word.

In spelling a word with a prefix, first spell the prefix, then the original word. Do not leave out any letters of the original word. Be especially careful in spelling prefixed words with double letters, one from the prefix and one from the original word. It is easy to leave out one of the *n*'s in *unnatural* or one of the *r*'s in *irregular*, for example.

EXAMPLES

in-	+	complete	=	incomplete
mis-	+	conduct	=	misconduct
re-	+	pay	=	repay
dis-	+	please	=	displease
mis-	+	spell	=	misspell

Some prefixed words, such as those with the prefix *ex-*, are spelled with a hyphen. For a more detailed discussion of prefixes, see 4.f.

EXERCISE 10. Write the following phrases, combining the prefix in parentheses with the italicized word.

1. an *exact* measure (in-)
2. *happy* travelers (un-)
3. *claim* the ring (re-)
4. *wrap* the gifts (un-)
5. *necessary* parts (un-)
6. *spell* a word (mis-)
7. *appear* suddenly (dis-)
8. *value* yourself (under-)
9. *regular* towels (ir-)
10. *legal* acts (il-)
11. *movable* objects (im-)
12. *legible* writing (il-)
13. *migrate* annually (im-)
14. *mature* child (im-)
15. *replaceable* vases (ir-)
16. *rational* means (ir-)
17. a *satisfied* look (dis-)
18. the *rated* actor (over-)
19. *elected* mayor (re-)
20. *moderate* plans (im-)

5.b.4 Adding suffixes

A suffix is a group of letters that can be added to the end of a word to form a new word with a related meaning. For example, the suffix *-or*, meaning "one who," can be added to the word *direct* to form *director*, meaning "one who directs." With some words, such as *director*, the addition of a suffix does not require a spelling change. Sometimes, however, the spelling of the original word changes when a suffix is added. The three most common spelling changes are as follows:

- changing a final *y* to *i*
- dropping a final silent *e*
- doubling a final consonant

■ Words ending in *y*

When adding a suffix to a word that ends in a consonant + *y*, change the *y* to *i*.

EXAMPLES

BEAUTY: beautiful
DUTY: dutiful
LAZY: lazily, laziness
HAPPY: happier, happiest, happiness
GLORY: glorious

EXCEPTIONS

With suffixes beginning with *i*: crying, worrying, babyish
With words formed from certain one-syllable words: dryly, dryness, shyly, shyness, spryly, spryness

When adding a suffix to a word that ends in a vowel + *y*, generally keep the *y*.

EXAMPLES

betray + -al = betrayal
employ + -er = employer
destroy + -ing = destroying

EXCEPTIONS

day + -ly = daily
gay + -ly = gaily
pay + -d = paid
say + -d = said

EXERCISE 11. Combine the following words and suffixes, and write the new words.

1. happy + -ness
2. employ + -er
3. lazy + -est
4. buy + -er
5. copy + -er
6. ally + -ance
7. annoy + -ance
8. angry + -ly
9. glory + -ous
10. carry + -er

11. fury + -ous
12. convey + -or
13. beauty + -ful
14. marry + -age
15. sloppy + -ness
16. cozy + -er
17. portray + -al
18. crazy + -ness
19. duty + -ful
20. clumsy + -ly

EXERCISE 12. Add the suffix *-ed* to each of the following words, and write the new words.

1. hurry
2. dignify
3. study
4. supply
5. amplify

6. betray
7. employ
8. volley
9. journey
10. annoy

11. empty
12. try
13. pity
14. destroy
15. mystify

16. simplify
17. beautify
18. signify
19. convey
20. portray

■ Words ending in silent e

When adding a suffix that begins with a consonant to a word that ends in a silent *e*, keep the *e*.

EXAMPLES

late	+ -ly	= lately
excite	+ -ment	= excitement
extreme	+ -ly	= extremely
hope	+ -less	= hopeless
hate	+ -ful	= hateful
sure	+ -ly	= surely

In words like these, the *e* is kept so that the vowel sound of the original word remains the same. In addition, the *e* sometimes helps to prevent possible confusion of the suffixed word with another word. Look at the word *surely*, for example. If the *e* of *sure* were dropped when the *-ly* was added, the new word would be *surly*, a word with a different sound and a different meaning.

EXCEPTIONS

argue + -ment = argument
judge + -ment = judgment
nine + -th = ninth
true + -ly = truly

When adding *y* or a suffix that begins with a vowel to a word that ends in a silent *e*, generally drop the *e*.

EXAMPLES

amuse + -ing = amusing   come + -ing = coming
arrive + -al = arrival   ice + -y = icy
believe + -ing = believing   move + -able = movable

EXCEPTIONS

In words ending in *ce* or *ge*, keep the *e* before a suffix beginning with *a* or *o*.

marriage + -able = marriag**e**able
courage + -ous = courag**e**ous

In one-syllable words ending in *ie*, change the *ie* to *y* when adding *-ing*.

die + -ing = d**y**ing
lie + -ing = l**y**ing
tie + -ing = t**y**ing

EXERCISE 13. Combine the following words and suffixes, and write the new words.

1. come + -ing
2. arrive + -al
3. ice + -y
4. advantage + -ous
5. move + -able
6. argue + -ment
7. hate + -ful
8. nine + -th
9. dine + -ing
10. use + -ful

11. scarce + -ity
12. pursue + -ing
13. intense + -ity
14. acknowledge + -ment
15. awe + -some
16. judge + -ment
17. state + -ment
18. manage + -able
19. use + -able
20. love + -able

EXERCISE 14. Add the suffixes indicated to the following words, and write the new words.

-less	-able	-ment	-ly
1. care	6. love	11. excite	16. sure
2. use	7. desire	12. amuse	17. bare
3. hope	8. believe	13. move	18. pure
4. taste	9. adore	14. abate	19. fine
5. shape	10. live	15. debase	20. entire

■ Doubling the final consonant

Double the final consonant before a suffix beginning with a vowel (1) if the word ends in one vowel + one consonant and (2) if the word has only one syllable or is accented on the final syllable.

Below are questions that you can ask yourself to help you decide whether or not to double a final consonant before a suffix:

- Does the word end in one vowel and one consonant?
- Is the accent on the final syllable, or does the word have only one syllable?
- Does the suffix begin with a vowel?

If the answer to all three questions is yes, you double the final consonant.

ONE-SYLLABLE WORD

$$\text{PLAN} \ + \ \text{-ER} \ = \ \text{PLANNER}$$

ends in one vowel + one consonant

suffix begins with a vowel

EXAMPLES

DROP: dropped, dropping

MAN: mannish

RUN: runner, running

STRIP: stripped, stripping

In words like these, the consonant is doubled to keep the vowel short. The word *strip*, for example, becomes *stripped* to retain the short *i* sound. If the *p* is not doubled, the word becomes *striped*, which not only has a different sound but also is a word with another meaning.

EXAMPLES

hop + -ing = ho**pp**ing BUT hope + -ing = hoping

plan + -ed = pla**nn**ed BUT plane + -ed = planed

TWO-SYLLABLE WORD

O·MIT′ + -ING = OMITTING

ends in one
vowel + one
consonant

suffix begins
with a vowel

stress on
final syllable

EXAMPLES

ad · mit′: admi**tt**ed, admi**tt**ing, admi**tt**ance

e · quip′: equi**pp**ed, equi**pp**ing

pre · fer′: prefe**rr**ed, prefe**rr**ing

Do not double the final consonant if the stress does not fall on the last syllable.

EXAMPLES

hap′ pen: happe**n**ed, happe**n**ing

ben′ e · fit: benefi**t**ed, benefi**t**ing

la′ bel: labe**l**ed, labe**l**ing

Do not double the final consonant before a suffix beginning with a consonant.

EXAMPLES

annul + -ment = annulment BUT annu**ll**ed, annu**ll**ing

equip + -ment = equipment BUT equi**pp**ed, equi**pp**ing

EXERCISE 15. Combine the following words and suffixes, and write the new words.

1. run + -ing
2. plan + -ed
3. strip + -ed
4. man + -ish
5. permit + -ed
6. label + -ed
7. equip + -ment
8. happen + -ing
9. occur + -ence
10. forget + -ful
11. benefit + -ing
12. red + -est
13. glad + -en
14. commit + -ment
15. win + -less
16. commit + -ed
17. compel + -ing
18. open + -er
19. color + -ing
20. confer + -ed

EXERCISE 16. Write each of the following sentences, choosing the correctly spelled word from the parentheses.

1. Leila's radio is old, and it has a (tiny/tinny) tone.
2. George (taped/tapped) his talk to the assembly.
3. The police (questioned/questionned) all the witnesses.
4. Sally (exhibited/exhibitted) her paintings in the school gallery.
5. The accident (occured/occurred) at a crowded intersection.
6. Raoul has been (offered/offerred) scholarships by two colleges.
7. Lynne (developed/developped) a strong tennis serve.
8. Air traffic (controlers/controllers) have a difficult job.
9. The sign on the office door said "No (Admitance/ Admittance)."
10. Julio (exceled/excelled) in chemistry.

5.b.5 Spelling noun plurals

As you know, the basic way to form plurals in English is to add an *s* or *es* to the singular form. For some nouns, however, it is necessary to make an additional spelling change. The chart on the following page summarizes the rules for spelling noun plurals.

SPELLING NOUN PLURALS

1. To form the plural of most common nouns and proper nouns, add *s*.

    bat, bat**s**   Shaw, Shaw**s**

---

2. To form the plural of nouns ending in *s*, *sh*, *ch*, *x*, and *z*, add *es*.

    boss, boss**es**   inch, inch**es**
    dash, dash**es**   box, box**es**

---

3. To form the plural of nouns ending in a consonant + *y*, change the *y* to *i* and add *es*.

    factory, factor**ies**   bully, bull**ies**

One exception is proper names:

    Blatty, Blatty**s**   Mary, Mary**s**

To form the plural of nouns ending in a vowel + *y*, add *s*.

    play, play**s**   valley, valley**s**

---

4. To form the plural of nouns ending in a vowel + *o*, add *s*.

    cameo, cameo**s**   studio, studio**s**

To form the plural of nouns ending in a consonant + *o*, generally add *es* but sometimes add *s*.

    echo, echo**es**   banjo, banjo**s**
    hero, hero**es**   dynamo, dynamo**s**
    potato, potato**es**   solo, solo**s**

---

5. To form the plural of most nouns ending in *f* and all nouns ending in *ff*, add *s*.

    chief, chief**s**   tariff, tariff**s**
    roof, roof**s**   whiff, whiff**s**

To form the plural of some nouns ending in *f* or *fe* and many nouns ending in *lf*, change the *f* to *v* and add *es*.

    leaf, lea**ves**   half, hal**ves**
    life, li**ves**   self, sel**ves**

---

6. Some nouns have irregular plural forms; that is, they do not follow any spelling rule. Learn the most common irregular plurals.

    crisis, cris**es**   foot, f**eet**
    oasis, oas**es**   tooth, t**eeth**
    parenthesis, parenthes**es**   goose, g**eese**
    child, child**ren**   man, m**en**
    mouse, m**ice**   woman, wom**en**

---

7. Some nouns have the same form in both the singular and plural.

deer	series
sheep	species

8. To form the plural of compound nouns written as one word, follow the preceding rules.

handkerchief**s**	housedress**es**
cupful**s**	grandchild**ren**

To form the plural of compound nouns that are hyphenated or written as more than one word, make the most important part of the noun plural.

brother**s**-in-law	m**e**n-of-war
attorney**s** general	high school**s**

9. To form the plural of numerals, words, signs, and letters treated as words, add **'s**.

10**'s**   two j**'s**   ?**'s**
confused her *there***'s** and *their***'s**

EXERCISE 17. Write the plural form of the following.

1. man	6. child	11. cupful	16. radio
2. sheep	7. bush	12. watch	17. monkey
3. promise	8. studio	13. desk	18. echo
4. half	9. Smith	14. library	19. woman
5. series	10. kiss	15. bully	20. leaf

EXERCISE 18. Write each of the following phrases, choosing the correct plural form from the parentheses.

1. saw two (deer/deers)
2. sang three (solos/soloes)
3. a gaggle of (gooses/geese)
4. the howling (wolfs/wolves)
5. cleaned out the (chimnies/chimneys)
6. the two (crises/crisises) in his life
7. a field of (potatos/potatoes)
8. his helpful (brother-in-laws/brothers-in-law)
9. the two widely separated (oases/oasises)
10. flags of many (countrys/countries)

EXERCISE 19. Write the following phrases, correcting any incorrectly formed plurals.

1. built new bookshelves
2. carts with donkies
3. the two *m*s in *commit*
4. species of insects
5. loud stereos
6. wifes of the astronauts
7. dank factorys
8. echoes from the past
9. climbed the rooves
10. visited the Dalys
11. the nine lives of a cat
12. Use parenthesises.
13. all by ourselfs
14. two cupsful of sugar
15. a history of tariffs
16. spotted a herd of deers
17. defeated their enemies
18. the giraffes in the zoo
19. cut apples into halfs
20. cities in the valleys

5.b.6 Spelling possessives

The possessive form of nouns and some pronouns, the form that shows ownership or possession, is formed by adding an apostrophe and, often, an s to the end of the word. There are several variations in the use of the apostrophe and s, depending on whether the noun is singular or plural and on the letter with which the noun ends. The following rules summarize the spelling of possessive forms:

Add **'s** to form the possessive of singular and plural nouns that do not end in *s*.

EXAMPLES
a student**'s** desk
Owen**'s** tickets
the children**'s** toys
women**'s** rights

Add an apostrophe alone, without *s*, to form the possessive of singular nouns of more than one syllable that end in *s* and of all plural nouns that end in *s*.

EXAMPLES
Doris' job
the actress' wig
the players' uniforms

NOTE: You may also use 's to form the possessive of singular nouns of more than one syllable that end in *s*: *Doris's job*, *the actress's wig*.

Add 's to form the possessive of singular nouns of one syllable ending in *s*.

EXAMPLES
Gus's friend
the boss's lunch

Add 's to form the possessive of indefinite pronouns such as *anyone* and *everyone*.

EXAMPLES
anyone's coat
everyone's favorite
someone's yogurt

Write personal pronouns without any apostrophes.

EXAMPLES
I met his uncle.
The paintings are hers.
Is this ours or theirs?
These tickets are yours.

EXERCISE 20. Write the following phrases, making each italicized word possessive.

1. the *country* future
2. the *countries* alliance
3. *Paris* boulevards
4. the *iris* lovely colors
5. the *irises* lovely colors
6. *Carlos* tennis racket
7. the *dentist* office
8. the *dentists* offices
9. Robert *Burns* poems
10. *someone* lost book

11. their *children* school
12. *Chris* nephew
13. the *Davises* new house
14. the *woman* neighbor
15. the *women* neighbors

16. the *Jets* next game
17. the *sun* brilliance
18. *nobody* responsibility
19. an *artist* style
20. my *brother-in-law* leg

EXERCISE 21. Write the following phrases, changing each group of italicized words into a possessive noun.

1. the wishes *of the boy*
2. the wishes *of the boys*
3. the novels *of Charles Dickens*
4. the appearance *of this actress*
5. the roles *of these actresses*
6. a visit *from my Aunt Agnes*
7. the broadcast *by my favorite orchestra*
8. performances *by American orchestras*
9. the city-states *of ancient Greece*
10. the last time at bat *of the Orioles*

5.c SPELLING HOMOPHONES

Homophones are words that sound alike and may cause spelling problems.

English has dozens of groups of words that are pronounced the same or almost the same way but are spelled differently and have different meanings. Such words are called homophones. Examples are *aisle* and *isle*, *morning* and *mourning*, and *their* and *there*. Homophones are often a source of spelling difficulty. The problem is usually not so much spelling itself as remembering which spelling goes with your intended meaning. Clearly, the solution is to learn the meaning of each word that has a sound-alike companion and to use it in the right place. In addition, it is sometimes helpful to exaggerate or make up differences in pronunciation between the words of a group, such as **add**ition and **ed**ition.

Here is a list of some commonly confused words. Study the definitions in each group carefully, and then choose the correct word in parentheses in each sentence.

addition a joining of numbers; something added; an increase

edition form in which something is published; number of copies of a work printed

This book is now in its fifth (addition/edition).

In (addition/edition) to *The Crucible* we read *The Zoo Story*.

aisle a narrow passageway

isle a body of land surrounded by water [Notice the similarity to *island*.]

The ship landed on the beautiful (aisle/isle) of Capri.

The flight attendant walked down the (aisle/isle) to my seat.

all together all in one place; all persons in a group

altogether completely, entirely

This answer is (all together/altogether) wrong.

The family is planning to be (all together/altogether) again for the holidays.

brake a device for stopping

break to smash or crack; to destroy; an interval

We took a ten-minute coffee (brake/break).

Tanya applied the (brake/break) just in time.

capital a city that is the seat of government; wealth

capitol building in which a legislature meets

The dome of the (capital/capitol) is covered with gold leaf.

A state's (capital/capitol) is usually not its largest city.

All his (capital/capitol) is invested in real estate.

choral pertaining to a chorus

coral a substance made up of the skeletons of marine animals

Frieda sings alto in the (choral/coral) society.

Her necklace is made of (choral/coral).

chord a combination of musical tones; a feeling or emotion

cord rope, string; a measure of wood

cored past tense and past participle of the verb *core*, meaning "to remove the central part"

The box was tied with strong (chord/cord/cored).

Paul (chord/cord/cored) the apple with his pocketknife.

The overture opened with a loud (chord/cord/cored).

coarse rough; vulgar

course way of action, movement, or development; subject of study

The sand on the beach was surprisingly (coarse/course).

Under the circumstances, moving is our only (coarse/course) of action.

complement to complete or balance; something that completes [hence the *e* before *-ment*]

compliment to praise; an expression of praise

The director paid the cast a (complement/compliment) on its performance.

The crew was two short of its full (complement/compliment) of sailors.

council an assembly or group of advisers

counsel advice; to give advice

I belong to the neighborhood tenants' (council/counsel).

King Arthur followed the wise (council/counsel) of the magician Merlin.

dew light moisture in small drops

do to act or perform

due payable; owed; expected to arrive

He did not want to (dew/do/due) what his parents suggested.

The first payment is (dew/do/due) next Wednesday.

The (dew/do/due) glistened in the morning sun.

do (dō) the first tone of a musical scale

doe a female deer

dough material from which bread or pastry is baked

Our headlights spotted a young (do/doe/dough) nibbling on the grass.

Machines now knead the (do/doe/dough) for bread.

The conductor asked all the sopranos to sing "(do/doe/dough)."

for preposition with many meanings, including "in place of," "in favor of," "with the purpose of"

fore in front; in a prominent position; in golf, a warning shout

four the whole number between three and five

Watch out (for/fore/four) the traffic.

I ducked when I heard her yell "(For/Fore/Four)!"

Franklin D. Roosevelt was the only President elected to (for/fore/four) terms.

hear to be aware of sounds; to listen [Notice the *ear* in *hear*]

here in this place

It was (hear/here) that Lincoln delivered the Gettysburg Address.

Not everyone in the audience could (hear/here) him.

hole a hollow place in something solid; an opening

whole complete, entire

We enjoyed the (hole/whole) game, especially the last quarter.

One player ripped a (hole/whole) in his uniform.

holy sacred

wholly completely

To Muslims, Mecca is a (holy/wholly) city.

I was not (holy/wholly) convinced by his argument.

its belonging to *it* (possessive form of the pronoun *it*)

it's contraction of *it is* or *it has*

The cat was licking (its/it's) paws.

(Its/It's) a Siamese cat.

meat the flesh of animals used as food

meet to come into contact with; to assemble

Prices for (meat/meet) have risen sharply this year.
The governors of all the states (meat/meet) each year.

morning   the early part of the day
mourning   expressing grief; the expression of grief
   The telephone has been ringing all (morning/mourning).
   Not all peoples regard black as a color of
      (mourning/morning).

pain   suffering, discomfort
pane   a flat piece, especially of glass
   Every (pain/pane) in the window was shattered.
   Under the anesthetic Joanna felt no (pain/pane).

peace   the absence of conflict or war
piece   a part or section of a whole
   Paris was the site of the (peace/piece) conference after
      World War I.
   A (peace/piece) of Germany was given to Poland.

plain   simple; a level expanse of land
plane   a flat surface; an airplane; a carpenter's tool
   Irish food is (plain/plane) and hearty.
   Our (plain/plane) circled over the city.

plum   a fruit; a prize
plumb   perfectly vertical; to make vertical; to discover
      the contents of
   The job of supervisor is regarded as quite a (plum/plumb).
   Scientists now regularly (plum/plumb) the ocean depths
      with electronic instruments.

principal   the head of a school; the greatest or most
      important
principle   basic truth; a rule of conduct; integrity
   The (principal/principle) dancer was enthusiastically
      applauded.
   Archimedes discovered an important (principal/principle)
      of physics.

profit   financial gain; to benefit
prophet   a religious leader; one who predicts

A large part of the company's (profit/prophet) is spent on research.

Cassandra was a Trojan (profit/prophet) of doom.

rain water falling to earth from the sky
reign to rule as a monarch; to prevail; a period of rule
rein part of a horse's harness; a means of guiding or restraining

The forecast is for more (rain/reign/rein) tomorrow.

Queen Victoria's long (rain/reign/rein) ended in 1901.

The budget director holds a tight (rain/reign/rein) on all expenditures.

right correct; suitable or proper; opposite of left; what a person has a just claim to
rite ceremony, procedure
write to form letters, words, or symbols on a surface; to produce a literary composition

Please (right/rite/write) more legibly.

Do you have the (right/rite/write) time?

The (right/rite/write) of ordination was performed by the bishop.

role a part performed by an actor; a function
roll to move by turning over and over; paper in the form of a scroll; a small form of bread

President Theodore Roosevelt played an important (role/roll) in ending the Russo-Japanese War.

One (role/roll) of wallpaper is all we need.

rout a disorderly retreat; an overwhelming defeat
route a road; a regular course of travel

The turnpike is the shortest (rout/route) from here to Philadelphia.

Scoring five runs in the eighth inning, the Dodgers turned the game into a (rout/route).

seam place where two pieces of material join
seem to appear

All trains (seem/seam) to be on time today.

The quilt had a (seam/seem) in the middle.

serf   a person bound to a master's land; a kind of slave
surf   the waves of the sea breaking on the shore

> The lifeguards launched their boat into the heavy (serf/surf).
>
> The (serf/surf) was the backbone of agriculture in the Middle Ages.

stationary   not moving; unchanging
stationery   paper for writing

> The startled deer stood (stationary/stationery) in the glare.
>
> I need more (stationary/stationery) for my correspondence.

steal   to take without permission
steel   a metal; great strength or hardness

> Randolph was thrown out trying to (steal/steel) second base.
>
> With bases loaded and the score tied, a pitcher has to have nerves of (steal/steel).

their   belonging to them [Notice the word *heir*, pertaining to possession, in *their*.]
there   in that place [Notice the word *here*, pertaining to location, in *there*.]
they're   contraction of *they are*

> The movie crew set up (their/there/they're) lights.
>
> The director stood (their/there/they're), next to the camera.
>
> (Their/There/They're) now ready to shoot.

threw   past tense of *throw*
through   in one side and out the other; from beginning to end; finished

> Hunter (threw/through) the next ball wide of the plate.
>
> The pitch was hit (threw/through) the infield.

to   in the direction of; as far as
too   also; excessively
two   the whole number between one and three

> It's (to/too/two) early for lunch.
>
> Let's go (to/too/two) the play.
>
> I have (to/too/two) tickets for tonight's performance.

wares goods for sale
wears has on the body as clothing
    Ron usually (wares/wears) jeans to school.
    The craftsman sold his (wares/wears) at the bazaar.

weather atmospheric conditions
whether if
    Channel 9 has a (weather/whether) forecast every hour.
    I do not know (weather/whether) the forecast is accurate.

who's contraction of *who is* or *who has*
whose possessive form of *who*
    (Who's/Whose) the new quarterback?
    (Who's/Whose) cassette player did you use?

your belonging to you
you're contraction of *you are*
    Is this (your/you're) glove?
    (Your/You're) just in time.

EXERCISE 22. Write the following sentences, correcting any misspelled words. Some of the sentences are correct as written.

1. Dogs can here very high-pitched sounds that humans cannot.
2. Woody Allen usually plays the lead roll in his films.
3. Queen Elizabeth wares a crown only on state occasions.
4. Be sure to use suitable stationery for business letters.
5. In most European trains the isle runs along one side of the cars.
6. Each state elects too United States senators.
7. The Oregon Trail was the route followed by many settlers of the West.
8. "Whose Afraid of the Big Bad Wolf?" was a popular song during the Depression of the 1930s.
9. The French visitor Alexis de Tocqueville was an accurate profit of many developments in American society.
10. Many Pacific islands are surrounded by choral reefs.

11. Famous people today often rite their memoirs when they are still young.

12. Thomas Jefferson designed the Virginia capital on the model of a Roman temple.

13. Vice Presidential candidates are often chosen on the principal of "balancing the ticket."

14. A first addition of a Jane Austen novel is very valuable.

15. The woman's suffrage movement had to brake down strong male resistance.

16. Katharine Hepburn has played many kinds of parts in the course of her career.

17. A cat cleans itself by licking it's fur.

18. Queen Victoria was in mourning for her husband, Prince Albert, during much of her rein.

19. Gray and pink are colors that compliment each other well.

20. Dietary experts say that most Americans eat more meet than they need.

21. Since World War II steel and glass have been used in the construction of most office buildings.

22. Scientists are still unable to change the whether significantly.

23. Under the Constitution your entitled to freedom of speech.

24. Emily Dickinson spent almost her hole life in the same house in Amherst, Massachusetts.

25. The footnotes in a research paper can be placed at the bottom of each page or altogether at the end of the paper.

5.d FREQUENTLY MISSPELLED WORDS

There are many English words that cause spelling problems even for those people who consider themselves good spellers. The list that follows contains four hundred of these so-called *spelling demons*. Many fall into the categories of words that have been treated earlier in this section. Some, however, do not follow any particular rule or logic. These words must simply be memorized.

In dealing with this list of words, the first thing to do is to look at them in groups of ten or twenty to see which ones give you trouble. Then concentrate on these problem words. You will need to find a way of fixing them in your mind. Have someone dictate these words to you. Say each word syllable by syllable as you write it, and identify the trouble spot in the word. Try to invent a memory device for particularly troublesome words. For example, if you regularly misspell *separate* as *seperate*, it may help you to remember that the word has "a rat" in it.

If you take on these and other spelling demons as a challenge, you can improve your spelling tremendously. Never hesitate, however, to consult a dictionary when in doubt about a correct spelling.

FOUR HUNDRED SPELLING WORDS

abdomen	almost	athletics
abhor	alphabet	attendance
absence	already	attitude
accessible	although	audience
accommodate	aluminum	autumn
accumulate	always	auxiliary
accuracy	analysis	awful
accustomed	analyzed	
ached	answered	bachelor
acquire	antiseptic	baggage
acquit	anxiety	balloon
across	apology	banana
address	apparatus	banquet
advantageous	apparently	basis
advertisement	appearance	battalion
aerial	approval	beautiful
agency	arctic	beggar
aggravate	argue	beginning
aggressive	argument	behavior
allot	ascend	believe
all right	assassinate	beneficial

benefited
bicycle
biscuit
bookkeeper
bruise
budget
bureau
business
butcher
buttress

cactus
cafeteria
caffeine
calculator
calendar ·
calorie
camera
camouflage
campaign
canceled
cannibal
cannon (gun)
canoe
cantaloupe
capable
career
careless
carnival
cashier
cassette
casual
catastrophe
cemetery
centennial
certificate
chandelier
changeable
channel
chief

chocolate
choir
college
colonel
colossal
column
commercial
committee
commune
compass
compatible
competent
complexion
concede
condemn
conscience
conscientious
consensus
consistent
contemptible
controlled
convalescent
convenient
counterfeit
criticize
crochet
cylinder
cynical

dazzle
dealt
debris
debtor
deceive
decision
defendant
deficient
deficit
definite
dependent

descendant
descent
detour
develop
dictionary
different
dilemma
disappoint
disastrous
discern
discipline
disease
dissatisfied
dissident
dynasty

eccentric
ecology
efficient
eighth
elegant
elementary
eligible
eliminate
eloquent
embarrass
emphasize
endeavor
environmental
equipped
essential
etiquette
exaggerate
exasperate
exceed
excellent
exhaust
exhilarated
existence
expel

experience
extraordinary
extravagant

facial
facility
familiar
fantasy
fascinate
fatigued
feasible
February
fiend
fierce
fiery
fluorescent
foreign
forty
fourteen
fulfill
furlough

gadget
gaiety
gauge
ghetto
government
grammar
guarantee
gymnasium

handicapped
handkerchief
harangue
harass
hatchet
height
heroes
hoarse
hostile

hygiene
hypocrisy
hysteria

idol
immature
immediate
inconvenient
incredible
ingenious
inhabitant
insistent
intelligible
interference
interruption
irrelevant
irresistible
itinerary

jealous
jeopardize
juvenile

label
laboratories
laborious
legitimate
leisure
library
license
lightning
likelihood
livelihood
luxury

maintenance
mammal
maneuver
martyr
mathematics

medicine
medieval
miniature
miscellaneous
mischievous
misspell
moccasin
murmur
myth

naive
necessary
neighbor
neither
neurotic
nuclear
nuisance

occasion
occupant
occurrence
opponent

pagan
pageant
pamphlet
pantomime
parallel
paralysis
parentheses
    (plural)
parliament
pedestrian
permissible
perseverance
petroleum
physician
physique
picnicked
picturesque

plaintiff
pneumonia
pollution
possession
possible
practice
precede
preference
prevalent
privilege
probable
procedure
proceed
pronunciation
psychology
pursue

questionnaire
quizzed

radar
rarity
raspberry
receipt
receive
recognize
recommend
reference
reign
relevant
remembrance
reminisce
renown
repetition
restaurant
rhyme
rhythm
righteous
route
rustle

sacrifice
sacrilege
salmon
salve
scenario
scenic
schedule
scissors
seize
separate
shepherd
sheriff
shoulder
significant
similar
sincerely
skeptical
skiing
smoggy
solar
solemn
spaghetti
specimen
succeed
succumb
sufficient
sugar
supersede
syllable
synthetic

tactics
tangible
tariff
technique
teammate
temperament
temperature
tenant
thorough

though
tomatoes
traffic
trivial
truly
twelfth

umbrella
unanimous
unnatural
unnecessary
usual
utensil
utilize

vaccine
vacuum
vague
variety
vehicle
vessel
veteran
villain
vinegar
vulgar

warrant
Wednesday
wizard
women
wrestle
wretch
writhe

yacht
yield

zigzagged
zinc
zoology

THE DICTIONARY

The Dictionary

The dictionary is an important source that will help you in your reading, speaking, research, and writing. It is organized to answer many questions you might have about individual words. The dictionary also contains certain basic facts, such as data on people and places.

You can use three main kinds of dictionaries: unabridged dictionaries, college dictionaries, and high school dictionaries. These three kinds do not differ much in their arrangement of information about individual words. They do differ, however, in the number of entry words and in the amount of detail given to each.

An unabridged dictionary contains a greater number of entry words and more detailed definitions than you will find in college and high school dictionaries. (The word *unabridged* means "complete, not shortened.") *Webster's Third New International Dictionary of the English Language, Unabridged* has more than 450,000 words. In contrast, a typical college dictionary contains about 150,000 words. A high school dictionary, such as the *Macmillan Dictionary,* has approximately 90,000 entries. The following examples show the same word as it is treated in each kind of dictionary.

unabridged
dictionary

> **mem·brane** \'mem,brān *sometimes* -ˌbrən\ *n* -s [L *membrana* skin, membrane, parchment, fr. *membrum* member — more at MEMBER] **1 :** a thin soft pliable sheet or layer esp. of animal or vegetable origin   **2 :** a limiting protoplasmic surface or interface — see CELL 5   **3 :** a piece of parchment forming part of a roll ⟨the pages in the . . . ∼ usually were square and had two to four columns to the page —A.T.Robertson⟩

Webster's Third New International Dictionary of the English Language, Unabridged

college dictionary

mem·brane \'mem-ˌbran\ *n* [L *membrana* skin, parchment, fr. *membrum*] **1** : a thin soft pliable sheet or layer esp. of animal or plant origin **2** : a piece of parchment forming part of a roll — **mem·bran·al** \mem-'brān-ᵊl\ *adj* — **mem·braned** \'mem-ˌbrand\ *adj*

Webster's New Collegiate Dictionary

high school dictionary

mem·brane (mem′brān) *n.* thin layer of tissue that lines a cavity or passage in the body or covers a body surface. [Latin *membrāna*.]

Macmillan Dictionary

6.a INFORMATION FOR READERS: DEFINITIONS

When you are puzzled by the meaning of a word you have read, turn to the dictionary. You will find the word listed alphabetically. If the word has more than one meaning, read through all of the definitions to determine which meaning fits the use in your reading.

■ Definitions organized by part of speech

The definitions of a word are organized by part of speech. You will find, for example, all of the meanings of the word as a noun listed together. Then you will find listed together meanings of the word as an adjective, adverb, verb, and so on. Within the definitions for each part of speech, specific definitions are listed in order from older to newer meanings or from more common to less common meanings.

The following list shows the abbreviations for the parts of speech that are used by most dictionaries.

noun	n.
transitive verb	v.t. *or* vt.
intransitive verb	v.i. *or* vi.
adjective	adj.
adverb	adv.
pronoun	pron.
preposition	prep.
conjunction	conj.
interjection	interj.

Homographs

Homographs are words that have the same spelling but different meanings and origins. Dictionaries generally list homographs as separate entries with superscripts.

Idioms

An **idiom** is an expression the meaning of which cannot be determined from the words composing it. For example, *let the cat out of the bag* is an idiom that means "reveal a secret." Idioms are listed in a dictionary under their key words, such as *cat* or *bag*.

Multi-word verbs

A **multi-word verb** is a verb made up of more than one word. *Put away* and *put up with* are multi-word verbs. Dictionaries may list multi-word verbs after the main verb entry (such as *put*) or as separate entries.

The following entries illustrate definitions organized by part of speech, homographs, and the listing of idioms and multi-word verbs within entries.

Rack¹ *(def. 5)*

homographs part of speech

rack¹ (rak) *n.* **1.** framework or stand for hanging, displaying, or storing things. **2.** hayrack. **3.** former instrument of torture used to stretch or pull a victim's body in different directions. **4.** *Pool.* triangular frame in which the balls are set before the opening shot. **5.** bar with teeth on one surface that meshes with a toothed gear or wheel. **6.** state or cause of acute mental or physical suffering. **7.** strain: *a tree bent by the rack of storms.* **8. on the rack.** suffering acute pain, tension, or anxiety. —*v.t.* **1.** to cause to suffer mentally or physically; torment: *a body racked with pain.* **2.** to put pressure on; strain: *to rack one's brains.* **3.** to torture on a rack. **4.** *Pool.* to arrange (the balls) in the rack. **5. to rack up.** *Informal.* to score or achieve, esp. impressively: *to rack up points.* [Possibly from Middle Dutch *rec* framework.]

rack² (rak) *n.* **1.** destruction. **2. to go to rack and ruin.** to deteriorate; fall apart. [Form of WRACK.]

— idiom
— part of speech
— multi-word verb
— idiom

EXERCISE 1. Use your dictionary to find the meaning of the italicized word in each of the following sentences. Indicate whether the word is a homograph or a single entry word with several meanings.

1. In the snow the *husky* frolicked with the leader of the sled team.
2. The hotel guest asked politely, "Please *page* me in the dining room at 6:30."
3. Janet found the first four *measures* of the song difficult to sing.
4. When Ned visited England, he attended a *tattoo*.
5. The *dimples* on the lake were more noticeable in the afternoon.

EXERCISE 2. Look up each of the following idioms and multi-word verbs. Explain the meaning of each idiom. Use each multi-word verb in a sentence.

1. keep to oneself
2. lose out on
3. in the least
4. pass off
5. start off on the right foot
6. give up
7. put aside
8. down on one's luck
9. keep up with
10. puzzle over

6.b INFORMATION FOR SPEAKERS: PRONUNCIATION

Most likely when you look up the meaning of a word, you will also want to learn its pronunciation. The pronunciation directly follows the entry word and appears between parentheses or slanted lines. It is indicated by symbols called phonetic symbols and by stress marks.

■ Phonetic symbols

Although English has only twenty-six letters in its alphabet, there are approximately forty-five sounds in spoken English. Clearly, there are more sounds than letters to represent them. In order to show all the sounds of English, there are special symbols called **phonetic symbols**. These consist of letters of the alphabet, diacritical marks (usually placed above vowel sounds), and the schwa. (The schwa, represented by the symbol ə, is an unaccented vowel sound that is frequently used in English.) For each of the more than forty sounds in the English language, there is a phonetic symbol.

Each dictionary, however, has its own system of phonetic symbols. You must, therefore, familiarize yourself with the system that your dictionary uses. You can usually find a complete key to your dictionary's system of phonetic symbols in the front of the dictionary. In addition, a shortened form of the key often appears at the bottom of each page spread. You need not memorize the key because you can easily refer to it. You should, however, understand the sound that each symbol represents. The following list explains some phonetic symbols that you might encounter in your dictionary.

- •• as in /kär/ for *car*
- ∧ as in /lô/ for *law*
- — as in /dāt/ for *date*
- — as in /mēt/ for *meet*
- — as in /bīt/ for *bite*
- ə as in /ə gō/ for *ago*

■ Stress

English words of more than one syllable are pronounced with greater stress or force on one of the syllables. Dictionaries indicate the degree of stress by **stress marks**. Some words require only **primary**, or **heavy**, **stress**. Other words require both primary and **secondary**, or **light**, **stress**. A heavy mark, or a mark above the line, shows primary stress. A lighter mark, or a mark below the line, shows secondary stress. Some dictionaries place the stress marks before the syllables. Others place them after the syllables.

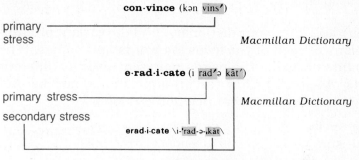

primary
stress

con·vince (kən vins′)

Macmillan Dictionary

primary stress
secondary stress

e·rad·i·cate (i rad′ə kāt′)

Macmillan Dictionary

erad·i·cate \i-'rad-ə-ˌkāt\

Webster's New Collegiate Dictionary

■ Variant pronunciations

Some words may be pronounced in more than one way. These words are said to have **variant pronunciations**. Variant pronunciations may be due to regional differences, national differences, or differences in the use of the word as more than one part of speech. The variant pronunciation follows the first pronunciation. Usually only the part of the word that differs in pronunciation is shown.

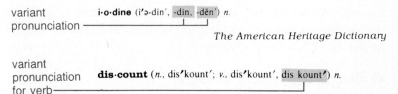

variant
pronunciation

i·o·dine (i′ə-din′, -din, -dēn′) *n.*

The American Heritage Dictionary

variant
pronunciation
for verb

dis·count (*n.,* dis′kount′; *v.,* dis′kount′, dis kount′) *n.*

Macmillan Dictionary

EXERCISE 3. Look up each of the following words in a dictionary. Give one definition of the word. Also, copy the phonetic pronunciations, and be prepared to pronounce each word.

1. matriarchy
2. xylophone
3. thyme
4. senescence

5. chagrin	8. Ariadne
6. puma	9. wanderlust
7. apothegm	10. arpeggio

EXERCISE 4. In your dictionary, find the variant pronunciations of each of the following words and names. (The variants of two of the words represent uses as different parts of speech.) Copy the pronunciations, and be prepared to give each pronunciation out loud.

1. juvenile	6. rococo
2. leisure	7. conduct
3. convert	8. wash
4. Don Quixote	9. gangrene
5. Sancho Panza	10. cerebral

6.c INFORMATION FOR RESEARCHERS

In addition to giving the meanings and pronunciations of words, dictionaries contain concise facts useful to researchers. Information on the origins of individual words is found in all dictionaries in brackets after the pronunciation or the definitions of the word. Other data, such as facts about famous people and places, may be included among the word entries or in separate sections at the back of the dictionary.

■ Word origins (etymology)

Dictionaries give the **etymology**, or history, of words to show their place in the development of English. English is a Germanic language, but it has imported and adapted many words from other languages. The etymology presents more recent non-English forms of the word first and moves back to the earliest non-English form. Meanings and explanations of the forms are given, and abbreviations (explained in the front of the dictionary)

are sometimes used. In the following example, you see that the word *etymology* is traced first to its French form, then to its Latin form, and finally to its original Greek form.

etymology ⎯
(in brackets)

et·y·mol·o·gy (et′ə mol′ə jē) *pl.,* **-gies.** *n.* **1.** history of a word, tracing it from its origin to its present form, including the changes in spelling and meaning that have taken place. **2.** study of the history of words. [French *étymologie* science of explaining the origin and derivation of words, from Latin *etymologia* analysis of the origins of words, from Greek *etymologiā,* from *etymon* true sense of a word according to its origin + *-logiā.* See -LOGY.]

Macmillan Dictionary

EXERCISE 5. Use your dictionary to trace the etymology of each of the following words. Indicate the previous form or forms each word has had in its development.

1. meander
2. pedigree
3. scent
4. Dalmatian
5. bagel
6. magnolia
7. sparse
8. candy
9. boomerang
10. progress

■ People

Dictionaries provide very basic information on men and women who have made contributions in many fields. Their names are listed either alphabetically among the word entries or in a special section at the back of the dictionary. Pronunciation of names, birth and death dates, nationalities, and fields of endeavor are given.

■ Places

Dictionaries also list the names of important places throughout the world: countries, states, cities, mountains, rivers, and so on. Their names are listed either alphabetically among the word entries or in a special section at the back of the dictionary. Information given includes pronunciation, location, and relevant statistics, such as population, height, and area.

■ Science

The scientific names of many species of plants and animals, the periodic table of chemical elements, and tables of weights and measures are included in dictionaries.

The following sequence of entries illustrates some of the information useful to a researcher in a dictionary.

data on people —————

Harte (härt), **Bret** (bret) (born *Francis Brett Hart*) 1836–1902; U.S. writer, esp. of short stories

scientific data —————

har·te·beest (här′tə bēst′, härt′bēst′) *n., pl.* **-beests′**, **-beest**′: see PLURAL, II, D, 1 [obs. Afrik. < *harte*, hart + *beest*, beast] a large, swift South African antelope (*Alcelaphus caama*), now rare, having a reddish-brown coat with a yellow patch on each haunch, and long horns curved backward at the tips

data on places —————

Hart·ford (härt′fərd) [after HERTFORD] capital of Conn., in the C part, on the Connecticut River: pop. 158,000 (met. area 664,000)

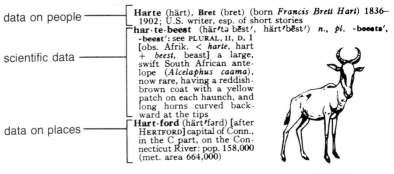

HARTEBEEST
(4–5 ft. high at shoulder)

Webster's New World Dictionary

EXERCISE 6. Use your dictionary to supply answers for the following questions.

1. What is the approximate population of Anchorage, Alaska?
2. John James Audubon was a renowned painter of North American birds. In what year was he born, and when did he die?
3. To what genus does the linden tree belong?
4. What is the scientific name of the cougar?
5. How many feet are in one fathom?
6. What is the area in square miles of the state of Mississippi?
7. Where is Mindanao?
8. Of what nationality was Mozart? What was his full name?

9. How many quarts are in one peck?
10. What is the approximate height in feet of Pikes Peak?

6.d INFORMATION FOR WRITERS

Writers constantly have questions about the spelling, syllabification, capitalization, and specialized uses of words. A dictionary gives them instant answers to questions in all these areas.

6.d.1 Spelling

Some words have more than one spelling. These variants usually follow the entry spelling. Although variant spellings are acceptable, the first spelling shown is the most common form. Writers must use one of the spellings consistently in a composition.

Dictionaries are particularly helpful in spelling the **inflected forms** of certain words. Inflected forms include the plurals of nouns, the tenses of verbs, and the degrees (comparative and superlative) of adjectives. There are rules for inflecting these parts of speech. For example, add -*s* or -*es* to form the plural of nouns, add -*d* or -*ed* to form the past tense of verbs, and add -*er* to form the comparative and -*est* to form the superlative degrees of adjectives. Dictionaries always list irregular forms. They also list the regular spellings of inflected forms about which questions might arise.

EXERCISE 7. Using your dictionary, find the variant spellings of the following words.

1. caliber
2. program
3. traveling
4. fulfill
5. theater
6. Djakarta
7. idyl
8. pretense
9. guerrilla
10. judgment

EXERCISE 8. Use a dictionary to find the correct spelling of each of the following inflected forms.

1. the plural form of the noun *alumnus*
2. the past tense of the verb *journey*
3. the past tense of the verb *shine*
4. the comparative degree of the adjective *red*
5. the superlative degree of the adjective *lonely*

6.d.2 Syllabification

In words of more than one syllable, each point of division between syllables is indicated by a centered dot. This division into syllables shows where you may hyphenate a word at the end of a line. Do not confuse the division of syllables for writing purposes with the division of pronounced syllables shown in parentheses or slashes. The two may differ.

EXERCISE 9. Use a dictionary to find all the points at which you can hyphenate each of the following words.

1. logarithm
2. saga
3. ticket
4. venerable
5. preposition
6. organism
7. rubbish
8. filling
9. dual
10. method

6.d.3 Capitalization

Dictionaries indicate which words are always capitalized. They also indicate which particular uses of a word, if any, require capital letters. Some dictionaries use the label *cap.* ("capitalized") and *not cap.* ("not capitalized"). Others actually show (sometimes partially) the capitalized or noncapitalized form.

capitalized use for ⎡ **har·le·quin** (här′lə-kwən, -kən) *n.* **1.** *Capital* **H**. A conventional
one definition │ buffoon of the commedia dell'arte, traditionally presented in a
⎣ mask and parti-colored tights. **2.** A clown; buffoon. **3.** A small
duck, *Histrionicus histrionicus*, having a short bill and distinc-
tively patterned plumage. In this sense, also called "harlequin
duck." —*adj.* **1.** Bright; parti-colored; spangled; suggesting the
dress of Harlequin. **2.** Having frames that flare in an upward
noncapitalized uses ⎯ slant, suggesting the slits of Harlequin's mask. Said of eyeglasses.   [Variant (influenced by obsolete French *harlequin*) of
earlier *Harlicken, Harlaken,* from Old French *Herlequin, Hel-*
lequin, leader of a troop of demon horsemen riding at night,
probably from Old English *Herla cyning,* King *Herla,* a mythi-
cal figure who has been identified with Woden.]

The American Heritage Dictionary

EXERCISE 10. Use your dictionary to find the definition
of each of the following capitalized words. Then find one
meaning of the noncapitalized form of each of the words,
and use it in a sentence.

1. Hydra
2. Sphinx
3. Mecca
4. Genesis
5. Renaissance

6. Colossus
7. Chimera
8. Pygmy
9. Pueblo
10. Thoroughbred

6.d.4 Special labels

Some definitions of a word apply only to certain subject areas. **Subject labels**, such as *Baseball, Biology,*
Law, or *Physics,* precede such specialized definitions.

Usage labels indicate that a word or a definition is
restricted to a specific time (*Archaic*), geographic area
(*British*), or level of language use (*Slang*). Other usage
labels include *Obsolete, Rare, Colloquial,* and *Informal.*

EXERCISE 11. Look up the following words in your dictionary. For each, find the specialized meaning indicated
by the label in parentheses.

1. occult (Astronomy)
2. cradle (Mining)

3. widow (Printing)
4. eye (Meteorology)

5. crank (Colloquial)
6. weird (Archaic)

7. conscience (Obsolete)
8. lift (British)

6.d.5 Synonyms and antonyms

To add interest and variety to your writing, you can use synonyms. **Synonyms** are words similar in meaning to one another. To produce contrasts in your writing, such as pointing out differences, you can use **antonyms**, words opposite in meaning to each other.

Not all word entries in your dictionary will list synonyms and antonyms. When they are listed, you will find them at the end of the entry, following the abbreviated labels *Syn.* and *Ant.* Some dictionaries also include discussions of slight differences in meanings of certain synonyms. Look at the following entry for *bright*.

bright (brīt) *adj.* [ME. < OE. *bryht*, earlier *beorht* < IE. base **bhereg-*, to gleam, white, whence Goth. *bairhts*, E. BIRCH] **1.** shining with light that is radiated or reflected; full of light **2.** clear or brilliant in color or sound; vivid or intense **3.** lively; vivacious; cheerful [a *bright* smile] **4.** mentally quick; smart, clever, witty, etc. **5.** *a*) full of happiness or hope [a *bright* outlook on life] *b*) favorable; auspicious **6.** glorious or splendid; illustrious —*adv.* in a bright manner —*n.* [Poet.] brightness; splendor —**bright'- ly** *adv.*

synonym label ——— **SYN.**—**bright**, the most general term here, implies the giving forth or reflecting of light, or a being filled with light [a *bright* day, star, shield, etc.]; **radiant** emphasizes the actual or apparent emission of rays of light; **shining** implies a steady, continuous brightness [the *shining* sun]; **brilliant** implies intense or flashing brightness [*brilliant* sunlight, diamonds, etc.]; **luminous** is applied to objects that are full of light or give off reflected or phosphorescent light; **lustrous** is applied to objects whose surfaces gleam by reflected light and emphasizes gloss or sheen [*lustrous* silk] See also INTELLIGENT —**ANT.** dull, dim, dark

discussion of synonyms

antonym label

Webster's New World Dictionary

EXERCISE 12. Use your dictionary to find synonyms for words 1-5 and antonyms for words 6-10.

1. punish
2. inactive
3. tardy
4. hesitate
5. meaning

6. clear
7. kind
8. lean
9. silent
10. rare

CAPITALIZATION
AND PUNCTUATION

7 Capitalization and Punctuation

Capitalization and punctuation are the mechanics of writing. Learning the correct uses of capital letters, abbreviations, numbers, numerals, and the various marks of punctuation is important for all writers.

The rules of capitalization and punctuation are partly a matter of tradition. For example, you use a colon in the greeting of a business letter and a comma in that of a personal letter. Such elements of mechanics are very important, however, in helping your reader to understand your message. Putting commas around a nonessential clause, for instance, may make a difference in the way a sentence is understood. When used properly, periods, question marks, quotation marks, and the like help the reader understand your meaning.

This section will help you master the rules of capitalization and punctuation. Learn the rules, study the examples, and do the exercises. Make a habit of checking, or *proofreading*, all your writing for the proper use of mechanics.

7.a CAPITALIZATION

Capital letters are used to identify the first word in a sentence as well as to designate proper nouns, proper adjectives, important words in titles, and some abbreviations. Capital letters are also called upper-case letters.

Unfortunately, there is no one set of capitalization

rules that everyone follows. You will probably notice different patterns even among the magazines that you read. For example, a university publication might capitalize terms such as *professor* or *dean*, whereas a general-interest publication might not. You should be aware of the reasons for capitalizing certain words and not capitalizing others. Most important, you should be consistent in your own use of correct capitalization.

The following rules indicate general current trends in capitalization. Remember always to check your dictionary when you are unsure about whether to capitalize a particular word.

7.a.1 Capitalization of sentences

Capitalize the first word of a sentence.

Soccer has been called the only international language.
Who said so?
Well, I am not sure.

7.a.2 Capitalization of direct quotations

Capitalize the first word of a direct quotation that is a complete sentence.

Henry James once wrote to a friend, "It's a complex fate, being an American."

Do not capitalize the first word of a direct quotation that is only a partial sentence.

Churchill said he had "**n**othing to offer but blood, toil, tears, and sweat."

Do not capitalize the first word of an indirect quotation. (An indirect quotation does not quote a person's exact words. It often follows the word *that*.)

Steve McQueen once said that **h**e would rather wake up in the middle of nowhere than in any city on earth.

7.a.3 Capitalization of the pronoun *I* and the interjection *O*

Capitalize the pronoun *I* and the interjection *O*.

O is used mainly in poetry and religious writing, usually before the name of the person or thing being addressed. The interjection *oh* is less formal. *Oh* is not capitalized unless it occurs at the beginning of a sentence, a quoted sentence, or a line of poetry.

> Because **I** studied hard, **I** found the biology test easy.
> Our national anthem begins, "**O** say can you see."
> Spring arrived yesterday, and **o**h, what a glorious day it turned out to be!

EXERCISE 1. Rewrite each sentence in the following passage, correcting all errors in capitalization. You can assume that all quotation marks are used correctly. (The passage contains ten errors.)

¹when Cathy Rigby was born two months early in 1952, she was so weak that her family feared for her life. ²"we almost lost her several times, but she always came back," her mother remembers. ³"i don't admit defeat in anything, and neither does she." ⁴little did her parents dream that Cathy would grow up to be an internationally famous gymnast. ⁵Mr. Rigby recalls that when his eight-year-old daughter was introduced to acrobatics, she was able to do backflips "on the very first night." ⁶Olympic coach Bud Marquette remembers that Cathy looked like a "ragamuffin" when he first met her. ⁷after only two months, however, she was better than girls who had trained for two years. ⁸when other girls were faced with a tricky leap, they seemed to freeze, as if to say "oh, forget it!" ⁹Cathy, on the other hand, insists that She cannot be afraid because Bud expects her to be brave. ¹⁰although she did not win a medal in the Olympics, Cathy says she was "Just excited about getting to compete."

EXERCISE 2. Rewrite each of the following sentences, correcting all errors in capitalization. You can assume that all quotation marks are used correctly. (One sentence is correct as written.)

1. "happiness comes from the health of the soul," said Aeschylus in 458 B.C.

2. It was Mrs. Fezziwig whom Dickens described as "One vast substantial smile."

3. Emerson once said, "whenever you are sincerely pleased, you are nourished."

4. Carl Sandburg once expressed thanks for "The laughter of children who tumble barefooted and bareheaded in the summer grass."

5. Charles Schulz thinks that Happiness is a warm puppy.

6. Dorothy Parker said there were four things she would have been better off without: "love, curiosity, freckles, and doubt."

7. It was an anonymous person who said, "love is a transitive verb."

8. Ella Wilcox said, "laugh, and the world laughs with you."

9. Aaron Burr once wrote, "the rule of my life is to make business a pleasure and pleasure my business."

10. It is one of Edith Wharton's characters who says that She lives in the moment when she is happy.

7.a.4 Capitalization of proper nouns

Capitalize a proper noun.

Remember that a proper noun is the name of a particular person, place, or thing (see 1.a.1). For example, the proper noun *Wyoming* is the name of a particular state. The word *state*, on the other hand, is a common noun, or the name of a general class of things.

Proper nouns	Common nouns
Phoenix	city
Tracy Austin	tennis player
the American River	river
"The Pasture"	poem
The Pearl	book

In proper nouns of more than one word, capitalize only the important words. Do not capitalize articles, conjunctions, or prepositions of fewer than five letters.

Congress of **V**ienna	**P**eter the **G**reat
Secretary of **D**efense	**U**niversity of the **S**outh

Here are some of the kinds of proper nouns that should be capitalized:

1. **names of people and animals**

Diane **K**eaton	**T**ecumseh
Arthur **A**she	**F**rances **H**odgson **B**urnett
William **W**ordsworth	**R**over

2. **titles of people**
Capitalize titles used before a name.

Vice **P**resident **H**umphrey	**P**resident **L**ópez **P**ortillo
Princess **G**race	**C**ardinal **S**pellman
Mayor **L**a **G**uardia	**A**dmiral **N**imitz

Do not capitalize titles used alone or used after a name unless you wish to show respect or unless the person is a high official. For example, always capitalize the word *President* when you refer to the President of the United States. Do not capitalize titles used as common nouns.

Mayor **J**anet **H**ayes   *but*   the duties of the **m**ayor

Capitalize titles of family relationships when they are used before a name or in place of a name. Do not capitalize a word of family relationship if a possessive pronoun is used before it (unless the word is part of a name).

Can you help me, **F**ather?	*but*	Nancy's **f**ather
I saw your **U**ncle Joe.	*but*	I saw your **u**ncle.

3. **names of nationalities, ethnic or regional groups, and languages**

Yugoslavians	**C**herokee
the **I**rish	**G**erman

4. **organizations, institutions, government bodies, political parties and their members, business firms**

a **D**emocrat
Republican party
American **A**irlines

March of **D**imes
Garden **C**lub of **A**merica
University of **U**tah

Do not capitalize common nouns such as *court* or *university* unless they are part of a proper noun. The word *party* is not capitalized in the name of a political party.

She planned to attend the **s**tate **u**niversity.
She attended the **U**niversity of **M**innesota.

5. **buildings, monuments, bridges, dams**

Fanueil **H**all
Beverly **W**ilshire **H**otel
Houston **S**pace **C**enter

Jefferson **M**emorial
George **W**ashington **B**ridge
Tellico **D**am

6. **trade names**

Ajax
Tide

Crest
Lincoln **C**ontinental

Do not capitalize a common noun that follows a trade name.

Levi's jeans

Pepperidge **F**arm cookies

7. **documents, awards, laws**

Articles of **C**onfederation
Magna **C**arta

Emmy
Voting **R**ights **A**ct of 1965

8. **geographical terms**
Capitalize the important words in the names of continents, regions, countries, states, counties, cities, parks, geographical features, and streets.

South **A**merica
Iran
Tennessee
Alameda **C**ounty
Minneapolis
Caribbean **S**ea

White **M**ountains
San **F**ernando **V**alley
San **F**rancisco **B**ay
Catalina **I**sland
Middle **E**ast
Newbury **S**treet

9. compass points

Capitalize compass points such as *west* and *northeast* when they refer to a specific area of the country or the world or when they are part of a proper name. Do not capitalize compass points if they merely indicate direction.

> The **M**iddle **E**ast is known for its historical sites.
> Bananas are an important crop in **S**outh **A**merica.
> Canada lies **n**orth, but we visited the **W**est for vacation.

10. planets and other heavenly bodies

Mercury	**A**lpha **C**entauri
Pluto	**N**orth **S**tar

Do not capitalize *sun* and *moon*. Do not capitalize *earth* unless it is used with the names of other planets. *Earth* is never capitalized when it is preceded by the word *the*.

> Today's weather should permit good visibility of both the **s**un and the **m**oon.
> Scientists believed that the meteor had fallen to the **e**arth many years ago.
> **J**upiter is much larger than **E**arth.

11. ships, planes, trains, spacecraft

U.S.S. *Independence* [ship]	*Spirit of* **St.** *Louis* [plane]
Southern **C**rescent [train]	**S**kylab 4 [spacecraft]

12. historical events and eras

Wars of the **R**oses	**G**ay **N**ineties
Battle of **S**talingrad	**D**ark **A**ges

13. days of the week, months, holidays, events

Saturday	**T**hanksgiving
March	**Y**om **K**ippur
Mother's **D**ay	**W**orld **S**eries

Do not capitalize the names of the seasons (spring, summer, autumn, fall, winter).

14. religious terms

Capitalize names of religions, denominations, and their members, and words referring to the Deity.

Islam	Baptists
Hinduism	Catholics
Judaism	God
Eastern Orthodox Church	the Almighty

Do not capitalize the word *god* when it refers to the gods of mythology.

In Roman mythology Neptune is the god of the sea.

Do not capitalize *church* unless it is part of a name.

a Presbyterian church *but* First Presbyterian Church

15. school courses

Capitalize school courses that are languages or that are titles of specific courses. Do not capitalize general names of subjects.

Latin	*but*	geology
Geometry I	*but*	geometry
Topics in American History	*but*	history

EXERCISE 3. From each of the following pairs select the phrase that is capitalized correctly.

1. a) the new Mayor
   b) the new mayor
2. a) U.S.S. *constitution*
   b) U.S.S. *Constitution*
3. a) Easter Sunday
   b) Easter sunday
4. a) astronomy 202
   b) Astronomy 202
5. a) Father's Day
   b) father's day
6. a) Zion National Park
   b) Zion national park
7. a) the Far East
   b) the far East
8. a) Catherine the great
   b) Catherine the Great
9. a) the sun
   b) the Sun
10. a) the bill of rights
    b) the Bill of Rights

EXERCISE 4. Rewrite each of the following sentences, correctly capitalizing all proper nouns.

1. Baseball's hall of fame is located in cooperstown, new york.
2. One well-known breakfast cereal is cheerios.
3. The better business bureau works to assure high standards of service.
4. The symbol of the democratic party is the donkey.
5. "Hello, mother. This is leslie."
6. Did you know that west virginia was formerly a part of virginia?
7. His sister hilary hopes to be elected president of the student body.
8. In 1898 the spanish were defeated at manila bay by commodore dewey.
9. Next month is the sierra club hike to vogelsang point, yosemite.
10. Ivan the terrible was the first czar of russia.

EXERCISE 5. Rewrite each of the following phrases, correcting all errors in capitalization.

1. dole pineapple
2. acadia national park
3. the battle of saratoga
4. sears tower
5. the moons of saturn
6. explore the southwest
7. nobel prize
8. a methodist church
9. a history major
10. the salvation army
11. the ohio turnpike
12. may, june, july
13. university of california
14. lake tanganyika
15. crenshaw boulevard
16. arlington cemetery
17. the city of chicago
18. mojave desert
19. middle ages
20. lake placid

EXERCISE 6. Rewrite each of the following sentences, correctly capitalizing all proper nouns.

1. The city of pompeii lies fourteen miles southeast of naples.
2. Until A.D. 79, when it was buried by an eruption of mount vesuvius, pompeii was an important port city.
3. We know about pompeii today from the work of archeologists like giuseppe fiorelli and institutions like the national archeological museum in naples.

4. We know that pompeii's citizens lived in villas near the mediterranean sea.

5. Citizens of pompeii might have discussed the problems of emperor vespasian in rome.

6. Pompeians worshiped the god apollo.

7. They might have also revered the goddess isis.

8. It is possible that pompeii was founded by greeks.

9. By 80 B.C., however, pompeii had been settled by romans.

10. Preserved graffiti reveal the names and home towns of people like speratus.

EXERCISE 7. Rewrite each of the following sentences, correctly capitalizing all proper nouns.

1. The biggest volcanic eruption of recent centuries took place at krakatau, indonesia, in august 1883.

2. Tidal waves caused by the eruption killed 36,000 people in nearby java and sumatra.

3. The tidal waves were felt as far west as cape horn.

4. In 1902 on the island of martinique in the west indies, mount pelée erupted.

5. The mountain was originally named after a local god, pelée.

6. The eruption destroyed the city of st. pierre, killing many west indians.

7. Several thousand years ago mount mazama erupted in what is now southern oregon.

8. The ash spread over what is now the northwest and even reached saskatchewan, canada.

9. Mount mazama now contains crater lake.

10. Most volcanoes lie within a zone that runs down the western coast of north america and south america and down the eastern coast of asia.

7.a.5 Capitalization of proper adjectives

Capitalize proper adjectives; do not capitalize common adjectives. Proper adjectives are adjectives formed from proper nouns.

Some words, such as *Norwegian*, are used as both proper nouns and proper adjectives; that is, the noun and the adjective have the same form.

Here are some of the kinds of proper adjectives that should be capitalized:

1. **formed from names of people**

   Victorian   **B**yronic
   Jeffersonian   **C**opernican

2. **formed from place names and names of national and ethnic groups**

   Asian   **B**ostonian
   German   **A**fro-**A**merican
   Egyptian   **P**uerto **R**ican

3. **formed from political and religious terms**

   Democratic   **B**uddhist
   Congressional   **P**resbyterian

EXERCISE 8. Change each of the following proper nouns into a proper adjective. Use your dictionary if necessary.

    EXAMPLE America
    ANSWER   *American*

1. Tibet	8. Israel	15. Homer
2. Philadelphia	9. Iceland	16. Ireland
3. Shakespeare	10. Washington	17. Mohammed
4. Germany	11. Napoleon	18. Dickens
5. Ethiopia	12. Vienna	19. Yugoslavia
6. Stalin	13. Islam	20. Peru
7. Japan	14. Brazil	

EXERCISE 9. Rewrite each of the following sentences, correctly capitalizing all proper adjectives and proper nouns.

1. Just west of the italian border, on the mediterranean sea, is the tiny nation of monaco.

2. Monaco is ruled by prince rainier, whose family was awarded the territory in 1297 by the holy roman emperor.

3. Princess grace of monaco is a former actress from philadelphia.

4. Another small nation is new hebrides, a series of islands under joint british and french rule.

5. The new hebrideans actually have two police forces, two sets of laws, and two chief colonial officials.

6. In the central mediterranean sea is the tiny island of malta.

7. Malta's strategic location has caused it to be occupied by many foreign peoples, including the phoenicians, the greeks, and the french.

8. The island of tonga in the pacific ocean is the last polynesian monarchy.

9. Tonga's economy is based on agriculture, and tongan children are taught early to cultivate the land.

10. Vatican city is located in the heart of rome, near the west bank of the tiber river.

11. Vatican city attracts both roman catholic pilgrims and italian tourists interested in great art.

12. The vatican railroad line, only three hundred yards long, is the shortest in the world.

13. Belize occupies the southeast corner of the yucatán peninsula.

14. Before the arrival of europeans, belize was the site of several mayan ceremonial cities.

15. Liechtenstein is nestled between austria and switzerland.

16. Established in 1719, liechtenstein is the only independent country outside the arab world where women cannot vote.

17. Most of greenland lies within the arctic circle off the extreme northeast coast of north america.

18. The people of greenland, mostly eskimos, are ruled by the danish.

19. Seychelles, a country that consists of eighty-five islands in the indian ocean, was used mostly by pirates until the eighteenth century.

20. Still governed by the british, seychelles is famous for exotic plant and animal life.

7.a.6 Capitalization of titles of works

Capitalize the first and last words and all important words in titles of works.

Titles of artistic works are proper nouns. They name particular things. Capitalize the first and last words and all important words in titles of books, short stories, poems, plays, movies, television shows, newspapers, magazines, paintings, and musical compositions. Do not capitalize articles, coordinating conjunctions, or prepositions unless they are the first or the last words or unless they have more than four letters. Capitalize all words that are part of a verb, such as *make* **up** or *pick* **out**.

Most titles of works are either italicized or enclosed in quotation marks. (For a discussion of quotation marks and italics with titles of works, see 7.l.2 and 7.m.1.)

Portrait of a Lady	*60 Minutes*
"The Lady or the Tiger?"	the *Boston Globe*
"Birches"	*Fortune*
A Midsummer Night's Dream	*American Gothic*
Casablanca	*Rhapsody in Blue*

Capitalize an article at the beginning of a title only when it is part of the title itself. In general, do not capitalize (or italicize) articles preceding the name of a newspaper or periodical or the word *magazine* following the title of a periodical.

The Age of Innocence	but	the *New Yorker*
"A Christmas Carol"	but	a *Life* magazine

EXERCISE 10. Rewrite each of the following sentences, correctly capitalizing all titles.

1. In his poem "i hear america singing" Walt Whitman salutes America's mechanics, shoemakers, and masons.
2. Ferde Grofé portrays the natural beauty of Arizona in his musical composition *the grand canyon suite*.
3. Katharine Hepburn and Cary Grant starred in the popular film *the philadelphia story*.

4. Henry James's *the bostonians* is set in that city.
5. In the song "i left my heart in san francisco" Tony Bennett sings about cable cars climbing halfway to the stars.
6. The *new yorker* contains news and reviews of current plays, films, and books.
7. The *augusta chronicle* is published in Georgia.
8. Some of Rodgers and Hammerstein's most popular songs are from the musical *oklahoma!*
9. Seven-story skyscrapers are celebrated in the song "everything's up to date in kansas city."
10. California is the home of *sunset* magazine.
11. A song from the Southwest is "the yellow rose of texas."
12. Betty Frye Leach has written many poems about Boston, including "flowery talk in the public garden."
13. In *abe lincoln in illinois* playwright Robert Sherwood shows Lincoln as a youth and as a young adult.
14. The television show *happy days* is set in Milwaukee.
15. Brian Friel's play *philadelphia, here i come!* looks at the relationships between parents and children.
16. *A tree grows in brooklyn* is a popular novel by Betty Smith.
17. Washington Irving's story "the legend of sleepy hollow" takes place in Tarrytown, a town on the Hudson River.
18. In "crossing brooklyn ferry" Walt Whitman uses the ferry crossing as a metaphor of time and life.
19. The *sacramento bee* reports the news in the capital of California.
20. In her painting *red hills and the sun* Georgia O'Keeffe portrays the landscapes of New Mexico.

7.a.7 Capitalization of abbreviations

Capitalize abbreviations of proper nouns and proper adjectives. Also capitalize the abbreviations *A.M.*, *P.M.*, *A.D.*, and *B.C.*

A.M.	B.C.	RCA	Dr.	Minn.
P.M.	UNESCO	Prof.	Corp.	Nov.
A.D.	NATO	Jr.	U.N.	Wed.

REVIEW EXERCISE A. From each of the following pairs, select the phrase that is capitalized correctly.

1. a) Russian Revolution
   b) russian revolution
2. a) Fenton's Ice Cream
   b) Fenton's ice cream
3. a) Puget Sound
   b) Puget sound
4. a) dr. Jerome Carbone
   b) Dr. Jerome Carbone
5. a) Fenway park
   b) Fenway Park

6. a) Christmas Eve
   b) Christmas eve
7. a) a Buddhist priest
   b) a buddhist priest
8. a) 9 a.m. to 5 p.m.
   b) 9 A.M. to 5 P.M.
9. a) Yale University
   b) Yale university
10. a) a junior college
    b) a Junior College

REVIEW EXERCISE B. Rewrite each of the following sentences, correcting all errors in capitalization.

1. The longest river in the world is the nile river in africa.
2. The southernmost city in south america is punta arenas in argentina.
3. The largest and longest ship of any kind is the french tanker *pierre guillaumal.*
4. The world's tallest mountain is mount everest.
5. The lowest temperature ever recorded was taken at vostok, antarctica.
6. The most influential american newspaper is the *new york times.*
7. The longest-running television show in history is nbc's *meet the press.*
8. The windiest city in the united states is great falls, montana.
9. *The maltese falcon* by dashiell hammett is one of the most popular detective stories ever written.
10. Most towns in the united states have a street named main street.

REVIEW EXERCISE C. Rewrite each of the following phrases and sentences, correcting all errors in capitalization.

1. the film *lawrence of arabia*
2. a course on american Civilization
3. ceres, the Goddess of the harvest
4. standard oil of california
5. the song "joy to the world"
6. murphy's law
7. the *christian science monitor*
8. the story "but the one on the right"
9. the planets earth, mars, and venus
10. the poem "the rime of the ancient mariner"
11. an emersonian philosophy
12. a balkan folk dance
13. a quaker college
14. 140 b.c.
15. the song "o how lovely is the evening"
16. the painting "after the hunt"
17. the president of the united states
18. professor arthur schlesinger
19. the battle of little big horn
20. a bowl of wheaties

REVIEW EXERCISE D. Rewrite each of the following sentences, correcting all errors in capitalization.

1. What do *the king and i*, *the sound of music*, and *south pacific* have in common?
2. The three musicals are linked by a single name: richard rodgers.
3. With lorenz hart and later with oscar hammerstein, rodgers wrote some of the world's most memorable songs.
4. Alden Whitman of the *new york times* credits rodgers with transforming american musical comedy into a true art form.
5. Over forty rodgers musicals were performed during his lifetime, many of them in other countries.
6. At one point in 1975, sixty productions of *oklahoma!* were under way in the united states, europe, africa, and asia.

7. "Oh, what a beautiful mornin'!" has been sung in both japanese and italian.

8. One critic declared, "probably not a day goes by without a show of his being performed somewhere in the world."

9. One line from a song in *oklahoma!* proclaims, "all the sounds of the earth are like music."

10. It was no surprise in 1944 when rodgers won a pulitzer prize for *oklahoma!*

11. Even more successful was *south pacific*, his musical adaptation of james michener's *tales of the south pacific*.

12. Generations of americans hum and sing "i'm in love with a wonderful guy" and "some enchanted evening."

13. The latter song begins with the line "some enchanted evening, you may meet a stranger."

14. Another rodgers classic is *carousel*, a tale of clambakes and fishers in a small town in maine.

15. "If i loved you" and "you'll never walk alone" are two tunes from *carousel* that have become popular classics.

16. Much of rodgers' music portrays american scenes, ranging from the west in *annie get your gun* to new england in *carousel*.

17. Rodgers received an oscar for the song "it might as well be spring" from *state fair*.

18. In 1978 president carter honored richard rodgers at a white house reception.

19. Rodgers also received the lawrence langner award for "a lifetime of distinguished achievement in the american theater."

20. Rodgers composed his first song, "auto show girl," at age fourteen, and he wrote his first musical comedy while still a student at columbia college.

7.b ABBREVIATIONS

Abbreviations are shortened forms of words. They are used to save space and time and to avoid wordiness. For example, it is easier and more concise to write *50 mph* than *50 miles per hour*.

You can use some abbreviations (such as *Mrs.*) in your regular prose writing. Others (such as the abbreviations for the months) should not be used in such prose.

7.b.1 Abbreviations of titles of people

Use abbreviations for some personal titles.

Titles such as *Mr.*, *Mrs.*, *Jr.*, and *Sr.* and those indicating professions and academic degrees (*Dr.*, *M.D.*, *M.A.*) are almost always abbreviated when used with a person's name. *Ms.* and *Miss* are not abbreviations, although *Ms.* is followed by a period. Titles of government and military officials and members of the clergy are often abbreviated when used before a name.

Mrs. Carter	**Sen.** Margaret Chase Smith
Mr. Vincent Lopez	**Rev.** Martin Luther King, **Sr.**
Rep. Patricia Schroeder	Alvin F. Poussaint, **M.D.**
Dr. Juanita M. Kreps	Vicki Young, **J.D.**
Adm. Stansfield Turner	Kathleen Peterson, **M.A.**

7.b.2 Abbreviations of businesses, organizations, government agencies

Use abbreviations for names of business firms, organizations, and government agencies.

Most of these abbreviations do not require periods.

NBC	**VISTA**	**NASA**
UNICEF	**AFS**	**NHL**

In regular prose writing you should spell out such names the first time they are used and give the abbreviation in parentheses after the name. In later references you may use the abbreviation alone.

The Organization of African Unity (**OAU**) meets yearly to promote African solidarity and to work for the rights of its members. The **OAU** was founded in 1963.

7.b.3 Abbreviations of places

Spell out the names of countries, states, and streets in regular prose writing.

Places may be abbreviated in addresses in informal letters but should not be in business letters.

Spartanburg, **S.C.**   666 Fifth **Ave.**

The names of most states may be abbreviated in two ways. The abbreviation that consists of two capital letters with no periods should be used only when the ZIP code is also used.

Michigan   **Mich.**   **MI**

EXERCISE 11. Match the abbreviations in the left column with the words they represent in the right column.

1. OAS	1. Missouri
2. Corp.	2. Central Intelligence Agency
3. ABC	3. Street
4. Rep.	4. Argentina
5. CIA	5. Organization of American States
6. La.	6. Louisiana
7. MO	7. Corporation
8. Arg.	8. American Broadcasting Company
9. M.A.	9. Representative
10. St.	10. Master of Arts

EXERCISE 12. Match the abbreviations in the left column with the words they represent in the right column.

1. USMC	1. Alabama
2. Blvd.	2. Hawaii
3. TVA	3. European Economic Community
4. CIA	4. Federal Communications Commissic
5. Ala.	5. Central Intelligence Agency
6. FCC	6. Tennessee Valley Authority
7. HI	7. Union of Soviet Socialist Republics
8. USSR	8. United States Marine Corps
9. USIA	9. United States Information Agency
10. EEC	10. Boulevard

7.b.4 Abbreviations of dates and times

Do not abbreviate the names of months and days of the week in regular prose writing.

NOT The Great Chicago Fire started on ~~Sun.~~, ~~Oct.~~ 8, 1871.

BUT The Great Chicago Fire started on **Sunday, October** 8, 1871.

The following abbreviations are used in writing dates and times. These abbreviations are acceptable in all kinds of writing.

A.D. (*anno Domini*), "in the year of the Lord"; placed before the date—*A.D. 27*

B.C. (before Christ); placed after the date—*44 B.C.*

A.M. (*ante meridiem*), "before noon"

P.M. (*post meridiem*), "after noon"

EXERCISE 13. Rewrite the following passage, spelling out in words all of the *misused* abbreviations. (The passage contains twenty misused abbreviations.)

[1]Most people consider the Wright bros. to be the pioneers of aviation, but there were actually several other experimental aviators before them. [2]As early as 1503, one daring adventurer broke a leg trying to fly a glider from a church tower in Perugia, It. [3]In the yr. 1783 the Montgolfier bros. set aloft a smoke-filled balloon carrying a rooster, a duck, and a sheep to a ht. of six thousand ft. for a one-and-a-half-mi. flight. [4]Then, on Nov. 21 of that yr., the Marquis d'Arlandres became the first to fly an airborne vehicle. [5]His seventy-ft. balloon traveled five mi. before coming down. [6]He was followed shortly by the first women to fly: Mrs. Thimble of Fr. and Mrs. Sage of Eng.

[7]The first steerable glider to fly was built in the U.K. by Geo. Cayley in 1804. [8]Later models could carry people for several yds. [9]At the turn of the cent., the leading Am. authority on gliders was Octave Chaute. [10]In 1903 Chaute rec'd. a letter from a Mr. Wright from the state of OH asking for advice on airplanes, but that is of course another story.

7.c NUMBERS AND NUMERALS

In most prose writing some numbers should be spelled out as words, and some numbers can be expressed in figures. If a number can be written in one or two words, it is generally spelled out. If a number requires more than two words, however, it is usually written in figures.

7.c.1 Numbers expressed in words

In general, in prose spell out numbers that can be written in one or two words and numbers that occur at the beginning of a sentence.

Saturn is now thought to have **eleven** moons.

Four hundred and seventy-five people attended the conference.

Aunt Sylvia's **sixty-fifth** birthday was celebrated at a surprise party.

Having placed **first** in the jumping competition, Dorrit's horse was awarded a blue ribbon.

7.c.2 Numbers expressed in figures (numerals)

Use figures to express numbers of more than two words.

In addition, use figures (numerals) in the following situations:

1. **dates, times, addresses (except numbered streets up to 10th)**

In **1876** Alexander Graham Bell invented the telephone.

The concert was scheduled to begin at **8:15** P.M.

The Apollo Theater is located at **253** West **125th** Street in Harlem.

The Macmillan Publishing Company has its offices on **Third** Avenue.

2. **money, decimals, percentages**

The apartment was renting for **$225** a month.
Use **3.14159** for *pi*.
The stock paid a **13** percent dividend quarterly.

3. **measurements**

Hitters love Fenway Park's left-field fence, which stands
only **315** feet from home plate.
Mount McKinley, the highest mountain in the United
States, is **20,320** feet high.

If a sentence (or a paragraph) contains more than one
number, express all the numbers in either words or numerals. Do not mix words and numerals. The only exceptions are dates and times. Use a date or time in numerals
even with a number in words in the same sentence.

The number of women runners in the local marathon went
from **55** to **429** within a few years. [In a sentence where
it was the only number, *55* would appear as *fifty-five*.]
In **1889** Nellie Bly traveled around the world in **seventy-
two** days, thereby beating Phineas Fogg's record of
eighty days. [Because you are expressing a date, you may
use words and numerals in the same sentence.]

Actually, there is often more than one correct way to
express an amount of money, a fraction, or a percentage.
Make sure that you use the same form throughout your
sentence, paragraph, or paper. That is, do not write
twenty-five percent in one sentence and *25%* in another.

EXERCISE 14. Rewrite each of the following sentences
that has errors in the use of numbers and numerals. One
of the sentences is correct as written.

1. New Yorkers frequently insist that their city is number 1.
2. New York City includes 5 boroughs—Brooklyn, Queens,
the Bronx, Staten Island, and Manhattan.
3. 7,000,000 people live in the city.
4. New York has no tall mountains, but its World Trade Center stands one hundred and ten stories high.

5. The Empire State Building has 102 stories, with an observation platform on the eighty-sixth story.

6. Yankee Stadium, at East 161st Street, was built in 1923 and rebuilt in nineteen hundred and seventy-six.

7. 5th Avenue is one of the world's famed shopping streets.

8. The Avenue of the Americas and 6th Avenue are two names for the same street.

9. Duke Ellington Boulevard is actually another name for West One Hundred and Sixth Street.

10. A traditional Christmas movie, *Miracle on 34th Street*, is set in New York.

EXERCISE 15. Rewrite each of the following sentences, correcting all errors in the use of numbers and numerals.

1. A baseball weighs just over five ounces and measures around two point eighty-six inches in diameter.

2. Its cork core is covered with 2 layers of rubber, 1 black and 1 red.

3. The cork is surrounded by 121 yards of blue wool yarn, forty-five yards of white yarn, and fifty-three more yards of gray yarn.

4. Then come one hundred and fifty yards of cotton yarn and a coat of rubber cement.

5. The exterior is cowhide, which is held together with two hundred and sixteen red cotton stitches.

6. Baseballs are now made in Taiwan, but before nineteen hundred and seventy-three they were made in Chicopee, Massachusetts.

7. A good fastball travels 90 to ninety-five miles per hour.

8. A great fastball pitcher was Sandy Koufax, a Dodger from nineteen hundred and fifty-five to nineteen hundred and sixty-six.

9. Also impressive is Ron Guidry, who in 1978 won twenty-five games and lost three, compiling an earned-run average of one point seven four.

10. Babe Ruth, the 1st to hit sixty home runs in a season, was also a pitcher and pitched 29 consecutive scoreless innings in the 1916 and 1918 World Series.

FORMING THE PLURALS OF NUMBERS AND NUMERALS

1. Numbers that are spelled out form their plurals like other nouns (see 1.a.3).

   The telephone operator's **nines** sound as if they have two syllables.

   Chemise dresses and pointed shoes became popular in the **fifties**.

2. Numbers that are expressed in figures form their plurals by adding an apostrophe and *s*.

   Some people cross their **7's** to distinguish them from **1's**.

   NOTE: Do not use an apostrophe between the numeral and the *s* in showing a span of time.

   The **1890s** are sometimes called the Gay Nineties.

EXERCISE 16. Rewrite each of the following sentences, correcting all errors in the use of numbers and numerals.

1. Before nineteen hundred Henry Ford was one of 1000s who worked in the booming bicycle industry.
2. By the 1880s bike wheels were 50 inches in diameter in the front and seventeen inches in the rear.
3. These early bikes weighed anywhere from twenty-one to 150 pounds.
4. "Diamond Jim" Brady once gave Lillian Russell a gold-plated bicycle worth $10 thousand.
5. One of the longest bikes was 35 feet four inches long.
6. This bike had over one hundred feet of chain and weighed 1,000 pounds.
7. Today a good bicycle can cost as much as two hundred and twenty-five dollars.
8. A bicycle with poor brakes going fifteen miles per hour on a wet road can take 100 feet to stop.

9. An average of $100 million worth of bikes are sold each year, 1/3 of them to adults.

10. For more information about bicycles, write to the Bicycle Institute of America, 122 East Forty-second Street, New York, NY 10017.

7.d PERIODS

Use a period at the end of a sentence, in initials and abbreviations, and as a decimal point in writing numerals.

Use a period at the end of the following kinds of sentences: a declarative sentence, a polite command, and a statement including an indirect question.

> *Flying Down to Rio* is the film in which Fred Astaire met Ginger Rogers. [declarative sentence]
> Be sure to see *Flying Down to Rio*. [polite command]
> She asked them if they had ever seen *Flying Down to Rio*. [indirect question]

Use periods with initials and with most other abbreviations (see 7.b).

F. Scott Fitzgerald	Sept.
Dr. Diana Lee	B.C.
U.S.A.	oz.

Do not use periods with the abbreviations of some businesses, organizations, and government agencies. Also do not use periods with the two-letter abbreviations of states that are used with ZIP codes, with abbreviations of metric measurements, or with acronyms (abbreviations that are pronounced as words). Be sure to check your dictionary whenever you are unsure whether to use periods with a particular abbreviation.

ITT	CA	GSA
FBI	GOP	NOW

EXERCISE 17. Rewrite the following sentences, inserting any necessary periods.

1. La Donna Harris is the founder of Oklahomans for Indian Opportunity
2. This group trains Native Americans to work with Latin American Indians
3. One might ask why she is so active in Native American affairs?
4. Perhaps it is because Ms Harris is herself a Native American.
5. Her husband is Fred R Harris, who formerly represented Oklahoma in the US Senate.
6. Mr Harris, you may remember, was once a candidate for President
7. People ask how Ms Harris has time for so many concerns?
8. She has been a board member of the National Association of Mental Health
9. Antioch College in Ohio has been another of her concerns
10. Ms Harris is indeed a very active American

7.e QUESTION MARKS

Use a question mark to indicate a direct question.

Where is the best place to live?

A traditional Christmas carol asks the question, "Do you hear what I hear?"

Notice that you use a period rather than a question mark after an indirect question. (An indirect question does not quote a person's exact words.)

He asked what period of history I liked best.

AVOIDING ERRORS WITH QUESTION MARKS

Always place the question mark at the *end* of the question.

NOT How long ago⤬ did you visit Yosemite.
BUT How long ago did you visit Yosemite?

EXERCISE 18. Rewrite the following sentences, supplying either a question mark or a period at the end of each sentence.

1. One might well wonder why someone would spend sixty-three days in a cave
2. Have you heard of Michel Siffre of France, who did just that
3. Siffre wanted to find out how people act after being alone for a long time
4. He wanted to see how a person would react to constant dampness, cold, and darkness
5. He also wondered if time would seem to slow down under such circumstances
6. Are these not reasonable curiosities
7. What do you think of someone who would undertake such an experiment
8. Do you think Siffre was merely performing a stunt
9. Are you surprised that he suffered few ill effects after sixty-three days underground
10. How would you like to spend that much time in a cave

7.f EXCLAMATION POINTS

Use exclamation points to show strong feeling and to indicate a forceful command.

I never thought you'd make it!
You set a new world record!
Watch out!
Don't ever do that again!

NOTE: Use a period, not an exclamation point, after a polite command.

Work as fast as you can.

REVIEW EXERCISE E. Rewrite the following sentences, inserting any necessary periods, question marks, and exclamation points.

AVOIDING ERRORS WITH EXCLAMATION POINTS

Remember that it is usually better to use a period rather than an exclamation point in regular prose writing. The effectiveness of the exclamation point depends on its being used infrequently.

NOT At the age of seven, Mozart was already going on concert tours⟩

BUT At the age of seven, Mozart was already going on concert tours.

1. Have you read *The Man Who Rode the Thunder*
2. What a hair-raising tale it is
3. The man was William H Rankin
4. He had joined the U S Marines seeking travel and adventure
5. As a lieutenant colonel he flew jet missions in Korea
6. For two years Col Rankin served as a squadron leader
7. He first met adventure, however, on a routine flight over the U S South
8. What would you do if your engine suddenly went dead 47,000 feet above the ground
9. Imagine bailing out into a thunderstorm and taking 40 minutes to reach the ground
10. Rankin had to jump from a plane that was traveling 600 miles per hour at an altitude of 9 miles
11. How terrified he must have been
12. Put yourself in his place
13. His first problem was getting his parachute open
14. Without the parachute he was falling at a rate of 10,000 feet per second
15. As his oxygen supply was about to give out, Rankin's parachute flew open

16. What a close call
17. The thunderstorm slowed his descent
18. He had bailed out in Virginia but finally landed in North Carolina
19. How would you like to "ride" thunder
20. Read *The Man Who Rode the Thunder* for all the details

7.g COMMAS

A comma is a mark of punctuation that signals a small pause in a sentence. A comma's main purpose is to help the reader follow, and therefore understand, the sentence. Because commas are used in so many different situations, writers often have trouble deciding exactly where to use them. There are, however, logical patterns to the use of commas and several rules that will help you to use commas properly.

Commas are used in many standard positions, such as between personal titles and names, between parts of a place name or date, and between items in a series. Commas are also used to separate clauses, phrases, and extra expressions from each other or from the rest of the sentence.

In this section you will learn the various situations that call for the use of a comma. Study the rules and the examples, and do the exercises. Try to develop a sense of when to use a comma and when not to. Remember that commas should never be used unnecessarily.

CONVENTIONAL USES

7.g.1 Commas for personal titles

Use commas to set off titles when they follow a person's name.

In a complete sentence the title should be set off with commas *before* and *after* it.

Margaret Coleman, M.D.
Jane M. Byrne, mayor of Chicago
Whitney M. Young, Jr.
Dianne Feinstein, mayor of San Francisco, has played an
    active role in restoring that city's old residential
    neighborhoods.

7.g.2 Commas in addresses

Use commas to set off the various parts of an address or
of a geographical term.

If the address or place name is in the beginning or
middle of the sentence, place a comma after the last part
to set it off from the rest of the sentence.

Amarillo, Texas
The American Hospital Association is located at 840 North
    Lake Shore Drive, Chicago, Illinois, and has no branch
    offices.

Do not use a comma between the street number and
the name of the street or between the state and the ZIP
code. Do use a comma after the ZIP code when it comes in
the middle of a sentence.

My grandparents lived at 1870 Hampshire Avenue, St.
    Paul, Minnesota 55116, for many years.

7.g.3 Commas in dates

Use commas to separate the parts of a date.

Place a comma between the day of the week and the
month and between the day of the month and the year. In
a complete sentence always use a comma after the last
part of the date.

October 15, 1905
Thursday, March 20, 1941
On Sunday, January 20, 1957, Dwight D. Eisenhower was
    inaugurated as President.

Do not use the comma with dates in military form (as in *3 July 1941*). Do not use the comma if only the month and the numeral or only the month and the year are given.

May 1981   November 22

Election Day is on November 7 this year.
In July 1969 the first Americans walked on the moon.

7.g.4 Commas in letter writing

Place a comma after the salutation of an informal letter and after the closing of all letters.

Dear Sonia,   Dear Aunt Milly,
Love,   Yours truly,

Use a colon, not a comma, after the salutation of a business letter (see 16.c).

Dear Sir or Madam: Members of the Board:

EXERCISE 19. Rewrite the following letter, inserting any necessary commas. You should put in ten commas.

239 Dunmore Road
Denver Colorado 80201
November 3 1981

Ms. Roberta Rommer Publisher
Healthline News
19 River Avenue
Lancaster Pennsylvania 17604

Dear Ms. Rommer:

I enjoyed reading the story on bicycling in the August 25, 1981 issue of *Healthline News*. I have always believed that people who ride bikes stay healthy. I am writing to ask where I might get a copy of the government study referred to in the article.

I would also like to commend you on the feature articles by June Caruso M.D. and John Master Ph.D. I particularly enjoyed the item on Vitamin C that they recently reprinted from the Mamaroneck *Daily Times*.

Sincerely yours

James Gibbs, Jr.

James Gibbs Jr.

ITEMS IN SERIES

7.g.5 Commas and words in series

Use commas with nouns, verbs, adjectives, and adverbs in a series.

Notice that a series can appear in three different ways:

apples, oranges, and pineapples [This is the most common form.]
apples, oranges, pineapples
apples and oranges and pineapples [Commas are not used in this form.]

Although newspapers and some periodicals omit the comma before the *and*, it is always better to use the comma because it helps avoid confusion. For example, in the sentence "I am looking for a dress, blazer, skirt and blouse," it is not clear whether the writer wants a matching skirt and blouse or two separate items that need not match. If the writer wants separate items, a comma after the word *skirt* would make the meaning clear.

The backpackers carried bandanas, canteens, insect repellent, and cameras.
Our campfire smouldered, flickered, and glowed under the stars.
The cool, calm, cloudless evenings were refreshing.
After a summer in the Sierra Nevada, John Muir wrote, "I gladly, gratefully, hopefully pray I may see it again."

Do not use a comma between adjectives in a series if they sound unnatural with their order changed or with *and* between them. Adjectives that do not need commas between them usually describe different aspects, such as size and color, of the word to which they refer.

A large black bear stood on the trail.

EXERCISE 20. Rewrite each of the following sentences that needs commas. One of the sentences is correct as written.

1. The American Revolution brought out the courage of many men women and children.
2. Susan Livingston of New Jersey was especially brave imaginative and intelligent.
3. She was the daughter of the governor and lived in a big white clapboard house.
4. The countryside in those days consisted of dirt roads green farmland and small villages.
5. The British held nearby Staten Island, Long Island and New York.
6. One evening British troops entered searched and seized the Livingston house.
7. Susan Livingston faced the British troops coolly calmly and bravely.
8. They insisted on searching the kitchen the dining room and the upstairs bedrooms.
9. She boldly cleverly and successfully prevented the British from noticing a stack of valuable papers.
10. Susan Livingston's courage nerve and spirit are remembered to this day.

7.g.6 Commas and phrases in series

In general, use a comma after every phrase (except the last) in a series of prepositional, participial, gerund, or infinitive phrases.

Abraham Lincoln believed that government should be "of the people, by the people, and for the people."

Speaking loudly, gesturing forcefully, and gazing earnestly, the speaker held her audience spellbound.

Eating properly, exercising regularly, and getting enough sleep will keep you in good health.

For the new year Judy resolved to finish her quilt, to study Latin, and to learn tennis.

7.g.7 Commas and main clauses in series

Use a comma after every main clause (except the last) in a series.

The lights dimmed, the conductor came out, and the orchestra began to play.

AVOIDING ERRORS WITH COMMAS AND ITEMS IN A SERIES

1. Do not place a comma after the conjunction in a series.

   NOT The local diner is fast, convenient, and, cheap.
   BUT The local diner is fast, convenient, and cheap.

2. Do not use commas between items in a series if all the items are joined by *and*, *or*, or *nor*.

   NOT In a well-known song Dionne Warwick sings of "trains, and boats, and planes."
   BUT In a well-known song Dionne Warwick sings of "trains and boats and planes."

EXERCISE 21. Rewrite each of the following sentences that needs commas. Two of the sentences are correct as written.

1. Robert Shields and Lorene Yarnell are two mimes who are known for their wit and imagination and agility.
2. They perform in public squares in formal theaters and on nationwide television.
3. Their routines manage to touch to amuse and to enchant audiences everywhere.
4. Using only gestures, Shields and Yarnell are able to convey actions characters and moods.
5. They first performed in San Francisco's Union Square, where they appeared daily attracted crowds and entertained for free.
6. Everyone stops to watch the pair, smiling left and right beating invisible drums and taking bows.
7. Shields and Yarnell capture people's attention make them see themselves and make them laugh at themselves.
8. They often select someone from the crowd to stare at or to imitate or to follow playfully.
9. Some "victims" become furious others act amused and many eagerly join the act.
10. The mimes' impish charm usually enables people to shed reality to consider fantasy and to have a good laugh.

CLAUSES AND PHRASES

7.g.8 Commas and main clauses (compound sentences)

Use commas between the main clauses in a compound sentence.

Place the comma before the coordinating conjunction (*and, but, or,* or *for*).

> Robert Frost never finished college, but he became one of America's most celebrated poets.
>
> Frost lived in Vermont and New Hampshire, and his poems contain many images from New England.

The comma may be omitted if the main clauses are very short, but it is always a good idea to use the comma.

The lights dimmed and the hall became quiet.
The lights dimmed, and the hall became quiet.

Always use a comma if the sentence might be confusing without it.

NOT   I opened the window✗and the door slammed shut.
BUT   I opened the window, and the door slammed shut.

Main clauses may also be separated by a semicolon instead of a comma and a coordinating conjunction. Always use a semicolon when a conjunctive adverb is used.

I do not usually enjoy opera music; however, I adore every note of *The Magic Flute*.

EXERCISE 22. Rewrite each of the following sentences that needs commas. Two of the sentences are correct as written.

1. More food is produced today than ever before but only one third of the world is well fed.
2. One sixth of the people in the world are often hungry and one half suffer from malnutrition.
3. Many people are unaware of the hunger problem in the world for the poor often lack the means to publicize their problems.
4. The rich nations are mostly in the northern hemisphere and poor nations are mainly in the southern hemisphere.
5. The average Indian family spends more than half of its income on food and still does not have enough to eat.
6. India's population will almost double in the next thirty years but its food supply may not keep pace.
7. New kinds of wheat and rice have already helped greatly but cannot by themselves eliminate hunger.
8. More than half of the new grain has gone to the richest 30 percent of the world's population and less than half has gone to the poorest 70 percent.
9. New "miracle" seeds will not solve the hunger problem for better farming methods are needed.
10. Rich nations must do more to help the poor and poor nations must do more to help themselves.

AVOIDING ERRORS WITH COMMAS AND MAIN CLAUSES

1. In a sentence with two main clauses, remember to use a coordinating conjunction or a semicolon between the clauses. If you use only a comma between main clauses, you will create a run-on sentence (also called a comma splice or comma fault).

   NOT   It was early in the season⨯every team was still a contender.

   BUT   It was early in the season, **and** every team was still a contender.

   OR   It was early in the season; every team was still a contender.

   OR   It was early in the season; therefore, every team was still a contender.

2. Do not confuse a sentence that has a compound verb (see 2.g) with a sentence that has two main clauses. A compound verb with two parts does not require a comma between the parts. A sentence with two main clauses does require a comma between the clauses.

   NOT   Our team rarely wins the pennant⨯ but every year has the league's most loyal fans.

   BUT   Our team rarely wins the pennant but every year has the league's most loyal fans. [compound verb]

   NOT   Our team rarely wins the pennant⨯but every year it has the league's most loyal fans.

   BUT   Our team rarely wins the pennant, but every year it has the league's most loyal fans. [compound sentence]

7.g.9 Commas and adjective clauses

Use commas to set off a nonessential adjective clause.

A nonessential adjective clause is not necessary to the meaning of the sentence. A nonessential (or nonrestrictive) adjective clause can be thought of as an *extra* clause. It gives *extra* information about a noun or pronoun. Remember that an *extra* adjective clause calls for *extra* commas.

Castroville, which is a city in northern California, is the artichoke capital of the world. [nonessential clause: *which is a city in northern California*]
Our cousin Ken, who is a dentist, keeps bees as a hobby. [nonessential clause: *who is a dentist*]

Do not use commas with a clause that is essential to the meaning of the sentence. An essential (or restrictive) adjective clause gives necessary information about a noun or pronoun.

People who dislike warm weather should not vacation in Florida. [essential clause: *who dislike warm weather*]
The state that I want to visit is Virginia. [essential clause: *that I want to visit*]

EXERCISE 23. Rewrite each of the following sentences that needs commas. Some of the sentences are correct as written.

1. Marian Anderson who is one of the world's most celebrated contralto singers was born in Philadelphia in 1902.
2. She began singing in the choir of the local Baptist chapel that her family attended.
3. The first song that Anderson remembers singing in public was "Dear to the Heart of the Shepherd."
4. Her voice which has enormous range was already remarkable at age six.
5. The church community which recognized the young girl's talent helped her to begin a singing career.

6. A special fund which was raised at a church concert enabled Anderson to study voice with Giuseppe Boghetti.

7. She soon won a contest that was sponsored by a Philadelphia choral society.

8. Anderson next won first prize at a singing competition that was held in New York City.

9. Her 1933 concert tour of Europe and South America which received rave reviews established her reputation.

10. The conductor Toscanini called Anderson's voice one that "comes only once in a hundred years."

11. It is a deep contralto voice which handles spirituals as well as opera.

12. Anderson excels in music that expresses pensiveness and humility.

13. In 1939 she sang at the Lincoln Memorial in a concert that was sponsored by Eleanor Roosevelt.

14. In 1955 Anderson made her debut with the Metropolitan Opera which is the leading American opera company.

15. Her performance which marked the first time that a black had sung there earned thunderous applause.

16. By then she was one of the most praised singers who had ever performed in the United States.

17. Her walls are now covered with honorary degrees that colleges and universities have awarded her.

18. In 1958 she was one of the delegates who represented the United States at the United Nations.

19. One of the greatest honors that Anderson has received was the Presidential Medal of Freedom.

20. Anderson's voice is one that is not easily forgotten.

7.g.10 Commas and adverb clauses

Use commas to set off introductory adverb clauses.

After I hiked in Yosemite, nothing else could impress me.
Although it was a rugged climb to Nevada Falls, the vista from the top was worth every step.
If you ever have the chance, be sure to visit Yosemite.

Use commas to set off adverb clauses in an internal position that interrupt the flow of the sentence.

> The mountains, because they were formed by glaciers, have spectacular shapes.

In general, do not use a comma before an adverb clause at the end of a sentence unless the clause is parenthetical (or extra) or unless the sentence would be misread without the comma.

> Let's go to the beach tomorrow if the weather is good.
> It is supposed to be in the seventies, if we can believe the forecast. [comma because clause is parenthetical]
> It looked like a gloomy day, when the sun suddenly came out from behind the clouds. [comma to avoid misreading]

Use a comma if an adverb clause at the end of a sentence begins with *although* or *though*.

> The skiing was terrific that day, although it never did stop snowing.

Use a comma if an adverb clause at the end of a sentence begins with *while* meaning "whereas."

> Some people like downhill skiing, while others prefer cross-country skiing.

Use a comma before an *as* or *since* clause at the end of the sentence if the clause tells "why."

> We skied on Mount Lincoln, since the lift lines were too long on Mount Disney.

Do not use a comma before *while, as,* or *since* if the clause tells "when."

> Lois and Linda have been skiing since they were old enough to walk.

EXERCISE 24. Rewrite each of the following sentences that needs commas. Some of the sentences are correct as written.

1. While most of the United States is developed much land still remains as wilderness.
2. When Congress passed the Wilderness Act in 1964 some people objected.
3. Although wild rivers and forests are important people need electricity and wood.
4. Conservationists lobby for more wilderness areas while utility companies insist on the need for more hydroelectric power.
5. Many people after they see Yellowstone or the Grand Tetons begin to sympathize with conservationists.
6. Conservationist groups have been arguing against dams since the Glen Canyon Dam was built in 1964.
7. Because trees can be replanted lumber companies defend logging as not harmful.
8. Before Florida's Okefenokee Swamp was made a refuge thousands of trees were cut down.
9. The Okefenokee was not permanently destroyed because trees grow rapidly in swamps.
10. If the Wilderness Act proves effective no more wilderness land will be needlessly destroyed.

7.g.11 Commas and participial phrases and infinitive phrases

Use commas to set off participles, infinitives, participial phrases, and infinitive phrases that are not essential to the meaning of the sentence.

Remember that an *extra* (nonessential) participle, infinitive, participial phrase, or infinitive phrase requires *extra* commas.

NOTE: Always use a comma after an introductory participle or participial phrase.

> Jogging along the beach, I had not a care in the world. [introductory participial phrase]
> The copper teapot, sparkling, looked like new. [participle]

The children ripped open their presents, giggling excitedly. [participial phrase]

To stay fit, John plays squash. [infinitive phrase]

I am not quite sure, to be honest, what you are trying to say. [infinitive phrase]

She sounded unenthusiastic, to tell the truth. [infinitive phrase]

Do not set off participles, infinitives, participial phrases, or infinitive phrases if they are essential to the meaning of the sentence.

The young lady *selling programs* looks just like Veronica. [essential participial phrase]

The white car *parked out front* belongs to Nancy and Tim. [essential participial phrase]

To perform at Carnegie Hall is her dream. [essential infinitive phrase]

He wants *to move to the country*. [essential infinitive phrase]

I always have too many errands *to run* on Saturdays. [essential infinitive]

7.g.12 Commas and introductory prepositional phrases

Use a comma to set off a single short introductory prepositional phrase only if the sentence would be misread without the comma.

In the distance we saw Aspen Mountain.

On her lap sat a large marmalade cat.

During the rush hour, traffic is worse than ever. [comma to avoid confusion in reading]

Use a comma after the final phrase in a succession of connected introductory prepositional phrases unless it is immediately followed by the verb. Do not use commas *between* introductory prepositional phrases unless the phrases are a series (see the following examples and 7.g.6).

On the morning of the day of graduation, Margot woke up early. [comma after a succession of connected prepositional phrases]

On the left burner of the stove was a huge pot of beans. [no comma after a succession of connected prepositional phrases immediately followed by the verb]

EXERCISE 25. Rewrite each of the following sentences that needs commas. Some of the sentences are correct as written.

1. Looking through the 1922 edition of Emily Post's *Etiquette* one realizes how much life in America has changed since that time.

2. Some of Post's topics and concerns sound like those of another world to tell the truth.

3. In Emily Post's world after-dinner finger bowls were commonplace.

4. Walking across a ballroom a lady took steps of medium length and never swung her arms.

5. The butler dressed in a black waistcoat and a white lawn tie guarded the combination of the silver safe.

6. A gentleman accompanying a lady anywhere at night offered his arm.

7. For some occasions footmen wore buff satin waistcoats and lace cravats.

8. To be polite ladies always wore their stylish hats in the dining room.

9. A lady never asked a gentleman to dance.

10. "Roughing it" meant sitting in steamer chairs around a roaring fire.

11. Gracious hostesses greeted guests shaking hands and smiling sweetly.

12. Polite folk held debutante balls to present young ladies to society.

13. Young couples engaged to be wed announced their good news formally.

14. After the announcement of the engagement came the formal dinner honoring the happy couple.

15. During the salad course of the elaborate dinner the young lady's father toasted the health of his daughter and future son-in-law.
16. During the engagement dinner conversation was always about the happy event.
17. Gentlemen knew not to bow to a lady from a window.
18. To wear tweed coats and flannel trousers in town showed bad taste.
19. Elbows on the table were considered bad form to be sure.
20. There was no occasion requiring greater dignity than the opera.

EXTRA EXPRESSIONS

7.g.13 Commas and appositives

Use commas to set off an appositive unless it is essential to the meaning of the sentence.

An appositive is a noun or pronoun (sometimes with modifiers) that is placed next to another noun or pronoun to identify it or to give additional information about it. A nonessential (or nonrestrictive) appositive can be considered an *extra* appositive that needs *extra* commas.

Nonessential appositives
John Muir, the naturalist and explorer, founded the Sierra Club.
Our dog, an Irish setter, needs a lot of exercise.
I am reading *Emma*, the novel by Jane Austen.

A nonessential appositive is sometimes placed before the word to which it refers.

A doctor, William Carlos Williams wrote poetry between office visits.

Do not use commas for an appositive that is essential to the meaning of the sentence. An appositive is essential if it gives necessary information about the noun or pronoun that it precedes or follows.

Essential appositives

Louisa May Alcott's novel *Little Women* describes incidents from the author's life. [If commas were placed around the essential appositive *Little Women*, the sentence would seem to mean that this was Alcott's *only* novel.]

Franklin Roosevelt married his distant cousin Eleanor. [no comma before *Eleanor* because Roosevelt had more than one distant cousin]

EXERCISE 26. Rewrite each of the following sentences that needs commas. Some of the sentences are correct as written.

1. The American writer Gertrude Stein was born in 1874 and died in 1946.

2. She was the daughter of Daniel and Amelia Stein two German immigrants.

3. At Radcliffe College Gertrude studied under William James the eminent American philosopher.

4. After college she settled in Paris the home of many important writers and artists.

5. Pablo Picasso and Henri Matisse both unknown artists at the time became her friends.

6. Stein was one of the first to realize the importance of Cubism and Fauvism two experimental movements in painting.

7. She greatly encouraged the American poet E. E. Cummings.

8. She also helped Ernest Hemingway a young American newspaper reporter at the time.

9. Her memoirs *The Autobiography of Alice B. Toklas* describe those years in Paris.

10. Her other works include a book of stories *Three Lives* and an opera *The Mother of Us All*.

7.g.14 Commas and parenthetical expressions

Use commas to set off conjunctive adverbs, interjections, and other parenthetical expressions.

The term *parenthetical expression* does not mean that the words are surrounded by parentheses. A parenthetical expression is simply an extra expression.

By the way, the jazz festival was a great success.
It was, to tell the truth, almost impossible to get tickets.
Tania wrote early for tickets; consequently, she got front-row seats.
She did not like some of the experimental pieces, however.

No, reindeer are not deer.
The name reindeer is misleading, isn't it?

7.g.15 Commas and direct address

Use commas to set off words or names used in direct address.

Mr. Watson, come here.
No, my friend, you are not mistaken.
Thank you for the information, Mrs. Winant.

EXERCISE 27. Rewrite each of the following sentences, inserting any necessary commas.

1. Believe it or not many well-known "facts" are not true.
2. Yes a falling apple may have inspired Isaac Newton.
3. To tell the truth we have only one biographer's word for it.
4. John Fitch invented the steamboat; nevertheless Robert Fulton has gotten all the credit.
5. Fulton's boat in fact came twenty years after Fitch's.
6. Fitch died poor and unknown sad to say.
7. The American Revolution moreover has unfactual "facts."
8. Contrary to many accounts Lexington was not the first town to resist the British.
9. That honor Salem residents goes to you.
10. No guns were actually fired at Salem however.
11. Did you know sports fans that baseball was *not* born in America?
12. Indeed references to baseball appeared in England in 1744.

13. Baseball was not played in the United States in point of fact until 1839.

14. Abner Doubleday never wrote a single word about baseball by the way.

15. No most people in Columbus' day did *not* believe the world was flat.

16. On the contrary Ptolemy had proved the earth round as early as the second century A.D.

17. Ptolemy's estimate of the earth's size however was far off.

18. You think it surprising don't you that so many "known" facts are not all factual?

19. Well rest assured that some things are still sacred.

20. Yes Virginia there really is a Santa Claus.

REVIEW EXERCISE F. Rewrite each of the following sentences that needs commas. One of the sentences is correct as written.

1. Richard "Pancho" Gonzales the famous tennis player got his start in tennis by accident at age twelve.

2. He had asked his mother for a bicycle but she bought him a tennis racket instead.

3. That tennis racket was the start of a career that would one day be legendary.

4. Noted for his powerful serve Gonzales soon became a championship amateur tennis player.

5. In 1949 he was the top amateur player in the United States playing on the U.S. Davis Cup team.

6. After playing on that team Gonzales quit amateur tennis in 1949.

7. Turning professional Gonzales again scored many successes.

8. In 1969 for example he won the longest Wimbledon match ever played.

9. In that match Gonzales who was forty-one defeated Charles Pasarell who was twenty-five.

10. A great athlete Pancho Gonzales still plays tennis regularly.

AVOIDING ERRORS WITH COMMAS (GENERAL)

1. When you use commas to set off an expression in the middle of a sentence, do not forget to place a comma both *before* and *after* the expression.

   NOT   There is, however✕one other possibility.
   BUT   There is, however, one other possibility.

   NOT   Calliope music, the squeaky music on a carousel✕is made by steam whistles.
   BUT   Calliope music, the squeaky music on a carousel, is made by steam whistles.

2. Do not place a comma between the parts of a compound subject or a compound object if all the parts are separated by *and* or *or* (see 2.d and 2.j).

   NOT   One week in Maine✕and one week in Boston turned out to be a great vacation.
   BUT   One week in Maine and one week in Boston turned out to be a great vacation.

   NOT   He should bring his camera✕and plenty of film.
   BUT   He should bring his camera and plenty of film.

3. Do not place a comma before an indirect quotation or an indirect question. (An indirect quotation or an indirect question does not quote the person's exact words.)

   NOT   Carlos Alberto said✕that he loved soccer.
   BUT   Carlos Alberto said that he loved soccer.

   NOT   The sportscaster asked him✕if he ever tired of playing soccer.
   BUT   The sportscaster asked him if he ever tired of playing soccer.

REVIEW EXERCISE G. Rewrite each of the following sentences that needs commas. Three sentences are correct as written.

1. Writers thinkers and philosophers have long dreamed of utopia.
2. Utopia is a land where everything is ideal including laws government and social conditions.
3. The word *utopia* which means "no place" in Greek was coined in 1516 as a book title by Sir Thomas More.
4. More's *Utopia* tells of an island where all people are equal and prosperous and wise.
5. Although More was the first to use the word Plato had described a utopian world as early as 375 B.C. in *The Republic.*
6. In the society of Plato's utopian world the state controls education art and religion.
7. Ancient utopias existed only in literature but in recent centuries people have tried to establish real utopian communities.
8. Brook Farm a community founded near Boston in 1841 was based on agriculture and education.
9. To combine thinking and working to guarantee mental freedom and to permit a wholesome life were the goals of Brook Farm.
10. Members believed in the value of work intellect and leisure.
11. Nathaniel Hawthorne was a charter member and Ralph Waldo Emerson was an interested visitor.
12. Hawthorne later wrote a novel *The Blythedale Romance* based on his experience at Brook Farm.
13. People who lived there earned a dollar a day for all work.
14. Income for the community came from the school which was one of the finest of the day.
15. Students studied Latin philosophy and music and they also got training in agriculture.
16. Although Brook Farm was a noble experiment the community broke up in 1849.
17. Today people often use the term *utopian* to describe plans of reform that seem impractical or impossible.

18. Literary utopias are often satirical; for example the title of the novel *Erewhon* is almost the word *nowhere* spelled backwards.

19. Gilbert and Sullivan poked fun at utopian visions in their operetta *Utopia Ltd.*

20. Until someone discovers a real Shangri-La utopia will continue to exist in our imaginations only.

REVIEW EXERCISE H. Correct all errors in comma usage in the following business letter. Rewrite each phrase or sentence, adding commas that are needed and deleting those that are incorrect. You should find twenty-five errors.

400 Walnut Street
Louisville Kentucky 40201
January 4 1980

Ms. Lydia Stone Sports Editor
Louisville *Star*
456 Post Street
Louisville Kentucky 40201

Dear Ms. Stone:

[1]Your recent article of December 20 1979 discusses what you call problems with the Olympic Games. [2]I found your article incomplete, because it fails to make any suggestions for improvement.

[3]For a different view of the subject let me refer you to an article in the September 1, 1979 issue of *Saturday Review*. [4]The article by Roger M. Williams senior editor offers three good pieces of advice. [5]To begin Williams suggests that the team aspects of the Games be played down. [6]Athletes could Williams suggests be grouped by sport. [7]If they were grouped by sport rather than by country there would be more emphasis on individual athletes, and less emphasis on national teams.

[8]Furthermore athletes should not share housing only with teammates Williams believes. [9]Getting athletes from Canada, Poland and China to share rooms, is a small

but important step toward increasing understanding among different peoples.

[10]His last suggestion to give the Games a permanent home is also worth considering. [11]The Summer Games could be held in Greece and the Winter Games could take place somewhere else.

Although I do not agree with all of Mr. Williams' suggestions, I found his article helpful because it offered ideas to consider.

Sincerely

Scott Horton, Jr.

Scott Horton Jr.

7.h SEMICOLONS

A semicolon is a mark of punctuation that is used to indicate a pause in a sentence that is too strong for a comma but not strong enough for a period. Semicolons are used to separate main clauses in a compound sentence. They are also used to separate clauses or items in a series that themselves contain commas. Except for those two situations, semicolons are not often used. Learn to use semicolons properly, but be careful not to overuse them.

7.h.1 Semicolons to separate main clauses

Use a semicolon to separate two main clauses that are not joined by a coordinating conjunction (*and, but, or,* or *for*).

It is sometimes difficult to decide whether to separate two main clauses with a semicolon or whether to make the clauses into two separate sentences. Use a semicolon if the two clauses are very closely related and seem to belong together in the same sentence.

Claes Oldenburg designs sculptures and monuments of familiar objects; the sculpture *Hamburger with Pickle and*

Tomato Attached is one of his best-known works. [The two clauses are closely related; use a semicolon.]

Claes Oldenburg is an American sculptor who was a leader in the pop art movement in the sixties. He is best known for his sculptures of such common objects as electric fans and vacuum cleaners. [The clauses are both about Oldenburg, but they deal with different aspects of his work. Therefore, make them into two separate sentences.]

Use a semicolon to separate main clauses joined by conjunctive adverbs such as *however, therefore, nevertheless, moreover, furthermore,* and *consequently*, or by such expressions as *for example* and *that is*.

In general, a conjunctive adverb or an expression like *for example* is followed by a comma.

Oldenburg once designed a giant pair of scissors as a monument; moreover, he has done sculptures of electric fans and vacuum cleaners.

EXERCISE 28. Rewrite each of the following sentences, inserting semicolons where necessary.

1. Everyone knows the importance of a balanced diet few people can plan or prepare a healthful meal, however.
2. Food should be fresh and natural in fact, many vegetables are more nutritious raw than cooked.
3. Boiling destroys vitamins therefore, steamed vegetables are more healthful.
4. Our bodies need protein and vitamins therefore, it is essential for us to know which foods provide them.
5. Dairy products supply large amounts of protein cheese and milk are especially good sources.
6. Beef is only about 25 percent protein you actually get more protein from turkey, soybeans, and some cheeses.
7. Proteins eaten together are better than those eaten separately for example, wheat and beans provide one-third more protein when eaten together than when eaten separately.
8. Vitamin A is supplied by eggs and liver it can also be obtained from some fruits and vegetables.

9. Citrus fruits and juices contain Vitamin C oranges and grapefruits are particularly good sources of Vitamin C.

10. Vitamin E is found in wheat germ it can also be obtained from vegetable oils.

7.h.2 Semicolons to separate expressions containing commas

Use a semicolon to separate clauses or items in a series that themselves contain commas.

Three well-known American writers are Nikki Giovanni, who is a poet; Margaret Walker, who is a novelist; and Lorraine Hansberry, who is a playwright.

Three former Olympic medal winners are Dorothy Hamill, a skater; Nadia Comaneci, a gymnast; and Micki King, a diver.

EXERCISE 29. Rewrite each of the following sentences, inserting semicolons where necessary. In some sentences you will have to replace a comma with a semicolon.

1. George Washington was born on February 22, 1732 became President on April 30, 1789 and died on December 14, 1799.

2. Many historic inns and buildings are said to have housed Washington, his career took him numerous places.

3. Places where Washington stayed include Cambridge, Massachusetts Philadelphia, Pennsylvania and Mount Vernon, Virginia.

4. Most people probably assume that Washington attended college, however, his education was probably rather limited.

5. It is true that Washington was tall, strong, and commanding, furthermore, he was noted for his honesty and intelligence.

6. He was not always popular with women in fact, he was turned down by the first woman he wanted to marry.

7. Washington was not always a victorious general his first campaign ended in his own surrender.

8. Washington was a gifted politician, many consider him one of our best Presidents.

9. His cabinet included Thomas Jefferson, a Democratic Republican, Alexander Hamilton, a Federalist, and John Adams, a Federalist.

10. Famous likenesses of George Washington were done by Gilbert Stuart, the American painter, Jean Antoine Houdon, the French sculptor, and John Copley, the American portrait painter.

7.i COLONS

Use a colon to introduce a list, especially after such expressions as *the following* or *as follows*.

A colon is a rather formal punctuation mark that is used to introduce lists and quotations. A colon also has several conventional uses, including the following:

- writing the time
- referring to sections of the Bible
- writing business letters

My grandparents' garden contains the following flowers: camellias, pansies, peonies, tulips, marigolds, and chrysanthemums.

Try the following methods to break in a new pair of jeans: 1) Roll them in the dirt, 2) rub them with sandpaper, and 3) wear them in the bathtub.

Samuel Taylor Coleridge's poem "The Rime of the Ancient Mariner" includes the following often-quoted lines: "Water, water, everywhere,/Nor any drop to drink."

7:05 A.M.	4:30 P.M.
Genesis 5:23	Proverbs 12:2-3
Dear Madam:	Dear Sir:

EXERCISE 30. Rewrite each of the following sentences, inserting colons where necessary.

1. Tracing your family history requires at least three things time, patience, and the ability to listen.

2. It is probably best to begin by interviewing members of your family your parents, your aunts and uncles, your grandparents, your great-grandparents.

3. Your close relatives may have tales about other family members great-uncles, third cousins, great-great-grand-mothers, and others that you have never met.

4. Try the following ways of finding information about your family history 1) Look in attics and cellars, 2) inquire about old pictures, and 3) try to find old clothing and jewelry.

5. Drawing your family tree may require research into several sources oral histories, family albums, and public records.

6. Family records include the following materials letters, diaries, and bills.

7. Family information can also be found in the following books, trophies, and recipes.

8. Along with information you will probably gather several keepsakes your father's war medal, your grandmother's first embroidered handkerchief, and your great-uncle's pocket watch.

9. Heed the warning of one family historian "The longest list in my life is the list of people I wish I had interviewed before they died."

10. Studying your family history has several results getting to know your immediate family better, learning about more distant family members, and learning some history.

7.j HYPHENS

Hyphens have two main uses in English. First, they are used in certain compound words and compound numbers. Second, they are used to divide words at the end of a line.

7.j.1 Hyphens in compound words and numbers

Use hyphens in some compound words and numbers.

There are many compound words that require hyphens as an essential part of their spelling. If you are unsure whether a hyphen is required in a particular compound word, check your dictionary.

brother-in-law	audio-visual
vice-president	sharp-witted
secretary-general	pan-fry

In addition, compound numbers from *twenty-one* through *ninety-nine* require hyphens.

fifty-five	fifty-fifth

7.j.2 Hyphens to divide words at the end of a line

In order to keep the right-hand margins of your paper fairly even when writing or typing, you may want to use a hyphen to divide a word at the end of a line.

Do not divide one-syllable words or a single syllable within a word.

NOT	fri̶n̶ge	ask̶e̶d	gasoli̶n̶e
BUT	fringe	asked	gas-o-line

In general, divide multisyllable words that have double consonants between the double consonants.

puz-zled	pos-sess	rab-bit
shop-ping	slip-per	mis-spell

If a suffix such as -*ing* or -*est* has been added to a word that ends in two consonants, divide the word after the two consonants.

crush-ing	pick-ing	bill-ing
press-ing	fast-est	tall-est

If a word contains two consonants standing between two vowels, ordinarily divide it between the consonants.

prin-cess	pow-der
pub-lic	thun-der

Divide a word with a prefix or a suffix after the prefix (such as *ex-*, *re-*, and *un-*) or before the suffix (such as *-able*, *-ish*, and *-ous*).

ex-President	reli-able
re-nominate	squeam-ish
un-tie	fam-ous

To divide a compound noun or a compound adjective that is generally written as one word, place the hyphen between the two base words.

ant-eater	keep-sake
home-made	key-hole

Divide a hyphenated compound word at the point where the hyphen occurs.

anti-hero	law-abiding
hand-me-down	pro-Austrian

Do not divide proper nouns, proper adjectives, or abbreviations.

NOT	Hep⁄burn	Dickens⁄ian
BUT	Hepburn	Dickensian
NOT	ab⁄brev.	UN⁄ICEF
BUT	abbrev.	UNICEF

The dictionary should be your final authority for word division (see 6.d.2).

EXERCISE 31. Decide whether or not each of the following words could be divided if it appeared at the end of a line. Rewrite each word that could be divided, adding hyphens at the point or points of division.

1. greatest	8. somewhere	15. returnable
2. introd.	9. flood	16. pothole
3. Jeffersonian	10. trapping	17. backpacker
4. Bradbury	11. walked	18. mother-in-law
5. complaining	12. wiggled	19. Kennedy
6. center	13. timber	20. UNESCO
7. nonsense	14. repeat	

7.k APOSTROPHES

Apostrophes are used to form the possessive of nouns and indefinite pronouns; to form contractions; and to form the plural of letters, numbers, signs, and words used as words.

7.k.1 Apostrophes for the possessive

Remember that *possessive* means "belonging to." The expression *Mary's book* means "the book that belongs to Mary." The apostrophe is often used in showing that something belongs to someone.

1. **nouns not ending in *s***
   Use the apostrophe and *s* to form the possessive of singular and plural nouns not ending in *s*. This rule applies to both common and proper nouns.

Ron Guidry's fastball	men's department
Canada's mountains	the children's zoo
the poet's life	the alumni's reunion

   NOTE: Do not italicize the 's in the possessive of italicized titles of works.

   Business Week's feature story
   Annie Hall's theme

2. **plural nouns ending in *s***
   Use the apostrophe alone to form the possessive of plural nouns ending in *s*. This rule applies to both common and proper nouns.

the Beatles' album	the players' association
the Rotarians' meeting	the planets' orbits
the Jets' victory	the skiers' lodge

3. **singular nouns ending in *s***
   When forming the possessive of a singular noun ending in *s* (or an *s* sound), count the number of syllables in the word. If the noun has only *one* syllable, use the apos-

trophe and an *s* to form the possessive. If the noun has *more than one* syllable, usually add the apostrophe alone.

Willie Mays's fans   the duchess' title
the press's rights   C. S. Lewis' works
Langston Hughes's poetry   Richard Rodgers' music

NOTE: Some books do not follow the preceding rule. Although the rule states the preferred usage, it is not incorrect to use both an apostrophe and an *s* after a singular noun of more than one syllable ending in *s*.

the duchess's title   C. S. Lewis's works

4. **indefinite pronouns**

Use the apostrophe and an *s* to form the possessive of indefinite pronouns such as *someone, one, anybody, everybody, somebody else,* and *each other.*

one's own room   someone else's plan
everybody's vote   anybody's guess

5. **compound words**

Use the apostrophe and an *s* (or the apostrophe alone) after the last part of a hyphenated or nonhyphenated compound.

my great-grandmother's pearls
his sister-in-law's birthday
the district attorney's victory
the court of law's rule

6. **joint possession**

If two or more persons possess something jointly, use the possessive form of only the last name mentioned. The names of businesses and organizations should also be treated in this way.

Iris and Steve's new house
Rodgers and Hammerstein's musical
Bell and Howell's equipment
Fortnum and Mason's marmalade

7. **individual possession by more than one person**

If two or more persons (or things) each possess something individually, put each name in the possessive form.

Hemingway's and Fitzgerald's biographies
Peggy's and Bill's apartments
Haydn's and Mozart's music

AVOIDING ERRORS WITH APOSTROPHES IN POSSESSIVES

1. Do not forget to use the apostrophe to form the possessive.

   NOT   This is Tania office.
   NOT   This is Tanias office.
   BUT   This is Tania's office.

   NOT   He forgot the visitors names.
   BUT   He forgot the visitors' names.

2. Do not misplace the apostrophe in the possessive of a noun that ends in *s*.

   NOT   They studied E. E. Cumming's poetry.
   BUT   They studied E. E. Cummings' poetry. [The poet's name is E. E. Cummings with an *s* at the end.]
   OR   They studied E. E. Cummings's poetry.

3. Do not use an apostrophe with the possessive personal pronouns that end in *s* (*his, hers, its, ours, yours, theirs*). These pronouns are already possessive in form.

   NOT   Is this book your's?
   NOT   Is this book yours'?
   BUT   Is this book yours?

EXERCISE 32. Write the possessive form of each of the following items. Two of the items are correct as written.

1. the Palmers
2. geese
3. oxen
4. theirs
5. flowers
6. high schools
7. three dollars
8. spices
9. tomatoes
10. ribbons
11. the Cardinals
12. jazz songs
13. everybody
14. mice
15. yours
16. swimmers
17. the actresses
18. grandparents
19. ten days
20. many cats

EXERCISE 33. Write the possessive form of each of the following nouns.

1. Los Angeles
2. school district
3. class
4. *Jane Eyre*
5. Greece
6. Frank Norris
7. apple
8. children
9. bicycle
10. Beverly Sills
11. oxen
12. trees
13. tug-of-war
14. peonies
15. Sanders
16. pepper
17. princess
18. jeans
19. Socrates
20. Ecuador

EXERCISE 34. Rewrite each of the following items that has errors in the formation of the possessive. Some of the items are correct as written.

1. womens' wear
2. a cat and it's kittens
3. the Whites children
4. The prize is yours.
5. a man coat
6. the brother's noses
7. Jimmy Carters election
8. my sister's-in-law dog
9. two cousins friendship
10. Ann's and Ed's wedding
11. Dicken's novels
12. Angela scrapbook
13. *Silas Marner's* ending
14. Bob and Al's names
15. Mrs. Jones's job
16. the class' project
17. Laurel and Hardy's film
18. men's colleges
19. two cents worth
20. everyones' opinion

7.k.2 Apostrophes in contractions

Use the apostrophe in place of letters omitted in contractions.

A **contraction** is a single word made up of two words that have been combined by omitting letters and substituting an apostrophe for them. The following list contains some familiar contractions:

contraction	original words
I'm	I am
you're	you are
it's	it is (or it has)
there's	there is (or there has)
who's	who is (or who has)
I've	I have
they've	they have
he'd	he had (or he would)
you'd	you had (or you would)
couldn't	could not
doesn't	does not
weren't	were not
wouldn't	would not
won't	will not
we'll	we will
we're	we are

Use the apostrophe in place of omitted numerals in such expressions as "the class of '95" and "the '84 Presidential race."

EXERCISE 35. Write the contracted form of each of the following pairs of words.

1. we will
2. she is
3. you have
4. do not
5. should not
6. they had
7. I have
8. she would
9. can not
10. who has

AVOIDING ERRORS WITH CONTRACTIONS

1. Do not forget to use the apostrophe in contractions.

   NOT I dont remember the combination to my locker.
   BUT I **don't** remember the combination to my locker.

2. Do not confuse the contraction *it's* (*it is*) with the possessive pronoun *its*. Use the apostrophe only when you mean *it is*.

   NOT Its going to be a beautiful house as soon as you take care of it's garden.
   BUT **It's** going to be a beautiful house as soon as you take care of **its** garden.

3. Do not misplace the apostrophe when writing contractions.

   NOT You should'nt plan to go to the beach.
   BUT You **shouldn't** plan to go to the beach.

EXERCISE 36. Choose the expression in parentheses that correctly completes each of the following sentences.

1. Meg is the one (who's/whose) paying.
2. I am sure that the Palmers (wont/won't) be late.
3. The cat was licking (its/it's) fur.
4. Margot (doesn't/does'nt) live here any more.
5. Chris and John (could'nt/couldn't) go with us tonight.
6. (Were/We're) sitting on top of the world.
7. (It's/Its) only a paper moon.
8. Look what (they've/theyv'e) done to that street.
9. (Shell/She'll) be here any minute now.
10. (You're/Your) the greatest!

7.k.3 Apostrophes for special plurals

Use the apostrophe and an *s* to form the plural of letters, numerals, signs, and words used as words.

Italicize (underline) the letter, numeral, sign, or word, but do not italicize the *'s*.

His *r*'s look just like *v*'s.
Some of the *4*'s look like *9*'s.
Please be sure to write *and*'s instead of *&*'s.
The editor changed all the *round*'s to *around*'s.

EXERCISE 37. Select the expression in parentheses that correctly completes each sentence below.

1. Catherine got all (*As/A*'s) last semester.
2. My little brother already knows his (*ABC*'s/*ABC*s).
3. There are three (Smith's/Smiths) in our class.

4. Dot all your (*i*'s/*i*s) and cross all your (*t*'s/*t*s).
5. All the (*for*'s/*for*s) should be (*four*'s/*four*s) in this paper.
6. Count by (threes/three's) to twenty-one.
7. Mind your (*p*'s/*p*s) and (*q*'s/*q*s)!
8. The animals all came in (two's/twos) on Noah's Ark.
9. First of all, change all the (*percent*s/*percent*'s) to (%s/%'s).
10. Sometimes I use too many (*and*'s/*and*s) in my writing.

REVIEW EXERCISE I. Rewrite each of the following sentences, inserting apostrophes where necessary.

1. Its often surprising to see the names of some cities and countries in their own languages.
2. In Italian, for example, Venices name is Venezia.
3. The Germans name for their country is not Germany, but Deutschland.
4. Some people dont know that Poles call their country Polska.
5. The Finns name for their country is *not* Finland; it is Suomi.
6. The Germans name for the city that we call Munich is München.
7. If you were Russian, youd know Moscow as Moskva.
8. Your writing would also be different: Your *s*s would look like *c*s, and your *r*s would look like *p*s.
9. Moreover, youd know many more Romanovs than Smiths!
10. Spains name in Spanish, by the way, is España.
11. A rose may be a rose, but Switzerland isnt Switzerland; its Schweiz, Suisse, or Svizzera.
12. Thats one other confusing thing about some names: Countries occasionally *change* their names.
13. Leningrads name is the same in Russian, but it was once called Petrograd and St. Petersburg.
14. Thailands name used to be Siam.
15. Irans ancient name was Persia.
16. Not long ago Zaires name was Congo.
17. Istanbul wasnt always Istanbul; it used to be Constantinople.

18. Todays Sri Lanka was yesterdays Ceylon.

19. Of course, dont forget that New York was once New Amsterdam.

20. Whos to say that New York wont someday be New Something Else?

7.1 QUOTATION MARKS

Quotation marks are used most often to indicate other people's words. They are also used to punctuate titles of short works. Quotation marks are placed both at the beginning and the end of the material you wish to enclose.

7.1.1 Quotation marks for direct quotations

Use quotation marks to enclose a direct quotation.

1. **capitalization of quotations**

Capitalize the first word of a quotation that is a complete sentence. Do not capitalize a quotation that is only a partial sentence.

> Samuel Clemens once said, **"A** classic is something that everybody wants to have read and nobody wants to read."
> It was Ambrose Bierce who defined a novel as **"a** short story padded."

2. **setting off quotations**

Set off a quotation with a comma (or a colon) only if the quotation is a complete sentence. Do not set off a quotation that is a partial sentence.

> G. K. Chesterton once said, "Golf is an expensive way of playing marbles."
> Bill Veeck described baseball as "almost the only orderly thing in a very unorderly world."

3. **interrupted quotations**

When a quotation is interrupted by such words as *she wrote* or *he said*, enclose both parts of the separated quotation in quotation marks. Set off each part with some kind of punctuation. If the second part of the quotation is a complete sentence, be sure to begin it with a capital letter.

> "Luis Tiant," Reggie Jackson once declared, "is the Fred Astaire of baseball."
>
> "Since baseball time is measured only in outs, all you have to do is succeed utterly; keep hitting, keep the rally alive, and you have defeated time," wrote Roger Angell. "You remain forever young."

4. **indirect quotations**

In writing you may want to use someone else's words without quoting them exactly. This is called using an indirect quotation. An indirect quotation is often preceded by *that*. Do not use quotation marks in an indirect quotation (or in an indirect question).

> **EXACT WORDS:** "Writing free verse is like playing tennis with the net down." —Robert Frost
>
> **INDIRECT QUOTATION:** Robert Frost said that writing free verse was like playing tennis without a net.

5. **single quotation marks**

Use single quotation marks to enclose a quotation within a quotation.

> It was George Bernard Shaw who said, "Some men look at things as they are and wonder, 'Why?' I dream of things that never were and ask, 'Why not?'"

6. **quotation marks in dialogue**

In writing dialogue, begin a new paragraph and use a new set of quotation marks every time the speaker changes.

> As she drank her coffee, Mrs. Rosen tried one subject after another to engage Mrs. Harris's attention.
>
> "Do you feel this hot weather, Grandma? I am afraid you

are over the stove too much. Let those naughty children have a cold lunch occasionally."

"No'm, I don't mind the heat. It's apt to come on like this for a spell in May. I don't feel the stove. I'm accustomed to it."

"Oh, so am I! But I get very impatient with my cooking in hot weather. Do you miss your old home in Tennessee very much, Grandma?"

"No'm, I can't say I do. Mr. Templeton thought Colorado was a better place to bring up the children."

"But you had things much more comfortable down there, I'm sure. These little wooden houses are too hot in summer."

"Yes'm, we were more comfortable. We had more room."

"And a flower-garden, and beautiful old trees, Mrs. Templeton told me."

"Yes'm, we had a great deal of shade."

—Willa Cather

EXERCISE 38. Rewrite each of the following sentences, changing each direct quotation into an indirect quotation.

EXAMPLE When she came from Japan to dance with Martha Graham's company, Takako Asakawa said, "I couldn't believe I was performing with them."

ANSWER *When she came from Japan to dance with Martha Graham's company, Takako Asakawa said that she couldn't believe she was performing with them.*

1. She recalled walking into the office and saying, "I want to see my teacher, Martha."
2. Asakawa explained, "This is our tradition."
3. She also explained, "When you go to study with a master, the first thing you must do is introduce yourself."
4. She then laughed, remembering, "The way I spoke, no one understood me."
5. Asakawa smiled and said, "I have learned a great deal from Martha."

7.1.2 Quotation marks for titles of short works

Use quotation marks to enclose titles of short works such as stories, poems, essays, newspaper and periodical articles, chapters, songs, and television episodes.

"The Diamond as Big as the Ritz" [short story]
"Casey at the Bat" [poem]
"Self-Reliance" [essay]
"Come Back, Dizzy" [newspaper article]
"Salutations of Courtesy" [chapter]
"This Land Is Your Land" [song]

NOTE: Italicize (underline) titles of long works, such as books, films, and plays, and the names of periodicals, newspapers, television series, and paintings (see 7.m.1).

EXERCISE 39. Rewrite each of the following sentences, adding quotation marks where necessary.

1. Age before beauty, said Clare Boothe Luce as she stepped aside to let Dorothy Parker pass.
2. Pearls before swine, replied Parker without a moment's hesitation.
3. The cynical humor of Dorothy Parker is seen in such poems as Epitaph for a Darling Lady.
4. Big Blonde is one of her many short stories about New York in the twenties.
5. The story The Standard of Living gives a witty description of two stenographers who go window-shopping on Fifth Avenue.
6. One article, Mrs. Post Enlarges on Etiquette, is Parker's review of Emily Post's *Etiquette*.
7. Far from Well is the title of her review of *The House at Pooh Corner*.
8. Parker's complimentary and appreciative essay on Ernest Hemingway is entitled The Artist's Reward.
9. She was one of the wittiest people in the world and one of the saddest, wrote Brendan Gill about Dorothy Parker.
10. Indeed, Parker asked to have the following epitaph: Excuse my dust.

QUOTATION MARKS WITH OTHER MARKS OF PUNCTUATION

1. Always place a comma or a period *inside* closing quotation marks.

   "The frog," states an old African proverb, "does not jump without a reason."

2. Always place a semicolon or a colon *outside* closing quotation marks.

   Baseball French includes the following terms: *circuit*, which means "home run"; *programme double*, which means "double-header"; and *gaucher*, which means "left-handed pitcher."

   Russian contains no fewer than four basic verbs that mean "go": *khodit*, *idti*, *ezdit*, and *ekhat*.

3. Place the question mark or exclamation point *inside* closing quotation marks when the question mark or exclamation point is part of the quotation.

   In his poem "Jordan" George Herbert asks, "Is there in truth no beauty?"

   Walt Whitman's poem "O Captain! My Captain!" is about President Lincoln.

   Place the question mark or exclamation point *outside* quotation marks when the question mark or exclamation point is part of the entire sentence.

   Have you read "Mending Wall"?

   How I adored "After Apple-Picking"!

   NOTE: If both your sentence and the quotation at the end of your sentence need a question mark or an exclamation point, use only *one* question mark or exclamation point placed *inside* the quotation marks.

   What film star is supposed to have asked, "Tennis, anyone?"

AVOIDING ERRORS WITH QUOTATION MARKS

Do not forget to place quotation marks (single or double) both *before* and *after* the quoted material. Omitting the closing quotation marks is a frequent error.

NOT   "Everybody leave the room! he shouted.
BUT   "Everybody leave the room!" he shouted.

NOT   Have you read "The Garden Party?
BUT   Have you read "The Garden Party"?

EXERCISE 40. Rewrite each of the following sentences, adding quotation marks where necessary. One of the sentences is correct as written.

1. Someone once said, It is good to be witty and wise.

2. James Howell seemed to think differently when he remarked, God send you more wit, and me more money.

3. Another thought comes from Ralph Waldo Emerson, who commented that true wit never made us laugh.

4. Better a witty fool than a foolish wit, wrote Shakespeare.

5. One of today's most common meanings for *wit* is given in the *Macmillan Dictionary*: ability to make keenly perceptive observations and express such observations in an amusing, ingenious, or unusual way.

6. True wit is nature to advantage dressed, /What oft was thought, but ne'er so well expressed, said Alexander Pope.

7. Wit is the salt of conversation, maintained William Hazlitt, not the food.

8. In 1771 Tobias Smollett wrote, One wit, like a knuckle of ham in soup, gives a zest and flavour to the dish, but more than one serves only to spoil the pottage.

9. Was George Herbert warning us when he said, Wit's an unruly engine, wildly striking/Sometimes a friend, sometimes the engineer ?

10. The following proverb seems to offer good advice: If you have wit, use it to please and not to hurt.

7.m ITALICS (UNDERLINING)

Italic type is a special slanted type that is used in printing. (*This sentence is printed in italics.*) Indicate italics on the typewriter or in handwriting by underlining. (This sentence is underlined.)

7.m.1 Italics for titles of long works

Italicize (underline) titles of long artistic works, including books, films, plays, long poems, and long musical compositions. Also italicize the names of newspapers, periodicals, television series, and works of art.

> *Jane Eyre* [book]
> *North by Northwest* [film]
> *Our Town* [play]
> *Leaves of Grass* [long poem]
> *An American in Paris* [long musical composition]
> *Starry Night* [painting]
> *Chicago Tribune* [newspaper]
> *Newsweek* [periodical]
> *The Today Show* [television series]

NOTE: Use quotation marks, not italics, to enclose titles of short works such as stories, poems, essays, newspaper and periodical articles, chapters, songs, and television episodes (see 7.1.2).

7.m.2 Italics for names of spacecraft, airplanes, ships, trains

Italicize (underline) names of spacecraft, airplanes, ships, and trains.

Apollo-Soyuz [spacecraft]
U.S.S *Independence*[1]
  [ship]

Air Force One [airplane]
San Francisco Zephyr
  [train]

---

[1]Do not italicize *U.S.S.* in the name of a ship.

EXERCISE 41. Rewrite each of the following sentences, underlining those elements that should be italicized.

1. One theme of the play Peter Pan is the universal desire to remain forever a child.
2. Novels such as Charlotte's Web and The Adventures of Huckleberry Finn explore the world from the point of view of a child.
3. The French painter Renoir portrayed children in such paintings as Little Girl in a Pinafore.
4. Henry James's novel What Maisie Knew describes an adult's world through the eyes of a child.
5. Fantasia is only one of many children's films that appeal to adults as much as to young people.
6. The Children's Corner is one of Claude Debussy's well-known compositions for the piano.
7. Boats with names such as Daisy-O or Molly M are often named after children.
8. People of all ages love Dylan Thomas' long poem A Child's Christmas in Wales.
9. Another traditional holiday favorite is Tchaikovsky's ballet The Nutcracker Suite, which tells the story of a child's dream.
10. Youngsters who visit New York's Central Park can play near a statue based on the novel Alice's Adventures in Wonderland.

7.m.3 Italics for foreign words

Italicize (underline) foreign words and expressions that are not used frequently in English.

Do not italicize a foreign word or expression that is commonly used in English. For example, *vice versa* is usually not italicized, although it is a Latin expression. The French expression *comme il faut* ("as it should be") is normally italicized because it is less frequently used. Enclose in quotation marks the English translation of a foreign word or expression.

If you are unsure about whether to italicize a foreign word or expression, check your dictionary.

My boss said to do the report ***tout de suite***. [foreign expression not used frequently in English]
We spent the afternoon baking **éclairs**. [foreign word commonly used in English]

7.m.4 Italics for words and letters used to represent themselves

Italicize (underline) words, letters, numbers, and signs used to represent themselves.

Be careful not to mix up the words ***gorilla*** and ***guerilla***.
The letters ***q*** and ***w*** sometimes stick on this typewriter.
Some people expect good luck from the number **7**.
Use the **$** sign to express amounts of money.

NOTE: Use an 's to indicate the plural of words, letters, numbers, and signs used to represent themselves. This 's is not italicized.

She crossed all her ***t*'s** but forgot to dot her ***i*'s**.
I changed all the ***round*'s** to ***around*'s**.

EXERCISE 42. Rewrite each of the following sentences, underlining those items that should be italicized.

1. The word alphabet is a combination of the Greek words alpha and beta.
2. Alpha and beta come from the Hebrew words aleph ("ox") and beth ("house").
3. From alpha and beta we get the letters a and b.
4. The dollar sign ($) was formed from the letters U and S.
5. The so-called Arabic numerals—1, 2, 3—probably originated in India.
6. For some reason the first Arabic system had no numeral 0.
7. The Roman numeral V seems to represent the fingers of an open hand.

8. The word algebra comes from the Arabic word al-jabr ("the reuniting").

9. The English word safari traces its origin to the Arabic word safara ("to travel").

10. The informal expression so long may come from the Arabic word of greeting and farewell, salaam ("peace").

EXERCISE 43. Rewrite each of the following items, underlining those elements that should be italicized and adding quotation marks where necessary.

1. H. T. Moore's book The Novels of John Steinbeck
2. Steinbeck's novel East of Eden
3. the play Of Mice and Men
4. Woody Guthrie's song Tom Joad
5. Steinbeck's short story The Leader of the People
6. the film Viva Zapata!
7. the essay John Steinbeck, Californian
8. the newspaper article Nobel Prize for Literature Goes to John Steinbeck
9. Steinbeck's short novel The Moon Is Down
10. the film The Grapes of Wrath

7.n PARENTHESES

Use parentheses to set off extra material.

Commas are also used to set off extra material. The difference between the two marks is one of degree—that is, how much you want to set off the extra material. Commas are used to set off extra material that is fairly closely related to the rest of the sentence. Parentheses are used for material that is less closely related. Use parentheses for material that is not part of the main statement but is, nevertheless, important enough to include.

Heinrich Schliemann (German archaeologist, 1822–1890) discovered the ruins of ancient Troy.
Troy is located in Turkey, about 4 miles (6.4 kilometers) from the mouth of the Dardenelles.

NOTE: Use commas, not parentheses, to enclose material closely related to the sentence.

> Schliemann, unlike most archaeologists, had a career in business until he was forty-one.

If a sentence (or phrase) within parentheses is contained within another sentence, it is not capitalized (nor does it need a period). If such a sentence or phrase appears at the end of the other sentence, be sure to place the period *after* the closing parenthesis. If a complete sentence in parentheses stands by itself, a capital letter and a period are needed.

> Archaeologists debated for years which layer of the excavation (nine different cities were built on the site) was the Troy of Homer's poem.
> Troy was a city of some importance in Roman times (when it was called Ilium).
> Schliemann had been a student of Homer since childhood. (In fact, he knew the verses of Homer by heart.)

EXERCISE 44. Rewrite each of the following sentences, adding parentheses where necessary.

1. Nancy Caldwell Sorel's book *Word People* published by American Heritage Press tells surprising stories of people who became words.
2. (Another book with similar stories is Robert Hendrickson's *Human Words*.
3. The unit of electrical power called the watt was named after James Watt 1736-1819.
4. The ohm admittedly a strange-sounding name for an electrical term was named after George Ohm.
5. Even the humble sandwich was named after John Montagu, fourth Earl of Sandwich 1718-1792.
6. The earl was supposed to have been the first to eat food between two pieces of bread. (Such a meal allowed him to eat on the run.
7. The saxophone no, it was not named after the telephone takes its name from its inventor, Joseph Sax.

8. The next time you eat something made of graham graham crackers or graham bread, for example think of Sylvester Graham.

9. Silhouette portraits are named for Étienne de Silhouette, a frugal French finance minister. (Silhouettes were less expensive than regular portraits.

10. The circus performer Jules Léotard popularized and named leotards worn now by dancers as well as circus artists).

SECTION REVIEW EXERCISE. Rewrite each of the following sentences, correcting all errors in capitalization and punctuation. You should find fifty errors.

1. Do you know anything about ragtime music.

2. If youve ever listened to a player piano you have probably heard ragtime.

3. Ragtime originated with black pianists along the mississippi river at the end of the nineteenth century.

4. Its rhythms show the influence of many different kinds of music minstrel songs show tunes and sentimental ballads.

5. Elements of Africa of the Caribbean and of the U.S. south can be heard in the ragtime beat.

6. The left hand plays a slow regular beat the right hand plays a fast syncopated beat.

7. Because of the tricky rhythm the music was called "ragged time" which then turned into ragtime.

8. The greatest ragtime composer was a black pianist Scott Joplin.

9. Joplin the son of a former slave was born in Texarkana, Texas in 1868.

10. He left home at fourteen, and began playing the piano in saloons in the Mississippi valley.

11. He studied music at George Smith college a methodist institution.

12. Joplin performed regularly at will and walker williams' Maple Leaf Club.

13. As a tribute to that club he composed "The Maple Leaf Rag in 1899.

14. "The Maple Leaf' will make me the king of ragtime compos-
    ers, he told a friend.
15. Joplins prediction came true, The Maple Leaf Rag became a
    nationwide hit.
16. As enthusiasm for ragtime swept America Joplin left the
    club circuit moved to St Louis and turned to composing.
17. He considered ragtime a unique and serious form of music,
    that was Americas answer to european music.
18. He went on to compose a ballet *The Ragtime Dance* and an
    opera Treemonisha.
19. Although they were both dismal failures at the time *Tree-
    monisha* was revived with great success in the 1970s.
20. Interest in ragtime continues, in fact, the Ragtime Society
    publishes the journal The Ragtimes.

8

GLOSSARY OF USAGE PROBLEMS

8 Glossary of Usage Problems

As a speaker and a writer of English, you must be concerned with usage because you need to know that different language is appropriate in different situations. Some words and expressions are appropriate for casual uses, such as speaking with your family and friends and writing friendly letters. A more formal kind of language is required when you write compositions, test answers, or business letters or when you speak in an interview or a class report.

There are certain uses of English that are considered "preferred usage" because they are, as the term implies, preferred by most educated speakers and writers. Preferred usage is the language you should use in your writing for school and in formal speaking situations.

The glossary that follows presents some particularly troublesome matters of preferred usage. The glossary will give you guidance, for example, in choosing between two words that are often confused. It will also discuss certain words and expressions that you should avoid completely in speaking and writing.

a, an The article *a* is used when the word that follows begins with a consonant sound. Therefore, words that begin with a sounded *h* and the sound /yū/ are preceded by *a*: *a day, a book, a heart, a hen, a universe.* The article *an* is used when the word that follows begins with a vowel sound: *an accordion, an herb.*

about, at about Do not use the word *at* before *about* when expressing an approximation.

We will be leaving for the airport **about** 3:00 P.M.

ad, photo *Ad* and *photo* are short versions of *advertisement* and *photograph*. These abbreviated forms should be used only in informal circumstances. Use the longer words in all formal writing.

There was a four-color **photograph** in the magazine **advertisement**.

ain't *Ain't* is unacceptable in speaking and in writing unless you are quoting the exact words of a character or real person. Say or write, instead, *I am not, she is not, he is not,* and so on.

all right Never make one word out of this expression. *Alright* is incorrect.

Is the baby **all right**?

all the farther, all the faster These are very informal expressions. It is much better to use *as far as* and *as fast as* in speaking and writing.

Is this **as fast as** you can walk?

bad, badly See page 81.

beat, win *Beat* implies action done to something or someone else. *Win* refers to the act of gaining a victory. You *beat* an opponent in order to *win* a game, prize, or contest.

I am watching the Dallas Cowboys **beat** the Philadelphia Eagles.
If the New York Giants **win** most of their remaining games, they can make the playoffs.

beside, besides These are different words; use each of them carefully. *Beside* means "located at the side of." *Besides* means "in addition to."

The cat sat **beside** the refrigerator.
I lost two buttons **besides** a shoelace!

between, among *Between* should be used in reference to two things or persons. *Among* should be used in reference to groups of three or more.

I stood **between** my mother and father.
I sat **among** my seven cousins.

EXERCISE 1. In each of the sentences below, select from the choices in parentheses the word or phrase that represents preferred usage.

1. George Washington was the son of (an/a) wealthy planter.
2. Washington did not have to (beat/win) an election; he was unanimously chosen as the first President.
3. (Besides/Beside) intelligence, Washington was also noted for honesty and poise.
4. Important (between/among) the many debated issues of Washington's administration were taxation and state debts.
5. Washington's policies were accepted as (alright/all right) by most people.
6. There are no (photographs/photos) of Washington available, but there are many fine portraits.
7. While President, Washington traveled (all the farther/as far as) he could through the country.
8. Washington's wisdom and his friendly nature helped keep the American Revolution free of (a/an) usual byproduct of revolutions—a reign of terror.
9. It (is not/ain't) true that Washington accepted a third term in office.
10. Washington died (about/at about) 10 P.M. on December 14, 1799.

EXERCISE 2. Write ten sentences, each of which uses one of the following words or expressions correctly: *a, an, about* (meaning "approximately"), *all right, beat* (meaning "defeat"), *win, beside, besides, between, among.*

bring, take   Do not use these words interchangeably. *Bring* means to move something to the speaker or writer. *Take* means to move something away from the speaker or writer.

Will you **bring** my glasses to me?
Jeff will **take** my dog out for a walk.

cannot help but   This is a double negative because the word *but* is used in a negative sense. Leave the *but* out and you will be speaking and writing correctly.

I **cannot help** liking that old jazz record.

climb up   *Climb* means "to go up." Therefore, to add *up* after *climb* is redundant and incorrect.

These stairs are steep; **climb** them slowly.

could of, might of   These incorrect expressions result from the careless pronunciation of *could have* and *might have*. Speak clearly, and use the correct expressions when writing.

I **might have** won the singing award if I had not lost my voice the day before the contest!

different from, different than   Use *different from* before a noun or pronoun. It is all right to use *different than* before clauses and some phrases.

Ice dancing is **different from** figure skating.
The cloud formations are **different than** they were yesterday.
His whole appearance was **different** in the morning **than** at night.

discover, invent   These words are not interchangeable. When you discover something, you are the first person to learn about its existence. When you invent something, you have thought up or created something brand new.

Balboa **discovered** the Pacific Ocean.
Elias Howe **invented** the sewing machine.

doesn't, don't   These are different contractions. *Doesn't* is a shorter form of *does not* that is used with *he, she, it,* and singular nouns. *Don't* is a shorter form of *do not* that is used with *I, you, we, they,* and plural nouns.

My dad is one commuter who **doesn't** mind long bus rides.
Subway riders **don't** expect comfortable traveling conditions.

done   Never use *done* alone. Always add a form of *be* or *have,* as in *is done, had done.* Also, do not use *done* when you mean *did.*

We **have done** all we can with this messy room.
We **did** all we could.

each other, one another   Use *each other* when talking or writing about two people (or animals). Use *one another* when talking or writing about three or more.

The two lovebirds gave **each other** a kiss.
The people in my ten-member club all trust **one another**.

end result   A *result* is anything that comes about as a consequence of something else; it happens after something else or at the end of it. For that reason, to speak of an *end result* is to be redundant—and incorrect.

The **result** of the voting was the reelection of the incumbent candidate.

EXERCISE 3. In each of the sentences below, select from the choices in parentheses the word or phrase that represents preferred usage.

1. At the name *Lincoln*, one (cannot help but think/cannot help thinking) of a tall, gaunt man with a homely face.
2. One of Abraham Lincoln's early business ventures failed, but he was able to (climb up/climb) out of debt.
3. Possessed of great physical strength as a young man, Lincoln (discovered/invented) that he could easily handle bullies.
4. Lincoln's failure to support an extension of slavery (might have/might of) caused his defeat in a race for the Senate.
5. As President, Lincoln said he learned a great deal from citizens who (brought/took) their problems to him.
6. Many people (doesn't/don't) know that Lee surrendered to Grant only one month after Lincoln's second inauguration.
7. One of the most famous things Lincoln (did/done) was to issue the Emancipation Proclamation, freeing the slaves.
8. The (end result/result) of the Emancipation Proclamation was renewed enthusiasm for the war.
9. There were other issues besides slavery dividing the North and South from (each other/one another).
10. Reality turned out to be (different from/different than) Lincoln's dreams because his plans to restore the Union to harmony were demolished by an assassin's bullet.

EXERCISE 4. Write ten sentences, each of which uses one of the following words or expressions correctly: *bring, take, different from, discover, invent, doesn't, don't, done, each other, one another.*

farther, further   *Farther* should be used in reference to physical distance. *Further* should be used in reference to degree or time.

> Compact cars can go **farther** than big cars on a gallon of gasoline.
> Argue no **further**—I will do as you suggest!

fewer, less Use *fewer* when referring to nouns that can be counted. Use *less* when referring to nouns that cannot be counted. *Less* can also be used with figures that are seen as a single amount or quantity.

> **less** rice
> **fewer** apples
> The rent was **less** than $400. [The money is treated as a single sum, not as individual dollars.]

frightened of Use *frightened by*. Do not use *frightened of*. *Afraid of* is correct, however.

> I was **frightened by** the sudden clap of thunder.
> Are you **afraid of** lightning?

good, well See page 81.

had of See *could of*, page 413.

had ought Do not use *had* before *ought*.

> You **ought** to do your homework early in the evening.

in, into, in to *In* means "within." *Into* indicates movement, usually from the outside to the inside. *In to* is a separate use of *in* and of *to* that should not be confused with the single word *into*. Here, *in* is used as an adverb, and *to* introduces a prepositional phrase.

> The baby was **in** the bassinet.
> Gillian put the rabbit **into** the basket.
> Cara went **in to** her piano class.

in regard to Do not add *s* to *regard* in this particular expression. *As regards* is fine, however.

> The President was reluctant to institute new policies **in regard to** the oil situation.
> **As regards** your question, I will not be able to give you an answer until next week.

irregardless, regardless Use *regardless*. The prefix *ir-* and the suffix *-less* both have negative meanings. When used together, they produce a double negative, *irregardless*, which is incorrect.

Regardless of the snow and cold temperatures, Robby always runs in his red jogging shorts.

this kind, these kinds Always use two words that agree with each other in number. *This* and *that* are singular and should be used with *kind, sort,* and *type* and with a singular noun. *These* and *those* are plural and should be used with *kinds, sorts,* and *types* and with a plural noun.

this kind of injury
these types of figurines

kind of a Do not add *a* to the expression *kind of*. This rule also applies to *sort of* and *type of*.

What **kind of** costume is that?

lay, lie People often confuse these two words in both writing and speaking. *Lay* means "put" or "place"; it takes a direct object. *Lie* means "recline" or "be positioned"; it never takes an object.

Lay the bar of soap on the sink edge.
I like to **lie** under a shade tree in summer.

Problems arise particularly in using the principal parts of these verbs. Notice, for example, that the past tense of *lie* is *lay*. Learn all the principal parts of these verbs.

BASIC VERB	lay	lie
PRESENT PARTICIPLE	laying	lying
PAST TENSE	laid	lay
PAST PARTICIPLE	laid	lain

EXERCISE 5. In each of the sentences below, select from the choices in parentheses the word or phrase that represents preferred usage.

1. Theodore Roosevelt was not (frightened by/frightened of) the tremendous power he assumed at President McKinley's death.
2. (In regards to/In regard to) Roosevelt's great spirit and determination, it could already be seen when he was a young child.
3. Roosevelt was told that he (had ought/ought) to build up his frail health by participating in rough physical activities.
4. The "teddy bear" became a (kind of/kind of a) symbol of Roosevelt.
5. Roosevelt's conservation efforts went (farther/further) than those of previous Presidents.
6. Roosevelt wrote no (less/fewer) than forty books in his lifetime.
7. Always adventurous in spirit, Roosevelt was the first President to step (in/into) one of the new "horseless carriages" and go for a ride.
8. (Irregardless/Regardless) of the hostility of business to his "trust busting," Theodore Roosevelt had much domestic support.
9. Explorations and big-game expeditions were an important part of his life; (these kind/these kinds) of activities made Roosevelt an interesting man.
10. Roosevelt died on January 6, 1919, as he (lay/laid) asleep in his bed.

EXERCISE 6. Write ten sentences, each of which uses one of the following words or expressions correctly: *farther, further, fewer, less, frightened by, into, this kind, these kinds, that type, those types.*

EXERCISE 7. Write five sentences, each of which uses a different principal part of *lie* or *lay*.

learn, teach These words have different meanings. *Learn* means to receive knowledge, and *teach* means to give knowledge.

I **learned** how to find the hypotenuse of a triangle.
My brother **teaches** history to freshmen at Ithaca College.

leave, let *Leave* means "go away" and *let* means "allow" or "permit." Some people use the expressions *leave alone* and *let alone* to mean the same thing, but these expressions have different meanings. *Leave alone* means "go away from" and *let alone* means "permit to be alone."

The speaker threatened to **leave** the meeting.
Let him try to open the door by himself.
Do not **leave** me **alone** with this terrible head cold.
Let your sister **alone** so she can do her homework.

like, as *Like* is a preposition and introduces a prepositional phrase. *As* is a subordinating conjunction and introduces a subordinate clause. Therefore, do not use *like* before a clause.

He drives **like** a maniac.
She thinks **as** I do.

moral, morale The word *moral* relates to the distinction between right and wrong. *Morale* means "mental condition," in terms of enthusiasm, confidence, willingness to endure hardship, and the like. Be careful to distinguish between these two words.

The lawyer said that he could not make a **moral** judgment.
The **morale** of the losing team was very low.

most, almost *Most* means "greatest in amount." It should not be used to mean *almost*.

Beth wants to learn the **most** she can about biology.
It is **almost** time to lock up.

off of   Use *off* without *of*.

> Please take your hat **off** the bed.

or, nor   *Or* must be used with *either*. *Nor* goes with *neither*.

> Julie will play **either** Scrabble **or** Monopoly.
> Tarikh wants **neither** the carrot **nor** the celery stalk.

raise, rise   *Raise* means "to cause to move upward." The verb *raise* always takes an object. *Rise* means "to go up of itself." *Rise* is an intransitive verb and does not take an object.

> We will **raise** the flag at sunrise.
> A helium-filled balloon will **rise** high into the air.

reason is because   *Because* means "for the reason that." Therefore, do not use *because* after *reason is*. That expression is repetitive. Use *that* after *reason is*, or use *because* alone. Your writing will be more direct if you use *because*.

> The **reason** Nazale is tired **is that** she stayed up too late last night.
> Dan loves the summer **because** swimming in the ocean is his favorite pastime.

respectfully, respectively   Use these two words carefully. *Respectfully* means "with respect." *Respectively* means "in the order named."

> The man shook the President's hand **respectfully**.
> Ann and Arlene are, **respectively**, my aunt and cousin.

EXERCISE 8. In each of the sentences below, select from the choices in parentheses the word or phrase that represents preferred usage.

1. One reason John F. Kennedy inspired American youth is (because/that) he was the youngest elected President in our history.

2. Kennedy lifted the nation's (moral/morale) in a rousing inaugural address.

3. He had (learned/taught) much at Harvard, from which he had graduated with honors.

4. Commander Kennedy was (most/almost) killed in World War II when his PT boat was sunk by an enemy destroyer.

5. Miraculously, Kennedy was neither killed (nor/or) rendered incapable by the accident, and he was able to help rescue his crew.

6. Kennedy had to (leave/let) public life behind temporarily when he was operated on in 1954 and 1955 for a spinal injury suffered during the war.

7. There were two crises involving Cuba during Kennedy's administration: the Bay of Pigs invasion and the Cuban Missile Crisis. These crises were a defeat and a victory, (respectfully/respectively).

8. Kennedy compelled the Soviet Union to take its offensive missiles (off of/off) the island of Cuba.

9. Kennedy entertained at the White House (like/as) a man interested in literature and the arts.

10. Unfortunately, all the spirits that (rose/raised) at the young President's election were dashed at his assassination in Dallas.

EXERCISE 9. Write ten sentences, each of which uses one of the following words correctly: *learn, teach, leave, let, moral, morale, raise, rise, respectfully, respectively.*

rob, steal *Steal* is the general word meaning to take away dishonestly, usually in a secret manner. *Rob* is a stronger word and involves the idea of force or violence. These verbs differ in the objects they take. The object of the verb *steal* is the thing taken; the object of *rob* is the person from whom something is taken. Remember: A thief steals *something* but robs *someone*.

The thieves **stole** my television set while no one was at home.

I was **robbed** of my purse in the subway.

says, said *Says* is the present tense. *Said* is the past tense. Be careful not to use *says* when you mean *said*.

Dad **said** we should feed the fish daily while he was away.

seeing as how This expression is incorrect. *Since* and *because* are correct, and they sound better in speaking and in writing.

Since it's so late, why don't you stay for dinner?

sit, set *Sit* means "place oneself in a sitting position." *Sit* rarely takes an object. *Set* means "place" or "put" and usually takes an object.

Sit down and stop talking.
Set the flowers on the mantelpiece, please.

try and, try to Do not use the phrase *try and* in speaking or writing. It is incorrect. Use *try to*.

Try to climb into that saddle one more time.

varied, various *Varied* means "made up of different things." *Various* means "different from one another" or "of different kinds." It is usually used with a plural noun.

This restaurant has a **varied** menu.
Marge shows **various** breeds of dogs.

way, ways Do not use *ways* to mean distance, as in the expression *a long ways off*. The correct word is *way*.

Graduation is a long **way off**.

where, that *Where* is often used incorrectly to mean *that*, as in the expression *I read where*. Do not use *where* when you mean *that*.

I read **that** the price of oil is still going up.

where . . . at Use *where* without *at*.

Where **are** you going to stay?

who, whom See pages 66, 166–67.

EXERCISE 10. In each of the sentences below, select from the choices in parentheses the word or phrase that represents preferred usage.

1. (Seeing as how/Since) he led the nation through the Great Depression and World War II, many people consider Franklin Roosevelt one of the greatest Presidents.
2. Roosevelt had been (robbed/stolen) of the ability to walk in 1921 by an attack of infantile paralysis.
3. It was Warm Springs, Georgia, (where/where at) he took winter treatments to recover from the illness, although he never regained the use of his leg muscles.
4. His wife, Eleanor, encouraged him to (try and/try to) continue his political career in spite of his paralysis.
5. When Roosevelt took office in 1933 in the midst of the Great Depression, the nation's recovery seemed a long (way/ways) off.
6. Roosevelt would not (set/sit) content, however, while the nation faced such hard times.
7. People today read in history books (where/that) Roosevelt conducted the most daring Presidential leadership in American history.
8. He (set/sit) more bills before Congress during its seventy-third session than any other President has in a comparable time period.
9. His (varied/various) legislative program included the Tennessee Valley Authority, the National Recovery Act, and the Social Security Act.
10. Roosevelt often (said/says), "The only thing to fear is fear itself."

EXERCISE 11. Write five sentences, each of which uses one of the following words correctly: *rob, steal, sit, set, varied.*

REVIEW EXERCISE A. In each of the sentences below, select from the choices in parentheses the word or phrase that represents preferred usage.

1. (Since/Seeing as how) miniature objects have fascinated people since early civilizations, it is no wonder that doll-houses are very popular today.

2. A (kind of/kind of a) miniature house was made as far back as Egypt's Twelfth Dynasty.

3. Most collectors want to know (where/where at) the first miniature dollhouse was built.

4. The first actual dollhouse (might of/might have) been the one constructed for the Duke of Bavaria in 1558.

5. Miniature fanciers (cannot help thinking/cannot help but think) that the Queen's Dolls' House, presented to Queen Mary of England in 1924, is the most fabulous structure of its kind.

6. Work on the Queen's Dolls' House began in 1920, but it was four years before the builders (done/had done) the finishing touches.

7. Many adults will go (all the farther/as far as) young people do in putting together a collection of miniatures.

8. The National Association of Miniature Enthusiasts has helped collectors (invent/discover) other collectors.

9. (Almost/Most) all of the dollhouses put together today are furnished in the styles of earlier periods.

10. The success of miniatures (lays/lies) in how closely they duplicate the original objects.

11. Most serious collectors believe their pieces (had ought/ought) to be based on a scale of one inch to one foot.

12. Miniaturists try to put pieces from the same historical period (into/in to) each room.

13. It is also important to coordinate rooms of miniatures that go with (each other/one another).

14. Miniaturists always (try to/try and) collect originals.

15. Reproductions are neither as valuable (or/nor) as charming as originals.

16. (Beside/Besides) a good tweezers, a would-be miniature maker needs a pliers, a metal rule, and a contour marker.

17. Along with (these kind/these kinds) of tools, the miniature maker must have agile fingers and a careful nature.
18. Handling of miniatures should be done (respectfully/respectively) so as not to break delicate pieces.
19. Many collectors travel a long (way/ways) to find a sought-after piece.
20. (Irregardless/Regardless) of the funds a collector has available, miniatures can be a rewarding hobby.

REVIEW EXERCISE B. In each of the sentences below, select from the choices in parentheses the word or phrase that represents preferred usage.

1. Photography was (discovered/invented) about 1839.
2. The hobby of collecting photographs is (different from/different than) that of taking them.
3. People have been collecting (photographs/photos) since the earliest days of photography.
4. Historical evidence (don't/doesn't) show a strong interest in the hobby, however, until the early 1970s.
5. (Almost/Most) all serious photograph collectors do more than simply assemble old family snapshots.
6. Collectors (learn/teach) about the outstanding photographers and the different schools of photography.
7. The reason some people hesitate to collect photographs is (because/that) prints seem easy to duplicate.
8. Actually, (in regards to/as regards) collectible photographs, many are quite rare and some are even one of a kind.
9. Some photographers destroy (various/varied) negatives after a limited number of prints have been made.
10. The (fewer/less) the number of prints of a particular photograph, the higher is the value of each of those prints.
11. A person who is (frightened of/frightened by) the thought of paying more than $100 for a collectible photograph should probably find a cheaper hobby.
12. At auctions, collectors are thrilled at (beating/winning) others in bidding on particular prints.
13. Dealers offer helpful advice to the collector who is ready to (bring/take) a new print home.

14. To be certain the condition of a photograph remains (all right/alright), several precautions should be taken.
15. A photograph should not be pressed (among/between) two other photographs.
16. Care should be taken to insure that light and humidity (are not/ain't) allowed to age and warp precious prints.
17. To display a photograph to best advantage, it is often appropriate to place it (beside/besides) another photograph.
18. The (result/end result) of good care is collectible prints that frequently increase in value.
19. A beginning collector whose (moral/morale) is low while looking for a fine print will not stay unhappy for long.
20. The discovery of a rare photograph will (raise/rise) the spirits of any collector.

REVIEW EXERCISE C. Write twenty sentences, each of which uses one of the following words or expressions correctly: *a, bring, farther, learn, rob, ought, lying* (meaning "reclining"), *about* (meaning "approximately"), *different from, fewer, moral, set, regardless, beat* (meaning "defeat"), *invent, frightened by, raise, climb, let, varied.*

REVIEW EXERCISE D. Write twenty sentences, each of which uses one of the following words or expressions correctly: *an, take, further, teach, leave, steal, could have, in regard to, all right, discover, less, morale, sat, various, lain, win, doesn't, into, this kind, respectfully.*

REVIEW EXERCISE E. Write twenty sentences, each of which uses one of the following words or expressions correctly: *beside, don't, these kinds, respectively, sit, might have, different than, result, lay* (past tense of *lie*), *raised, besides, between, done, each other, rise, lay* (meaning "put"), *among, one another, lie* (meaning "recline"), *nor.*

CATCHING, CLASSIFYING, AND CORRECTING ERRORS

9 Catching, Classifying, and Correcting Errors

Errors in sentences spoil writing. Grammatical errors annoy and often confuse readers. As a writer, you should learn to avoid errors. Now is a good time for you to do this. You can do it in two ways: (1) You can learn to reduce the chances of making errors when you first write a sentence, and (2) you can learn as an editor to spot and correct errors by looking back over what you have written.

One thing is certain: You cannot learn to *avoid* errors unless you can recognize them. Part of your job in learning to write is to get to know errors. You should also learn not to be afraid of making errors. Everyone learning to write makes errors now and then. Smart people learn from errors, their own and others'. You already probably learn from errors in other activities, in sports and music, for example. You can do the same in writing. Learning from errors is what this section helps you do.

How should you deal with errors? First, you must not let making an error frighten you. You do not have to write perfect sentences in your first draft. It is more important at that point simply to get your thoughts down on paper—with or without errors. Then, however, you should learn to edit your writing so that you can present a better second draft.

To edit means "to correct, revise, or prepare for presentation." Both movies and books are edited before they get to an audience. Only by being edited are they able to be just what the director or writer wanted.

When you edit your own or someone else's work, you have to look at the piece of writing as a whole *and* at the individual sentences. Sections 10–12 provide guidelines for judging a paragraph or a composition as a whole. Here, in Section 9, you will have a chance to focus on ways to edit individual sentences.

Look at the Editing Chart that begins on this page. The chart is divided into the seven most common kinds of sentence errors. The center column contains sentences that were written with errors. (These sentences were, for the most part, written by students between the ages of thirteen and seventeen.) On the left you will see the editing signal that an editor can use to point out a certain error in a sentence. On the right you will see a cross-reference to the part of the book that explains in more detail why the sentence has an error.

Look again at the center column on the Editing Chart. The red cross-outs and the handwritten revisions suggest ways of correcting errors.

Remember one more point as you go about editing your own or someone else's work or as you have your own work edited by others: Recognizing and complimenting what is creative, original, and refreshing about a piece of writing is also part of the process of being an editor.

EDITING CHART

ERRORS IN SUBJECT–VERB AGREEMENT

agree

1. A verb must agree in number with its subject.

   The President always seem*s* to put the
   United States before anything.   2.c

   Johnny Carson get*s* to meet many new and
   unusual people.

   In other words, he like*s* all people.

We ~~was~~ **were** hoping to get tickets for the Super Bowl. [2.c]

She ~~don't~~ **doesn't** know the answer to the problem.

Each of us need**s** friends.

My mother and my father make~~s~~ my good life possible. [2.d]

Such determination, courage, and ability make~~s~~ him the person I admire most.

Optimism or courage ~~are~~ **is** essential for someone like Helen Keller.

The long-term goal ~~have~~ **has** always been peace and prosperity. [2.l.1]

ERRORS IN CASE

case 2. Pronouns that are objects of action verbs, objects of prepositions, or appositive objects must be in the *objective* case. [1.d.1]

Who **m** do you want?

The project brought Jeremy and **me** together.

The audience showed who **m** they liked.

We sent greetings to Charles and ~~she.~~ **her**

I will go along with who **m** ever you want.

case 3. Pronouns that are subjects and predicate nominatives must be in the *nominative*, or *subjective*, case. [1.d.1]

We
~~Us~~ children have never had much responsibility.

Mary and h~~im~~ *he* have tickets for the ballet.

She
~~Her~~ and Tom had lunch together last week.

The audience knew who*m* was best.

they
It was ~~them~~ who began the argument.

Could it be h~~er~~ *she* on the phone right now?

case 4. Pronouns must be in the appropriate case after *than* or *as*.

1.d.1; p.59

Jane knows Wilma better than h~~e~~ *him*. [The

writer means to say that Jane knows

Wilma and knows *him*.]

Jane knows Wilma better than h~~im~~ *he*. [The

writer means to say that Jane and *he*

know Wilma.]

REFERENCE ERRORS WITH PRONOUNS

Incorrect Reference

ref 5. A personal pronoun must agree with its antecedent in number.

1.d.1

A person can look all over, and t~~hey~~ *he* will

never find a greater quarterback than Joe

Namath.

one
One can always dream, can't t~~hey~~?

ref 6. In writing, *that* and *which* should not be used to refer to people.

1.d.6

who
The person t~~hat~~ taught Helen Keller was

Annie Sullivan.

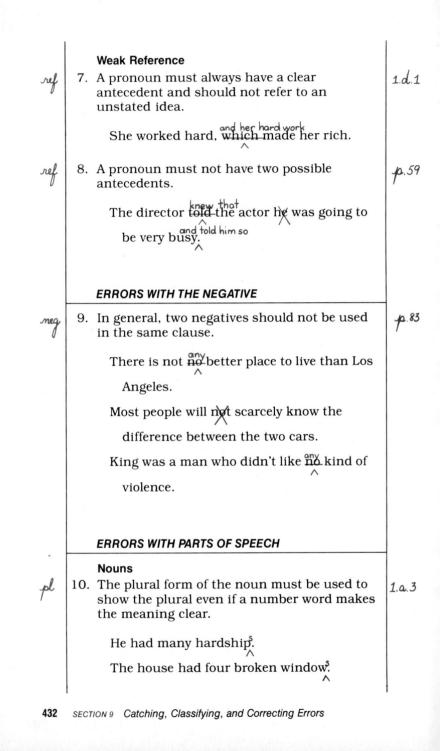

Weak Reference

ref

7. A pronoun must always have a clear antecedent and should not refer to an unstated idea.

1.d.1

She worked hard, ~~which~~ ^and her hard work^ made her rich.

ref

8. A pronoun must not have two possible antecedents.

p.59

The director ~~told~~ ^knew that^ the actor ~~he~~ was going to be very busy ^and told him so^.

ERRORS WITH THE NEGATIVE

neg

9. In general, two negatives should not be used in the same clause.

p.83

There is not ~~no~~ ^any^ better place to live than Los Angeles.

Most people will n~~o~~t scarcely know the difference between the two cars.

King was a man who didn't like ~~no~~ ^any^ kind of violence.

ERRORS WITH PARTS OF SPEECH

Nouns

pl

10. The plural form of the noun must be used to show the plural even if a number word makes the meaning clear.

1.a.3

He had many hardship^s^.

The house had four broken window^s^.

poss

11. The possessive form of a noun must include an apostrophe.

    We can now foresee the series' end.

    Are those John's red socks?

    Do you remember Ted Williams' number?

Verbs

tense

12. Past-time verbs must have the appropriate word endings.

    He like^d all people whether they were rich or poor.

    It has work^ed for me before.

    Michelle use^d to live in Pennsylvania, but now she lives in New York.

    Have you ever stud^ied another language?

    She did ~~tried~~ ^try her best!

tense

13. The present tense should not be used if another tense is more logical.

    She ~~is~~ ^was said to be very pretty as a young girl.

tense

14. The past perfect must be used to describe the earlier of two past actions.

    By the time I told him the news, he ^had already heard.

tense

15. A sentence should not shift verb tenses unnecessarily between clauses.

    He ~~is~~ ^was faithful to his team and stood by them.

1. a. 5;
7. k. 1

1. b. 15-
1. b. 18

1. b. 14

1. b. 18

p. 39

Adjectives

adj 16. A comparative adjective must be used when comparing two items, and a superlative adjective must be used when comparing more than two.

1.c.3;
1.c.4

Between Maui and Kauai, Kauai is the ~~most~~ more beautiful.

Of Maui, Kauai, and Hawaii, Kauai is ~~more~~ the most beautiful.

adj 17. A double comparison must be avoided.

p.49

I admire Winston Churchill because I think he was one of the m~~os~~t fittest men during World War II.

adj 18. An incomplete comparison must be avoided by adding *other* or *else*.

p.49

Henry Kissinger spent more time overseas than any other Secretary of State.

adj 19. Some adjectives do not logically have comparative or superlative forms—for example, *perfect, unique, round*.

1.c.3;
1.c.4

Some would say that the Beatles' music is more ~~perfect~~ interesting than the Rolling Stones'.

Pronouns

pro 20. *Hisself* and *theirselves* are not words; *himself* and *themselves* should be used instead.

p.62

He did the problem ~~hisself.~~ himself

pro | 21. In writing, *this* should not be used to mean simply *a* or *an*. | *p.64*

There is ~~this~~ $\overset{a}{\wedge}$ building in San Francisco that is shaped like a pyramid.

pro | 22. *This here* should not be used to mean *this*. | *p.64*

Is this ~~here~~ book yours?

pro | 23. *Them* should not be used to mean *those*. | *p.64*

For three hours we studied ~~them~~ $\overset{those}{\wedge}$ verbs.

Adverbs

adv. | 24. The *-ly* ending must not be omitted from adverbs of manner. | 1.*f*.1

The Panovs seem to dance effortless $\overset{ly}{\wedge}$

ERRORS IN COMPLETING AND JOINING CLAUSES

run-on | 25. A comma alone should not be used to join main clauses. (The error results in a *run-on sentence*.) | *p.149*

I admired John F. Kennedy $\overset{.\ H}{\wedge\ \wedge}$ he was an honest man.

frag | 26. A sentence must have both a subject and a linking verb or an action verb; without both elements a group of words is a *sentence fragment*. | 2.*b*; *p.112*

$\overset{Martin\ Luther\ King\ was\ a}{\wedge}$ A man who liked to help others.

The two girls $\overset{were}{\wedge}$ jogging through Tilden Park.

27. Main clauses should not be joined with *so* or
yet, but rather with *and so* and *and yet*.

p. 90

Robert Kennedy knew that going out into

big crowds was like playing Russian

roulette, ~~yet~~ ^and^ he continued to go out.

Katherine Anne Porter grew up in the

South, ^and^ ~~so~~ she often writes about life in

the South.

voice | 28. A sentence should not shift unnecessarily
from the active voice to the passive voice, or
vice versa, between clauses.

1. 6.20

Although she had a lot of talent, the poet

was ~~known to be~~ undisciplined.

ERRORS IN CLARITY AND STYLE

Dangling or Misplaced Words, Phrases, and Clauses

dang-
ling | 29. A phrase or clause should clearly modify a
word in the sequence; if there is any
confusion, the phrase or clause is said to be
dangling.

p. 102;
p. 225

^When I was young,^
~~At an early age,~~ my parents explained the

difference between right and wrong.

mis-
placed | 30. A phrase or clause should be placed as close
as possible to the word it is modifying.

p. 102;
p. 225

Adlai Stevenson discussed peace and

prosperity at the Democratic Convention

*mis-
placed*

31. An adverb of degree should be placed as close as possible to the word it refers to.

p.83

We had (only) completed four of the six

games.

Sagging Subjects

sag

32. If a subject and a verb are not clearly connected—both logically and grammatically—the sentence *sags*. The performer that is logically the most important performer in that particular sentence should be the subject of the main clause.

3.i

A sagging sentence can be improved in one of the ways listed below. Some rewriting is usually required.

1. Make the word or words that are most important the subject of the main clause.

2. Select a new, and more logical, word as the subject of the main clause.

3. Substitute a logical word for a weak pronoun as the subject of the main clause.

The camera can fool the human eye, and in

conjunction with makeup and costuming

makes for an enjoyable film.

[This sentence sags because the most important performer is not the subject of the main clause. What makes a film enjoyable? The camera? No. More likely, *clever photography* makes for an enjoyable film. These words should be the subject.]

Clever photography in conjunction with

makeup and costumes makes for an

enjoyable film.

[Now the subject *clever photography* has the main role.]

~~Plays~~ don't have the advantages of ~~camera~~
angles and ~~editing techniques~~ that film
~~directors~~ have.

[This sentence sags because the subject
plays does not serve as the logical subject
of *don't have advantages*. The logical
subject of the sentence should be *stage
directors*.]

Stage directors don't have the advantages of

camera angles and editing techniques

that film directors have.

sag

33. The subject should not be lost in a prepositional phrase.

~~In the job~~ that I really want, I ~~need to know~~
~~Spanish.~~

[This sentence sags because it places the
most important word or words—*the job*—
in an introductory prepositional phrase.
The job should be the subject of the main
clause.]

The job that I really want requires a

knowledge of Spanish.

[In this rewrite the subject is indeed *job*,
which is connected to the verb *requires*.]

~~As to the~~ energy crisis and the ~~recent~~
gasoline ~~shortage, it is~~ upsetting for all
~~Americans.~~

The energy crisis and the recent gasoline

shortage are upsetting for all Americans.

~~By limiting gasoline sales may not completely solve the problem.~~

Limiting gasoline sales may not completely solve the problem.

sag | 34. The subject should not be lost in a subordinate clause.

Although soccer has for many years been popular in South America, it is still fairly new in North America.

If Brazilians were asked to choose between the San Francisco Giants and the Los Angeles Dodgers, they would first have to find out what baseball is.

Wordiness

wordy | 35. A sentence should contain no unnecessary words. | 3. j

Willa Cather ~~still continues to~~ live s on in the words and actions of ~~the people in her~~ her characters ~~stories and novels~~.

■ Other editing signals

On the next page you will find other editing signals that you can use when looking over sentences. Make sure that you understand what each signal indicates. The column on the right also tells where in this book you can learn more about how to improve your abilities as a writer and editor in certain areas.

SIGNAL	ERROR
vocab	Vocabulary: word choice (see Section 4)
sp	Spelling (see Section 5)
cap	Capitalization (see Section 7)
p	Punctuation (see Section 7)
use	Usage: commonly confused words and common misused forms (see Section 8)
∧	Omitted word or letter

When you edit paragraphs and compositions, you will need at least one more editing signal:

SIGNAL	ERROR
¶	Problem in paragraphing (see Section 10)

USING EDITING SIGNALS

If you edit your own work, you are doing self-editing. If you edit a classmate's work or a classmate edits yours, you are involved in peer editing. There is also the possibility that teachers may edit your work. In all cases, though, you can use the editing signals from the preceding Editing Chart.

As an illustration, look at the sample composition on the facing page, which was written by a student who was asked to write about someone admirable. The student made quite a few sentence-level errors. A few more were introduced into the sample so that you could see how to handle them.

A second student then edited the sample composition. You will see the editing signals in the margins. In the body of the composition itself, you will see circles, brackets, and carets to pinpoint the errors.

The student who wrote the composition can easily see what the problem areas are and find the same signals on the Editing Chart. There, the student can find suggestions for how to correct those particular errors. The student can also use the cross-references on the Editing Chart to read more about why the item is considered an error and to get additional exercise practice.

Sample Composition with Editing Signals

I admire Jacques Cousteau for many reasons. Cousteau fought physical disabilities. He was almost crippled in a car accident, and the doctors thought he would have to have his arm amputated. He refuse *tense* to let them take his arm, he worked for months just *run-on* to [regain the use of it once more.] *wordy*
　[In the invention of the aqua lung almost killed *sag* him] on several occations by poisonous gas, *sp* crippling pressure, the diseases of Neptunes *poss* kingdom, and dangerous marine life. Cousteau is a great man, he is a leader and a great team man. *run-on*
　[Jacques one of the last great explorers left on *frag* Earth.] He has witnessed scenes no man has ever scene before. He has gone deeper and discovered *sp* more than any oceanographer. There is still much *adj* we haven't learned, but now with his help the mysteries of the sea are being unveiled.

■ Editing exercises: general instructions

Rewrite each sentence in the following exercises correctly. You may use the Editing Chart on pages 429–439 as follows if necessary:

1. Find on the chart a sentence that has the same kind of error.
2. Correct the sentence in the exercise the same way that it is corrected on the Editing Chart.
3. Use the cross-reference in the right column of the Editing Chart to review the grammar rules.

EXERCISE 1. Each of the following sentences has an error in subject-verb agreement. (Note the editing signals.) Rewrite each sentence correctly.

1. The dolphin send out air waves in order to "see" what is around it. *agree*
2. The mammal breathe air into the water through which it is swimming. *agree*
3. The air bounce off any object in the water. *agree*
4. The echo return to the dolphin who can then measure the object based on the echo. *agree*
5. Without this system a dolphin do not know what is in front of it. *agree*
6. Each of these intelligent water mammals have several stomachs. *agree*
7. Problems and stress gives a dolphin an ulcer. *agree*
8. Scientists, animal lovers, and even a child finds dolphins irresistible. *agree*
9. Either the intelligence or the affection of a dolphin are the subject of many studies. *agree*
10. The goal have been breakthroughs in human-dolphin communication. *agree*

EXERCISE 2. Each of the following sentences has an error in case. (Note the editing signals.) Rewrite each sentence correctly.

1. Who does a lawyer help? *case*
2. Sometimes a defendant expects the court to bring a lawyer and he together. *case*
3. The jury members sometimes hint who they favor. *case*
4. The jury system brings both justice and responsibility to millions of other citizens and we. *case*
5. Us voters must accept our responsibility to serve on juries. *case*
6. The French and us have very different principles in the courtroom. *case*
7. The French court considers whomever is on trial guilty until proven innocent. *case*
8. The people whom are brought to trial in the United States are considered innocent until proven guilty. *case*
9. It is us who have to prove guilt. *case*
10. Us lawyers have a responsible job. *case*

EXERCISE 3. Each of the following sentences has an error in pronoun reference. (Note the editing signals.) Rewrite each sentence correctly. Each sentence is a paraphrase of a quotation.

1. The person that has health has hope, and the person that has hope has everything.—Arabian proverb *ref*
2. Every man is a volume if you know how to read them. —William Ellery Channing *ref*
3. Last year more Americans went to symphonies than went to baseball games, which may be viewed as an alarming statistic, but I think that both baseball and the country will endure.—John F. Kennedy (1962) *ref*
4. Some people take no pride in the achievements of their ancestors, and they will therefore never be remembered. —Macaulay *ref*
5. There is no king that has not had a slave among his ancestors and no slave that has not had a king among his. —Helen Keller *ref*

EXERCISE 4. Each of the following sentences has a double negative. (Note the editing signals.) Rewrite each sentence correctly.

1. Never give no advice in a crowd.—Arabian proverb *neg*
2. Never advise no one to go to war or to marry.—Spanish proverb *neg*
3. It is a bad bargain when nobody gains nothing.—English proverb *neg*
4. Do not sign nothing without reading it.—Spanish proverb *neg*
5. Sticks and stones will break my bones, but no names will never hurt me.—English proverb *neg*

EXERCISE 5. Each of the following sentences has an error with one part of speech. (Note the editing signals.) Rewrite each sentence correctly.

1. There are many career related to biology. *pl*
2. For example, both the anthropologists and the farmers work involves biology. *poss*
3. Many forest rangers and game wardens have study biology before finding their jobs. *tense*
4. A medical secretary must know more about biology than any secretary. *adj*
5. There are these other fields requiring training in biology, such as landscape architecture, herpetology, and home economics. *pro*
6. Obviously, nurses and surgeons must study biology thorough. *adv*
7. Them students who study biology may choose to work in either a greenhouse or a lab. *pro*
8. In fact, it becomes more harder to choose a biology-related career the more you know about your choices. *adj*
9. Some students have a hard time choosing careers for theirselves. *pro*
10. They should talk to other people who have various career in biology-related fields. *pl*

EXERCISE 6. Each of the following numbered items contains an error in the way the two clauses were put together. (Note the editing signals.) Rewrite each item.

1. The baseball season seems to start earlier and earlier, spring training arrives before the March winds. *run-on*

2. The thrill of throwing out the first ball of the season. *frag*

3. Astounding prices of major-league contracts. *frag*

4. It is pleasant to remember that baseball has long been called the American pastime, yet American teams play Canadian teams during the regular season. *join*

5. The *Baseball Encyclopedia* is an endless source of fascination, it includes every baseball statistic. *run-on*

EXERCISE 7. Each of the following sentences has an error in clarity or style. (Note the editing signals.) Rewrite each sentence correctly.

1. Enchanted by its romance, ballooning has long been popular. *dangling*

2. Begun in the late 1700s by the French, Americans soon heard the news. *dangling*

3. Today, ballooning ranches have been set up in some states that charge reasonable fees. *misplaced*

4. A sky full of hot-air balloons makes beautiful pictures that have colorful decorations. *misplaced*

5. The first balloon caused quite a stir as it rose before 300,000 Parisians, drifting twenty-four kilometers before being attacked by frightened farmers. *misplaced*

6. By taking balloon trips will give you a sense of how quiet motorless travel can be. *sag*

7. As to their use for mass transportation, it is unlikely. *sag*

8. An ascending balloon going up in the air makes viewers rethink again about *Around the World in Eighty Days*, the book written by the author Jules Verne. *wordy*

9. Although ballooning has revived in the United States, unlikely that it will replace other transportation. *sag*

10. Still, there was a day in the year of 1870 when balloons carried and transported soldiers, flew mail by air, and rescued people from the city of Paris. *wordy*

EXERCISE 8. Rewrite the Sample Composition on page 441, correcting all the errors that the editor found. (You may also want to change some of the other words to make the writing sound more like your own.)

THE PARAGRAPH

10 The Paragraph

A **paragraph** is a group of sentences that relate to one main idea or incident.

You do not need to read a page of print such as this one to identify the paragraphs on it. They are obvious to you the moment you see the page. Clearly, then, you know what a paragraph looks like. A paragraph is to some extent a visual device. Paragraphs make a page easier to read.

Paragraphs are writing aids as well. Just as sentences can be put together into paragraphs, so paragraphs follow each other to form a composition. Each paragraph is a link in a chain. You can work your way through a composition more easily if you think about it paragraph by paragraph.

The sentences in a paragraph must all relate to one another and to one central idea. Look at the individual sentences in the following paragraph, for example.

> The sea is a most silent world. I say this deliberately on long accumulated evidence and aware that wide publicity has recently been made on the noises of the sea. Hydrophones have recorded clamors that have been sold as phonographic curiosa, but the recordings have been grossly amplified. It is not the reality of the sea as we have known it with naked ears. There are noises underwater, very interesting ones that the sea transmits exceptionally well, but a diver does not hear boiler factories.
>
> —Jacques Cousteau

In the preceding paragraph every sentence has to do with the sounds (or lack of them!) of the sea. The sentences are related to an idea, which is stated in the first sentence. Together the sentences in the paragraph produce a unit of thought.

As you know, most paragraphs are composed to work with other paragraphs in the creation of a whole composition. To do so effectively, each paragraph must be well constructed in itself. In this section you will be studying ways of building strong paragraphs. In Section 11 you study ways of linking them together to form whole compositions.

THE TOPIC SENTENCE

10.a THE TOPIC SENTENCE: GUIDE TO THE PARAGRAPH

The **topic sentence** of the paragraph states the main idea of the paragraph.

For the reader a topic sentence is a guide. It states the main idea of the paragraph. For you as a writer the topic sentence is a way of helping you to organize the paragraph. Once you have a topic sentence, you know the direction that your paragraph must take. For example, once the writer Cousteau had written the sentence *The sea is a most silent world*, in the paragraph quoted earlier, he must have known that the other sentences in the paragraph would have to defend that statement.

Most of the time a topic sentence is a *generalization*, a statement that draws a conclusion from a number of specifics. If, for example, you learn that in recent years speed records in swimming, skating, or track have been broken, you draw a conclusion from these specifics. The conclusion is a generalization. You generalize that people are swimming faster, skating faster, or running faster— or all three.

Once you have a topic sentence, it will guide you in completing your paragraph. You will know what specifics to include. These are often the specifics that led you to make your generalization. You will now share them with your reader, and they will convince your reader that your topic sentence is in fact true. In the preceding paragraph by Jacques Cousteau, you find certain specifics: hydrophones, underwater noises amplified, the naked ear, a diver's hearing. These specifics all become part of the paragraph that began with a generalization about the silence of the sea.

An experienced writer may place the topic sentence in the middle or at the end of a paragraph. As you become more experienced at writing, you too may want to vary the placement. It is easier for a student writer to start thinking about a paragraph by thinking about the topic sentence and to start writing the paragraph with the topic sentence. After you have written the topic sentence, you will find it easier to decide what other ideas are directly related to your main idea.

The following exercises will give you practice in recognizing and writing topic sentences.

EXERCISE 1.   Read each of the following three paragraphs. Identify the topic sentence in each. Remember that the topic sentence states the main idea of the paragraph and is usually a generalization.

PARAGRAPH A

The Otis Elevator Company's Elevonic 101 introduces a new generation of elevator. A series of microcomputers control virtually every aspect of elevator operation: car speed, position and direction, passenger-travel door operation, and car assignments. In this way, it offers up to 40 percent reduction in operating costs and provides passengers with a more efficient ride. It also minimizes waiting time and can diagnose trouble spots such as faulty door openings.

PARAGRAPH B

Embroidery is the art of needlework. Although there are many kinds of embroidery—crewel, bargello, and needlepoint are among the most popular—they all have one thing in common. They are all methods of stitching a pattern on cloth using threads of many colors. The huge tapestries on museum walls, each tapestry composed of hundreds of tiny stitches in a myriad of colors, are a beautiful and traditional form of embroidery. In recent years embroidery has regained its old popularity. Today one sees on the streets jackets with colorful scenes stitched on them. Tablecloths, napkins, chair seats, and footstools decorated with patterns in varicolored threads are other modern examples of this art.

PARAGRAPH C

By all odds, the most ancient "building" ever to serve as a local landmark was the General Noble Redwood Tree House in Tulare County, California. This giant Sequoia was 2,000 years old when it was felled in 1892. Fellers built a scaffold 50 feet above the ground around the trunk (26 feet in diameter, 85 feet in circumference). It took a week to cut through the tree. When the 300-foot-high tree fell, it struck the scaffold. The woodcutters, jumping to the stump, were unable to stand for 20 minutes because of the shock from the vibration.

EXERCISE 2. Each of the following paragraphs lacks a topic sentence. After you read the paragraphs, choose the best topic sentence for each paragraph from the list of sentences that follows.

PARAGRAPH A

Laws now give renters protection against excessive charges, lack of services, and general neglect of their buildings. Tenants can now successfully protest the lack of upkeep and services such as poor paint, neglected hallways, and inadequate lighting. Tenant groups have also established the right to hold meetings and organize without the interference or harassment of their landlords.

PARAGRAPH *B*

The first people to use paper money were the Chinese, as early as 2600 B.C. Europeans did not begin to use it until A.D. 1661 in Sweden. Soon after that, paper money began to be used in England, originating there with goldsmiths. People kept their gold with the goldsmiths, who gave the depositors receipts. People soon found it more convenient to exchange receipts than the gold itself.

PARAGRAPH *C*

In 1587, 120 colonists were left on Roanoke Island off the coast of Virginia. They were ill-prepared for setting up a colony, and their governor returned to England for more supplies. When he came again to the colony, in 1590, he could find no trace of the colonists. Even their buildings had been dismantled. All the supplies were gone, and there was no sign of a struggle. No message was ever found beyond the cryptic letters *CRO* and the word *CROATOAN*.

Topic sentences

1. American settlers often had grave problems.
2. Paper money, by no means a new invention, has been used for centuries.
3. Many people prefer to buy their own homes rather than rent an apartment.
4. One of the great mysteries of American history is the fate of the settlers on Roanoke Island.
5. Tenants are no longer completely at the mercy of their landlords.
6. Money is simply a symbol for the value of things being exchanged.

EXERCISE 3. Each of the following lists can be used to make up a paragraph. Each list contains one sentence that would be a good topic sentence. Read each list, and decide which sentence in each group you would select as a topic sentence. Be prepared to explain why you chose that sentence. (One way to do this exercise is first to eliminate the sentences that are obviously *not* general enough to be topic sentences for the list.)

LIST A

1. For example, ultraviolet rays in sunlight have wavelengths too short for our eyes to pick up, although we can feel them as they tan our skins.
2. Few people realize that light is only one part of the whole electromagnetic spectrum.
3. There are many wavelengths that we cannot see.
4. In addition, infrared rays, which are given off by all warm objects, have wavelengths that are too long for our eyes to see.
5. Again, we can feel but not see them.
6. In fact, visible light is only about 3 percent of all the electromagnetic waves that exist.

LIST B

1. As a young man, Schweitzer showed a major talent for the organ and became an internationally famous organist.
2. Schweitzer also studied philosophy and theology during his early years.
3. After receiving his Ph.D. in philosophy, he taught at the University of Strasbourg.
4. While he taught, he also wrote and published books of philosophy and theology, which were known worldwide.
5. Albert Schweitzer had a total of four careers in his lifetime, three of them before he was thirty.
6. Then, at the age of thirty, he began to study medicine.
7. At the age of thirty-eight, he established a hospital, in which he treated thousands of African people.

LIST C

1. Some vanes, those on city and town houses chiefly, often displayed the crafts of the people who owned them.
2. In rural areas farm animals were often used.
3. Near the ocean nautical themes such as fish, boats, or spyglasses were favorites.
4. The subjects used for weathervanes were as varied as the people who owned the vanes.
5. In Louisiana, for instance, a locksmith's weathervane was a door key on an anvil.

10.b WRITING THE TOPIC SENTENCE

Sometimes, especially when you have something that you want to say, the first sentence that occurs to you will be an effective topic sentence. You will have an idea, and your sentence will make a statement about it. Do not be afraid, therefore, of trying out the first sentence that occurs to you as a topic sentence. It may work with just a little changing after you have completed writing the whole paragraph.

Sometimes, however, you have information that you have to pass on to others in writing, but a sentence about it does not come readily to mind. Then is the time to remember that a topic sentence makes a generalization. Ask yourself *What general statement can I make about this information?* Your answer will probably turn out to be a useful topic sentence. With it you can begin your paragraph.

For example, listed below is some information about the "yellow pages" in an average-size city's telephone book. Think about the information for a minute, and then see what generalizations you can make about it.

LISTINGS IN A TYPICAL YELLOW PAGES

Kinds of Product or Service	Number of Advertisers
Beauty Salons	18
Book Stores	5
Bicycle Sales, Rentals & Service	7
Bumper Stickers	1
Cheese Stores	3
Children's Haircutters	5
Home Improvements	23
Jewelers	18
Murals	1
Music Instruction	3
Oil Paintings	1
TV Sales & Service	27
Tennis Court Construction	4
Theaters of all kinds	7
Travel Bureaus	9

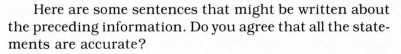

Here are some sentences that might be written about the preceding information. Do you agree that all the statements are accurate?

1. Many people in this community can afford to spend money on leisure-time activities.

2. People in the community spend much time and money on and in their homes.

3. There are nine travel bureaus.

4. Most people who have a business establishment in this city provide services rather than only products if this list is any indication.

All but one of the preceding sentences are generalizations. Which one is not?

One way to test whether a sentence is a generalization is to ask yourself whether it suggests a topic for further discussion. Is there anything else that can be said about it? If there is, the sentence is usually a generalization and will make a useful topic sentence. If the sentence seems to lead nowhere, it probably is not a generalization and will not make a practical topic sentence.

For example, what more can be said about Sentence 3 above? *There are nine travel bureaus.* Is nine a surprising number? Is nine a large number for travel bureaus? To do anything with this statement, you have to have some other piece of information to go along with it. Sentence 3 states a *specific* (a detail), and specifics need other specifics before anyone can make a generalization about them. Sentence 3 by itself will not make a topic sentence.

All the other sentences about the "yellow pages" will make topic sentences. They can all be further developed. For example, Sentence 4 can be developed by going back to the list and giving specific examples of the business establishments that provide (a) services or (b) products only. You can include in your paragraph specifics about the number and kinds of services and products offered by the businesses.

EXERCISE 4. Be ready to suggest how Sentence 1 or Sentence 2 about the "yellow pages" can be used as a topic sentence at the beginning of a paragraph. What more can be said about the idea that either of them introduces? Can you find specifics in the list from the "yellow pages" or from the "yellow pages" of a telephone book in your own town or city? Do you have ideas of your own that you can add to either Sentence 1 or 2 to develop it further into a convincing paragraph?

EXERCISE 5. Examine the information in the following table about the United Nations. Then complete the topic sentence below the table. Use the information in the table as a basis for completing the sentence.

	UNITED NATIONS MEMBERSHIP		
Year	Countries Given Membership	Year	Countries Given Membership
1945	51	1963	2
1946	4	1964	3
1947	2	1965	3
1948	1	1966	4
1949	1	1967	1
1950	1	1968	3
1951	0	1969	0
1952	1	1970	1
1953	0	1971	4
1954	0	1972	0
1955	16	1973	2
1956	4	1974	3
1957	2	1975	6
1958	1	1976	3
1959	0	1977	2
1960	17	1978	2
1961	4	1979	1
1962	5		

START OF TOPIC SENTENCE: Membership in the United Nations . . .

EXERCISE 6. Proceed as you did in Exercise 5. Examine the material in the following table, and complete the topic sentence below it.

POPULATION OF LARGE U.S. CITIES			
Name of City	**1900**	**1950**	**1970**
Atlanta	89,872	331,314	495,039
New York City	3,437,202	7,891,957	7,895,563
Chicago	1,698,575	3,620,962	3,369,357
Los Angeles	102,479	1,970,358	2,811,801
Philadelphia	1,293,697	2,071,605	1,949,996
Houston	44,633	596,163	1,282,443
Detroit	285,704	1,849,568	1,514,063
Dallas	42,638	434,462	844,621
Baltimore	508,957	948,708	905,787
San Diego	17,700	334,387	697,471
San Antonio	53,321	408,442	708,582

START OF TOPIC SENTENCE: Between 1900 and 1970 the population of large cities in the United States . . .

EXERCISE 7. Below you will find three sets of information in the form of phrases. This information can be used as the basis for a paragraph on the topic indicated. Write a topic sentence for a paragraph about each set.

1. TOPIC: The South American llama
   forebears evolved in South America
   adapted to high altitudes   thick, durable wool
   also thrives at low elevations   gentle and good-natured

2. TOPIC: Yoga as an exercise
   increases flexibility
   no abrupt movements   beginning stages are simple
   aids relaxation   no special equipment

3. TOPIC: Woman's right to vote
   Susan B. Anthony: voted in 1872, fined $100,
       refused to pay
   Victoria Woodhull: first woman candidate for
       President, 1872
   Aug. 18, 1920: Constitutional Amendment 19 passed;
       allowed women to vote

EXERCISE 8. The paragraphs that follow do not have topic sentences. Read each paragraph carefully; then write a topic sentence to start each paragraph.

PARAGRAPH *A*

(*First sentence missing*) A glass blower shapes glass by blowing through a tube into a mass of extremely hot glass. As the tube is rotated, the glass takes shape, pushed out by the air blown into it. Thus a glass blower must have powerful lungs, skilled hands, and the ability to withstand heat.

PARAGRAPH *B*

(*First sentence missing*) One function of a crafts guild was regulation of standards of quality. A guild member had to achieve a certain level of expertise before moving to the next class of membership. Guilds also regulated the fees to be charged so that members in good standing were protected financially. A third function, possibly the most important, was education. Guild members were taught not only the skills of their crafts but also, at the least, reading, writing, and arithmetic.

PARAGRAPH *C*

(*First sentence missing*) Three popular songs about streets are "Abbey Road," "Penny Lane," and "Positively Fourth Street." Others include "Second Avenue," "Nights on Broadway," and "South Street." As for cities, there are songs titled "Memphis," "San Francisco," and "El Paso." Still others are "Please Come to Boston," "By the Time I Get to Phoenix," "Philadelphia Freedom," and "Do You Know the Way to San Jose?"

EXERCISE 9. For each of the next topics, information is given. Read the information, and then choose one of the topic sentences that follow.

TOPIC *A*

PALINDROME: a word or phrase that reads the same backward as it does forward; examples: *Madam, I'm Adam; Able was I ere I saw Elba.*

ANAGRAM: a word or phrase formed by reusing all the letters in another word or phrase; examples: *Florence Nightingale* and *Flit on, cheering angel*; *Queen Victoria's Jubilee Year* and *I require love in a subject*. An anagramic phrase is often related in meaning to the original phrase.

Topic sentences

1. The words *palindrome* and *anagram* came originally from Greek words.
2. Two amusing ways to play with words are called palindromes and anagrams.
3. It can be great fun to make up your own anagrams.

TOPIC *B*

January comes from the name of the Latin god Janus; March comes from the Latin god Mars; April comes from the Greek goddess Aphrodite; May comes from the Latin goddess Maia; June comes from the Latin goddess Juno; Tuesday comes from the Norse god Tiu; Wednesday comes from the Norse god Odin; Thursday comes from the Norse god Thor; Friday comes from the Norse goddess Frigga; Saturday comes from the Latin god Saturn.

Topic sentences

1. Our names for the months of the year and the days of the week often come from various mythological sources.
2. Nearly all names in our language have a distinct and sometimes mythological meaning.
3. Many of our names for the days of the week come from Norse mythology.

10.c STRONG VS. WEAK TOPIC SENTENCES

As the preceding discussion in 10.b pointed out, a sentence that states a specific (a detail) does not make a good topic sentence. This kind of sentence takes a very narrow view of a limited subject, maybe focusing on a concrete detail. It does not suggest a topic that can be opened up for development. A sentence that is limited in the statement that it makes does not make a good topic sentence.

On the other hand, a sentence that introduces too broad a topic is not a good topic sentence either. If a sentence is too broad, it often comes close to saying nothing, at least nothing worth more discussion. For example, look at the ingredients needed to make Welsh rabbit, a famous cheese dish.

> Cheese, grated, 3/4 pound
> Dry mustard, 1 teaspoon
> Cayenne, few grains
> Paprika, 1/2 teaspoon
> Salt, 1/2 teaspoon
> Cream or milk, 1/2 cup

Here are two possible but poor topic sentences:

A. To make a Welsh rabbit, you will need one-half teaspoon of paprika.
B. Various kinds of food are needed to make a Welsh rabbit.

Sentence *A* is too narrow and limited. It leaves the reader with a very specific piece of information, a detail. There is no generalization, no idea.

Sentence *B* is so broad as to be almost useless. It states a generalization, to be sure. The generalization is too broad to be useful, however. As a topic sentence it is so dull and useless that a writer could not blame a reader who read it and then left the rest of the paragraph unread. A writer who was trying to develop a paragraph after this opening sentence would have to start all over and try to come up with a more powerful topic sentence.

A stronger topic sentence to replace Sentences *A* and *B* might be the following:

> Making a Welsh rabbit, a famous cheese dish, is easy and fun because to cheese and milk you add only four spicy, tasty, but common items.

With this as a topic sentence, you hope to have interested your reader and told the reader what to expect in the paragraph. The sentence has an idea: that making a Welsh rabbit is easy and interesting. To develop your paragraph, you will simply fill in the details about each ingredient.

To summarize then, to be a strong topic sentence, a statement should not be too broad or too narrow.

EXERCISE 10. Following each of the next two paragraphs you will find three possible topic sentences. The paragraphs themselves have no topic sentence. First read each paragraph, and then decide which of the possible topic sentences is the strongest.

PARAGRAPH *A*

. . . In the first place, penguins do not fly. While there are a few other birds that do not fly, penguins combine their lack of flight with a swimming ability unmatched by any other bird. Their wings have become flippers. Secondly, penguins have solid bones. All other birds have hollow bones, which help them to stay airborne. Finally, penguins' feathers are tiny, hard, and very numerous. They resemble fish scales more than they do the feathers of other birds.

Possible topic sentences

1. There are seventeen different species of penguin.
2. Penguins differ widely from other birds.
3. Penguins can swim faster and longer than any other kind of bird.

PARAGRAPH *B*

. . . People with excellent voices can sing with an opera company or pursue a career as a popular singer. For those who enjoy acting, there is television, the film industry, or the stage. Someone with the gift for making others laugh may become a comedian. Others, who work best with ideas and objects, might try animated films. People who have a gift for a musical instrument can join an orchestra or a band. Still others have strong, graceful bodies, and enjoy movement. Such people may become dancers or athletes.

Possible topic sentences

1. The field of entertainment offers a variety of exciting careers.
2. Many people hope to earn a living by acting.
3. Lawyers, doctors, artists, and entertainers in general make their livings by offering services.

EXERCISE 11. Read each of the paragraphs below. Then reread the topic sentence underlined in each paragraph. Decide how this underlined sentence can be improved. Then rewrite it to make it stronger. Make sure it is neither too narrow nor too broad.

PARAGRAPH *A*

<u>The U.S. Geological Survey is an agency that employs many mapmakers</u>. Scientists in the agency have explored our continent's wildernesses. They have brought back reports on the geology and landforms of the continent. They also have compiled accurate maps of the explored areas. Over the years these scientists have hauled measuring instruments to the tops of high mountains and wrestled with bulky equipment of various kinds. Photographers and artists have produced photographs and detailed sketches of geological formations, as a result. The reports, pictures, and maps provided by the survey greatly aid us in understanding the geography of our continent. This understanding is invaluable in planning the use of our natural resources.

PARAGRAPH *B*

<u>In recent years many married women have joined the workforce</u>. In 1948, 31 percent of the women in the United States were working. Thirty years later, in 1978, 50 percent of American women were working. By 1988, according to projections, at least 66 percent of American women will hold jobs. The largest growth in the numbers of working women has not been among single women, however. It has been among married women, especially among mothers. By 1980 most mothers in the United States were working at jobs outside the home.

DEVELOPING THE TOPIC SENTENCE WITH SPECIFICS

10.d WAYS TO DEVELOP THE TOPIC SENTENCE

Among the ways of developing a topic sentence with specifics are the following: (1) concrete details, (2) examples, (3) facts or statistics, and (4) incidents.

A topic sentence gives you an idea of what a paragraph will cover. As you know, a topic sentence makes a general statement. Once you have written a topic sentence, therefore, you must find ways to convince your reader that the statement is true. A good way to do so is to use specifics (or details) to support the general statement. Look at the following examples:

EXAMPLES

GENERAL STATEMENT: People who grow plants should take precautions if small children or pets will be in the area. [Here is a topic sentence. It makes a generalization. People are going to say, "Why?" or "How do I know that that is true?" Your plan for the paragraph is now to explain and support your topic sentence. You do so by giving specifics.]

Developing statement with specifics: One popular plant, the oleander, has leaves that are poisonous when eaten.

GENERAL STATEMENT: Science fiction is by no means a new field of writing.

Developing statement with specifics: The famous science fiction novel *Frankenstein* by Mary Wollstonecraft Shelley was written in 1818.

In both of these examples, the writers can begin to support their topic sentences with a specific that happens to be a statement of fact. The facts are convincing and checkable.

As you know, facts are just one form of specific that can be used to support a topic sentence. Statistics, a kind of "fact," concrete details, examples, and incidents are other forms of specifics that can be used to support a topic sentence. All of these are discussed in the following pages.

EXERCISE 12. Read the topic sentence and the two specific developing sentences. Then write at least two more sentences of your own that support the topic sentence and that, therefore, can be used to complete the paragraph.

> TOPIC SENTENCE: Tastes in popular music keep changing over the years.
>
> *Developing sentences:* (1) The beat and the rhythm of the recordings that won prizes just a few years back are quite different from those that you hear on the most popular discs today. (2) Lyrics, almost always an important part of popular music, express different feelings today than they did five years ago.

10.e DEVELOPING TOPIC SENTENCES WITH CONCRETE DETAILS

Sometimes the best way to support a topic sentence is to use concrete details. Concrete details can include objects themselves (nouns) and also descriptive words that help us to see or hear or otherwise form an impression of an object. These important descriptive words are usually adjectives.

EXAMPLE
TOPIC SENTENCE: The state of Maine has one of the most beautiful coastlines in the world.

Use of concrete details: nouns
Rocks and beaches line the coast. Forests run down to the ocean's edge where waves break high across the jetties, spuming up jets of spray. Between the rocks tidal pools glisten in the sunshine.

10.e

Use of concrete details: adjectives to form an impression

<u>Wet-black</u> rocks and <u>white sandy</u> beaches line the coast. <u>Green</u> forests run down to the ocean's edge, where <u>giant white-plumed</u> waves break high across the <u>sturdy</u> jetties, spuming up jets of <u>lacy</u> spray. Between the rocks <u>dark-blue</u> tidal pools glisten in the <u>golden</u> sunshine.

If you have a topic sentence that needs to be developed with concrete details, it is a good idea to ask yourself questions such as the following:

QUESTIONS TO DEVELOP A TOPIC SENTENCE WITH CONCRETE DETAILS

1. What does it look like, sound like, smell like, taste like, act like?
2. What does it remind me of?
3. What, if anything, is unique about it?
4. What is its most outstanding feature?

EXERCISE 13. Using concrete details, write a paragraph to support each of the following topic sentences. Several questions follow each topic sentence to help you to select concrete details that will give your reader a good picture of the river (for Topic Sentence *A*) and a strong impression of the Fourth of July celebration (for Topic Sentence *B*).

TOPIC SENTENCE A: The long, dusty climb was well worth the effort when I reached the river.

Questions: How did the water feel? What did the banks of the river look like? Were there many plants? Was the water clear or muddy? What animals were there? What sounds did I hear?

TOPIC SENTENCE B: This year's Fourth of July celebration made previous ones seem tepid.

Questions: How many people were there? What kind of fireworks were there, if any? How long did the celebration last? What did it sound like? What smells were there? What was the weather like?

10.f DEVELOPING TOPIC SENTENCES WITH EXAMPLES

Using examples is a very common and useful way to develop a topic sentence. How often have you heard some-one say, perhaps to you, "Give me an example of what you mean?" Usually several examples are better than just one in supporting a topic sentence. Here is a topic sentence that needs support, and one example is not enough.

EXAMPLE

Some of the most interesting dwellings in the history of the human race have not been designed by licensed archi-tects. For example, the adobe huts of the American Indians were not designed by an architectural firm.

One example makes a point, but it does not satisfy the reader. You should go on and give several more examples to prove your point.

EXAMPLE

In Africa, huge trees have been hollowed out and used as houses. Whole underground towns were built in China by masses of people without benefit of blueprints supplied by an architect. Although most architects are not the least bit interested in them, tents have served as dwellings for mil-lions of people across the world.

EXERCISE 14. Using the topic sentence and, if you wish, the suggestions for examples that follow each topic sen-tence, develop three paragraphs of your own. Include at least three examples as support for each topic sentence. You can use examples of your own.

A. **TOPIC SENTENCE:** The oceans are probably a future source of energy.

Suggestions for examples: oil already discovered under the ocean floor; fish and plankton (seaweed) farms as a source of food; waves and tide-flows turning generators; great, deep ocean currents turning generators

B. **TOPIC SENTENCE:** Do-it-yourself hobbies such as making your own clothes can help you expand your material possessions.

   Suggestions for examples: costs of cloth less than costs of clothing; color choices of cloth wider; personal variations easier

C. **TOPIC SENTENCE:** Sweet fragrances of kitchen and garden are now captured, bottled, and marketed.

   Suggestions for examples: to bring the smell of a springtime meadow into a snowbound house; to give a kitchen the aroma of a local pie store; to bring the scent of salt into a city hospital room

10.g DEVELOPING TOPIC SENTENCES WITH FACTS OR STATISTICS

Facts or statistics are another kind of specific that you can use to support a topic sentence. A fact is a statement that can be checked or that your reader will take at face value. That an aircraft left the airport at 12:05 P.M. is a fact. It can be checked, on a flight log, for example. That Mexico is south of the United States, that the astronauts actually went to the moon, that a certain player played better than anyone else on the team—statements like these will be accepted as facts.

Statistics are numbers that have been collected with care for a purpose, recorded accurately, and classified into groups. That the Republican candidate Gerald Ford received 27,873 votes for President in Delaware in 1976 is a statistic. When you use statistics as specifics to support a topic sentence, your writing is convincing. To provide accurate statistics, you almost always have to do some kind of research or reading.

Sometimes you will want to support a topic sentence with facts only. Sometimes when you have developed a paragraph with facts, you should ask yourself whether you should not add some statistics to make your paragraph clearer and more convincing. The two paragraphs below show you the difference that statistics can make to a paragraph. The first paragraph has only facts. In the second paragraph statistics have been added. The topic sentence is the first sentence in both paragraphs.

FACTS ONLY

In several ways the Republic of the Philippines is one of the most interesting nations in the world. A population about one quarter that of the United States inhabits a land area only slightly larger than our state of Nevada. What is especially interesting, however, is that the country consists of many islands. These islands stretch for many miles north and south across the South Pacific Ocean. Most of the people live on comparatively few of the largest islands, however.

STATISTICS ADDED

In several ways the Republic of the Philippines is one of the most interesting nations in the world. A population of approximately 46,350,000 people, about one quarter that of the United States, inhabits a land area of about 115,700 miles, only slightly larger than our state of Nevada. What is especially interesting, however, is that the country consists of 7,100 islands. These islands stretch for more than 1,000 miles, north and south, across the South Pacific Ocean. Most of the people live on only eleven of the largest islands, however.

EXERCISE 15. Write a complete paragraph for the topic sentence below by using the facts and statistics provided for you. Not all of the facts provided are useful or relevant to the topic sentence. You must decide which you will use.

TOPIC SENTENCE: The world's major ocean areas vary greatly in size and in depth.

Facts and Statistics:

—Pacific Ocean: average depth—13,739 feet; size—64,186,300 square feet
—Yellow Sea: average depth—121 feet; size—113,500 square feet

—17 deep trenches in Pacific Ocean
—Gulf of California: average depth—2,375 feet; size—
59,100 square miles
—four major oceans recognized by geographers and
mapmakers
—the Gulf Stream: major current in Atlantic Ocean
—Mediterranean Sea: average depth—4,926 feet; size—
969,100 square feet
—Hudson Bay: average depth—305 feet; size—281,900
square feet
—Atlantic Ocean: average depth—12,257 feet; size—
33,420,000 square feet

10.h DEVELOPING TOPIC SENTENCES WITH INCIDENTS

An incident is a small and simple story. We think of an incident as being true. Usually people recall or relate an incident to prove a point—or a topic sentence. Usually one incident is enough to make a point, as you can see from the following example.

EXAMPLE

Every high school student in the country should take a course in cardiopulmonary resuscitation (CPR). In a comparatively few hours, anyone can learn this technique for helping people to survive the first three minutes of a heart attack. As more and more people are taking courses in CPR, reports of its uses in saving lives grow in number. When Tom Clark, a high school sophomore at Brayton High School, finished his nine hours of training in CPR, he never dreamed that he would have to use it the next evening. The evening after Tom finished his course, he was at dinner with his parents and grandparents. Suddenly, toward the end of the meal, Tom's grandfather slumped over in his chair. Tom knew immediately what to do. While someone else phoned the rescue squad, Tom applied the techniques of CPR to his grandfather. The rescue squad arrived in time, and Tom's grandfather is now up and around.

EXERCISE 16. Write complete paragraphs in which you support the following topic sentences with an incident or incidents. If you know any real incidents that can be used to support any one of these topic sentences, retell them as part of your paragraph. You can invent incidents if you wish, or follow out the suggestions given below each topic sentence.

A. **TOPIC SENTENCE:** The way in which some people overcome physical handicaps inspires all of us.

Suggestion for incident to support topic sentence: Perhaps you can recall an incident involving someone with a physical injury performing well in an athletic event. Perhaps you can recall an act of kindness or other contribution made by a handicapped person.

B. **TOPIC SENTENCE:** Sometimes animals outsmart people.

Suggestion for incident to support topic sentence: Cats are a good source of smart animal incidents.

C. **TOPIC SENTENCE:** Growing anything is a source of satisfaction.

Suggestion for incident to support topic sentence:
An incident that relates success with a flower or vegetable garden or indoor plants; an incident that reveals the results of hard work or a new idea such as playing soft music to help an indoor plant grow.

10.i DEVELOPING TOPIC SENTENCES WITH A COMBINATION OF METHODS

In newspapers, magazines, or textbooks you will find that professional writers develop paragraphs by using a combination of specifics. If you can think of a number of different kinds of specifics with which to support a topic sentence, do not hesitate to use all of them. A paragraph of this sort creates variety and interest for your reader.

If you combine specifics in your paragraphs, pay careful attention to organization. Jumping from one kind of

specific to another does not create a strong clear paragraph. You should not jump from a statistic to an incident to a concrete detail, for example, without having a good reason for this order.

Often a clear, well-organized way of combining specifics is to start with an incident. You can use concrete details to make the incident seem more vivid and interesting. Then you can follow the incident with brief examples of events similar to the one related in the incident. Finally, in summary, toward the end of the paragraph, you can include a fact or two and perhaps a statistic.

An outline of this combination would look like this:

> Topic Sentence
> > Incident
> > > Concrete details
> > Examples
> > Facts
> > Statistics

You can apply this organization to the topic sentence *Every high school student should take a course in cardiopulmonary resuscitation (CPR).* You can expand the paragraph on page 469 in the following way:

EXAMPLE

. . . The evening after Tom finished his course, he was having a pleasant Italian dinner with his parents and grandparents at Marco Polo's, the popular restaurant at the end of Elm Street. There were family jokes and laughter. Suddenly toward the end of the meal, Tom's grandfather slumped over in his chair. Tom knew immediately what to do. While the owner phoned the rescue squad, Tom applied the techniques of CPR to his grandfather. Within minutes, the wail of sirens could be heard...

Another way of combining different kinds of specifics is shown in the following paragraph, which uses facts, statistics, examples, an incident, and concrete details.

EXAMPLE

Modern medical techniques have changed the quality of American life considerably. In general, life expectancy has increased greatly. In 1900 the average life expectancy was 47.3 years of life; in 1977 it was 73.2 years, an increase of 54.8 percent. It is not simply in the number of years people may live that modern medicine has improved our lives. Diseases are now controlled better than ever before. For example, smallpox, once a disease people lived in fear of, is virtually eradicated today. Further, doctors can replace some vital organs damaged beyond repair. Replacement of kidneys, hearts, and arthritic joints is possible and relatively common. Now, too, having a limb severed may no longer mean that one has to live without it. In a recent incident, a young woman's hand was severed by a train. The hand was rushed to the hospital with her, and in a long and difficult process of surgery, doctors were able to reattach the hand. These are but a few of the differences modern techniques have made in our lives. Many others exist, from surgical techniques through control of chronic diseases to vaccines against common viruses.

| topic sentence |
| fact |
| statistic |
| fact |
| example |
| fact |
| example |
| fact |
| incident |
| details |
| examples |

In the preceding paragraph, all the specifics help to support the topic sentence. They also support one another so that the paragraph as a whole is clear and organized.

EXERCISE 17. Choose one of the given topic sentences, and write a paragraph about it. Use at least two of the four kinds of specifics: (1) concrete details; (2) examples; (3) facts or statistics; (4) incidents. Be careful to organize

the specifics you choose so that your paragraph is clear and logical.

1. My favorite kind of entertainment is . . .
2. Visiting a place one has never seen before offers excitement that outweighs anxiety.
3. Making one's living in any artistic field demands sacrifices.

REVIEW EXERCISE. In this exercise you are to choose three of the topic sentences given. Write a paragraph about each of them, using the indicated kind of specifics.

1. Owning a car can be more trouble than seems to be worthwhile, at times. (EXAMPLES: what can go wrong)
2. People's theories about the solar system have changed greatly over the centuries. (FACTS: Use the following facts and statistics. Ancient Greece: Ptolemy developed a theory that said the sun circled the earth and that the other planets circled the sun. The Middle Ages: people believed that the sun, moon, planets, and stars were on different shells circling the earth. The early 1500s: Copernicus developed the theory that the earth and other planets all circled the sun, in perfect circles. The late 1500s: Kepler showed that the orbits of the planets are not circles but ovals.
3. Moving from a house or apartment to a new one is usually a long, difficult, and sometimes funny process. (INCIDENTS)
4. A room that would please most decorators would be decorated in the following way. (CONCRETE DETAILS)

UNIFYING AND ORGANIZING THE PARAGRAPH

10.j UNITY

A good paragraph has **unity**: All the sentences have a relationship to one another and to the main idea.

Lack of unity in a paragraph weakens the writing. It can also be confusing to a reader. To see how lack of unity affects a paragraph, compare the following examples.

PARAGRAPH *A*

Doing crossword puzzles is a skill that can be developed. The first time you try one, perhaps, you find that you must leave half of it or more blank. As time goes on, however, you begin to be able to fill in more and more of the puzzles. At last you finish puzzles more often than not. At that point, you have developed a memory for words that are often used in crossword puzzles. You have also developed the ability to make good guesses about how unfamiliar words are spelled. Other word games, such as finding smaller words in a large word, develop other skills.

PARAGRAPH *B*

Doing crossword puzzles is a skill that can be developed. The first time you try one, perhaps, you find that you must leave half of it or more blank. As time goes on, however, you begin to be able to fill in more and more of the puzzles. At last you finish puzzles more often than not. At that point, you have developed a memory for words that are often used in crossword puzzles. You have also developed the ability to make good guesses about how unfamiliar words are spelled. In short, you have developed a special kind of word skill: that of doing crossword puzzles.

Of the two example paragraphs, Paragraph *B* has better unity. In Paragraph *A*, the last sentence is only indirectly related to the topic sentence and the other sentences. It does not deal with the skill of doing crossword puzzles, and so it does not belong in the paragraph. It might, however, be a good topic sentence to start the next paragraph in an article.

The last sentence in Paragraph *B* relates directly to the topic sentence and to the other sentences. It sums up the points given in the paragraph and returns the reader's attention to the main idea.

After you have written a paragraph, examine it carefully to be sure it has unity. Rewrite or remove altogether any sentences that destroy the unity. Sometimes you will find that your paragraph has more than one sentence that spoils the unity.

EXERCISE 18. Read each of the following paragraphs carefully. Find the sentence or sentences in each that destroy the unity of the paragraph.

PARAGRAPH *A*

Payse Weston was the champion pedestrian of the United States. His major accomplishments were in long-distance walking. In 1871 Weston walked 400 miles in four days, 23 hours, and 32 minutes, at the Empire Rink in New York City. Then, in 1879, Weston won the Astley Belt, the British prize for pedestrian perfection. He walked 550 miles in 142 hours—5 days and 22 hours—to win the belt. The greatest speed walk of his career was his "farewell appearance" in England, a month after he had won the belt. Weston walked 127 miles in 24 hours, setting a record for speed walking of 5.29 miles an hour. Weston was a reporter for the *New York Times* before he began his walking career.

PARAGRAPH *B*

Many famous rock stars changed their names as they became popular. Among these is Ringo Starr of the Beatles, who was born Richard Starkey. Ringo was the drummer for the Beatles when they became popular. Bob Dylan also changed his name, from Robert Zimmerman. Carole King and Marcie Blane changed theirs; they were originally Carol Klein and Marsha Blanc. Some stage names are much more changed from the originals than the ones above. For example, David Seville was Ross Bagdasarian.

PARAGRAPH *C*

There are many unusual, interesting, and amusing facts about wildlife. For instance, ostriches, which weigh up to 375 pounds, can attain speeds of fifty miles an hour, faster than lions run. Another example is the butterfly, which can really be quite a fighter. When other insects invade a butterfly's territory, the butterfly will chase them away, pursuing them for as far as 500 yards. Many butterflies migrate each year. Then there is the world's largest minnow, the Colorado River Squawfish. It can weigh as much as 80 pounds. Finally, the giant squid has the largest eyes in the world. Its eyes are each the size of a basketball.

10.k COHERENCE

A paragraph should have **coherence**: The sentences should be sequenced according to a clear, logical plan of development.

Each sentence in the paragraph needs to be related to the main idea of the paragraph. Each sentence also should have a logical relationship with the other sentences in the paragraph. Each sentence should fit in at an appropriate point in the paragraph.

Coherence is important because you want your reader to feel that you know where you are going. You want your reader to sense that your paragraph has a plan.

As you will see, the paragraphs below treat the same subject. Read and compare them. Then decide which version has better coherence.

PARAGRAPH *A*

In 1969 the New York Mets surprised everyone. They began their 1969 season in last place in their league. In mid-July the Mets were in second place and six games out of first place. By mid-August the Mets were still in second place and were then nine and one half games out of first place. By mid-September, however, the Mets were in first place. They went on, incredibly, to win their league championship, the National League pennant, and at last the World Series.

PARAGRAPH *B*

In 1969 the New York Mets surprised everyone. By mid-August, the Mets were still in second place and were then nine and one half games out of first place. They began their 1969 season in last place in their league. By mid-September, the Mets were in first place. In mid-July the Mets were in second place and six games out of first place. They went on, incredibly, to win their league championship, the National League pennant, and at last the World Series.

Clearly, Paragraph *A* is more coherent. It follows a definite plan: the order of the months of the season.

There are several kinds of order that can give coherence to a paragraph.

1. **Chronological order**, or time order, is the natural progression of time. See Paragraph *A*, page 476.
2. **Spatial order**, or order in terms of space, is the natural order of things in relationship to each other. An example of spatial order would be a paragraph that described a fish from mouth to tail fins.
3. **Order of importance** deals with the order of ideas. The most important idea is given first and the least important is given last, or vice versa. Specifics such as examples, facts, or statistics are often ordered according to their importance.

ORDER OF IMPORTANCE

<u>Painting a room requires a number of steps.</u> One cannot simply decide to paint and then plunge in and begin painting. <u>The first, and most important, step is preparation.</u> Without proper preparation, the finished paint job will look sloppy. It will probably not last as long, either. Preparation includes filling holes in walls and ceiling, smoothing rough plaster, and washing any particularly dirty places. <u>The next order of business is to be sure one has all necessary supplies.</u> It is most frustrating to be forced to stop in order to go out and buy that essential brush or bucket. Supplies include paint (of course), brushes of several sizes, one or two buckets, rollers and a paint pan, and drop cloths to spread on furniture and the floor. A good step ladder also helps. <u>At last, after the preparation and buying spree, it is time to begin painting.</u> It is somewhat paradoxical that, in doing a paint job, it is the actual painting that is the least important step.

topic sentence

most important item

second most important item

least important item

■ Logical connectives

A **logical connective** is a word or phrase that connects one sentence to another in a logical way. Logical connectives are important in maintaining the organized structure of a paragraph.

In the following paragraph, the topic sentence and the logical connectives are underlined.

EXAMPLE

Building the bookcase I needed took me some time but it was well worth every minute I spent on it. The first thing I did was to think about the project very carefully. I took several weeks to plan exactly what I needed and revised those plans several times. Then I measured, carefully, three or four times, the space the bookcase would go into. After that I bought the wood and the stain for the bookshelves. The next step was to measure again. I planned exactly how I would cut each piece of wood and how I would put all the pieces together. The fifth step was the actual cutting and construction. Because I had planned carefully, this step took little time. Finally, I stained the finished shelves. Taking my time with this project gave me a bookcase that is both sturdy and pretty.	topic sentence logical connective: step one logical connectives: steps two and three logical connectives: steps four and five logical connective: step six

Each of the underlined logical connectives helps to relate the sentences to one another in an orderly way.

Some logical connectives relate to time, such as *first, next, last, then,* or *after that.* Other logical connectives relate to spatial order, such as *here, there, overhead, underneath,* or *beside.* Still others relate to importance and sequence of ideas. Some of these are *furthermore, in the first place, also, another example,* or *finally.*[1]

---

[1]See Section 11 for detailed lists of logical connectives. See Section 12 for the other kinds of transitional devices.

EXERCISE 19. Read the following paragraphs. They contain no logical connectives. After you have read each paragraph, choose logical connectives from the list that follows. Indicate where each logical connective should be inserted in the paragraph to give it more coherence.

PARAGRAPH A

¹The late 1600s and the 1700s were a time of great musical importance. ²Four greatly loved and respected musicians and composers were born and died during those years. ³In 1685, both Bach and Handel were born. ⁴Bach lived from 1685 to 1750, Handel from 1685 to 1759. ⁵In 1756 Mozart was born, and he lived until 1791. ⁶Near the end of this period, in 1770, Beethoven was born. ⁷He died in 1827. ⁸Truly, the 142 years from 1685 to 1827 gave our culture some of its finest music.

Logical connectives
then
also
finally
first

PARAGRAPH B

¹My first sight of my new apartment was anything but inspiring. ²The rug was unbelievably dirty, covered with sand and bits of paper. ³The walls caught my attention. ⁴They were covered with dirty hand prints and a few lighter squares where pictures had hung. ⁵Two high, deepset windows faced the street, each window blocked by a crust of grime. ⁶A three-bulb fixture was attached to the ceiling, in a slightly lopsided manner. ⁷It had, of course, only one bulb. ⁸The floor, walls, and ceiling, however, were all sound. ⁹Soap and paint would do wonders, and so, indeed, it proved.

Logical connectives
overhead
next
to begin with
at the top
directly in front of me

PARAGRAPH C

¹Building a terrace from chips of granite was a memorable experience. ²I examined the area I wanted to cover. ³Most of it was sand, packed hard and six to twelve inches deep, easy to work with. ⁴I went to a nearby quarry to select my stones. ⁵All the stones were of different sizes and shapes; I took any with at least one flat side. ⁶I could begin to set the stones. ⁷Using a trowel, I dug out the shape of each stone in turn. ⁸Finding the right stone for each spot was like doing a three-dimensional jigsaw puzzle. ⁹I reached a small, steep drop. This was the place for steps, obviously. ¹⁰It was a most pleasurable and satisfying way to spend a summer.

Logical connectives

at that point	all in all	after that
then	to start with	finally

NARRATIVE, DESCRIPTIVE, AND EXPOSITORY PARAGRAPHS

10.l WRITING DIFFERENT KINDS OF PARAGRAPHS

Paragraphs can be grouped into three general types. Each of these types of paragraph serves a different purpose. In this section you can study the three basic kinds of paragraphs: narrative, descriptive, and expository.

As you write, you will discover that thoughts group themselves naturally into basic patterns. The different patterns demand different kinds of paragraphs.

10.m NARRATIVE PARAGRAPHS

Narrative is the kind of writing that tells a story, real or imagined.

A narrative paragraph tells a reader what happened. It relates a series of events. The paragraph may be an account of something that actually happened, or it may be imaginary, such as the kind of paragraphs that you would find in a short story or novel. The following narrative paragraph happens to be based on a real incident.

EXAMPLE

<u>Communication can be a chancy thing at times</u>. <u>Not long ago,</u> I was returning home on a bus. I happened to be carrying something that contained liquid. As the bus went over a particularly bad stretch of road, I was forced to juggle frantically to avoid spilling the liquid. <u>Then</u> the bus moved onto a smoother stretch, and I could relax. With a sigh of relief, I turned to the woman next to me and remarked that the roads were just terrible. She nodded and replied that they were bad all over. We shook our heads at each other sympathetically. <u>In the next moment</u>, she turned back to me and announced that boric acid did wonders for them. I was naturally mystified by this comment, and so I could only respond by saying, "Oh, yes." We smiled at each other, she knowingly, I rather confusedly. <u>Then</u> I turned back to wonder how exactly boric acid was supposed to help the bad roads. <u>At last</u> it dawned on me. The woman thought I had said that the *roaches* were terrible. Relieved at having finally understood, I turned to her again, smiled, and assured her that she was quite right. Boric acid did do wonders for them!

topic sentence

logical connective

logical connective

logical connective

logical connective

logical connective

The preceding paragraph tells a story. There are a series of events, related by logical connectives. The structure is chronological. A narrative paragraph should, in general, follow this pattern. Begin at the beginning, and move along to the end.

EXERCISE 20. Use the following topic sentences to write a narrative paragraph.

> TOPIC SENTENCE A: One of the best experiences I ever had was when I _____. (Fill in your own ending for this topic sentence.)
>
> TOPIC SENTENCE B: The series of events that left our group marooned on this (desert island, high mountain, uninhabited planet) was both absurd and incredible.

10.n DESCRIPTIVE PARAGRAPHS

Description is the kind of writing that creates an impression of a person, place, or thing.

A descriptive paragraph describes someone or something with sensory details. It tells a reader about the sights, sounds, smells, tastes, or feel of something. It gives a reader a clear mental picture of whatever is being described.

Descriptive paragraphs therefore deal largely with concrete details (10.e). The specifics used in description are generally sensory ones. The structure of a descriptive paragraph is generally spatial order (10.k).

EXAMPLE

<u>We were all disappointed when the fog closed in during the evening of July Fourth; yet we soon discovered that fireworks in the fog could be quite wonderful.</u> <u>To begin with,</u> each group of people was enclosed by shifting gray walls. The hill where we stood was <u>damp</u>, the air <u>warm and moist</u>. We could barely see others in the crowd and so felt quite private. The normal sounds of the crowd drifted faintly to us, as if from a distance. <u>Then</u> the fireworks began. The <u>opaque gray</u> ceiling was lit, suddenly, by <u>star-bursts of color</u>. Each spark was expanded by the fog into a <u>tiny sphere</u>, resem-	topic sentence logical connective concrete details logical connective concrete details

bling a comet as it fell. <u>Next</u> came the sound of the explosion, <u>echoing weirdly</u> from all around us, yet <u>softer</u> than usual. The <u>acrid</u> smell of the chemicals was softened by its passage through the fog. The <u>damp</u> air added its own smell, producing a unique aroma. The final burst of fireworks lit the whole sky in <u>shifting patterns of colored stars</u>. Never again will we complain if the fog joins us in celebrating the Fourth of July.

logical connective

concrete details

EXERCISE 21. Use the suggested topic sentences to write descriptive paragraphs. For the first paragraph, you are to describe a familiar object. For the second, describe an imaginary scene.

TOPIC SENTENCE A: I always enjoy looking at my _____. (old bicycle, house, new car, room, model planes, stuffed toys, etc.)

TOPIC SENTENCE B: The last time I visited my family on Mars, I was impressed by the progress of the major city there.

10.0 EXPOSITORY PARAGRAPHS

Exposition is the kind of writing that explains or clarifies.

Exposition can also be said to attempt to persuade or instruct a reader.

An expository paragraph may use examples or facts and statistics as specifics (see 10.f and 10.g). Examples, facts, and statistics are all suited to expository writing. A group of examples, facts, or statistics makes the most sense when it is organized according to the importance of the individual specifics.

There are several definite kinds of expository paragraphs. Here, you will find two of the more common kinds: (1) comparison and contrast paragraphs and (2) explanation-of-process paragraphs.

10.0.1 Comparison and contrast

Comparison is writing that tells about similarities. **Contrast** is writing that tells about differences.

A given expository paragraph may concentrate only on the similarities between two or more things. It may concentrate only on the differences between two or more things. On the other hand, an expository paragraph may include both comparison and contrast.

The following three examples are expository paragraphs. They are, respectively, a paragraph of comparison, a paragraph of contrast, and a paragraph that includes both. Note the strong topic sentence, the kinds of specifics, and the logical connectives used in each of these paragraphs.

PARAGRAPH OF COMPARISON

Surprising as it may seem, an orchestra conductor's job bears a similarity to a construction worker's job. Both expend large amounts of energy physically. A construction worker, of course, must expend his or her energy in carrying wood or stone, in hammering and sawing. Now consider what a conductor must do. There may be 100 or more members in a given orchestra, all of whom depend on the conductor to direct them. Pieces of music may last four or more hours. During this time, the conductor must be in constant motion, giving the beat and gesturing to tell the musicians what to do. In addition, the conductor must always be thinking ahead of the players, maintaining an exhausting double layer of thoughts. It is no wonder that a conductor may finish a performance as exhausted as someone who has been lifting and carrying all day.

[Margin annotations: topic sentence / example / logical connective / fact / fact / logical connective / logical connective]

PARAGRAPH OF CONTRAST

A constant discussion takes place be-
tween those who favor country living and
those who favor the city. The two lifestyles
are quite different, but each has its merits.
Supporters of country living enjoy the peace
and quiet that is available in the country.
Also, they say, country dwellers can be more
aware of the environment, more in contact
with nature. Finally, country dwellers point
out that the pace is slower. There is less
stress and more time to talk with neigh-
bors. On the other hand, city dwellers
praise the excitement of the city. Also, they
are proud of the many cultural benefits
available to them easily and quickly in the
city. Lastly, city dwellers find food, clothing,
and other products available within easy
reach. In the final analysis, it seems un-
likely that the argument will be resolved.
What it comes to is a matter of taste.

	topic sentence
	first example
	logical connectives; second and third examples
	logical connectives; fourth, fifth, and sixth examples
	logical connective

PARAGRAPH OF COMPARISON AND CONTRAST

The decision of whether to buy or to make
your own clothes is not an easy one. After
all, there are similar elements that you can-
not overlook. Although it takes time to
make clothes, it takes nearly the same
amount of time to shop for them. Further-
more, most of the same fabrics are available
both in bolts of fabric and in ready-made
clothes, and so choice of fabric is not a deci-
sive issue. Differences between shopping
and sewing do exist, however. New styles
are usually available in ready-made clothes
before they are available as patterns. Also,
clothes that you buy are often finished more

	topic sentence
	similarities
	differences

professionally than homemade clothes. On the other hand, the cost of homemade clothing is usually about half of the cost of ready-made clothing. In addition, an expert sewer can make clothes that look as nice and that fit better than factory-made clothes.

differences

EXERCISE 22. Use the given information to write your own paragraphs. Write as strong a topic sentence as you can, to begin with. Then use the information as specifics.

PARAGRAPH *A*

Write a paragraph comparing athletes and visual artists (such as painters, sculptors, etc.). You may wish to use some of the logical connectives listed below.

Information

ATHLETES: often have natural talent for athletics; must train for years to use talents; best athletes are creative about new ways to play; athletics takes complete concentration

VISUAL ARTISTS: usually have strong natural talents; takes much practice to use talents well; artists always experimenting to find new ways; often get completely involved in what they do

Logical connectives

also	secondly	to begin with
in addition	then	finally
besides that	furthermore	

PARAGRAPH *B*

Write a paragraph contrasting the use of private cars and the use of mass transit in the city. Some logical connectives are provided to help you.

Information

PRIVATE CARS: can go exactly where you want to go; no time schedule to follow; few parking spaces available; use much energy; expensive to pay for garage space

MASS TRANSIT: uses less energy per person; always available; costs less per ride to use; no traffic jams or parking problems; schedules may be inconvenient; do not go exactly where you want to go

Logical connectives

in the first place

secondly

finally

then

on the other hand

however

also

PARAGRAPH C

Write a paragraph of comparison and contrast about prepared foods in the supermarkets and food that you buy and prepare yourself. You may wish to use some of the logical connectives provided.

Information

PREPARED FOODS: easily available; wide variety of meals; available in many different serving sizes; quick and easy meals; taste is often bland; difficult to add your own spices, etc.; high energy usage; nutritional information may be scanty

FOODS YOU PREPARE: easily available; wide variety; any serving size you choose; costs less than prepared foods; taste is exactly what you want; sometimes long preparation work needed; vitamins and other nutrients are there naturally

Logical connectives

also

secondly

furthermore

however

in addition

when

on the other hand

finally

10.0.2 Explanation of process

An **explanation-of-process** paragraph explains how to reach a goal or how something works.

It tells a reader how to do something: what steps may be involved, what order the steps are in, and what the final result is. An expository paragraph that is an explanation of process is a paragraph that gives information in an easy-to-follow way.

Read the following example of an explanation-of-process paragraph. Notice the strong topic sentence, the specifics, and the logical connectives. What kind of structure does the paragraph have?

EXAMPLE

<u>Follow these directions carefully and completely to find the hidden treasure cave.</u> <u>First</u>, locate the double pine tree. Stand with it on your right. <u>Then</u>, walk 52 feet straight forward and turn to your left. <u>Now</u>, walk 12 feet forward to the side of the lake. Follow the edge of the lake to your left until you reach the stream. <u>At that point</u>, follow the stream downstream to the bridge. <u>Then</u> stand with your back to the bridge. Follow the very faint footpath until you reach Skull Rock. <u>Next</u> walk due east for 12 feet, <u>then</u> turn right and walk due south for 20 feet until you reach the stone wall. Follow the stone wall to your left until you reach the side of the hill. <u>Finally</u>, walk six steps to your left and stand facing the hillside. The hidden treasure cave will be directly in front of you.

topic sentence

logical connectives

logical connectives

The structure of the preceding paragraph is chronological (see 10.k). Any explanation of a process will have to discuss the process step by step. Since a process takes place during a certain amount of time, the explanation will have to be structured according to time. You will only confuse your reader if you jump around or if you leave out a step.

EXERCISE 23. Explain how to get to your school from your home.

EXERCISE 24. Explain how something familiar to you works: You may choose one of the following suggestions, or another subject with which you are more familiar. Possible subjects: how a light switch works; a telephone; a bicycle; a heating system; a camera; a folding chair; a typewriter; an elevator; a card trick.

10.p REVISING YOUR PARAGRAPHS

You should not consider a paragraph or any piece of writing finished until you have read it over and revised it. Even professional writers find it extremely difficult to write a polished paragraph the first time around. The last sentence that they have written may make them want to go back and change the first sentence, for example. Writers know that revising is a very important step in the writing process.

It is at the revision stage that you can clarify ideas, add details, and improve the flow of your sentences. As you read over your paragraph, ask yourself the questions on the following checklist. Look back to the material suggested in parentheses for review if necessary. Be aware that you may even decide to revise your revision. Writing is a continuous process.

■ Checklist for revising a paragraph

1. Does the topic sentence clearly state one main idea and give strong direction to the paragraph? (See 10.a–10.c.)
2. Does each sentence relate to the main topic of the paragraph but add more rather than just repeat? (See 10.d–10.j.)
3. Is there a logical order to the arrangement of the sentences in the paragraph? (See 10.k.)
4. Are logical connectives and other transitional devices used effectively to connect sentences and ideas? (See 10.k.)

10.q EDITING AND PROOFREADING

Once you have revised your paragraph, you should carefully edit and proofread it for matters of grammar and usage, capitalization and punctuation, and spelling. Use the questions on the following Editing and Proofreading Checklist as a guide. The cross references in parentheses indicate other sections of this book to check for review if necessary.

As you edit and proofread your own or someone else's paragraph, you may use Editing Signals, such as those below, from Section 9.

■ Editing and proofreading checklist

1. Are all sentences complete? (See 2.a.) *frag*
2. Are varied sentence structures used? (See Section 3.)
3. Have you used the voice (active or passive) that is most effective in each sentence? (See 1.b.20.) *voice*
4. Are verb tenses consistent? (See 1.b.12.) *tense*
5. Do subjects and verbs agree? (See 2.c and 2.e–f.) *agree*
6. Do pronouns agree with antecedents? (See 1.d.1 and 1.d.7.) *ref*
7. Is vocabulary precise but varied? (See Section 4.) *vocab*
8. Are words spelled correctly? (See Section 5.) *sp*
9. Is punctuation correct? (See Section 7.) *p*

11

PATTERNS OF THINKING AND WRITING

11

Patterns of Thinking and Writing

In compositions of more than one paragraph, each single paragraph is part of a larger pattern. Each paragraph becomes a link in a chain of thought. It is wise for you, therefore, to organize your writing into patterns.

The patterns that you will be studying in this section are ones that you use almost daily. These patterns are ways of thinking, talking, and writing. You use them in conversation with friends. You also use them when you think or write anything that communicates one of the following ideas:

1. "This is what happened."
2. "This is what it looks (sounds, tastes, smells, feels, acts) like."
3. "This is like (or unlike) that."
4. "This is how to do something."

PATTERN 1: "This is what happened."

This pattern is known as *narration.* You use it every time you tell someone what you have been doing, every time you tell a story, give a report, or record an event. Just as a single paragraph can be a narrative (see 10.m), so several narrative paragraphs can together tell a story.

PATTERN 2: "This is what it looks (sounds, tastes, smells, feels, acts) like."

This pattern is known as *description.* How do you tell someone about something? How do you describe it? You find words to tell the person what the "something" looked like (what one can see when one looks at it). Alternatively, you use words that appeal to the other senses. A few sentences can be descriptive, a single paragraph can be descriptive (see 10.n), or a few paragraphs can be used together.

PATTERN 3:   "This is like (or unlike) that."

PATTERN 4:   "This is how to do something."

These patterns are ways of explaining. Writing in which you explain is called *exposition*. To explain what something is you can compare it to something else. On the other hand, you can explain what something is by telling about it in a step-by-step way. You explain what squash is, for example, partly by comparing it to something else (say, tennis) and partly by explaining the way in which it is played. These two kinds of exposition are called *comparison and contrast* and *process*.

In this section you will find a discussion of each pattern, including a model of the pattern and a list of the skills that are essential to writing an effective passage. Then you will have a chance in the Warm-ups to practice each skill individually. Finally, in the Pattern Practices at the end of the section, you will use given information to write pieces of narration, description, and exposition. In several cases, you will work with the same set of information to produce three or four different kinds of writing.

NARRATIVE WRITING

11.a NARRATION: "This is what happened."

Narration is the kind of writing that tells a story, real or imagined.

You can use the pattern "this is what happened" to tell a true story or one that you have made up. You can also use it for a report on a current event such as you find in a newspaper or for a report on a past event such as you find in your history book.

11.b A NARRATIVE MODEL

The following model happens to be a true story. In it, as in all stories, certain events happen. Notice that the events are sequenced one after another in time. Notice, also, that the words and phrases underlined in red help to tell time. These words and phrases serve as **logical connectives**. They relate the events in the story to each other and help to order them in time.

■ Model: "This is what happened."

A few years ago a river tried to kill my father. My father, some friends of mine and their fathers, and I were on a white-water canoe trip. White-water canoeing is exciting because you must dodge between rocks as you are drawn swiftly downstream by the current. As you go, you must fight the "white water" that foams up as the river races over the jumbles of rocks and boulders that protrude at points along the way. White-water canoeing is dangerous, but I had yet to learn that.

My father was in one of the two-person lead canoes. I shared a canoe in the middle of the group with a friend's father. We were now paddling through a still section of the river. After a while I noticed that we had begun to put on speed, and I heard in the distance a hushed, hissing roar. I turned and grinned at my canoe mate, and he smiled back. The sound I heard was the sound of white water ahead.

In a moment we were in it, our canoe and all the others twisting under us like bucking horses, our paddles fighting to keep the canoes head on. Twice, our canoe was hung up on rock. The second time, we

Notice the underlined logical connectives, which help to relate the events in time.

swung around, using the rock as a pivot, and began to race downriver backward. Paddling as quickly as we could, we managed to get turned around again and finished bumping and bouncing our way safely to smooth water again.

We saw our canoes pulled up to the shore, and we joined them. There I found my father, looking dazed and soaking wet. He told his story as a sort of joke, laughing shakily, but it chilled me to the bone.

In the final hundred feet of the rapids, while I was just entering the white water, his canoe had struck a rock, slid up onto it, and turned over. His partner had been snatched into the main current and carried safely to deeper water. My father, however, had been pulled under by the current and had found himself in a tangle of tree roots that grew from the riverbank. The rushing water jammed him in tightly two or three feet beneath the surface. For precious seconds, he thrashed about in a blind struggle before he forced himself to be calm. Opening his eyes and deciding that he had to get out the way he came in, he hauled himself toward the gap in the tangle of roots. Working against the current, he squeezed through the opening. He broke surface and stood in the chest-deep water, taking in great lungfuls of air. Then he noticed, for the first time, that the water he stood in was freezing. Once on the riverbank, he walked down to the rest of the party.

From that time on, the river would look different to me. Its glittering, foaming surface would always seem to hide a private darkness below.

Notice the underlined logical connectives, which help to relate the events in time.

11.c SKILLS FOR WRITING NARRATION

When you set out to write a narrative and to follow the pattern "this is what happened," there are certain steps that you can follow. If you follow these steps and apply these skills, your writing will come more easily. Also, your entire composition will be more coherent. The steps that you should take and the special skills that you should apply to narrative writing are itemized here. You will also find a list of words that will help in writing narration.

■ Sequencing events in narration

To put the events or actions of a narrative into a logical sequence, you should:

1. **List the actions or events that you wish to include. Be sure to include all necessary events. Eliminate unnecessary events.**

   We launched our canoes into the river.
   We woke up at dawn.
   We rolled up our sleeping bags, cleared the tents, collapsed the tent rigging, and folded up the tents.
   We had a big breakfast of bacon and eggs.
   ~~It wasn't my turn to wash dishes that morning~~.
   We loaded the canoes and strapped everything down under waterproof plastic sheets.
   ~~I cut my finger slightly with a knife~~.

2. **Sequence the events in chronological, or time, order. You may find it helpful to put the events on a time line that moves from left to right.**

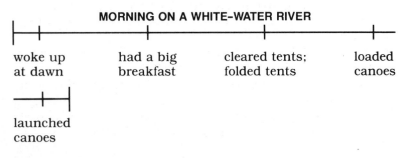

MORNING ON A WHITE-WATER RIVER

| woke up at dawn | had a big breakfast | cleared tents; folded tents | loaded canoes |

launched canoes

■ Using logical connectives in narration

Logical connectives are words and phrases that connect one sentence to the next. Logical connectives can also occur in the middle of sentences. In either position they make clear the order in which events occur or the way in which details are related to one another. Each of the patterns of thinking and writing has its own set of logical connectives.

In narrative writing logical connectives indicate the order in which events occur. They are time words.

Try to use these logical connectives as you write. You will not need to use a logical connective in every sentence, but you will find them useful whenever you need to make a complicated sequence of events clear.

The list below contains some common logical connectives for narrative writing.

after	finally
as soon as	just before
at the same time	next
before	soon
during	then
earlier	while

WARM–UP 1: Sequencing events. The historical events that follow are in no particular order. Rearrange the events, putting them into chronological order.

Oct. 24, 1962: Soviet ships carrying missiles to Cuba turn back to U.S.S.R.

fall 1962: U.S. spy planes discover missiles on Cuba.

Oct. 28, 1962: Khrushchev agrees to move missiles from Cuba.

summer 1962: Nikita Khrushchev, leader of U.S.S.R., secretly equips Cuba with nuclear missiles.

Oct. 22, 1962: President John F. Kennedy publicly denounces Soviet action, orders naval blockade of Cuba, and declares that any missile attack from Cuba will lead to a U.S. counterattack against the U.S.S.R.

WARM–UP 2: Sequencing events. The words of the following conversation are out of order. Rearrange them so that the conversation between Sheila and David makes sense.

> **SHEILA:** You don't know who Albert Finney is?
>
> **DAVID:** Friday, huh? Maybe. What's the movie?
>
> **SHEILA:** He starred in *Tom Jones* and *Murder on the Orient Express*. Do you want to go?
>
> **DAVID:** Sure, I'd be glad to.
>
> **SHEILA:** David, I was thinking of going to a movie on Friday. Do you want to go with me?
>
> **DAVID:** Who's he?
>
> **SHEILA:** *Wolfen*. It stars Albert Finney.
>
> **DAVID:** No. Should I know?

WARM–UP 3: Sequencing events. Notice that the events described in the model narrative in 11.b are not in chronological order throughout. The author first tells his own experience on the rapids and then relates his father's experience. In reality their experiences must have happened at nearly the same time. Make a time line that shows how the events of the two stories might have happened at the same time. The time line has been begun for you. Complete it up to the point at which the narrator reaches the group on shore.

WARM–UP 4: Using logical connectives. Rewrite the following paragraph, adding logical connectives where they will help the reader to understand the action. You may use the logical connectives listed after the paragraph or introduce your own.

The assault on the mountain took place in three stages. _____, the climbers hiked overland to the base of the mountain, where they established Camp One. _____ resting for a full day, they donned heavy clothes and began to climb the steep slopes. They were _____ among snowfields. Two thirds of the way up, they established Camp Two. A night's rest followed. _____ they rose and continued to climb. Two thousand feet below the summit, they established Camp Three and again rested. _____, a few hours before dark, they climbed the last two thousand feet and planted a flag on the summit. _____ they started down again.

Logical connectives

first	a little later
at dawn	after
soon	in the afternoon

11.d DESCRIPTION: "This is what it looks, sounds, smells, tastes, feels, or acts like."

Description is the kind of writing that creates an impression of a person, place, or thing.

In description you are dealing with details, not events as in narration. These are *sensory details*. In a description, you call on your senses of sight, hearing, taste, smell, and touch.

The examples, skills, and exercises that follow will help you to write descriptions in a long composition.

11.e A DESCRIPTIVE MODEL

As you read the model below, notice how the author uses sensory details to convey to you his impression of the scene. Notice also the logical connectives that help organize the details in the model. Do the logical connectives in the description order the details in time as in narration, or in some other way?

Model: "This is what it looks . . . like."

A few miles south of Soledad, the Salinas River drops in close to the hillside bank and runs deep and green. The water is warm too, for it has slipped twinkling over the yellow sands in the sunlight before reaching the narrow pool. On one side of the river the golden foothill slopes curve up to the strong and rocky Gabilan mountains, but on the valley side the water is lined with trees—willows fresh and green with every spring, carrying in their lower leaf junctures the debris of the winter's flooding; and sycamores mottled, white, recumbent limbs and branches that arch over the pool. On the sandy bank under the trees the leaves lie deep and so crisp that a lizard makes a great skittering if he runs among them. Rabbits come out of the brush to sit on the sand in the evening, and the damp flats are covered with the night tracks of 'coons, and with the spread pads of dogs from the ranches, and with the split-wedge tracks of deer that come to drink in the dark.

There is a path through the willows and among the sycamores, a path beaten hard by boys coming down from the ranches to swim in the deep pool, and beaten hard by tramps who come wearily down from the highway in the evening to jungle-up near water. In front of the low horizontal limb of a giant sycamore there is an ash pile made by many fires, the limb is worn smooth by men who have sat on it.

Evening of a hot day started the little wind to moving among the leaves. The shade climbed up the hills toward the top.

> Notice the underlined logical connectives, which help to order the details in space.

<u>On the sand banks</u> the rabbits sat as quietly as little gray, sculptured stones. And then from the direction of the state highway came the sound of footsteps on crisp sycamore leaves. The rabbits hurried noiselessly for cover. A stilted heron labored up into the air and pounded down river. For a moment the place was lifeless, and then two men emerged from the path and came into the opening by the green pool.

They had walked in single file down the path, and even in the open one stayed behind the other. Both were dressed in denim trousers and in denim coats with brass buttons. Both wore black, shapeless hats and both carried tight blanket rolls slung over their shoulders. The first man was small and quick, dark of face, with restless eyes and sharp, strong features. Every part of him was defined: small, strong hands, slender arms, a thin and bony nose. Behind him walked his opposite, a huge man, shapeless of face, with large, pale eyes, with wide, sloping shoulders; and he walked heavily, dragging his feet a little, the way a bear drags his paws. His arms did not swing at his sides, but hung loosely.

—John Steinbeck

A description of what the men look and act like begins. Notice that they are described in an orderly way: first their similarities and then their differences (see 11.g).

In this model of description, how are the details ordered? As you can see from this model, they are organized in space or, as it is said, spatially. When you are describing what something looks like, when sight is involved, details are organized by space usually. If taste were involved, space might not work. Notice the underlined phrases in the model. These are the logical connectives that help to organize the details in space. Notice that most of them are prepositional phrases. Prepositional phrases telling where and adverbs of space like *here* and *there* serve as logical connectives in description of this kind.

Usually, the details in a description are organized around a frame of reference of some kind—in this model a river. The details are introduced as being on one side or the other of the river.

You will seldom find description going on for several paragraphs as pure description. Usually description sets the stage for the reader or helps to introduce readers to characters in a story. Notice that, in the model, description serves both of these purposes, while some actions (narrative) are also included.

11.f SKILLS FOR WRITING DESCRIPTION

To write an effective description, you must learn to notice and order sensory details and to use logical connectives and other key words. These skills are discussed in more detail below. You will get a chance to practice what you have learned by doing the Warm-up exercises that follow.

■ Noticing and ordering sensory details

There are several steps involved in observing and ordering sensory details:

1. **Determine the dominant impression you want to convey.**
   A ride in a small airplane is thrilling and a bit frightening.

2. **Observe carefully with all your senses in order to list sensory details.**
   small size of single-engine airplane
   smell of oil and fuel
   cramped cockpit with only four seats
   deafening roar of the engine
   blurred whirling of propeller
   exciting race down the runway
   pressure of acceleration against my chest
   takeoff: a steep climb into the air
   houses, cars, and people shrinking beneath me
   feeling of wind buffeting the small plane

3. **Classify each detail by sense, using an observation table, perhaps.**

OBSERVATION TABLE

look	sound	smell	feel, movements

small size
cramped cockpit
blurred whirling
race down runway
takeoff
houses, etc.,
  shrinking away
	roar of
	  engine
		smell of
		  oil and
		  fuel
			pressure of
			  acceleration
			wind
			  buffeting
			  plane

4. **Put the details in the order that you wish to discuss them.**
As you know, you can order them in space, usually around an object (the river in the model above). There are other ways of ordering them, however. You may wish to order details according to which sense they affect. You may wish to order details in the same order in which you experience them. Generally, the organization of a description depends on what you are describing and on the sense affected. A description of an approaching parade involving sounds would be different from a description of a house that you walk through, for example.

■ Using logical connectives and key words in description

To help you establish directions

to the right	below
to the left	beneath
ahead	on the outside
under	on the inside
over	opposite to
horizontally	parallel to
vertically	overlapping with
diagonally	here, there

To help you describe shapes

rectangular	semicircular
circular	square

WARM–UP 5: Noticing sensory details. Take a few minutes to observe your surroundings. Do not move. Do not do anything. Simply think about what you are able to perceive with your senses of sight, hearing, smell, touch, and taste. After you have observed your surroundings for a few minutes, make an observation table and record on it as many of your sense impressions as you can.

WARM–UP 6: Remembering sensory details. Most of the time, people do not write about what they are experiencing at the moment. They write about experiences they have had in the past. It is important, therefore, to be able to remember sensory details from the past. Choose from the list below an activity that you have performed. Give yourself a few minutes to remember it in all its detail, and then make an observation table that records your sense impressions of that activity.

a. riding a ferris wheel
b. playing a fast-moving game like basketball, volleyball, or soccer
c. walking in a forest or park on a sunny day
d. gliding on a bicycle down a long or steep hill

WARM–UP 7: Ordering spatial details. Describe each of the following diagrams. Use logical connectives, such as those suggested.

across	diagonal	to the right
at the midpoint	on top of	to the left

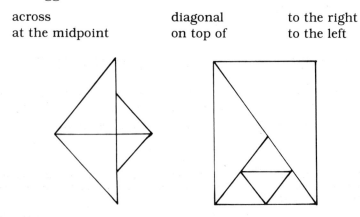

WARM–UP 8: Deciding how to organize details in description. Be ready to explain how you would organize descriptive details if you were describing each of the following:

a. a delicious dessert

b. an automobile

c. the marching band playing your school song

EXPOSITORY WRITING[1]

11.g COMPARISON / CONTRAST: "This is like (or unlike) that."

Comparison is the kind of writing that tells about similarities. **Contrast** is the kind of writing that tells about differences.

Comparison/contrast writing is unlike narrative or descriptive writing and yet combines elements of both. Unlike narration and description, which simply relate a story or list sensory details, comparison/contrast writing *examines* two or more items to see how they are similar or different. Yet comparison/contrast writing can often make use of descriptive and even narrative patterns. Before you can compare or contrast two events, you must first relate the actions that take place in each (narrative). Before you compare or contrast two objects, you must describe each.

11.h A COMPARISON / CONTRAST MODEL

The following model compares and contrasts two subjects. Note the underlined logical connectives. They help to make the comparisons and contrasts clear.

---

[1]The main kinds of expository writing are comparison/contrast, explanation of process, definition, cause-effect, and argument. The first two are covered in detail in this section.

■ Model: "This is like (or unlike) that."

Have you ever seen a play on stage? Many people have not. They have seen theater only in its recorded forms: on television and on film. To miss live theater is a great shame because a live performance is a unique experience, <u>unlike</u> anything seen through a camera's lens.

What is the <u>difference</u> between live and recorded theater, between a play seen on stage and the TV programs and films you see? Live and recorded theater certainly <u>resemble</u> each other in many ways. They are both composed of actors who perform a story in some kind of setting. Is not this process the same, whether live or recorded?

There is a <u>difference</u> between talking to someone face-to-face and talking to that same person over the telephone. The telephone transmits your words, <u>but</u> it cannot convey your gestures and facial expressions. The telephone also blocks other facets of face-to-face communication: those mysterious ways in which your personality and feelings can often be communicated to others without the benefit of words or gestures. A live performance is <u>similar</u> to a conversation. The audience and actors communicate with each other in many ways. The audience laughs, is bored, or listens and watches with deep concentration. The actors hear the laughter and somehow—by mysterious processes—feel the boredom or involvement of the audience.

The actors, in their turn, respond to the changing moods and reactions of the audience. If the audience is in a mood to laugh, the actors will often find ways to squeeze a few more laughs out of the play. An involved audience can often inspire actors to do their best work.

Recorded theater, <u>on the other hand</u>, makes this communication impossible. Once a performance has been recorded on film or videotape, it will never be changed. The actors never meet their audiences. The audience can laugh, or stare, or be bored, and it will not change the actors' performances one bit.

You may see a film or program over and over again, but you will always be seeing the same performance. <u>Compare</u> it to looking at a beautiful landscape. The landscape, seen live with your own eyes, changes from moment to moment as the sun moves in the sky and the wind comes and goes. A picture of that landscape, <u>however</u>, is the same from year to year. No two live performances are ever the same, because of the interplay of actor and audience.

11.i SKILLS FOR WRITING COMPARISON / CONTRAST

You will find the job of telling how "this is like (or unlike) that" easier if you make sure to select and order your points of comparison and contrast carefully and use logical connectives and key words effectively. The skills discussed here can be practiced by doing the Warm-Up exercises that follow.

■ Selecting and ordering points of comparison / contrast

There are several steps involved in selecting and ordering points of comparison/contrast:

1. **Decide whether you want to compare the items, contrast the items, or both compare and contrast the items.**

   Compare *and* contrast battery-operated and plug-in radios.

2. **Pick a few specific points that you wish to compare and/or contrast.**
   —quality of sound
   —portability
   —power supply
   —tuning range
   —durability

3. **Group the points of similarity together and give examples. Group the points of difference together and give examples. You may use a comparison frame.**

COMPARISON FRAME

points of comparison (+) points of contrast (−)	battery-powered radio	plug-in radio
quality of sound (−)	good	excellent
portability (−)	excellent	poor
power supply (−)	batteries	house current
tuning range (+)	standard	standard
durability (+)	good	good

4. **Put the points of similarity or difference in the order that you wish to discuss them.**

   Depending on your topic, you may want to place all of the similarities and all of the differences together. On the other hand, you may wish to discuss each point of similarity/difference separately.

   power supply (−)
   portability (−)
   tuning range (+)
   durability (+)
   quality of sound (−)

Note that in the preceding example, points of comparison/contrast are organized so that the greater portability and portable power supply of the battery-operated radio are discussed first. There then follows a discussion of the similar tuning range and durability of the two kinds of radios. The quality of sound, in which the plug-in radio is superior, is discussed last.

The composition written from this comparison frame might, therefore, begin with praise for the battery-operated radio's portability and then go on to explain the ways in which the two kinds of radios are similar. The composition would end with praise for the plug-in radio's superior quality of sound. In this way, the composition would be balanced in its examination of the positive and negative aspects of both kinds of radios.

■ Using logical connectives and key words in comparison/contrast

In comparison/contrast writing, logical connectives and key words are used to identify clearly points that are similar and points that are different.

To help you point out similarities

correspondingly	in like manner
in the same manner	similarly

To help you point out differences

although	in spite of
but	less than
differ from	more than
different from	on the contrary
however	on the other hand
in contrast to	unlike
in opposition to	whereas

WARM–UP 9: Finding similarities and differences. Look again at the comparison/contrast model in 11.h. Make a list of the similarities between live and recorded theater. Then make a list of the differences.

WARM-UP 10: Finding similarities and differences. Look at the two figures pictured below. Make a list of the ways in which the two figures are similar. Then make a list of the ways in which the two figures are different.

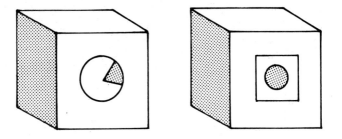

WARM-UP 11: Selecting points to compare and contrast. For each pair of items below, select some points of comparison and some points of contrast that you might use in writing a composition about them. Use (+) marks to indicate the points you plan to compare and (−) marks to indicate the points you plan to contrast.

a. a three-speed and a ten-speed bicycle

b. football and soccer

c. a traditional wind-up wristwatch and an electronic digital wristwatch

d. a sailboat and a power boat

WARM-UP 12: Using logical connectives for comparison/contrast. Rewrite the following passage, filling in the missing logical connectives. You may use those listed at the end of the passage, or you may supply your own logical connectives.

> Research into the way infants learn language has produced some startling results. Early in life, all of us go through a "babbling" stage, in which we make random noises in a steady stream. Studies have shown that, at this stage, infants produce all the sounds of all human language, from Chinese to Swahili to English.
>
> Infant monkeys go through a _____ "babbling" stage.

_____ human infants do, infant monkeys produce a stream of random noises that seems to test every possible combination of sounds their throats can produce.

A few months after they start babbling, human infants abruptly stop. The next sounds they are likely to make will approximate their specific native language. _____, infant monkeys stop babbling soon after they begin. But _____ human infants, they will never again produce the sounds of language. _____ the similarities between the babbling stages of humans and monkeys, monkeys fail to develop the complex ability to speak that humans easily master.

Logical connectives
in spite of
just as
unlike
corresponding
in the same manner

11.j EXPLANATION OF PROCESS: "This is how to do something."

Explanation of process is the kind of writing that tells how to reach a goal or how something works.

Much of what you learn about and most of what you hear about are not facts but processes. People are constantly explaining a process to you or you are to them. When you tell someone how to play a game or how to prepare a dish, you are also explaining a process. The examples, skills, and exercises that follow will help you learn how to write an explanation of process that will be clear to your readers.

11.k A PROCESS MODEL

The following model explains the process of erosion. Notice the use of logical connectives to help to make the steps in the process clear.

■ Model: "This is how to do something."

Erosion is a process by which water, wind, and other natural forces wear away the land. Erosion is a potent land-changer. The Appalachian mountains that run from Maine to Georgia were once a range of mountains higher and more rugged than the Rockies; the gentle slopes and low, rounded peaks they now wear are the result of erosion.

Erosion begins when water falls from the sky as rain or snow. Water soaks into stone and slowly dissolves the mineral "glue" that binds stone together. It liberates tiny particles and then washes them away. Rain and snow also fill cracks in rock and, since water expands when it freezes, forces these cracks to expand and exposes more stone surface to be slowly dissolved away. | step #1

| step #2

The next step in erosion occurs as the water that falls from the sky finds its way to rivers and to the sea. As it moves, it carries along its load of earth: grains of sand, flakes of rock, pebbles, and larger stones. Swept along in a river, the particles and grains strike at the riverbed and, like tiny chisels, knock off more grains and particles. The larger stones that roll and bounce along the riverbed do the same job, faster and more brutally. | step #3

| step #3 (continued)

The wind simultaneously erodes the land in much the same manner as running water. Strong winds carry fine dust and grains of sand and hurl them against the land. Each piece then cuts its tiny mark and creates more grains to be carried onward by wind and water. | another process going on at the same time: steps #1 and #2

11.1 SKILLS FOR WRITING PROCESS

To write an effective explanation of a process, you must be sure to include all the essential steps in their correct order. The use of logical connectives can help to make that order clear. The skills for writing process are explained fully below and on the next page. You will get a chance to practice what you have learned by doing the Warm-up exercises that follow.

■ Ordering steps in an explanation of process

To put the steps in an explanation of process into logical order, you should yourself follow certain steps.

1. **List the essential steps of the process in the correct (usually chronological) order. Exclude step or steps that are irrelevant.**

   ### How to Make Reservations on a Commercial Airline

   a. Collect information on available flights to your destination either by obtaining a printed schedule from an airline ticket office or by calling an airline information number. If you call, ask for daily flights.
   b. Examine the schedule information carefully.
   c. Talk over the schedule with friends and family.
   d. Decide which flight or flights would be most convenient for you.
   e. Before you call for a reservation, make sure you have all the information you need: day of departure, time of flight, and flight number. If you are making a round trip, you will probably want to reserve that, too, and you will need that information as well.
   f. Make a second choice of a flight or flights, since you may not be able to get a seat on the plane you want. Be prepared to discuss your needs with the reservations agent.
   g. Call the airline reservation number and ask for a seat aboard the flight of your choice.

   Step *c* can be safely excluded from an explanation of process. Not everyone will need to discuss the schedule with friends and family.

2. **Consider putting the steps into a different order—perhaps into distinct phases, stages, or actions. Decide whether or not these changes make the explanation clearer.**

    a. Collect information.
    b. Examine information carefully.
    c. Decide which flight or flights you want.
    d. Make a second choice.
    e. Before you call, make sure you have all needed information.
    f. Call airline reservation number and make reservation.

■ Using logical connectives in an explanation of process

Logical connectives in an explanation generally indicate the order in which steps are performed. Most of the time, the order in which you write the steps will make it clear how they are to be performed. When the order is not clear, however, be sure to use logical connectives like the ones below.

> first, second, third, etc.
> firstly, secondly, etc.
> in the first place, in the second place, etc.
> next, then, subsequently, at last, in conclusion, finally
> the most important, the least important, the most complex, the least complex

WARM–UP 13: Listing steps. List the steps involved in erosion by water. Then list separately the steps involved in erosion by wind. Use the explanation in the model in 11.k as your source.

WARM–UP 14: Sequencing steps. The following paragraph explains how rain forms. The steps in the explanation, however, are out of order. First, identify the connectives that relate the steps in the process. Second, using these connectives and the meaning of the sentences as a guide, order the steps in the formation of rain.

¹Rain forms when water vapor in clouds condenses around dust particles and falls in drops. ²Water vapor rises constantly from rivers and oceans in evaporation. ³When the water vapor reaches the cool air of the upper atmosphere, it condenses into tiny droplets that form clouds. ⁴These tiny droplets join together, usually around a particle of dust, and become larger and heavier. ⁵When they become heavy enough, they fall as rain. ⁶Before the tiny droplets can condense further, however, the temperature of the air must drop. ⁷In general, cooling a water vapor tends to make it condense into water. ⁸So rain falls when temperatures, in the upper atmosphere at least, fall.

WARM–UP 15: Sequencing steps. Erosion is a circular process that goes on and on. Draw a diagram that shows how erosion by water begins with rain and goes through a cycle to begin with rain again. (Use the corrected explanation from Warm-up 14.)

WARM–UP 16: Using logical connectives. Rewrite the following paragraph, filling in the missing logical connectives. You may use the logical connectives listed below the paragraph or introduce your own. Your goal is to make the process sound easy to follow.

Everybody seems to have his or her own system for washing a car. I begin by spraying the entire car with water from a hose. _____ I wash it all over with warm water and detergent. I use a terry-cloth rag for the washing. _____ I rinse it with the hose. _____, I wash any stubborn dirt again, and there are always some stubborn dirty places. _____, I rinse it again, and _____ I dry the car to keep water spots from showing up. I usually finish with a waxing, but that part is up to you.

Logical connectives
fourth
then
finally
third
next

11.m COMBINING PATTERNS IN ONE PIECE OF WRITING

Most writing, whether fiction or nonfiction, does not make use of just one pattern of thinking and writing.

Writers tend to use all the patterns to tell a story or provide information. Michael Crichton, for example, in his novel *The Andromeda Strain*, makes use of all four patterns.

The Andromeda Strain tells about scientists' attempts to deal with a disease brought back to Earth by a returning spacecraft. In the following excerpt a scientist is preparing to look at a sample of the green tissue of the disease under an electron microscope. Notice the author's use of all four patterns of thinking and writing.

■ Model: Combining patterns

In the room marked MORPHOLOGY, Jeremy Stone removed the small plastic capsule in which the green fleck had been imbedded. He set the now-hard capsule into a vise, fixing it firmly, and then took a dental drill to it, shaving away the plastic until he exposed barc green material. . . .

narrative pattern: "This is what happened."

He unscrewed the vise and lifted the plastic out. He took it to the microtome, a knife with a revolving blade that cut very thin slices of plastic and imbedded green tissue. These very thin slices were round; they fell from the plastic block into a dish of water. The thickness of the slice could be measured by looking at the light as it reflected off the slices—if the light was faint silver, the slice was too thick. If, on the other hand, it was a rainbow of colors, then it was the right thickness, just a few molecules in depth.

descriptive pattern: "This is what it looks . . . like."

That was how thick they wanted a slice

of tissue to be for the electron microscope.

When Stone had a suitable piece of tissue, he lifted it carefully with forceps and set it onto a small round copper grid. This in turn was inserted into a metal button. Finally, the button was set into the electron microscope, and the microscope sealed shut.

explanation-of-process pattern: "This is how to do something."

The electron microscope used by Wildfire was the BVJ model JJ-42. It was a high-intensity model with an image-resolution attachment. In principle, the electron microscope was simple enough: it worked exactly like a light microscope, but instead of focusing light rays, it focused an electron beam. Light is forced by lenses of curved glass. Electrons are focused by magnetic fields.

In many respects, the EM was not a great deal different from television, and in fact, the image was displayed on a television screen, a coated surface that glowed when electrons struck it. The great advantage of the electron microscope was that it could magnify objects far more than the light microscope. The reason for this had to do with quantum mechanics and the waveform theory of radiation. The best simple explanation had come from the electron microscopist Sidney Polton, also a racing enthusiast.

"Assume," Polton said, "that you have a road, with a sharp corner. Now assume that you have two automobiles, a sports car and a large truck. When the truck tries to go around the corner, it slips off the road; but the sports car manages it easily. Why? The sports car is lighter and smaller and faster;

comparison/contrast pattern: "This is like (or unlike) that."

it is better suited to tight, sharp curves. On large, gentle curves, the automobiles will perform equally well, but on sharp curves, the sports car will do better.

comparison/ contrast continued

"In the same way, an electron microscope will 'hold the road' better than a light microscope. All objects are made of corners, and edges. The electron wavelength is smaller than the quantum of light. It cuts the corners closer, follows the road better, and outlines it more precisely. With a light microscope—like a truck—you can follow only a large road. In microscopic terms this means only a large object, with large edges and gentle curves: cells, and nuclei. But an electron microscope can follow all the minor routes, the byroads, and can outline very small structures within the cell— mitochondria, ribosomes, membranes, reticula."

—Michael Crichton

WRITING ASSIGNMENTS: PATTERN PRACTICES

The following writing assignments will give you practice in using the four patterns of thinking and writing that you have studied in this section: narration description, comparison/contrast, and explanation of process.

The assignments will give you, or ask you to supply, information that you will then use in writing short compositions. The information given to you will include charts, dates, figures, and diagrams. Following the advice that you have received in this section, you should be able to transform this information into sentences and paragraphs.

You will see how the same information can lead to different kinds of compositions when you use different patterns of thinking and writing.

■ Assignment A: *Travel Writing*

You are going to be writing about a trip, real or imagined. If you wish, you can write about a real trip that you have taken. If not, use "A Trip Downtown" as the basis of the following writing tasks. "A Trip Downtown" is suggested by the map on the next page.

After you complete each writing task, be sure to edit and revise your work. See the checklists in 10.p and 10.q.

PATTERN PRACTICE 1: "This is what happened." Write a narrative of several paragraphs about your trip or some part of your trip that was especially interesting. Remember that you can use a real trip or an imagined trip. Use the map on the next page if it helps you.

PATTERN PRACTICE 2: "This is what it looks . . . like." Write a description of something or someone you encountered on your trip. Remember that you can use a real trip or an imagined trip. You can write about a famous landmark or an ordinary object.

If you use the map on the next page, you might write a description of one of the stores, businesses, or government buildings. Tell just where it is located in relation to other buildings and to the park.

PATTERN PRACTICE 3: "This is like (or unlike) that." Compare and contrast two places that you visited on your trip: two museums, two beaches, two restaurants.

If you use the map, compare and contrast two of the downtown streets (perhaps, Grand Avenue and Brook Avenue). In what ways are the two streets the same? (Consider their location.) In what ways are the two streets different? (Consider the kinds of stores on them.)

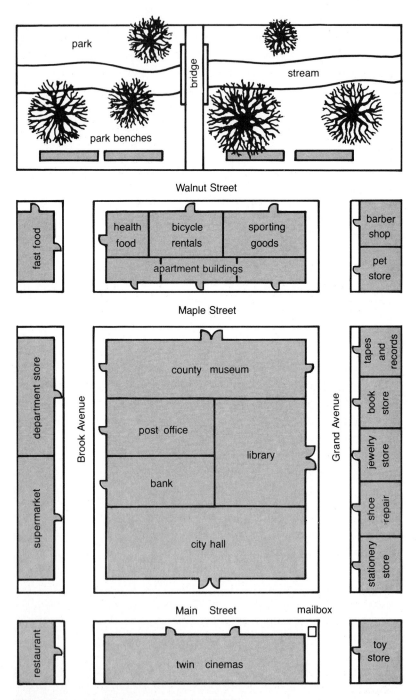

PATTERN PRACTICE 4: "This is how to do something."
Giving directions is a kind of explanation of process. Tell someone how to get to the place you visited on your trip.

If you are using the map on the facing page, assume that you want to plan an afternoon downtown for a visitor to town. Write a short composition telling the visitor how he or she can accomplish the following goals with the least trouble. Assume that you have left the visitor on the corner of Main and Brook and that the visitor wants to do the following:

> buy a take-out lunch and eat in a park
> buy postcards
> buy stamps
> buy a book
> see paintings by local artists in the museum
> pick up a basketball that was being repaired
> mail the postcards

PATTERN PRACTICE 5: Combination of patterns. Write four or five paragraphs in which you tell the story of your trip with descriptions, comparisons, contrasts, and explanations as you move from paragraph to paragraph. You will be using narration, description, and exposition together in one piece.

■ Assignment B: *Life Skills*

The following passage explains how to use a pay telephone. Notice that the steps are given in the wrong order and that the whole explanation is unclear.

After the explanation you will find four Pattern Practices. Using the passage about pay telephones, you will be asked to write a piece of description, an explanation of a process, and a piece of comparison/contrast. Then you will find one assignment that asks you to combine description, exposition, and narration in one piece of writing.

After you complete each writing task, be sure to revise and edit your work. See the checklists in 10.p and 10.q.

Pay phones may be dialed just like an ordinary phone. Some of them still have rotary dials, but most of them are now equipped with push-button dials.

If you read the directions printed on the phone carefully, you should have no trouble. First, lift the phone and listen for a dial tone. Then insert your money.

If the phone is a "Dial Tone First" phone, you will be able to hear a dial tone even before you insert your money. If you wish to call the operator, or make any other free call, you do not need to insert money at all.

If the phone is not a "Dial Tone First" phone, you will hear nothing when you listen to the receiver. If you dial a number that is outside your local area, the operator will come on the line and ask you to deposit more money. If you do not have the money, tell this to the operator, and he or she will stop your call from going through.

If the phone is not a "Dial Tone First" phone, simply lift the receiver, insert your money, and dial the number you want. If it is a "Dial Tone First" phone, listen for the dial tone to make sure that the telephone is working, then insert your money and dial.

PATTERN PRACTICE 6: "This is what is looks . . . like."
Describe a pay telephone. Assume that you are writing your description to someone who has never seen a pay telephone. Tell what it looks like. What parts does it have? What sounds does it make?

PATTERN PRACTICE 7: "This is how to do something."
Use the information in the paragraph to write a clear and logical explanation of how to use a pay phone. Rearrange the material, and add to it as necessary.

PATTERN PRACTICE 8: "This is like (or unlike) that."
Write a composition that compares and contrasts the process of making a telephone call (your explanation or the explanation above) with the process of writing and mailing a letter. Are any steps similar? Which takes more time, effort, thought?

PATTERN PRACTICE 9: Combination of patterns. Write four or five paragraphs in which you describe a pay telephone, compare and contrast a pay telephone to other kinds of telephones, explain how a pay telephone works (briefly), *and* relate an incident involving a pay telephone.

You will be combining description, exposition, and narration in one piece of writing.

■ Assignment C: *World History*

The information below and on pages 524–525 concerns an important development in world history: growth of the railroads. The development of the railroad in Great Britain was different in some ways from its development in the United States. After you have examined the information, you will be able to do Pattern Practices 10–13.

Remember to revise and edit your work. See the checklists in 10.p and 10.q.

Important Dates in the Railroad

Great Britain
1804: first locomotive invented by Richard Trevithick
1820: first modern railroad opened.
1829: George Stephenson's "Rocket," first modern locomotive
1845: peak of railroad age in Great Britain
1851: Great Britain recognized as the leading industrial nation in the world

United States
1830: first locomotive in the U.S.
1855: railroad crosses Mississippi River
1869: transcontinental railroad completed

PATTERN PRACTICE 10: "This is what happened." Using narrative, write a brief historical account giving the high points of the development of the railroad as a means of public transportation in Great Britain and in the United States.

NOTE: The following graph and maps provide information for Pattern Practices 11–13 on page 526.

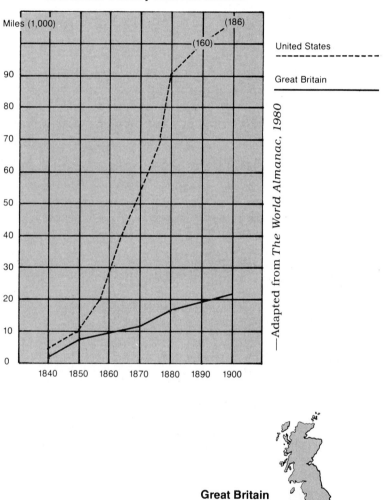

Nineteenth-Century Railroad Growth

United States
Great Britain

—Adapted from *The World Almanac, 1980*

Great Britain

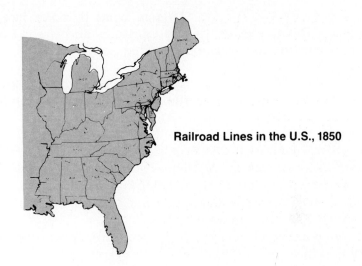

Railroad Lines in the U.S., 1850

Railroad Lines in the U.S., 1870

—Maps of U.S. courtesy of the Association of
American Railroads

PATTERN PRACTICE 11: "This is what it looks like." Describe the shapes of the United States and Great Britain, according to the maps provided here.

PATTERN PRACTICE 12: "This is what it looks like." Describe the two maps of the United States that show railroad lines in 1850 and 1870.

PATTERN PRACTICE 13: "This is like (unlike) that." Write a brief account comparing the development of railroads in Great Britain with their development in the United States. Were there similarities? What were the differences in time? The differences in extent?

From what you know about the geographical and population differences between the two countries and from your general sense of nineteenth-century history, explain why differences occurred in railroad development between the United States and Great Britain.

THE COMPOSITION

12 The Composition

A **composition** is a short paper composed of several paragraphs with a clear introduction, a body, and a conclusion.

Just how many paragraphs are needed in a composition depends upon how much you want to say about your topic. You may be asked to write a short composition of three to ten paragraphs (about 300 to 1,000 words).

In writing a composition, you will find it helpful to use the information from Section 10 about writing good paragraphs. The various patterns of thinking and writing that are discussed in Section 11 can also help you in developing your composition into several paragraphs. Your first job, however, is to select a topic unless a topic has been assigned to you.

12.a SELECTING A TOPIC

The job of selecting a topic will be made easier if you follow certain guidelines.

1. **Select a topic that interests you or that has various aspects that may interest you.** Writing about a topic in which you have some interest will make the work go more easily. You may find it helpful to make a list of possible topics. Do not be concerned about how long the list is. Simply write down your ideas. Then you can go on to eliminate one topic at a time.

2. **Your next step is to limit your topic.** Your composition is going to have to support your topic in much the same way that a paragraph supports a topic sentence. It is important to know in advance that you will be able to treat your topic adequately in the number of words that you plan to write. Even in a thousand words you are not going to be able to develop satisfactorily anything but a very limited and sharply defined topic. Keep trying to limit a topic until you are sure that you can handle it. You can limit your subject too much, however. Consider the following example of how a topic may be limited:

EXAMPLE

TOO BROAD:	*A.* television
LESS BROAD:	*B.* television news reports
TOO LIMITED:	*C.* reports at 6:00 on Mondays
ABOUT RIGHT:	*D.* weekday 6:00 news program

Topic *A* is so broad that it is almost meaningless. What about television? What in particular can you find to say about it? Topic *A* serves as a starting point only. You can begin with it and then start to limit it. Topic *B* is more manageable. Television news reports are a clear-cut part of a whole subject. You have begun the process of limiting by moving on to Topic *B.* Conceivably, you can watch all news reports at all hours of the day on television and write a composition about your experience. You must remember, however, that you are going to write only a short composition, not a research report. Can you limit the topic further? Topic *D* seems to be a good alternative: You can watch two or three evening news reports on different channels for a few days and write, for example, about their similarities or differences. Topic *C* certainly limits the topic: news reports on Monday evening only. Now it is too limited, however. "Why just Mondays?" one wonders. The topic is too limited to make sense or to be interesting to a reader.

An effective composition topic is one that will involve some thinking and activity on your part. Unless you are very familiar with the topic, you will not be able to sit right down and write it from start to finish. You will be dealing with real information. You will have to reflect upon that information and try to see how various pieces fit together. You may have to do some reading to fill in some general impression that you have or to back up an experience.

In selecting a topic for a short composition, however, be sure that you do not let yourself in for research involving more reading or more time than you have for the assignment. (When you do a research report, which is usually longer than a regular composition, you will have more time to read and find other information.

EXAMPLE

In selecting a composition topic, you should consider the information that you have gained in your other courses and subject areas. If, for example, you have been reading about the Industrial Revolution in England in your social studies class, you might draw your topic from this information. Some information might be fresh in your mind or in your class notes. You can go to your history book to get other information. Very little new research, if any, would be needed. Similarly, in your biology course, you might be reading about the cell. "The cell" would be too broad a topic. You would have to limit it in the same way that you saw the topic of television limited.

EXERCISE 1. Select the topic on each list that seems best for a short composition.

A

1. The world of biology
2. The world of the cell
3. The role of the cell in our daily life
4. The effects of pollution on cells

B

5. Origins of baseball
6. American sports
7. Growth of sandlot baseball, 1950–1970
8. Growth of baseball, 1950–1970

C
9. The Industrial Revolution in England
10. The effect of the Industrial Revolution on the growth of cities
11. Immigration, an effect of the Industrial Revolution
12. Factory life in England during the Industrial Revolution

12.b LIMITING A TOPIC FOR A BIOGRAPHY

The lives of people can be topics for compositions. These compositions are called **biographies**, or **biographical reports**. Often, when you choose to write about a person, you are also writing about the field in which the person worked. The Lindberghs, Charles and Anne, for example, led interesting lives, as individuals and as a married couple. When you write about them, however, you almost definitely will be writing about aviation, especially in its early days.

In choosing a person as a topic for a composition, you must be careful again to limit your topic. The entire life of anyone is seldom a good topic for a short composition. If you chose to write about the famous baseball player Babe Ruth, for example, you will have to select a topic from among several ideas that occur to you. The following ones vary from narrow to too broad:

A. Babe Ruth at bat in the eighth inning in Boston in 1938
B. Babe Ruth's finest year
C. Babe Ruth with the Yankees
D. The life of Babe Ruth

In choosing a biographical topic, be sure not to open yourself to too much reading and research. Ask yourself what reading you will have to do to write your composition on the topic you have selected. You may not have to do any reading at all. Perhaps you know about the life of someone already. Perhaps watching a movie or a television program will give you enough information. If you do some reading, you will probably be wise to select one book and stick to it as a basis for your information. Again, time is an important consideration when planning and writing a brief composition.

EXERCISE 2. For three of the broad topics listed below, name at least one person whose life relates to an aspect of that topic. Then write down a *limited* topic based on each of these people's lives.

1. music
2. some foreign country
3. basketball
4. the world of entertainment
5. exploration
6. literature

EXERCISE 3. At this point your teacher may ask you to begin the process of writing a short composition, perhaps one based on a person. If so, you may want to examine briefly the steps ahead as treated in the following pages of this section. You may at this point want to examine the biographical composition of Abigail Adams (12.p) as a sample. Exercises 4–14 provide a step-by-step procedure for preparing a composition. Each of these exercises is preceded by advice and sample material.

12.c SELECTING YOUR AUDIENCE AND STATING YOUR PURPOSE

Once you decide on your topic, limit it for a short composition, and find that you can easily get information about it, you should write out a formal statement of purpose. A **statement of purpose** makes clear what you will attempt to do in your composition. The statement of purpose is for your information. It usually will not appear in exactly those words within the composition itself.

For example, you may decide that because of your general interest in people, you will indeed write a biographical report for your composition. You are also inter-

ested in women's rights. You decide to write about Abigail Adams, the wife of the second President, John Adams, and the mother of the sixth President, John Quincy Adams.

You have heard that Abigail Adams was an interesting person and a leading woman in the early years of the country. You have watched a program about the Adamses on educational television. You have found a book or two in a library about Abigail Adams. You know that she wrote many letters that brought her fame in her own day. You then limit your topic to one like the following: "Abigail Adams, a famous woman, a famous letter writer and patriot."

Before you are ready to write out a statement of purpose, however, you need to consider for whom you will be writing your composition. You need to consider your **audience**. Your audience is important to your purpose. If you are writing for readers who know nothing much about America's past, for example, you will have to include more information about the time in which Abigail Adams lived than you will if you are writing for your classmates. If you are writing for a history class, you will have to be more precise and detailed about dates than you will in writing for a class studying composition. Your statement of purpose may be one like the following:

STATEMENT OF PURPOSE
I will explain to my classmates how Abigail Adams' life reflected through her letters shows her to be a strong voice for women's rights in the colonial period.

EXERCISE 4. Which of the following are good statements of purpose for a short composition? Explain in what ways the other statements fail.

1. I intend to write about music.
2. I will explain to my classmates how the basketball player Bill Russell enjoyed the job of playing with and at the same time coaching the Boston Celtics.

3. From basketball to Senator by Bill Bradley
4. I will show you how England survived World War II.
5. I will tell the readers of our high school magazine about the brightest moments in the life of Anne Lindbergh.

Prepare a statement of purpose for a composition that you may want to write. The composition can be about one of the people you listed for Exercise 2.

12.d MAKING NOTES

When you have written your statement of purpose, your next step is to get readily at hand the information that you will need in carrying out your purpose. If you are going to write about Abigail Adams, you need to have in front of you some essential facts about her life as well as the thoughts and opinions that you have formed about her. A biographical composition such as this one is not a research paper (see Section 15). You will not have to check several sources and to prepare footnotes documenting the information that you give in a brief composition. Your readers will want to be told or reminded about when Abigail Adams lived and about some of the high points of her life, however.

NOTES

born 1744   died 1818   colonial period   lived and died in Mass.   b. Abigail Smith in Weymouth   d. Quincy   At 20 married John Adams (he became second President)
Their son John Quincy—sixth President
Only woman to be First Lady and mother of a President
Little formal schooling—great reader and listener
Children and grandchildren loved and admired her.
Wrote letters all her life, to family and friends
Husband and son John Quincy traveled in Europe
Supported women's suffrage; against slavery
Letters give clear picture of her and her times.
Shown to hold strong opinions and ideals
Had deep understanding of people

12.e THE WORKING OUTLINE

A **working outline** will guide you as you think, plan, and gather any additional information that you need.

A working outline provides you with a way to structure the notes you have prepared. It is a means of organizing your ideas.

The first step in organizing your notes should be to group different kinds of notes together. In a biographical composition, one way of organizing is by date, in sequence, from birth to death. Groups of incidents that happened at nearly the same time will fit together.

Another way to group notes for a biography is to select the same *kinds* of incidents and put them together. If, for example, you were writing about Babe Ruth's years with the Yankees, you may choose to group events in his career as they occurred year after year. You may, on the other hand, choose to divide the events of his career into high points and low points.

There are several ways to begin grouping your notes about Abigail Smith Adams. The facts about when she was born, when she died, and when she was married can be grouped with the facts about her children and husband. Other groups may focus on her education and her reasons for writing so many letters. A third group may include your own judgment of what her letters reveal about her. Details of her personality and ideas about her political activism can be included here.

As you prepare your working outline, you should eliminate notes that do not relate directly to your purpose. For example, the notes about Abigail Adams' son's travel and about grandchildren are not necessary.

After you group related items together, you must order them. Decide which group should come first, second, and third in the outline. For example, in a biographical report on Abigail Adams, you may begin with the facts about her life. Next you can deal with her education and, finally, with what her letters show about her.

When you prepare your working outline, first write your statement of purpose. Then write down ideas in words or phrases. List each group of ideas under a Roman numeral and a heading. For example, the first group should be headed by I. *Personal life of Abigail Smith Adams*.

WORKING OUTLINE

Statement of purpose: I will explain to my classmates how Abigail Adams' life reflected through her letters shows her to be a strong voice for women's rights in the colonial period.

   I. Personal life of Abigail Smith Adams
      A. Born 1744 in Weymouth, Massachusetts
      B. Married John Adams in 1764, at age twenty
      C. Had five children; four became adults
      D. Had no career of her own
      E. Managed household and John Adams' business
      F. Was both wife and mother of Presidents
      G. Died 1818 in Quincy, Massachusetts
  II. Education
      A. Little formal education
      B. Avid reader and listener
      C. Letters as an education
 III. Her letters
      A. Written throughout her life
      B. Reveal honest and direct intelligence
      C. Reveal strong, well-examined ideals and opinions
      D. Give clear picture of her and her times
      E. Show her more politically knowledgeable than other women
      F. Indicate she was politically effective
      G. Show understanding of people
      H. Show she was socially adept as well
       I. Show her against slavery
      J. Show her supporting women's suffrage and other rights
          1. Wanted separate contracts for married women
          2. Wanted greater freedom than under English law as part of emancipation

After writing your working outline, check to see that it is complete. Do any sections of the outline need further details or development? For example, look at the boldfaced items that have been added to Section II of the outline you just read.

II. Education
    A. Little formal education
    B. Avid reader and listener
    C. Politics discussed at grandfather's
    D. Letters as education
    E. Classics in father's library

EXERCISE 5. Using your statement of purpose from Exercise 4, prepare notes, and then compose a working outline. Check to be sure it is complete when you have finished it. Add whatever may need to be added.

12.f THE FORMAL OUTLINE

A **formal outline** will guide you in writing your first draft.

The formal outline is based on the working outline that you developed. There are, however, several differences. First of all, your ideas must be in a clear and logical order in the formal outline. You must think about the order of the specific details within each group. You may also find yourself adding *more* details to the formal outline.

You should always, though, realize that an outline, no matter how formal, is supposed to help you, not limit you. An outline may be changed. As you write, you may start to move parts of your outline around. Still, the formal outline is a good place to start.

Many professional writers learned about formal outlines when they started to write and have continued to outline ever since. Other professional writers have found their own shortcuts to use instead of preparing formal outlines. If you learn the formal way of planning your writing, you will always be able to adjust it to your personal needs later.

■ Guidelines for formal outlines

1. **Numbering:** All major topics should be numbered with a Roman numeral: I, II, III, etc. These are the major headings in your outline. The next category, subtopics, should be indicated with capital letters. To divide your subtopics, use first Arabic numerals (1, 2, 3, etc.), then small letters. Should you need further divisions, use Arabic numerals in parentheses, then small letters in parentheses. An outline for a short composition will very seldom need the last two categories.

   In any one division you must have either no subdivisions or two or more subdivisions. In other words, you must not have only one subtopic under any particular topic.

   All Roman numerals should line up underneath one another, usually at the far left. Each division within the main topics should also line up. That is, all capital letters should line up throughout the outline, as should all Arabic numerals and small letters. (See sample outline on the opposite page.)

   Do not include a title or such terms as *introduction*, *body*, or *conclusion* in your formal outline. You do not need to include your statement of purpose.

2. **Capitalization and Punctuation:** Each entry should begin with a capital letter. This guideline applies whether or not your entries are sentences. Phrases should also begin with capital letters.

   Use normal punctuation in the entries as far as commas and quotation marks are concerned. End an entry with a period only if the entry is a sentence.

3. **Parallelism:** The divisions of an outline should be parallel in form. For example, if you use a sentence in main division I, you must also use sentences in the other main divisions. If you use a single word or phrase in subdivision A, all subdivisions should be similar.

FORMAL OUTLINE

I. Abigail Smith Adams' personal life
   A. Born in 1744 in Weymouth, Massachusetts
   B. Married John Adams in 1764
      1. Was twenty years old
      2. Had five children
         a. Death of girl at age two
         b. Survival of four boys
   C. Had no career of her own
      1. Managed household and farm
      2. Often managed husband's business
   D. Was wife and mother of Presidents
      1. Only such woman in history
      2. Great influence on both
   E. Died 1818 in Quincy, Massachusetts

II. Abigail Smith Adams' education
   A. Had little formal education
      1. Was ill as a child
      2. Could not afford formal schooling
   B. Became an avid reader and listener
      1. Read the classics
      2. Heard politicians at grandfather's
      3. Polished manners at aunt's
   C. Began exchanging letters with friends
      1. Polished her writing skills
      2. Kept her informed of events
      3. Sharpened her intellect

III. Abigail Smith Adams' letters
   A. Written throughout her life
   B. Show her personality clearly
      1. Had a deep understanding of people
      2. Was socially adept
         a. Met great people of the times
         b. Demonstrated powers of conversation
   C. Show her political opinions clearly
      1. Was politically knowledgeable
      2. Was against slavery
      3. Supported women's rights
         a. Wanted changes from English law
         b. Wanted rights for married women

IV. Abigail Smith Adams' political force

EXERCISE 6. The formal outline that follows has a number of problems in it. Read it, and correct the errors. Check the following items: numbering, indentation, capitalization, punctuation, parallelism. Add or delete items where necessary. If you have difficulty, refer to the guidelines for a formal outline.

A FAULTY OUTLINE

I. Outlet for imagination
II. Body of composition
   A. Fantasy has been around a long time.
      1. Fairy tales
      2. Legends and myths.
   B. Science fiction came in with technology
      1. Mary Shelley
      2. Jules Verne
      3. H. G. Wells
III. Recent developments
   A. Science-fiction magazines
      a. "Space opera"
         (1.) Monsters from outer space.
         (2.) Invasions of aliens
         (3.) Huge space battles took place.
      b. "Hard" science fiction
         (1.) High technology and new inventions
   B. Fantasy also changed.
      1. Full-length novels
      2. Complete world systems
IV. The field today
   A. Hundreds of novels are published each year.
      1. new authors
      2. many women are writing.
      3. growing numbers of fans.
   B. Magazines are still being published
      1. Encourage new authors
      2. more sophisticated stories
   c. Science fiction and fantasy have merged.
      (1.) other worlds, magic, and technology
   D. The field is producing literature.
  5. The field tomorrow

EXERCISE 7. Use the working outline you prepared in Exercise 5 to prepare a formal outline. Refer to the guidelines for formal outlines in 12.f as often as necessary. You may wish to change the order of entries from the working outline, add items, or delete items.

12.g THE THESIS STATEMENT

A **thesis statement** is a single statement that should appear at an early point in your composition. It performs three important tasks: (1) It states the main point of the composition; (2) it tells your reader your attitude toward the topic; and (3) it suggests the path that your composition will follow. Since the thesis statement acts as an introduction, it should appear in the first paragraph of your composition, perhaps as the last sentence in that paragraph.

You should not put your thesis statement in final form until the content and the structure of the composition are clear to you. Once you have finished the formal outline and examined it, try to write a single sentence that suggests most or all of the major divisions of the outline. You should also reread your statement of purpose. The sentence you now write may become part of the opening paragraph of your composition.

The thesis statement in a biography will be somewhat narrower in scope than one for a composition on, for example, the origins of baseball. The thesis statement for a biography should indicate what part of the person's life the paper will examine and from what point of view. It may also suggest the effect that the person's life has had on you.

The following thesis statement is for the composition about Abigail Smith Adams. Notice that it encompasses the main points of the formal outline (page 539). The thesis statement also suggests the order in which those points will be developed.

THESIS STATEMENT

Abigail Smith Adams, the wife of President John Adams, had little formal education, and yet she managed chiefly through her letter writing to promote the cause of women's rights.

EXERCISE 8. Use your formal outline and your statement of purpose to write a first-draft thesis statement.

12.h WRITING THE COMPOSITION

The first draft of a composition is not intended to be a polished piece of writing. It is intended to get your ideas on paper in sequences of sentences and paragraphs. Your major objective in the first draft is to have a basis from which you can work. Later, you will revise and reorder as necessary.

When you write the first draft, it is generally wise to follow the order of your outline. Each main division in the outline should have a separate paragraph. If the main division is a long one, you may need two paragraphs. You should feel free, however, to eliminate or add ideas from your outline as you write your first draft. The formal outline is a guide to your composition, not the paper itself.

Do not be too concerned with your introduction and conclusion at this point. After you write your first draft, you can write, expand, or revise your introduction and conclusion.

12.i USING PATTERNS OF WRITING AND THINKING

As you start to write your first draft, think about the different patterns of writing that you can use to develop a division or subdivision of your outline. At this point, you may want to review Section 11 to remind yourself that you can use narration, description, and exposition.

■ Narration

In biographical writing there are ample opportunities to use narration. A straightforward account of the events that occur in the lifetime of an individual is narration (11.a). Narration is the foundation of historical and biographical writing because it puts events into sequence as it tells "This is what happened."

■ Description

The pattern of description ("This is what it looked like") is also useful in biographical writing. It may be used to describe the person or to describe the person's town or house, for example. (See 11.d for more on description.)

The library in her father's house may be a place that you would want to describe if you were writing a biographical composition on Abigail Adams.

■ Comparison / contrast

Comparison and contrast (11.g) may come in handy. You may want to compare the rights of a woman in the colonial period with those of an American woman today.

■ Explanation of process

Explaining how a process works may be useful in writing about a phase of someone's life or in explaining what a person does. For example, you may explain a process of English law in the colonial period (one that Abigail Adams probably wished to see the new nation of Americans improve).

As you review your formal outline, therefore, add notes of where you may use various patterns of writing. Then you can look back into Section 11 at the specific writing skills (11.c, 11.f, 11.i, and 11.l) that are used in developing each pattern. Remember, also, the logical connectives and other special vocabulary that help you to write narration, description, or various forms of exposition.

12.j TRANSITIONS BETWEEN PARAGRAPHS

Transitional devices make the movement from one paragraph to another clear, smooth, and easy to follow.

When you write a composition of several paragraphs, you must make each paragraph connect smoothly to the paragraphs before and after it. Transitional devices are ways of making two paragraphs connect to each other. They provide bridges between two ideas.

Occasionally, you will find that two paragraphs treat ideas that are strongly connected already. In such cases, you may not need transitional devices. In general, however, you will find that using transitional devices helps your writing. There are several different devices that can be used. Three of the most important are: (1) determiners; (2) repeated key terms; and (3) logical connectives. Each of these devices is discussed in turn below.

■ Determiners

The determiners *this*, *that*, *these*, and *those* can be used as transitions between paragraphs. For example, you can introduce a second paragraph by saying, **This** *episode from the past was in her mind as she wrote.* . . . The next paragraph could then begin with **These** *years now seemed far behind Abigail, as she* . . . or **Those** *points are* . . .

In the following example the last sentence of one paragraph and the first sentence of the next are given. Notice how the determiner relates the two paragraphs to each other.

EXAMPLE

. . . and yet she achieved through her letters a considerable degree of political influence.

This political influence developed slowly during Abigail Adams' life, becoming more evident . . .

■ Repeated key terms

Throughout the composition, you will find that key, or important, terms are repeated. These key terms serve as transitional devices relating paragraphs.

The following example is from the sample composition on page 552. The first sentence is from one paragraph, the second is from the next paragraph. Notice that key words from the first paragraph are repeated in the second paragraph.

EXAMPLE

. . . She strongly **influenced** both men, not simply in their personal lives but in their **political actions** as well.

How did she achieve her **political influence**?

■ Logical connectives

Two paragraphs can be connected by using logical connectives. You may wish to review the logical connectives useful to various patterns of writing (see Section 11).

In the following example the logical connective that connects the two paragraphs is in bold type. Notice how it serves in this case to continue the ideas from the first paragraph into the second one.

EXAMPLE

. . . Abigail Adams settled into her life of maintaining her household and coping with a family of active children.

During this time and indeed for her entire life, Abigail Adams had no career of her own. . . .

EXERCISE 9. Review your statement of purpose and formal outline from Exercises 4–6. Then use the formal outline to write the first draft of your composition. Remember: You do not have to produce a polished piece of prose at this time. Concentrate on developing each idea fully. Try to use narration, description, comparison/contrast, and explanation of process.

12.k THE INTRODUCTION TO THE COMPOSITION

The time to work on your introduction is after you have finished your first draft. By then you have defined for yourself more clearly what you intend to say. The introduction to the paper will both make use of that added clarity and help to refine it further.

A good introduction should catch the reader's attention and also state the thesis of the composition. The following points are suggestions to consider when you write your introduction. They are general suggestions. You may find other ways.

1. **Ask a question**. For example, you may begin by saying *How can a woman who is allowed no possibility of entering politics on her own become effective politically in spite of this? Abigail Adams did.*

2. **Address the reader directly**. Ask what the reader would do or think about something; then go on to explain how the person in question handled it. In this case, you might find a specific event in Abigail Adams' life.

3. **State an interesting fact or statistic**. You may say that Abigail Adams holds a unique place in history for several reasons, one of which is the fact that she is the only woman in United States history to have been the wife of one President and the mother of another President.

4. **Tell an anecdote**. Find an amusing or interesting incident in your subject's life, one that supports the main point of your composition.

EXERCISE 10. Choose two of the suggestions from the list above, and write two different introductions for your topic. Use the composition you wrote a first draft for in Exercise 9.

12.l THE CONCLUSION TO THE COMPOSITION

The concluding paragraph completes your composition. It may be a summary of the ideas developed in the paper, or it may go on to give your own opinions about those ideas.

Be sure to make a smooth transition to the concluding paragraph. Again, the use of a logical connective may help in making this transition. Here are some suggestions that you should consider.

1. Restate the main idea of the composition.
2. Write a statement that sums up all your ideas about the subject.
3. Relate the topic directly to the reader's experience.
4. Use an anecdote that summarizes the main idea.
5. Ask a question that leads the reader to consider what has been said in your composition.

EXERCISE 11. Write a conclusion to the composition you began in Exercise 9.

12.m THE TITLE

After completing the first draft of your composition, including the introduction and conclusion, you must choose a title for your paper. The title is important, as it is the first thing a reader sees.

Your title should reflect the main idea of your composition. It must be neither too broad nor too narrow in scope. For example, as a title for a composition about Abigail Adams, "Abigail Adams" is not interesting enough. "A Strong Woman" does not tell us who is the subject of the biography. Furthermore, neither of these titles expresses the main idea of the composition. The title "Abigail Smith Adams: A Woman of Letters" is more appropriate. It tells a reader, first, that this is a biographical composition. It also includes the fact that Abigail Adams was a letter writer, an important aspect of the composition.

As you work with selecting a title, do not be afraid to try many different titles. Write down all your ideas. Play with them by switching the words around in them. Substitute part of one title for another.

EXERCISE 12. Choose a title for the composition you wrote in Exercise 9. After you have made your selection, list two alternative titles, and explain why you chose the one you did.

12.n REVISING THE FIRST DRAFT

When you have finished your first draft, including the introduction and conclusion, you will need to revise it. The first step is to put it aside for a time. When you come back to it later, your attitude toward the first draft will be more objective. Read your composition again, reading for content and looking closely at what you have said. The following checklist will be helpful in discovering specific problems:

■ Checklist for revising the first draft

1. Does this composition carry out my stated task (my statement of purpose)?
2. Are my ideas presented in a clear and logical order?
3. Does each main topic on my formal outline have its own paragraph or paragraphs?
4. Do all the ideas I discuss relate to my thesis statement?
5. Are the transitions between my paragraphs smooth, and do the ideas flow freely from paragraph to paragraph?
6. Will my audience understand my purpose?

After you go over your draft closely with the preceding questions in mind, you will have a better idea of where the problems are. You should begin to make changes at this point. You may need to develop some ideas more or to eliminate other ideas that do not fit. You may want to change the order of sentences in a paragraph or move a sentence from one paragraph to another. You may also wish to change individual words.

The following example is the second paragraph of the sample composition about Abigail Adams. It is the first draft version. Compare it to the final version on page 551. What kinds of changes were made? Why were they made?

EXAMPLE: FIRST DRAFT

This influence came to her slowly over the years of her life. She was born in Weymouth, Massachusetts, in 1744. She was the second daughter of a minister. Twenty years later, in 1764, she married John Adams. Over the next seven years, John and Abigail Adams had five children. John Adams was, at that time, a promising young lawyer. Four of their children were strong and healthy, but one child died before she was two. Abigail Adams settled into maintaining her household and raising four active children.

In the first version the beginning sentence bears less relation to the rest of the paragraph than it does in the final version. The order of sentences has been changed, and some sentences have been merged.

EXERCISE 13. Use the Checklist for Revising the First Draft to go over your composition. Work to improve the first draft you wrote in Exercise 9.

12.0 EDITING AND PROOFREADING

After you finish revising your first draft, go over your paper once more. This time you must check for any spelling, grammar, punctuation, and vocabulary errors or weaknesses. This is the final step in preparing a composition. No paper is complete until it has been edited and proofread. A paper may be beautifully written and be about an interesting subject. If it has errors throughout it, however, the overall effect will be negative.

The following checklist will help you in editing your own and other people's work. You may wish to ask a friend to check your paper against the list because it is often easier to catch errors in a paper you yourself did not write. Should you have difficulty with any of the points on the list, refer to the sections indicated in parentheses. You may wish to use the Editing Signals from Chapter 9, some of which are given below.

▪ Editing and proofreading checklist

1. Are all sentences complete? (See 2.a.) *frag*
2. Are varied sentence structures used? (See Section 3.)
3. Have you used the voice (active or passive) that is most effective in each sentence? (See 1.b.20.) *voice*
4. Are verb tenses used consistently? (See 1.b.12.) *tense*
5. Do subjects and verbs agree? (See 2.c and 2.e–f.) *agree*
6. Do pronouns agree with antecedents? (See 1.d.1 and 1.d.7.) *ref*
7. Is vocabulary precise but varied? (See Section 4.) *vocab*
8. Are words spelled correctly? (See Section 5.) *sp*
9. Is punctuation correct? (See Section 7.) *p*

EXERCISE 14. Edit and proofread your composition. Use the checklist for guidance, and refer to the appropriate sections of this book if you have any questions. Then rewrite or type your finished paper as a final draft.

12.p A SAMPLE COMPOSITION

The following sample composition is a biographical composition based on Abigail Smith Adams. You have followed the development of this composition throughout this section. Refer to the annotations in the margin as you read the composition. They indicate some of the points that have been raised throughout this section.

ABIGAIL SMITH ADAMS: A WOMAN OF LETTERS

Abigail Adams never held a public office. She had no formal recognition as an ambassador, Senator, or Representative. She is perhaps as famous today, however, as are her Presidential husband and son. Although she had little formal education and maintained throughout her life the traditional roles of wife and mother, she managed chiefly through her letter writing to promote the cause of women's rights.

Introduction deals with background information.

thesis statement

This political influence developed slowly during Abigail Adams' life, becoming more evident in her later years. She was born in Weymouth, Massachusetts, in 1744, the second daughter of a clergyman. In 1764, at the age of twenty, she married John Adams, a promising young lawyer. Over the next seven years, the young couple had five children. One of them, a girl, died before she was two, but the four boys were strong and healthy. As the years passed, Abigail Adams settled into her life of maintaining her household and coping with a family of active children.

Determiner connects two paragraphs.

Second paragraph is developed as narration.

Logical connectives useful to narrative help to sequence the narrative.

During this time and indeed for her entire life, Abigail Adams had no career of her own. She managed her household and a farm. When John Adams was away, which was often the case, she became a businesswoman, handling her husband's business affairs. In time, John Adams was

Logical connective connects two paragraphs.

elected the second President of the United States. Years later, her son, John Quincy Adams, became the sixth President, making Abigail Adams the only woman in our history to have been the wife of one President and the mother of another. She strongly influenced both men, not simply in their personal lives but in their political actions as well.

Third paragraph is developed as narration.

How did she achieve her political influence? The process is interesting to follow. She was a delicate child and for this reason could not attend school even if her parents could have afforded to send her. Nevertheless, she was curious and intelligent, and she soon became an eager reader and listener. In her father's library, its walls lined with books, including the great classics, Abigail began to read. As she read, she also learned to listen. At her grandfather's house she listened to and learned from politicians, lawyers, and educated men in all fields. In visits to other relatives, especially at her aunt's house, she learned to polish her manners and her conversational abilities, and she gained poise. By the time she married John Adams, Abigail was a very well educated person.

Repetition of key terms (*influence* and *political*) helps to make a transition between paragraphs.

Paragraph is developed as a process, a form of exposition.

All of these influences on Abigail appear in her letters to her friends. In exchanging letters with friends, she carried on discussions of politics. She kept up with current events and brought new ideas and opinions to them. Letter writing gave her a chance to develop writing skills and her ability to think and to sharpen her intellect, which was honest and direct.

Determiner connects two paragraphs.

The letters were a lifelong occupation for Abigail Adams. She exchanged hundreds of them with her family and friends. Her letters show clearly her personality. She had a deep understanding of people. Her reported conversations show that she was socially adept and an excellent conversationalist. She met and talked with many important people of her time.

Paragraphs are closely related; no connector needed.

It is through letters that we learn of her opinions. They show her to be very knowledgeable about politics and current events and firm in her opinions. They also show her love and respect for freedom. She took joy in the newly won freedom of her land. She opposed slavery long before battlelines were drawn up between the states. Most interesting of all, perhaps, is that she was a strong advocate of women's rights. She believed that some of the newly won freedom should be passed on to women. She did not believe that the English law affecting women should just blindly be carried out in the United States. Although a loyal wife, she believed that a married woman should be able to form separate business contracts. Most significant of all, as a woman living at a time when women were considered incapable of even learning about politics, Abigail Adams became recognized as a political force in her own right.

Notice the elements of comparison and contrast used within this expository paragraph.

The Abigail Adams revealed to us by her letters is deserving of our admiration simply as a fine, intelligent, knowledgeable, and dedicated person. In view of her lack of formal education and the low opinion in which women were held at that time, this

Conclusion sums up main idea.

achievement is remarkable. Abigail Adams went further, however. She became a strong voice for freedom and women's rights. Her opinions and the use she made of them added importance to the role of women in America.

12.q WRITING A BOOK REPORT

In writing a biographical composition you may have read a book that gave you your information. Perhaps it was a book that you enjoyed reading, and you would like to tell others about it. You can mention it in the course of your composition, of course, or you might write your composition as a book report. Furthermore, from time to time you may be asked to write a book review as a school assignment or for a school magazine, perhaps.

You can review and report on books of all kinds, of course. You can report on novels as well as nonfiction books such as biography, history, travel books, and how-to books.

You cannot tell everything about any book. You must, therefore, limit your topic (what you will say about the book) and decide on your purpose. You must organize your ideas, make notes, and write outlines and a first draft. You will also need an introduction and a conclusion.

In addition, you need to give several specific kinds of information in a book report.

1. It is essential that you give information about the book, its title and author.
2. You are expected in your introduction to reveal your attitude toward the book. You can do this briefly by simply describing the book as "fascinating" or "boring" or by using some other adjective that gets across your opinion of it. You can simply say that you enjoyed it, found it useful, found it instructive—or not.

3. If the author expresses a point of view about a topic (for example, about Abigail Adams), you should make clear in your review whether you agree with that point of view or not.

The following is the beginning of a book report that in general covers the same outline as the one for the biographical report on Abigail Adams (page 539). Notice, however, some of the differences between this paragraph and the opening paragraph of the preceding sample (page 551).

BOOK REPORT

<u>Abigail Adams: An American Woman</u>
by Charles W. Akers
Boston: Little, Brown and Company, 1980

> This instructive book describes the life of Abigail Adams, wife of John Adams, our second President. From it we learn about a remarkable woman of the colonial period. I share the author's enthusiasm for this famous woman who gained this spot in our history chiefly through her letters. The book quotes many of these letters, along with giving the facts of Abigail Adams' life.

In this example, reference is made to the book specifically. Much of the same information is present in the book report that was used in the composition. Observe, however, that no information *not* in the book should be used.

CLEAR THINKING
AND PERSUASION

13 Clear Thinking and Persuasion

Learning to think clearly and logically is the first step toward expressing your ideas in an intelligent and convincing way. Thinking clearly will help you whenever you have to argue in support of a position or when you have to defend a statement in an essay or on a written test.

The most important thing to remember when you try to persuade anyone is that there are very few people who will simply "take your word for it" without asking why. When people ask you why you do or say a certain thing, you must be able to convince them that you are right by defending your words or actions in some way. Persuasive techniques that you can learn include:

- using evidence to defend a statement
- using clear thinking to follow an argument through to its logical conclusion
- avoiding errors in reasoning

This section will help you train yourself to think clearly and to use persuasive techniques in writing and speaking.

EVIDENCE

In a court the lawyer who persuades a jury and wins a case is sometimes not the one who is "right" but the one who presents the strongest case. The lawyer who has the strongest case is the one who supports statements with

the best reliable evidence. That evidence must be precise, accurate, and relevant to the case. Similarly, in persuasive writing and speaking you must present your reader with reliable evidence to support your statements. Your evidence can take the form of facts and authoritative statements.

13.a FACT VS. OPINION

A **fact** is something that is known to be true. Most of the knowledge that you have is composed of facts. The following statements are examples of facts:

FACTS
Water boils at 212°F.
The capital of Alabama is Montgomery.
There are sixty seconds in one minute.
A soccer ball is shaped like a sphere, but a football is not.
Water is composed of molecules of hydrogen and oxygen.

Facts support your statements because everyone can agree that they are true. Most facts can be checked either through direct personal experience or in a reliable written source, such as an encyclopedia, an almanac, or a textbook. For instance, you can use a thermometer or read a science textbook to determine whether water boils at 212°F.

An **opinion** is a personal reaction about which other people may disagree. An opinion is based upon what one person *believes* or *feels* to be true, not upon what is known to be true. Opinions cannot be checked either by experience or in a written source. Compare the following list of opinions with the preceding list of facts.

OPINIONS
Ocean water is cold.
Montgomery, Alabama, is prettier than Miami, Florida.
An hour is a long period of time.
A soccer ball is easier to throw than a football.

Opinions play an important part in the decisions that you make every day. Although opinions cannot be proved either true or false, they are useful in making many personal decisions. For instance, you may rely upon your own opinions or the opinions of others in deciding what to eat for lunch, what film to see, or where to go on vacation.

■ Sound opinions

The value of an opinion depends upon how *sound* it is. A **sound opinion** is one that is based upon a sufficient number of precise and accurate facts. Before you form an opinion or believe someone else's opinion, gather as many facts about the issue as you can. If, for instance, you are trying to persuade your friend that Ms. Brossini is a good French teacher, gather as many facts about her as you can. *Why* is she a good French teacher? Does she make learning a foreign language seem exciting? Does she explain grammatical points in a way that is easy to understand?

Before you state your opinion, make sure that you can back it up with facts. The more precise and accurate your facts are, the sounder and more reliable your opinion will be. Remember that both facts and sound opinions (which are based upon facts) can be used as evidence to support a statement.

EXAMPLE

Imagine that you are supporting the following statement: *The Texas Wildcats are a better baseball team than the Colorado Mountaineers.* You must decide which of the following pieces of evidence presents the most convincing support for that statement.

1. The Wildcats' outfielders have higher batting averages than the Mountaineers' outfielders.
2. The Wildcats had a higher attendance total at their stadium this year than the Mountaineers had at theirs.
3. The Wildcats and the Mountaineers have played exactly

the same teams and the same number of games this year, and the Wildcats have won more games than the Mountaineers.

4. The manager of the Wildcats is firm and aggressive, and therefore he inspires his players.

The first statement is factual but misleading. Although the Wildcats' *outfielders* may have higher batting averages, the entire Wildcats team may have a lower batting average than the Mountaineers.

The second statement is also factual, but it is not relevant to the issue. The quality of a baseball team does not depend upon how many people go to watch them play.

The third statement is factual, precise, and relevant to the issue. The Wildcats have a better win/loss record than the Mountaineers against the same teams. On the basis of this evidence, most reasonable people will be persuaded that the Wildcats are the better team.

The fourth statement is an opinion that is not based upon facts. It is, therefore, unsound and unreliable. The manager's firm and aggressive manner may not, in fact, inspire his players but may discourage them. What may seem "firm" and "aggressive" to you may seem "offensive" to someone else. Remember that an opinion cannot be proved true or false and is always open to disagreement. This particular opinion, furthermore, is not relevant to the issue. Even if the Wildcats' manager does "inspire" his players, that does not necessarily make them a better team than the Mountaineers.

■ Authoritative statements

A special kind of fact or sound opinion that you can use as evidence is the authoritative statement. An **authoritative statement** is a piece of information from a reliable source, such as an encyclopedia, an almanac, a textbook, or an expert. Although you cannot use your own opinions to support your statements, you may use the sound opinions of recognized experts as evidence.

EXAMPLE

Suppose that your geography teacher tells you that Pikes Peak in Colorado has an elevation of 14,110 feet. Of course, you cannot measure the elevation for yourself. You may decide that your geography teacher is enough of an expert to know the elevation of Pikes Peak. If you wish to check the statement, however, you can consult a number of reliable references, such as an encyclopedia, an almanac, or a map.

Remember that whenever you wish to use an authoritative statement as evidence in your own writing you should choose a statement from the best authority available to you. For instance, you might consult a teacher, an encyclopedia, a dictionary, or an expert.

EXERCISE 1. Indicate which of the following items are facts and which are opinions.

1. A baseball diamond consists of a home plate and three bases.
2. Math is a difficult subject.
3. Television provides interesting entertainment.
4. Richard Rodgers was an American composer.
5. The United States has a Presidential election every four years.
6. The earth is shaped like a sphere.
7. Baseball is a very exciting sport.
8. There are twenty-four hours in a day.
9. Franklin D. Roosevelt was the greatest President of the twentieth century.
10. The United States is part of North America.

THE REASONING PROCESS

In persuasive writing and speaking you can use facts and sound opinions to support a statement. Another technique of persuasion is to use a logical reasoning process. Simply put, when you reason out an issue, you gather facts and sound opinions to help you arrive at a logical conclusion about the issue. This method of using reasoning to arrive at a conclusion is also called *argument*.

13.b MAKING A GENERALIZATION AND FINDING EVIDENCE TO SUPPORT IT

The first step in the reasoning process is to make a broad, general statement, often called a **generalization**. A generalization has not yet been researched and is based on too few facts and observations to be dependable. Consider, for example, the following generalization:

GENERALIZATION
Birds fly.

After forming the generalization *Birds fly*, the next step is to use evidence to test your statement. As discussed in 13.a, evidence can take the form of facts or of sound opinions.

You may wish to begin by using evidence based upon your personal knowledge of birds. Perhaps all of the birds you have seen are able to fly. Your experience with birds may be limited, however. You must, therefore, verify your knowledge by checking an authoritative source such as an encyclopedia. When you consult an encyclopedia, you will learn that there are many kinds of birds that do not fly, such as penguins, ostriches, kiwis, and emus. This evidence shows that your generalization is not true in all cases.

13.c FORMING A CONCLUSION

A **conclusion** is a statement arrived at after you have examined the evidence for your generalization. The conclusion must be as accurate and precise as possible. It must take into account all of the exceptions that a generalization does not. Given the generalization *Birds fly* and the evidence of various exceptions, a good conclusion is *Most birds fly*. Look at the following brief summary of this reasoning process:

GENERALIZATION: Birds fly.

EVIDENCE: Penguins, ostriches, kiwis, and emus are birds, but they do not fly.

CONCLUSION: Not all birds fly.

13.d THE LANGUAGE OF CONCLUSIONS: LIMITERS

A **limiter** is a qualifying word or phrase that is used to define a conclusion more precisely. As its name implies, a *limiter* limits a statement in order to account for exceptions. For instance, the word *most* in the conclusion *Most birds fly* is a limiter. There are a number of limiters that you can use to help make your conclusions as precise and accurate as possible. Consider, for example, the following lists of limiters and statements with limiters:

LIMITERS

almost never	mostly
a minority of	nearly all
as a rule	nearly always
certain	not all
few	occasionally
frequently	often
half	rarely
hardly ever	seldom
in general	several
in most cases	some
less than half	sometimes
many	the majority of
more than half	usually
most	

STATEMENTS WITH LIMITERS
Plants are **usually** green.
Some people are selfish.
He **often** takes the easy way out.

EXERCISE 2. After reading each of the following generalizations, produce a piece of evidence from your personal experience to test the generalization. Then write a precise conclusion. In your conclusion, use the limiters listed in 13.d or any of your own choice.

> EXAMPLE   <u>Generalization</u>: You need good physical endurance to play games.
>
> ANSWER   <u>Evidence</u>: *Checkers and Monopoly are games, but they do not require good physical endurance.*
>
> <u>Conclusion</u>: *You need good physical endurance to play certain games.*

1. Animals have four legs.
2. Encyclopedias contain lengthy articles.
3. Sports are played with a ball.
4. Rock music is harsh and loud.
5. Actors are handsome.
6. Pickled foods are sour.
7. Novels are long works.
8. Reading improves your mind.
9. Summer jobs are dull.
10. Desserts are fattening.

13.e STEREOTYPES

If you are not careful about adding the necessary limiters to your conclusions, you will end up with faulty conclusions known as stereotypes. A **stereotype** is an overgeneralization about someone or something that does not take into account exceptions. The word usually refers to a belief that is held by many people who have not thoroughly examined the facts.

For instance, the statement *College professors are absent-minded* is a stereotype because it does not take into account all of the college professors who are *not* absent-minded. If you knew that there are some absent-minded college professors, you could add the limiter *some* to form a more accurate conclusion: *Some college professors are absent-minded.* If you think about it, however, this conclusion does not mean very much. In any group of people, some will be absent-minded. You would have to make an extensive study of college professors to come up with an accurate statement about them.

When you use stereotypes, it indicates to others that you have not examined evidence logically and thoughtfully. Therefore, before you make a broad statement about someone or something, ask yourself if you have taken into account all of the exceptions.

EXERCISE 3. Each of the following statements is a stereotype. Pick five of the statements, and do the following for each: (A) Explain in a few sentences why it is an inaccurate overgeneralization, and (B) rewrite the statement, adding limiters to account for exceptions.

EXAMPLE Home-cooked food tastes better than restaurant food.

ANSWER (A) *There are many bad home cooks whose food cannot compare with the good food in many restaurants. Furthermore, very few home cooks can prepare food as delicious as that of master restaurant chefs.*

(B) *Good home-cooked food tastes better than some restaurant food.*

1. Artistic people are temperamental.
2. Poetry is difficult to understand.
3. Southerners talk slowly.
4. Politicians are dishonest.
5. Modern art is abstract.
6. Big cities are dirty and noisy.

7. Football players are tough and aggressive.

8. Television shows are for entertainment, not education.

9. Actors are conceited.

10. Business people dress conservatively.

ERRORS IN PERSUASIVE WRITING AND SPEAKING

Thinking clearly, giving evidence, and using logical reasoning will help you to be more persuasive in writing and in speaking. Once you have learned to reason properly, however, you must be on the lookout for the many kinds of errors in logic that can creep into your reasoning process and weaken your case. You must also be alert to errors in the reasoning of someone who is trying to persuade you.

Some errors involve sidetracking an issue or, in effect, changing the subject. Other errors involve trying to convince people of something by giving them false reasons or by telling them that "everyone else believes it." Some of the most common kinds of errors in persuasive writing and speaking are described in the following pages. You should learn to recognize them when others use them and to avoid them in your own writing and speaking.

13.f RED HERRING

A common error in reasoning that involves sidetracking a question or issue is called a **red herring**. This error consists of introducing a second issue in order to distract the opponent from the first issue. In other words, it is a way of changing the subject. People introduce side issues because they feel that they can no longer persuasively argue the first issue. The name comes from the practice in hunting of dragging a red herring (a strongly scented fish) across a trail. As a result, hunting dogs turn away from the scent of the hunted animal and follow the scent of the herring.

EXAMPLE

TEACHER: Jim, I'm concerned about your classroom behavior.

JIM: English bores me. Why can't English be as interesting as history?

Jim's feelings about history have nothing to do with the statement the teacher has made to him.

13.g EITHER-OR THINKING

You are committing the error of **either-or thinking** when you insist upon seeing things in terms of only two choices: right or wrong, kind or unkind, for you or against you. This is an error of oversimplification. It falsely implies that a situation is limited to one extreme or the other, without any possibility in between.

EXAMPLE

CARLOS THINKS: My friend Joseph did not volunteer to help me in my campaign for class president. Since he is not on my side, he must be campaigning for Eileen, who is running against me.

Carlos mistakenly thinks that because Joseph is not helping him in his campaign he must be helping the other side. Carlos thinks that Joseph is *either* for him *or* against him. In reality, Joseph may have chosen not to campaign for anyone.

13.h THE *POST HOC* ERROR

An error in reasoning that involves mistaking the cause of an event is the ***post hoc* error.** The complete

Latin phrase is *post hoc, ergo propter hoc,* which literally means "after this, therefore because of this." People who make the *post hoc* error mistakenly think that because something happened after something else the first event somehow caused the second. Actually, the two events were unrelated.

Many superstitions are based upon this error of reasoning. For instance, suppose that a superstitious person walked under a ladder and then immediately afterward tripped and sprained his ankle. He would mistakenly reason that because he tripped immediately after he walked under the ladder, the act of walking under the ladder was the cause of his accident. A more logical person would assume, however, that his accident was not related at all to his walking under the ladder; it was merely a coincidence.

EXAMPLE

PAO-CHEN SAYS: I am going to wear my blue shirt every time I play baseball from now on. The last two times I wore that shirt I hit a home run.

Pao-chen mistakenly reasons that because he hit a home run after putting on his blue shirt, the shirt brought him "luck" and, in some way, caused him to hit a home run. It is more logical to assume, however, that Pao-chen is a good hitter and would have hit a home run no matter what he was wearing.

13.i THE TESTIMONIAL

The **testimonial** is an attempt at persuasion that is based upon the advice, or testimony, of a famous person. It is a deceptive reasoning technique that is commonly used in advertising. The testimonial uses the glamour or prestige of famous people to give the impression that they are experts qualified to give good advice about almost anything.

EXAMPLE

FAMOUS HOCKEY GOALIE: When it comes to protecting the goal cage, I do a good job. When it comes to protecting my family, I like to do a good job, too. That's why I buy insurance from the Consolidated Insurance Company.

Although the goalie may be an expert at his job, he is not necessarily qualified to judge insurance.

13.j THE BANDWAGON

If your friends try to persuade you to do something merely because "everyone's doing it," they are using the **bandwagon** technique. The term *bandwagon* refers to the expression *jump on the bandwagon*, which means "join the crowd." The argument that "everyone does it," "everyone believes it," or "everyone wants it" is a very immature and weak argument, however. Do not be persuaded by it, and do not try to persuade others by it.

EXAMPLE

SOFT DRINK ADVERTISEMENT: Come on! People all over the country are quenching their thirst with Bubbli-Cola. Don't be left out! Join the fun!

The claim that many people drink a certain kind of soft drink, even if true, does not mean that you will necessarily like the product.

EXERCISE 4. Identify the error in reasoning in each of the following situations. Be prepared to explain why the reasoning used is faulty.

1. **SUSAN:** Should we ask Lois to go with us to the concert?
   LESLIE: Oh, she plays the flute. She won't want to go to a rock concert.

2. **MARK:** Angela, did you take that dollar from my desk?
   ANGELA: I didn't know the dollar was yours!

3. **TAMARA:** I knew if I picked the date for the class picnic it would wind up raining that day. Sure enough, here it is the day of the picnic, and it's pouring outside.

4. **LEGISLATOR Z:** Before we decide how much money we are going to allocate for the completion of Highway 61, shouldn't we decide whether we want to continue funding a transportation system that daily adds to our pollution problem?

5. **JACK:** I think I've finally figured out a trick for getting the TV picture to stop rolling. The last two times it was rolling, I glared at the set, concentrated, and mentally commanded it to stop. It worked!

EXERCISE 5. Identify the error in reasoning in each of the following situations. Be prepared to explain why the reasoning used is faulty.

1. **RADIO VOICE:** Join the thousands who have found relief from backache pain with Back-Ease.

2. **FAMOUS ACTOR:** I'm a professional in front of the cameras, but when it comes to taking pictures of my family and friends, I need a camera that makes everything as easy as 1-2-3. That's why I use the Simplex 123.

3. **CANDIDATE B:** More and more people in this fine state of ours are recognizing that I truly understand what needs to be done to revitalize this state. Join with your friends and neighbors on Election Day, and add your vote of support to theirs. With your vote we can have a better state.

4. **OLYMPIC ATHLETE:** As an Olympic athlete I've put in a lot of long, hard hours in training. I really understand the meaning of hard work and determination. That's why I want to talk to you about the hard-working people at Safeway Rent-A-Car. They know that to be good at anything you have to work at it, and that's why they can promise you the very best rental car service.

5. **BABYSITTER:** I don't think there's any question about it. If you give in to a child's demand to stay up "just fifteen minutes more," you won't get the child to go to bed at all.

REVIEW EXERCISE A. Several parents and teachers at a PTA meeting are discussing whether the school should build a new gymnasium. Identify the error in reasoning in each person's comment.

> **MR. AUSTIN:** A new gym would really help our athletic program. Look at the football stadium. The year after that was finished, we won the state championship. But the president of the school board is opposed to building a new gym.

> **MR. MARTINEZ:** Yes, she never comes to the football games, and so she must not be interested in sports.

> **MRS. YANG:** It's obvious that we need a new gym. Everybody knows that we need more space and a more modern facility.

> **MRS. WEINSTOCK:** Before we settle the question of the new gym, can't we talk about getting new uniforms for the teams? That seems the least we can do.

> **MR. CARSON:** Wait a minute. Before anyone says anything else, I just want to point out that the last time we built an addition to the school our property taxes went up 6 percent the following year! They are sure to go up this time, too.

> **MR. STANISLAWSKI:** Physical education is one of the most important aspects of a student's growth and development. If we don't build this new gym, it shows that we don't care about our students' physical fitness.

> **MRS. BARBIERI:** Besides, a new gym would discourage vandalism. Malcolm County built a new gym a couple of years ago, and I hear that vandalism in the schools there has decreased.

> **MS. SCHMIDT:** All the other high schools in this area have newer gyms than ours. We should have fiberglass backboards like everyone else.

REVIEW EXERCISE B. Have a class discussion about errors in reasoning that you have observed in newspaper and magazine articles, radio and television programs, and political campaigns.

14

LIBRARIES AND INFORMATION

14 Libraries and Information

"Knowledge is power," wrote the English philosopher Francis Bacon. He wrote the words at the end of the sixteenth century, but they remain truer than ever today in our complex technological world. One of the most important centers of knowledge is located right around the corner from home or perhaps just across the way from the cafeteria. This center of information is the library. (A library may also be called a learning resource center.)

14.a THE CARD CATALOGUE

The **card catalogue** is an alphabetical arrangement of individual file cards listing each of the books owned by a library.

The card catalogue is the first place you should check to locate a particular book in the library. Card catalogues are normally located in special cabinets in the lobby or circulation area of the library.

The card catalogue contains three kinds of cards for each nonfiction book in the library: an *author card*, a *title card*, and a *subject card*. The main entry on an author card is the author's (or editor's) name, last name first. For example, Jane Austen is listed as *Austen, Jane*. The card is filed under **A**.

The main entry on a title card is the title of the book, listed by the first letter of the first important word of the book's title (excluding *a, an,* and *the*). For example,

Emma is listed under **E**, whereas *The Watsons* is listed under **W**.

The main entry on a subject card is the book's principal topic. Works of fiction have only an author card and a title card; works of nonfiction have all three cards. The three kinds of cards are shown below.

Most card catalogues are divided into two sections. The *Author-Title Index* contains the author and title cards. The *Subject Index* contains the subject cards. Use the Author-Title Index if you know the title of your book or the author (or editor). Use the Subject Index if you want to find a number of books on a particular subject or if you cannot remember the title or author of a book.

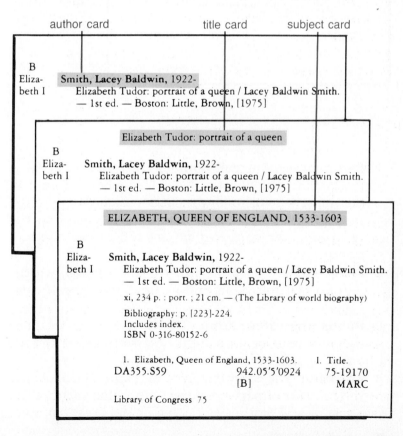

■ Catalogue card information

The annotated example of an author card that follows shows you the kind of information that you can expect to find.

Author Card

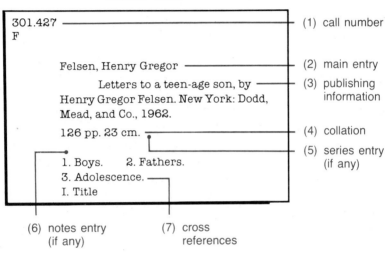

1. **Call number.** The **call number** marks the location of the book in the library. The call number is found in the upper left corner of the catalogue card and on the spine of the book itself. If the book is kept in the reference section, *Ref* is written above the call number.

2. **Main entry.** The **main entry** gives the book's title, author, or subject, depending upon the kind of catalogue card.

3. **Publishing information.** This information includes the name and location of the book's publisher and the date of publication.

4. **Collation.** The **collation** gives the size of the book and the number of pages, volumes, and illustrations.

5. **Series entry.** This entry tells whether the book is part of a series.
6. **Notes entry.** The **notes** provide information about any special features, such as introductions, appendixes, or bibliographies.
7. **Cross references.** The **cross references** list other subject headings under which the book is listed.

■ See cards and see also cards

There are two other kinds of cards that you will find in the card catalogue: *see* cards and *see also* cards.

See cards refer you to a different name, title, or subject card for the main entry that you have looked up. If you look up "National Basketball Association," for example, a *see* card may refer you to "Sports—Basketball, professional." Similarly, if you look up "Saki," a *see* card will refer you to the author's real name, "H. H. Munro."

See also cards refer you to other books or subjects related to the one you have already checked. If you look up "Television," a *see also* card may refer you to "Broadcasting," "Videotape," or "Advertising."

EXERCISE 1. Refer to the preceding sample catalogue cards to answer the following questions.

1. Who published *Elizabeth Tudor*? When?
2. How many pages is Lacey Baldwin Smith's book?
3. What is the call number for Henry Gregor Felsen's book?
4. Under what subject headings would you find catalogue cards for *Letters to a Teen-Age Son*?
5. Does *Elizabeth Tudor* have a bibliography? Does *Letters to a Teen-Age Son*?

EXERCISE 2. Refer to the card catalogue in your school library to find the following information.

1. the author of a book about sailing
2. the number of books in the library about Albert Einstein

3. the call number of a book about Nepal
4. the publisher of *The Great Gatsby*
5. the most recent book in the library about soccer
6. the title, author, and call number of a book about Vincent van Gogh
7. the author of a book about wildflowers
8. a book with illustrations of tropical birds
9. the number of books in the library by Pearl Buck
10. the author of a book about Antarctica

14.b CLASSIFICATION OF BOOKS: THE DEWEY DECIMAL SYSTEM

Use the **call number** from the catalogue card to locate the book in the library.

The call number on the catalogue card directs you to the shelf where the book is kept. There are two common systems for classifying books: the Dewey Decimal System and the Library of Congress System. The latter, a rather complicated but more flexible system, is used in most university, research, and state libraries. The Dewey Decimal System is used in most school and local libraries.

The Dewcy Decimal System usually separates novels from the rest of the fiction and from nonfiction. Novels are placed in their own section and are arranged alphabetically according to the last name of the author. To find a book by Helen Yglesias, for example, you look on the **Y** shelves; for one by Dylan Thomas, you look on the **T** shelves.

Nonfiction materials are divided into ten major categories according to subject matter. Each of these categories is designated by a three-digit number. These ten major categories are then further divided into ten subgroups each.

The following outline lists the categories of the Dewey Decimal System. It also shows one of the major subject categories, Pure Sciences, broken into its subgroups.

OUTLINE OF THE DEWEY DECIMAL SYSTEM

000	General Works	500	Pure Sciences
100	Philosophy	510	Mathematics
200	Religion	520	Astronomy
300	Social Sciences	530	Physics
400	Language	540	Chemistry
500	Pure Sciences	550	Earth Sciences
600	Technology	560	Paleontology
700	The Arts	570	Life Sciences
800	Literature	580	Botany
900	Geography and History	590	Zoology

Sometimes libraries classify books even more precisely than the above divisions. Smaller libraries often add the letter of the author's last name to the call number. Larger libraries will generally add a decimal point and more numerals to the number.

All nonfiction works are classified in this manner in the Dewey Decimal System, with the exception of biographies. Biographies are classified under the major category of General Works and are then shelved alphabetically according to the last name of their subject (not their author).

EXERCISE 3. Indicate the major Dewey Decimal System number (100, 200, 300, etc.) for each of the following books.

1. *Mars, The Red Planet,* Isaac Asimov
2. The New English Bible
3. *The Complete Poems,* Elizabeth Bishop
4. *Women on the Hollywood Screen,* Frank Manchel
5. *Economics,* Paul Samuelson
6. *F. Scott Fitzgerald,* Andrew Turnbull (a biography)
7. *Latin: An Introductory Course Based on Ancient Authors,* Frederic M. Wheelock
8. *Stilwell and the American Experience in China 1911–45,* Barbara W. Tuchman

9. *The Complete Works of William Shakespeare*
10. *Linotype Machine Principles*, Mergenthaler Linotype Company

14.c REFERENCE MATERIALS

The reference section of the library is the place to look for encyclopedias, dictionaries, almanacs, and atlases. It is also the place to find indexes to newspapers and periodicals, such as the *Readers' Guide to Periodical Literature*. The reference section is often the best place to check when you are beginning a research project.

14.c.1 Newspapers and periodicals

Current newspapers and periodicals are often kept in shelves or on racks in a reading room. Newspapers are alphabetized by the name of their city of origin, whereas periodicals are alphabetized by title.

Back issues of newspapers are normally kept on microfilm (see 14.d.1). Back issues of magazines are sometimes kept on microfilm and sometimes bound into hardcover volumes.

14.c.2 The *Readers' Guide to Periodical Literature*

The *Readers' Guide to Periodical Literature* is an index to articles published in over one hundred magazines. Use the *Readers' Guide* to find articles published in general, popular magazines such as *Newsweek* or *Popular Photography*. A new issue of the *Readers' Guide* is published approximately every two weeks and provides the most current listing of articles.

On the facing page is a sample column from the *Readers' Guide to Periodical Literature*.

GAS shipping terminals
Long, long LNG trail; two California utilities trying to bring liquefied natural gas from Indonesia and Alaska. il Forbes 124:21+ N 12 '79

GAS turbines, Automotive
Turbine with a new twist; Kronogard turbine/transmission system. J. Norbye. il Pop Sci 215:14+ O '79

GAS well drilling
Self-reliance, Buckeye style; Ohio companies producing their own gas. J. Grigsby. Forbes 124:154 O 15 '79

main entries ———
GASES, Rare
Atmospheric carbon tetrafluoride: a nearly inert gas. R. J. Cicerone. bibl il Science 206:59-61 O 5 '79

GASKILL, Gordon
Noble pizza prize. Read Digest 115:85-6+ O '79

GASOLINE
Catalytic production of high-grade fuel (gasoline) from biomass compounds by shape-selective catalysis. P. B. Weisz and others. bibl il Science 206:57-8 O 5 '79

subheading ———
Conservation
$2 a gallon for gas? Why not? M. Stone. U.S. News 87:92 N 5 '79

Prices
title of article ———
Cheap gas: gone and better forgotten. L. Grant. Pol Today 6:64 S '79

Rationing
Gas rationing: the latest plan. il U.S. News 87:13 O 29 '79

History
author of article ———
Sorry, no gas. S. W. Sears. il Am Heritage 30:4-17 O '79

Taxation
$2 a gallon for gas? Why not? M. Stone. U.S. News 87:92 N 5 '79

GASOLINE consumption, Motor vehicle. See Motor vehicle engines—Fuel consumption

GASOLINE supply
Energy and the skier. A. H. Greenberg. Skiing 32:4 O '79

In the wake of crisis '79. T. Orme. Motor T 31:14 O '79

source of article
(name of periodical,
volume number,
page numbers, and
date) ———
Running on empty; World Watch Institute study. L. J. Carter. Science 202:203 O 12 '79

GASTRONOMY
See also
Gluttony

GASTROPODS
see also reference
(directs you to
additional related
main entries) ———
See also
Snails

GAULLE, Charles de
House De Gaulle built. F. Lewis. il por N Y Times Mag p40+ N 11 '79 •

see reference
(directs you to a
different main entry) ———
GAULT, Charlayne Hunter-. See Hunter-Gault, C.

GAUNAURD, Guillermo C. and Überall, H. M.
Deciphering the scattering code contained in the resonance echoes from fluid-filled cavities in solids. il Science 206:61-4 O 5 '79

GAUTHIER, Mary Ann
What you can do about a phobia. Glamour 77:198+ O '79

GAY, Larry
Woodburning furnaces. il Blair & Ketchums 6:98-110 O '79

GEIL, P. H. See Lam, R. jt auth

GELATT, Roland
Liebermann, Losey and the libertine. il Opera News 44:10-12+ N '79

GELLES, Richard J.
Myth of battered husbands and new facts about family violence. Ms 8:65-6+ O '79

GENDELL, Milton
Venice. Art News 78:156+ S '79

EXERCISE 4. Refer to the sample *Readers' Guide* column on page 581 to answer the following questions.

1. When did Mary Ann Gauthier's article appear? In what magazine?
2. Under how many main entries can you find articles on gasoline and related topics?
3. How many subheadings are listed under the main entry on gasoline?
4. Who wrote the article on Charles de Gaulle?
5. How would you find the article written by P. H. Geil?
6. What is the title of the article on Gordon Gaskill?
7. How many articles can you find on gastronomy? Under what other main entries can you look for further information?
8. Give the source information (periodical, volume number, page number, date) for the article by Milton Gendell.
9. Under what main entry and subheading can you find an article about motor vehicle gasoline consumption?
10. In what periodicals can you find articles on gasoline supply?

EXERCISE 5. Find two articles on each of the following topics (or similar topics) in a recent issue of the *Readers' Guide*. Identify the author, title, periodical, volume number, page numbers, and date of each article.

1. Backpacking
2. Bees
3. Skiing
4. Sports on television
5. Rock music

14.c.3 Encyclopedias

Encyclopedias are alphabetically arranged collections of articles on almost every general topic.

Encyclopedias are often a good place to begin a research project. They provide a brief summary of each topic and frequently include a bibliography of other useful books on the topic. The most frequently used encyclopedias are the *Encyclopedia Britannica*, the *Encyclopedia Americana*, *Collier's Encyclopedia*, and *World Book Encyclopedia*.

14.c.4 Almanacs

Almanacs are annual collections of information on history, vital statistics, and current events.

Almanacs are an excellent source of information for recent statistical data and for general information about countries, states, and famous people. They also provide a general overview of the important events of the previous year. Some of the almanacs you may find helpful are the *American Year Book*, the *Official Associated Press Almanac*, the *World Almanac and Book of Facts*, and the *Information Please Almanac*.

14.c.5 Atlases

Atlases are collections of maps.

They are used for information about geography as well as for data about such related topics as population distribution or climatic profiles. Some atlases you may find useful are the *Hammond Contemporary World Atlas*, the *Historical Atlas of the United States*, the *National Geographic World Atlas*, and *The New York Times Atlas*.

EXERCISE 6. Refer to an encyclopedia to answer the following questions.

1. Who was Mother Goose?
2. Who was the first person to cross the Atlantic from New York to Paris alone in an airplane?
3. What was the name of the first island to which Napoleon was exiled?
4. What countries fought the Crimean War?
5. What is the largest national park in the United States?

EXERCISE 7. Refer to an almanac to answer the following questions.

1. What baseball team won the National League East in 1978?
2. What are the three principal exports of Sweden?
3. What is the average January temperature in Memphis, Tennessee?
4. Who won the Pulitzer Prize for fiction in 1976?
5. What is the nickname of the state of Indiana?

EXERCISE 8. Refer to an atlas to answer the following questions.

1. Where is Lake Titicaca?
2. Where is the Great Victoria Desert?
3. Name four mountain ranges in the United States.
4. Which country is larger: Ghana or Nigeria?
5. Where is the Baja Peninsula?

14.c.6 Other useful reference works

The following list describes some other specialized reference books that you may find useful.

1. **Biographical reference works** give short life stories of noteworthy people. Some useful books are *Who's Who, Current Biography, Webster's Biographical Dictionary*, and the *Dictionary of American Biography*.
2. **Language reference works** provide information about words and usage. Valuable language books include *Roget's Thesaurus, The Elements of Style*, and the *Dictionary of American-English Usage*.
3. **Books of quotations** contain memorable quotations arranged by subject or by key word. *Bartlett's Familiar Quotations* and the *Oxford Dictionary of Quotations* are two well-known sources for quotations.
4. **Literature handbooks** include *Book Review Digest*, the *Short Story Index*, the *Oxford Companion to*

American Literature, the *Oxford Companion to English Literature,* and the *Columbia Dictionary of Modern European Literature.*

5. **History books** that you might find useful include *Cambridge Modern History,* the *Oxford Companion to American History,* and the *Oxford Companion to World History.*

6. Two valuable **science books** are *A History of Technology* and Van Nostrand's *Scientific Encyclopedia.*

EXERCISE 9. Refer to the reference works cited in parentheses in each item below to find the answers to the following questions.

1. Where was Babe Ruth born? What was his real name? (*Webster's Biographical Dictionary, Dictionary of American Biography*)

2. Find five synonyms for each of the following verbs: *travel, hope (for), laugh,* and *find.* (*Roget's Thesaurus*)

3. Who said, "Rose is a rose is a rose"? (*Bartlett's Familiar Quotations,* the *Oxford Dictionary of Quotations*)

4. What was the Russian writer Dostoevsky's full name? Name three of his works. (*Columbia Dictionary of Modern European Literature, Webster's Biographical Dictionary*)

5. What other names has Leningrad had? When? (*Cambridge Modern History, Oxford Companion to World History*)

6. Who discovered radium? (*Scientific Encyclopedia*)

7. Who wrote, "A friend may well be reckoned the masterpiece of Nature"? In what work does it appear? (*Bartlett's Familiar Quotations,* the *Oxford Dictionary of Quotations*)

8. Who was Gertrude Stein? Where was she born? In what city did she settle? (*Webster's Biographical Dictionary, Dictionary of American Biography*)

9. What is the difference in meaning between *aggravate* and *irritate*? (*The Elements of Style,* the *Dictionary of American-English Usage*)

10. Who invented the hot-air balloon? (*A History of Technology,* Van Nostrand's *Scientific Encylopedia*)

PERIODICALS

The following list contains some of the general-interest magazines you may find useful or enjoyable. These magazines are available at most local libraries.

News

Time, Newsweek, U.S. News & World Report

Literature, art, and general culture

Harper's, The Atlantic Monthly, The New York Review of Books, Horizon, Saturday Review, Quest

Sports and the outdoors

Sports Illustrated, Sport, Sports Afield, Outdoors, Outdoor Life

Hobbies and recreation

Popular Photography, Modern Photography, Travel, Stereo Review

Science and technology

Scientific American, Science, Omni, Popular Mechanics, Popular Science

14.d USING THE LIBRARY

Many of the materials in the library can be borrowed for short periods of time. These are called **circulating** materials and include books, records, tapes, and sometimes works of art. You do, however, need a library card to check out circulating materials.

14.d.1 Microforms

Many libraries save space by using microforms, tiny photographs of printed pages that are stored either on film strips (microfilm) or on cards (microfiche). Materials that you will likely find on microforms include newspapers and those magazines frequently used for reference, such as *Time* or *Newsweek*. Microforms must be used with a special projector at the library. School libraries generally do not have microform materials, but most university and city libraries use them extensively.

14.d.2 The vertical file

The **vertical file** is a collection of news clippings, magazine articles, photographs, pamphlets, and other materials related to current events and topics. The vertical file is generally kept in a special cabinet or desk near the reference section. Although the contents of the vertical file are not listed in the card catalogue, the librarian can give you information about its contents. Nearly every library maintains a vertical file.

14.e PARTS OF A BOOK

Because you might find dozens of books on any topic, you must be able to determine which ones will be helpful to your research and which ones will not. Knowing the parts of a book will help you to look through a book quickly to see if it contains the information you are seeking. The following list describes the various parts of a book:

1. The *frontispiece* is an illustration relating to the book's author or subject.
2. The *title page* has the full title, the complete name of the author or editor, the edition number, the publisher, the place of publication, and often the date of publication.
3. The *copyright page* is usually on the back of the title page. It gives the name of the copyright holder and the year of copyright.
4. The *epigraph* is a relevant quotation at the beginning of the book.

5. The *table of contents* lists the contents of the book and the page number on which each chapter or section begins.
6. The *preface, foreword, introduction,* and *acknowledgments* explain the scope and purpose of the book and give credit to those whose ideas or efforts helped the author.
7. *Lists of tables or illustrations* act as tables of contents for graphic material, giving the page on which each entry appears.
8. The *epilogue* or *appendixes* include material such as diagrams, documents, charts, tables, or long quotations.
9. The *glossary* is a list of definitions for technical or unusual terms that are used in the book.
10. The *bibliography* is a list of sources either used by the author or recommended by the author for further reading. Bibliographies are usually placed at the end of the book but sometimes appear at the end of each chapter.
11. The *index* is an alphabetical list of names and topics covered in the book along with page numbers where they are mentioned.

THE RESEARCH REPORT

The Research Report

A **research report** deals with a limited topic and is based upon information from written sources or from interviews with experts on the topic. It usually uses three to five sources and is 500-1,000 words long (2-4 typed pages). Your teacher may specify a different length, however. Because the job of research usually involves working in a library, the kind of research report that you do for school is also called a **library paper**.

In writing a research report, you must use many of the skills discussed in the preceding parts of this book, such as using the library, writing an outline, writing topic sentences, and writing coherent paragraphs. You will probably also use some of the patterns of thinking and writing described in Section 11: narration, description, comparison/contrast, and explanation of a process.

Writing a research report is, of course, usually more work than writing a paper based only on your own knowledge and opinions. By researching what experts have to say about a subject, however, you have the satisfaction of adding to your knowledge and opinions and of becoming something of an expert yourself.

You should try to do more than merely report information from other sources, though. A good research report will include some of your own analysis of the information. Let your opinions about the subject give focus to your paper. You will see how a student made generalizations and gave focus to his paper in 15.m, "The Finished Research Report."

15.a SELECTING A TOPIC

Unless your teacher assigns a specific topic for your research report, selecting a topic will be your first step. Your major problem in choosing a topic will probably be finding one that is limited enough. For example, suppose that you want to write a research report about wildlife preservation. You will have to focus on a limited aspect of this broad subject. You could narrow the topic in the following way:

BROAD: Wildlife preservation
LESS BROAD: American wildlife preservation efforts
LESS BROAD: Campaigns to save American bird species
NARROW: The campaign to save the whooping crane

Although choosing a topic that is too broad is a more common error, be careful not to choose a topic that is too narrow. If you write about how to apply for a driver's license, for example, you cannot do much more than list the steps in the application process.

The other main consideration in choosing a topic for a research report is the amount of research material available on the topic. When you have an idea for a topic, check your library to make sure that you will be able to find enough information on it. If your topic is based on a very recent discovery or event or if it is highly technical, you may have trouble finding any books or articles about it. In this case you will have to choose another topic.

Ask yourself these questions about any topic that you are considering for a research report:

QUESTIONS FOR CHOOSING A TOPIC
1. Am I sufficiently interested in the topic?
2. Is the topic too broad to be covered adequately in the length specified?
3. Is the topic too limited?
4. Are there enough books or articles on the topic in the libraries available to me?

EXAMPLE

Randy Melick was assigned to write a research paper on a topic of his own choosing. He decided to write about Walt Disney World, the Florida amusement park, because he had recently vacationed there. The library did not have any books specifically about Walt Disney World, but Randy found that a large number of magazine articles on the subject had been published. Randy therefore felt that he would be able to find enough information on the topic "The Making of Walt Disney World."

EXERCISE 1. For five of the following broad topics, suggest a limited topic that can be handled in a brief research report. Then choose one of the limited topics (or another limited topic) for a research report of your own.

EXAMPLE Automobiles
ANSWER   *The Story of the Model T*

1. Country Music
2. Detective Stories
3. U.S. Political Campaigns
4. Canada
5. Texas
6. Early Days of Aviation

15.b BEGINNING YOUR RESEARCH

When you have chosen a limited topic for your research report, it is a good idea to begin your actual research by reading an encyclopedia article on the topic. Encyclopedia articles are designed to give an overview of basic factual material on all aspects of a topic. In addition, they often include a list of books on the article's topic.

Your topic may have its own entry in the encyclopedia, or you may have to use the encyclopedia index to find information about it in a more general article. For example, to find a discussion of the painting *American Gothic* you will probably have to look under the name of the artist, Grant Wood, or in a general article like "American Painting."

As you read the encyclopedia article, make a list of the important aspects of your topic. This list will help you to prepare a working outline and to take notes from other books and magazine articles.

EXAMPLE

Randy Melick consulted several encyclopedias. He found a short article "Disneyland and Disney World." Walt Disney World also received brief mention in articles on Walt Disney and Florida. To get a better overview of his topic, therefore, Randy read several magazine articles written about the park when it opened in 1971.

EXERCISE 2. Read one or two encyclopedia articles for general information on the research report topic that you chose in Exercise 1. Write down the most important aspects of the topic discussed in the article. If you cannot find general information about your topic in the encyclopedia, list the articles in which you looked for information.

15.c PREPARING A WORKING OUTLINE

A **working outline** will guide you in your reading and note taking.

When you have an overview of your topic, you can decide which aspects of the topic you want to cover in your paper and how you want to organize them. Prepare a working outline to guide your note taking. A working outline is a preliminary, less detailed form of the final, formal outline that you will follow in writing your report (see 15.g).

To prepare a working outline, use the list that you made when you read the encyclopedia article or other background source. Of the aspects of your topic that you listed, write down three or four that you want to treat in your paper. Try to arrange these aspects in logical order, asking yourself the following questions:

QUESTIONS FOR A WORKING OUTLINE
1. Is there a story that I can tell about this topic?
2. Can I describe one particular aspect of this topic?
3. Can I write about how two aspects of the topic are like or unlike each other? Can I write about how the topic itself is like or unlike another?
4. Can I explain how to do something related to this topic?

Keep your working outline in front of you as you read and take notes. It will help you to focus on the particular aspects of the topic that you want to treat.

EXAMPLE

After reading the background articles on Walt Disney World, Randy Melick prepared the following working outline:

The Making of Walt Disney World

I. Ideas behind Walt Disney World
II. Disneyland and Walt Disney World
III. Description of Walt Disney World
    A. Disney themes and characters
    B. Transportation

Randy planned to tell a story in the first section of his report. In the second section he planned to tell how Walt Disney World is like and unlike its predecessor, Disneyland. This section would include some description, but he planned to include most of the description of the park in a third section.

Look at Randy Melick's final outline in 15.g, and notice how he eventually changed the working outline before he began to write his paper.

EXERCISE 3. Prepare a working outline for the topic you have chosen for your research report. Your outline should have three or four main headings arranged in logical order. You need not include subheadings at this point. Use your outline to direct your reading and note taking.

15.d FINDING INFORMATION

When you have made a working outline, you are ready to look for possible sources for your report. A *source* is someone or something that provides information. For a brief research report, you should try to find six to eight books and articles that may be helpful.

FINDING SOURCES

- You will find lists of books at the ends of encyclopedia articles.
- You will find books classified in the Subject Index of the library's card catalogue.
- You will find periodical articles listed in the *Readers' Guide to Periodical Literature*.
- You can ask your librarian if there is information about your topic in the vertical file (see 14.d.2).

For complete information about doing research in the library, see Section 14, "Libraries and Information."

When you have made a list of six to eight sources, locate the books and articles in your library. You may find that some of them are not available. Some of the books may be checked out, and your library may not subscribe to the magazines in which some of the articles appear. A research report should be based on at least three sources. If you cannot find three usable sources, you must find another topic.

EXAMPLE

When Randy Melick looked under the subject heading "Walt Disney World" in the Subject Index of the card catalogue, he found no books listed. He found three books listed, however, under "Disney, Walter Elias," and two listed under "Amusement Parks—American." In recent issues of the *Readers' Guide to Periodical Literature*, he found ten articles on Walt Disney World. When he looked through the library, however, he found only three of the books and five of the articles.

15.e KEEPING A WORKING BIBLIOGRAPHY

A **working bibliography** is a list of books and other source materials that you will consult.

When you have located a source, skim over it quickly to decide whether it will be useful to you. If so, record the following information about the source on a 3 x 5-inch index card:

- the name of the author
- the title of the source
- the location and name of the publisher
- the date of publication

Make a card for each source, and use this group of cards as your working bibliography. Number each card in the upper left corner, in effect giving a number to each source. Later, when you take notes, number each note card (see 15.f) with the corresponding bibliography card number. This numbering system is a simple and efficient way of identifying the source of the information.

The information on a bibliography card is arranged in a standard style, shown in 15.k. Notice how Randy Melick followed the style.

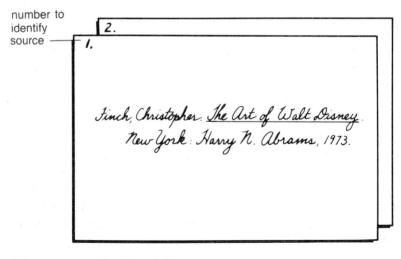

number to
identify
source

2.

1.

Finch, Christopher. *The Art of Walt Disney.*
New York: Harry N. Abrams, 1973.

EXERCISE 4. Locate and obtain at least three sources for the research report topic that you chose in Exercise 1. Use the book lists at the end of encyclopedia articles, the Subject Index of the library's card catalogue, the *Readers' Guide to Periodical Literature*, and the vertical file. Skim the sources quickly, and then write bibliography cards for those that you plan to use in your report. Follow the style shown in 15.k. Be sure to use at least one book and one encyclopedia article.

15.f TAKING NOTES

When you have made a working outline and collected your source material, you are ready to begin reading and taking notes. Most students find that large index cards (4 x 6-inch) are best for taking notes because it is easier to organize and rearrange notes on cards than on sheets of notebook paper. In the upper left corner of each note card, write the number of the bibliography source card (see 15.e). Below this number write the heading from your working outline that covers the information on the card.

Taking notes from a research source is somewhat different from taking notes on a lecture or a textbook (see 17.b). When you read the source, do not try to absorb all the ideas and information presented. Instead, look for information that is relevant to your topic. Write down the important facts and ideas in your own words, using either phrases or complete sentences. If you find an especially striking phrase, sentence, or passage that you think you may want to quote word for word in your paper, copy it carefully, and put quotation marks around it.

Be sure to write somewhere on every note card the page number(s) on which the information appears in the source. If the information is taken from more than one page, mark which information came from which page. Do not try to put too much information on one note card, however.

If you use an idea or a direct quotation from a source, you must credit the source in a footnote and in the final bibliography. Using someone else's ideas or exact words and presenting them as your own is called *plagiarism*. Plagiarism is not only dishonest; it can be a criminal offense.

EXAMPLE

Here is a sample note card from Randy Melick's research.

number to identify this source

heading from working outline

1.

Disneyland and WDW

Disney's regrets about Disneyland

-- no insulating area to prevent unsightly commercial devel.

-- no hotels - because of staff's inexperience

-- vowed not to repeat these mistakes

p. 396

page number on which information appears

EXERCISE 5. Take notes from the sources that you have assembled for your research report. Remember to identify the source by number and to write a heading from your working outline on each note card. Use your own words when you take notes. If you find a sentence or passage that you may want to quote in your paper, copy it carefully, and enclose it in quotation marks. Always write the page number of the source on the note card.

15.g WRITING A FORMAL OUTLINE

A **formal outline** will guide you in writing your first draft.

As you read and take notes, you will probably find that your working outline will require some changes. To prepare a formal outline, read over your note cards carefully and group them into piles, one for each important aspect of your topic. If any of your cards no longer seem to fit into your topic, set them aside. Compare your working outline with your piles of note cards, and ask yourself the following questions:

QUESTIONS FOR A FORMAL OUTLINE

1. Do the headings on the piles of note cards correspond to the main headings in my working outline? Have I discovered other main headings that should be added to the outline?
2. Do I have enough information to write about all the main headings in my working outline? If not, should I try to find more information, or should I eliminate headings?
3. Can I find logical subdivisions for the main headings?
4. What is the best order for presenting my ideas?

Using these questions as a guide, make changes in and add details to your working outline. Draw up a final outline that presents your ideas in a logical order. See 12.f for details on setting up a formal outline.

EXAMPLE

During his reading Randy Melick found so much descriptive material about Walt Disney World that he decided to devote more space to this part of his topic and less to a comparison of Walt Disney World with Disneyland. He also found an analysis of the reasons for Walt Disney World's success and decided to add a section on this subject. Making these changes and adding details, he revised his working outline into the following formal outline:

The Making of Walt Disney World

I. Ideas behind Walt Disney World

   A. Regrets about Disneyland

      1. Lack of insulating property

      2. Lack of revenue-producing hotels

   B. Ideas for new park

      1. Isolation

      2. Hotels

      3. Recreation

      4. Projects

   C. Follow-through by associates

II. Description of Walt Disney World

   A. "Visual magnets"

   B. Theme parks

   C. Disney characters

   D. "Main Street" attractions

III. Reasons for Walt Disney World's success

   A. Planned environment

   B. Controlled competition

EXERCISE 6. Prepare a final outline for your research report, using your note cards, your working outline, and the questions in 15.g. Follow the outline style shown in 12.f.

15.h WRITING THE FIRST DRAFT

Allow yourself two to three hours of uninterrupted time for writing the first draft of your research report.

Follow your formal outline, and refer to your note cards whenever necessary. Unless you are using a direct quotation, however, do not copy from your note cards.

In writing a first draft, you should concentrate on getting your ideas down on paper in a clear sequence. Do not spend too much time at this point looking for the ideal words or sentences to express your meaning. You can deal with these matters when you write your final draft. For now, try to keep moving from one part of the outline to the next.

Every research paper needs an introduction and a conclusion, although they are not listed as such on your formal outline. The introduction presents the topic and your main ideas about it. (See the discussion of *thesis statement* in 12.g.) The concluding paragraph should restate and tie together the main ideas of the paper.

Do not try to revise your rough draft immediately. Do something else, and come back to the paper after several hours or a day. By then you will be able to look at what you have written with a fresh mind.

EXERCISE 7. Using your note cards and formal outline, write the first draft of your research report.

15.i EDITING THE FIRST DRAFT

After you have been away from your first draft for a while, you will be able to look at it with a critical eye. Read through it carefully, asking yourself the following questions:

1. Does my paper have a clear beginning, middle, and end? Does the introduction state the topic, and does the conclusion summarize the main ideas and opinions effectively?
2. Does my paper follow the order of my outline? Are my ideas clearly and logically presented?
3. Are the sentences clear and easy to understand?

4. Have I included enough details and examples?
5. Is my paper free from errors in spelling, punctuation, grammar, and usage?

Follow these steps in changing and correcting your first draft:

1. Reword awkward sentences. (Review 3.i–3.k.)
2. Rewrite each paragraph so that every sentence is essential to the meaning of the paragraph. Rearrange sentences so that your ideas flow clearly from one sentence to the next. (Review 10.j and 10.k.)
3. Insert transitional phrases to link ideas and paragraphs. (Review 10.k and 12.j.)
4. Eliminate unnecessary words, and avoid monotony. (Review 3.j.)
5. If ideas are not developed enough, either develop them further or cut out paragraphs. Do not be afraid to rearrange sections of your paper.
6. Correct all errors in grammar, usage, spelling, and punctuation.

EXERCISE 8. Edit the first draft of your research report, following the steps listed in 15.i.

15.j USING FOOTNOTES

A **footnote** gives additional information, including source information, about a statement in your paper.

When you have rewritten your first draft to your satisfaction, you are ready to add the footnotes. You must use a footnote wherever you have borrowed an idea or a direct quotation from another author. The footnote gives credit to the author and also helps your readers to locate your sources in case they want to read the original material.

A footnote has two parts. The first part is a superscript, or raised number, placed in the text of your paper

at the end of the quotation or borrowed idea. The super-script usually appears at the end of a sentence. The second part of a footnote is the actual note that gives the information about the source. The notes may be placed either at the bottom of the pages on which their super-scripts occur or together at the end of the paper under the heading *Notes*. Follow your teacher's instructions.

The first line of a footnote is indented half an inch from the left margin of your paper, and the second line is even with the left margin. The information about the source must be given in a standard order with standard punctuation. Here are sample footnotes for a book, a periodical article, and an encyclopedia article.

FOOTNOTE FOR A BOOK
[1]Christopher Finch, The Art of Walt Disney (New York: Harry N. Abrams, 1973), p. 389.

FOOTNOTE FOR A PERIODICAL ARTICLE
[2]Horace Sutton, "Of Mouse and Man," Saturday Review, 8 Apr. 1972, p. 12.

FOOTNOTE FOR AN ENCYCLOPEDIA ARTICLE
[3]Howard Suber, "Walt Disney," Encyclopedia Americana, 1978 ed.

There are two ways of writing footnotes for a source that has already been cited in a previous footnote. The simplest way is to use just the author's last name and the page number. (If you are using more than one book by the same author, you must also include the title or a shortened form of the title after the author's name.) The older way of writing footnotes for a previously cited source is to use Latin abbreviations. The abbreviation *Ibid.* refers to the source of the footnote immediately preceding. *Op. cit.* refers to some earlier source, which you must specify by the author's last name.

FOOTNOTE FOR A SOURCE ALREADY NOTED
      [4]Finch, p. 391.
   or
      [5]Ibid., p. 391.
      [6]Griffin, op. cit., p. 67.

EXERCISE 9. Add the footnotes to the edited version of your research report, following the footnote styles given in 15.j.

15.k PREPARING THE FINAL BIBLIOGRAPHY

A **bibliography** lists all your sources.

   The bibliography is an alphabetical list of the sources that you have used in your research. It forms the last page of your paper. To prepare your final bibliography, alphabetize the cards of your working bibliography by the last name of the author. (For sources in which the author's name is not given, use the first important word of the title.) Your bibliography cards should already be in the correct style for entries in a final bibliography. Notice that this style differs from that of footnotes in a number of ways. For example, in a bibliography entry the author's last name is written first, and the punctuation is different. The indention of bibliography entries is the reverse of that in footnotes: The first line is not indented, while the second line is. Here are sample bibliography entries for a book, a periodical article, and an encyclopedia article.

BIBLIOGRAPHY ENTRY FOR A BOOK
Finch, Christopher. The Art of Walt Disney. New York:
      Harry N. Abrams, 1973.

BIBLIOGRAPHY ENTRY FOR A PERIODICAL ARTICLE
Sutton, Horace. "Of Mouse and Man." Saturday Review,
      8 Apr. 1972, pp. 12-14.

BIBLIOGRAPHY ENTRY FOR AN ENCYCLOPEDIA ARTICLE
Suber, Horace. "Walt Disney." <u>Encyclopedia Americana</u>,
    1978 ed.

EXERCISE 10. Prepare a final bibliography, using your
working bibliography cards.

15.l WRITING A FINAL DRAFT

The final draft of a research report may be either
typed or written neatly in ink. Follow your teacher's instructions. If you type, your report should be double-
spaced, with a one-inch margin on the left and right and
at the top and bottom. If your teacher asks you to put the
footnotes at the bottom of the page, be careful to leave
enough room for them on each page.

The first page of your report is the title page. It should
contain the title of the paper, your name, your teacher's
name, the name or number of the course, and the date.
The title and your name should be centered in the middle
of the page, and the other information should be listed in
the lower right corner.

Proofread your paper at least twice to catch errors in
typing, spelling, capitalization, and punctuation. Make
corrections neatly in ink.

EXERCISE 11. Using your revised first draft, write or type
the final draft of your research report. After adding the
footnotes and the final bibliography, proofread the entire
paper and make the necessary corrections.

15.m THE FINISHED RESEARCH REPORT

You have followed Randy Melick's steps in writing his
research report on Walt Disney World. His finished report
follows. (Notice that Randy's footnotes appear at the end
of the paper.)

title (not underlined)

The Making of Walt Disney World

by

Randy Melick

author

course name	English
teacher	Mrs. Comba
date	May 26, 1978

The introduction is a narrative paragraph. Notice the thesis statement in the last sentence.

More than fifteen years before the opening of Disneyland in 1955, Walter Elias Disney had paid several unsatisfying visits to local amusement parks with his young daughters.[1] He had wondered why such parks could not be made as entertaining for adults as they were for youngsters. Disney imagined a park that would be not merely a collection of rides and petty amusements but an entire land of adventure, of nostalgia, of progress, and of the exotic. Disneyland, in Anaheim, California, represented Disney's first attempt to fulfill his ambitious dream. Not until 1971, however, was Disney's dream fully realized with the opening of Walt Disney World in central Florida.

In the next two paragraphs the student writer tells how Walt Disney World was designed to be different from Disneyland.

Though Disneyland enjoyed unparalleled success, Disney hoped to improve upon the Anaheim complex in the park he envisioned for the East. He had several regrets about Disneyland and had vowed not to make the same mistakes twice.[2] The land surrounding Disneyland had been quickly bought up by speculators hoping to capitalize on the park's success; consequently, Disneyland had become completely hemmed in by unsightly motels and other counter-attractions.[3] Disney also regretted that no hotels had been built on the park grounds. This potential source of income had been disregarded because of the inexperience of his staff.[4]

Notice the transitional device in the next sentence.

Consequently, for his new park Disney had in mind a complete vacationland, isolated from the outside world. Campsites and hotel accommodations would be provided, along with a host of recreational activities ranging from birdwatching to golf. Visitors would be entertained by musical shows, strolling minstrels, parades, and simulated cowboy shootouts, train robberies, and stagecoach holdups.[5] In his zeal Disney also planned to include in his wonderland an industrial park as a showcase for American business, a small community of vacation and permanent residences, and an "experimental prototype community of tomorrow" (EPCOT). EPCOT, Disney said, would be a testing ground for new technology and a place where "people actually live a life they can't find anywhere else in the world."[6]

Though Walt Disney died six months before ground was broken for Walt Disney World, he had carefully planned the first stages of the park and had set rigid guidelines for the follow-through.[7] His associates in the WED organization carried out his ideas faithfully, and the project bears his unmistakable stamp.[8]

The next three paragraphs are a description of Walt Disney World.

The innovative amusement park concepts that Disney introduced at Disneyland are the main contributing factors in the Florida park's prosperity. By the use of "visual magnets," visitors are kept moving throughout the complex. Cinderella's Castle, looming in the background from all points in the "Magic Kingdom," is the major such magnet.[9] The castle is located in the center of Walt Disney World, directly in front of a traffic circle from which roads lead to the six theme parks. Access to any point in Walt Disney World from one of the theme parks—Adventureland, Fantasyland, Frontierland, Liberty Square, Tomorrowland, or Main Street, U.S.A.—is convenient and simple.[10]

The complex is filled with references to the many famous Disney cartoon characters and motion picture themes. Costumed figures of Mickey Mouse, Donald Duck, and others roam freely within the park, greeting visitors and posing for pictures with delighted children. Familiar motion picture and cartoon scenes, such as those from 20,000 Leagues Under the Sea and Peter Pan, are incorporated into many of the attractions.

Disney's love for trains, which helped to inspire Disneyland, is also evident in the physical format of Walt Disney World. A steam-powered railroad circles the perimeter of the park, and its quaint main station is situated at the main entrance. Beyond the station lies a small square with a fire house and town hall. A small park covered with flowers leads the visitor onto Main Street, U.S.A., a reproduction of the Main Street of a typical midwestern town. Built on a slightly smaller scale than life-size to enhance the sense of friendliness and intimacy, the street serves as a base for concessions.[11] Visitors to Main Street can browse through Mlle. Antoinette's Parfumerie, investigate the local cinema, or have their portraits drawn by talented artists much as they could in many bustling towns in the Gay Nineties.

In the next paragraph the student writer compares Walt Disney World to an animated cartoon and contrasts it with a world's fair.

The success of Walt Disney World is closely related to the success of the Disney cartoons and films, according to John Hench, a close associate of Disney.[12] Walt Disney World is a controlled environment like that of the Disney animated cartoons.[13] Every element is previously considered and carefully devised so that it complements all others. Unlike a world's fair, where exhibits attempt to outdo one another and ideas are constantly being introduced and then discarded, Walt Disney World has a noncompetitive format and a sense of progression and sequence.[14]

Notice how the student writer uses a quotation in his conclusion.

The Magic Kingdom is a symbol of all that the name Disney represents. It is a fantasy world in which the past and the future, the unknown and the exotic mingle harmoniously in the atmosphere of an animated cartoon. As one adult wrote at the sight of Mickey Mouse leading a marching band,

> there is a swell of joy in the part of one's heart that is still young, and the mind slips the shackles of reality, leaving one with naught to do but clutch the hand of a child and shout, "There's Mickey!"[15]

Notes

[1]Christopher Finch, The Art of Walt Disney (New York: Harry N. Abrams, 1973), p. 383.

[2]Finch, p. 396.

[3]Al Griffin, "Step Right Up, Folks!" (Chicago: Henry Regneri, 1974), p. 214.

[4]Finch, p. 396.

[5]Griffin, p. 67.

[6]Finch, p. 396.

[7]Finch, p. 398.

[8]Paul J. C. Friedlander, "What Has Mickey Mouse Wrought?" The New York Times, 21 Mar. 1971, Section 10, p. 45.

[9]Finch, p. 390.

[10]Peter Blake, "The Lessons of the Parks," in The Art of Walt Disney, p. 431.

[11]Finch, p. 390.

[12]Finch, p. 411.

[13]Finch, p. 411.

[14]Finch, p. 415.

[15]Horace Sutton, "Of Mouse and Man," Saturday Review, 8 Apr. 1972, p. 12.

Bibliography

Blake, Peter. "The Lessons of the Parks." The Art of Walt Disney. New York: Harry N. Abrams, 1973.

Finch, Christopher. The Art of Walt Disney. New York: Harry N. Abrams, 1973.

Friedlander, Paul J. C. "What Has Mickey Mouse Wrought?" The New York Times, 21 Mar. 1971, Section 10, p. 45.

Griffin, Al. "Step Right Up, Folks!" Chicago: Henry Regneri, 1974.

Sutton, Horace. "Of Mouse and Man." Saturday Review, 8 Apr. 1972, pp. 12-14.

15.n A RESEARCH REPORT CHECKLIST

Before you turn in your research report, check to be sure that it includes the following:

- a limited topic
- your own ideas supported by three to five outside sources
- a clear and logical organization
- footnotes giving credit for borrowed ideas and quotations
- a title page and a bibliography following the proper form

THE LETTER

The Letter

Even in today's age of instant telephone communication, there are many good reasons for writing letters. A letter has the following advantages over a telephone conversation.

- A letter gives you the best opportunity to organize your thoughts in an orderly fashion.
- A letter provides a dated record for further reference.
- People often hear what they want to hear in a conversation. A letter is specific and unmistakable.
- A letter is more likely to result in the action you request than is a phone call.

When writing a business letter, be brief and clear. A simple, direct message is always the most effective. Also, be sure to use correct grammar, punctuation, and spelling, and read the letter over carefully to check for mistakes. Make sure the final version is neat and correct.

A business letter should follow a standard style and format that enable the reader to understand and reply to it quickly and accurately. This standard format is composed of the following six parts:

- the heading
- the inside address
- the salutation
- the body
- the closing
- the signature

16.a THE HEADING

The heading of a business letter gives your address and the date on which the letter is written. It is single-spaced and is placed to the right of center. Avoid abbreviations unless they are necessary to prevent a line from running into the margin.

EXAMPLE

> 721 Mountain Drive
> Denver, Colorado 80201
> February 16, 19--

16.b THE INSIDE ADDRESS

The inside address is included in a business letter to ensure that the correct person receives the letter even if it is separated from its envelope. The inside address is single-spaced and is placed a few lines below the heading and even with the left margin. It should include the full name and address of the person and the organization to whom you are writing.

■ Titles of respect

The person's full name is preceded by a *title of respect*. The titles *Mr.*, *Mrs.*, and *Dr.* are normally abbreviated. Others, like *Professor* and *Reverend*, must be spelled out.

A business title may follow a person's name. It is usually written or typed next to the name and is separated from the name by a comma. If the title is more than one word, it may be placed on a second line. (See the sample letter on page 622.)

Sometimes a business letter is written to a company or organization rather than to a person. In this case, write the name of the company or organization as it appears in the company letterhead or advertisement, including the same punctuation and abbreviations.

EXAMPLES

Professor Carlos Muñoz, Chair
History Department
Angelo State University
San Angelo, Texas 76901

Miss Catherine Reilly
Director of Personnel
Sears Department Store
Kingston, New York 12401

L. L. Bean, Inc.
6995 Casco Street
Freeport, Maine 04033

16.c THE SALUTATION

The salutation of a business letter is a formal greeting to the reader of your letter. The salutation is placed two lines below the inside address, even with the left margin. It is followed by a colon.

Different kinds of salutations are used in different situations, as shown in the following examples.

1. When writing to a man whose name you know, use *Mr.*, *Dr.*, or other appropriate title.

   EXAMPLE
   When writing to:
   Adam Stein, Director
   Salutation:
   Dear Mr. Stein:

2. When writing to a woman whose name you know, use *Ms.*, *Miss*, *Mrs.*, *Dr.*, or other appropriate title, as she prefers.

   EXAMPLE
   When writing to:
   Miss Janet Chaney
   Salutation:
   Dear Miss Chaney:

3. When writing to a woman whose title of respect you do not know, use *Ms.*

   EXAMPLE
   When writing to:
   Susan Fenton
   Salutation:
   Dear Ms. Fenton:

4. If you do not want to use a title of respect, you may address people by both their first and last names.

EXAMPLE
When writing to:
Richard Sinkoski
Salutation:
Dear Richard Sinkoski:

5. When writing to a specific person whose name you do not know, use *Sir or Madam*.

EXAMPLE
When writing to:
Manager
King Record Store
Salutation:
Dear Sir or Madam:

6. When writing to a company, organization, or box number, generally use *Sir or Madam*.

EXAMPLE
When writing to:
Information Service
Chicago Public Library
Salutation:
Dear Sir or Madam:

EXERCISE 1. Write the correct heading, inside address, and salutation for letters to the following parties. Use your home address and today's date in the heading.

1. Mr. James Kwong, Hong Kong Tourist Association, 160 Sansome Street, San Francisco, California 94104

2. Dr. Sara Olson, Reading Improvement Clinic, University of Minnesota, Minneapolis, Minnesota 55455

3. Editor, *Photography Today*, 55 West 50th Street, New York, New York 10020

4. Consumer Information, Gulf Oil Corporation, P.O. Box 2001, Houston, Texas 77001

5. Mrs. Paula Campbell, Craft Kits Company, Box 25Y, Dayton, Ohio 45409

16.d THE BODY

The body of a business letter begins two lines below the salutation. It should be single-spaced, with double spaces between paragraphs, and may be written in either block style or semiblock style. In semiblock style, the first line of each paragraph is indented. In block style, the paragraphs are not indented. If your letter is very short, you may double-space the entire body. (See the sample letters on pages 622 and 623.)

16.e THE CLOSING

The closing of a business letter is placed two spaces below the body and to the right of the center of the page. It is followed by a comma. The tone of the closing may range from very formal to personal, depending on the tone of your letter.

EXAMPLES

VERY FORMAL: Respectfully yours,
FORMAL: Very truly yours,
LESS FORMAL: Sincerely,
PERSONAL: Cordially,

16.f THE SIGNATURE

Sign your full name below the closing in dark ink. Then type or print your name below the signature so that the spelling of your name is clear. Always check to see that you have signed a letter before mailing it.

If you have a title, you may put it below your typed or printed name. A woman may also indicate how she wishes to be addressed by writing a title of respect in parentheses before her typed or printed name.

EXAMPLES

Cordially,

Raphael Lopez

Raphael Lopez
Secretary

Sincerely yours,

Sandra Siegel

(Mrs.) Sandra Siegel

EXERCISE 2. Write the correct heading, inside address, salutation, closing, and signature for letters to the following parties. Use your own name and address for the heading and signature. Draw lines to indicate the placement of the body of the letter.

1. Bob Burke, Director, YMCA Basketball Clinic, 410 North Central Avenue, Shelbyville, Indiana 46176
2. Director, Information Service, National Aeronautics and Space Administration, 400 Maryland Avenue, S.W., Washington, D.C. 20546
3. Rosalie Lavaggi, Director, Bayside Health Club, 440 Beacon Street, Boston, Massachusetts 02109
4. Manager, Sportsgear Inc., Fifth and Union Streets, Seattle, Washington 98124
5. The governor of your state or the mayor of your city or town

16.g THE ENVELOPE

The envelope of a business letter is addressed in a standard style. The return address is placed in the upper left-hand corner of the envelope. You should include your name as well as your address.

Peter Depew
1480 Cedar Street
Berkeley, California 94701

Mrs. Cynthia Nichols
Membership Department
Paperback Book Club
Columbus, Ohio 43216

The name and address of the person to whom you are writing are placed just below and to the right of center on the envelope. The address on the envelope should be the same as the inside address of the letter, including any titles. Always include the ZIP code in the address. You can find the correct ZIP codes for local areas in your telephone directory. ZIP codes for the entire country are listed in a ZIP code directory that you can find at your local post office or library.

16.h KINDS OF BUSINESS LETTERS

Business letters serve a number of purposes. Among them are (1) to request information or services, (2) to order something from a company, and (3) to make a complaint to a company or organization.

■ The letter requesting information or services

You may write a business letter to an organization or company to request information about products, services, or possible employment. You may also write a business letter to request someone to do something for you. For example, if you are writing a paper on the Alaska Pipeline, you might write to a department of the state government or to one of the major oil corporations.

When you write a letter that asks for information or services, you should do the following:

- Identify yourself.
- Explain why you need assistance from the person to whom you are writing.
- State a specific request.
- Close courteously.

■ The order letter

Most mail order firms provide printed forms for ordering goods, but sometimes you must write an order letter. In an order letter be sure to do the following:

- Give necessary information about the quantity, size, color, and price for each item.

- If you are enclosing payment, state how much you are sending. Do not forget to enclose the payment. Send a check or money order. Never send cash.
- If necessary, provide a smaller envelope addressed to yourself.

■ The letter of adjustment or complaint

There are several reasons that you may want to write a letter of adjustment or complaint to a company or organization. For example, if you order goods by mail and they arrive in an unsatisfactory condition or not at all, you will need to write to the company. You may also want to write to a company or organization to complain about the poor quality of a service it provides.

In a letter of complaint or adjustment, be sure to do the following:

- Give all necessary details of the situation.
- Be polite but firm. A courteous tone is more likely to get a positive response than a rude tone.
- Ask for specific action, and indicate that you assume it will be taken.

EXERCISE 3. Each of the following items asks you to write a letter requesting information or services. Use your home or school address and today's date.

1. Write to the Maxwell Vacation School asking for a schedule of summer school courses and tuition costs. Address the letter to Alice Brenner, registrar of the school, at 141 East 56th Street, New York, New York 10022.

2. Write to your local medical association to request that one of its members speak to your biology class about heart transplant surgery.

3. For your science project you need information on solar energy for heating the home. Write to the Energy Information Administration to ask for pamphlets and other printed matter on the subject. The address is 1110 Independence Avenue, S.W., Washington, D.C. 20314

A Letter Requesting Services (*semiblock style*)

Hamilton High School
Provo, Utah 84601
May 4, 19 - - | Heading

Mr. Winston Rayburn
Executive Secretary
Chamber of Commerce
Provo, Utah 84601 | Inside address

Dear Mr. Rayburn: | Salutation

    On Friday, May 25, the sophomore class at our school is sponsoring a summer employment workshop. I would like to invite you to be our guest speaker.

    We hope that you can share with us your knowledge of summer job opportunities for students in our city. We would also appreciate advice on how to meet an employer's expectations and succeed on a job. | Body

    Please let me know if you can speak at our workshop. If you need more information, I would be glad to supply it.

Yours truly, | Closing

Ramona Newcomb | Signature

Ramona Newcomb
President
Sophomore Class | Typewritten name
| Title

A Letter of Complaint (*block style*)

1380 Peach Street, N.E.
Atlanta, Georgia 30309
September 15, 19--

Subscription Manager
Teen Life
Box 666
Denver, Colorado 80202

Dear Sir or Madam:

One June 3 I sent an order for a one-year subscription to
Teen Life along with a money order for $9.00 in payment.
It is now the middle of September, and I have not received
any copies of the magazine.

> Give the
> details of the
> situation.

Please send me the July, August, and September issues as
soon as possible. I hope I will receive all future issues of
the magazine on time.

> Ask for
> specific
> action.

Thank you for your attention to this request.

> Close
> courteously.

Yours truly,

Lisa Bolton

Lisa Bolton

EXERCISE 4. Each of the following items asks you to write a sample order letter. Use your home address and today's date in the return address.

1. Order two books of your choice at $6.50 each from Books on Tape, Inc., Department N, P.O. Box 7900, Newport Beach, California 92660

2. Order a model airplane kit, catalogue number 1304, from Hobby Craft Company, Box 797, Fairfield, Iowa 52556. The price is $12.00.

EXERCISE 5. Each of the following items asks you to write a sample letter of complaint. Use your home address and today's date in the return address.

1. Write to the Johnson Manufacturing Company to complain about excessive noise coming from the company's factory in your neighborhood. Ask the company to install sound-proofing or otherwise reduce the noise.

2. Write a letter of complaint to a made-up restaurant about the poor service or quality of the food or what you feel are unfair prices. Cite specific instances and details in your complaint.

EXERCISE 6. Write a letter to a company or organization about a *real* complaint that you have. Send the letter, and report to the class on any reply you receive.

EXERCISE 7. Have a class discussion on the advantages and disadvantages of writing business letters. When can a telephone call be as effective as a letter? Discuss how business letters can create a good or poor impression.

STUDY SKILLS AND TEST TAKING

Study Skills and Test Taking

This section will help you learn two skills that are very important to you as a student: how to study and how to take standardized tests. In this section you will learn ways to become a better listener, reader, and note taker. In addition, you will be given strategies for answering several kinds of questions that appear on standardized reading and vocabulary tests. Finally, you will see some questions similar to those on a specific test.

STUDY SKILLS

As a student, you are constantly learning facts and ideas. You have probably often thought about how much material you have to study, but have you ever thought about *how* you study? This section will help you understand ways to make the studying process easier and more effective.

17.a LISTENING AND READING SKILLS

Why do some people understand and remember more of what they hear and read than other people? Part of the

Sample questions in this section (except for synonym questions) are from *1979 PSAT/NMSQT Student Bulletin* and *Taking the SAT: A Guide to the Scholastic Aptitude Test and the Test of Standard Written English*. Reprinted by permission of the College Board and of Educational Testing Service, copyright owner of the sample questions.

reason may be that they have a better understanding of how to listen and read. Certain techniques that you can use to help you develop your listening and reading skills are discussed in the following pages.

■ Listening skills

Listening is a problem for almost everyone. The reason is that the average person thinks at a speed more than three times as fast as the average speaker talks. There is room in the listener's mind for more information. The listener's mind, then, tends to wander while it is waiting for the speaker to catch up. Simply trying to pay attention, therefore, is not enough to make you a good listener. You must be an *active listener*. That is, you must completely fill your mind by thinking about and analyzing what you hear as you hear it. The following five suggestions will help you to become an active listener:

1. As you listen, think from time to time about the main points the speaker has already made.
2. Try to think ahead of the speaker and to figure out the direction in which he or she is going.
3. Be alert for what the speaker may be suggesting but not actually saying. Listen "between the lines."
4. Try not to react emotionally to what the speaker is saying until you have heard all of it. If you start to think about how you feel about a particular statement, you may miss what the speaker is saying next.
5. Take notes on the important information if you will later need to recall what is being said (see 17.b).

■ Skills for reading textbooks

Many students do not learn as much as they could from their textbook reading because they do not use the helps provided in the textbooks themselves. Headings, introductions, conclusions, and review questions are included in textbooks for the specific purpose of making the material more understandable. Try to follow these suggestions in your textbook reading:

1. Before you begin reading, look at the chapter titles and headings, the introduction and/or conclusion, and any review questions.
2. Then, as you read, concentrate on the points mentioned in the headings, the introduction and/or conclusion, and the review questions.
3. Take notes on the important information in what you read (see 17.b).

17.b NOTE-TAKING METHODS

If your notes do not seem to be of much help to you, the problem may be that you are not sure what you are trying to accomplish when you take them. Notes have two purposes. First, they help you to learn the material as you take them. Not only does the very act of writing something on paper help to reinforce it in your mind, but note taking also forces you to organize the material in some way. Second, your notes will serve as reminders when you use them later to study for tests.

Two methods of note taking are discussed in the following pages: outlining and mapping. In addition to learning those methods, try to follow these general suggestions in taking notes.

1. Take notes in your own words. Putting ideas and information into your own language helps you learn the material.
2. Concentrate on the main ideas and important facts. Do not try to write down every word or detail.
3. Use words and phrases rather than complete sentences, and use as many abbreviations and symbols as you can. *Be sure, however, that whatever you are writing will make sense to you when you have to use the notes.*

■ Outlining notes

Outlining is the most common way of organizing notes. In an outline, numbers and letters are used to show the relationships among ideas and details. Outlining can be used in taking notes from a lecture, but it is more easily used for written materials. Follow these steps in outlining your reading from textbooks:

1. Read the material, applying the skills for reading textbooks discussed in 17.a.
2. Decide what the first main idea is, and write it down after the Roman numeral *I*.
3. Use capital letters to list important ideas or details below the main idea.
4. Use numbers to list more detailed points below the capital-letter points.
5. If the passage has more than one main idea, list the second one as Roman numeral *II*. Repeat steps 2-4 until you have outlined the whole passage.

OUTLINE FORM

I. First main idea
   A. Idea
   B. Idea
      1. Detail
      2. Detail
II. Second main idea

Read the following paragraphs from a biology textbook, and think about how you would outline them. Then look at the sample outline that follows the paragraphs.

EXAMPLE

Gnawing Mammals. The gnawers, or rodents, outnumber all of the other mammals. Of the more than 5,000 species of mammals, over 2,000 are rodents. Some, like the mouse, are tiny. Others, like the capybara of South America, may weigh more than 100 pounds. Most rodents are scattered all over the earth as small animals that make their homes in burrows. Some, however, like the squirrels, live in trees. A few, such as the muskrat and beaver, have become adapted to the water. Rats, guinea pigs, and porcupines are also members of this large order, which is called *Rodentia*.

All rodents have two pairs of large, chisel-like teeth, called *incisors*, in the front of the mouth. The upper and lower pairs work together like shears to gnaw their food. Although their cutting edges are gradually worn away in the process, the incisors keep on growing throughout the life of the animal. Similarly, if the incisors are not used enough, they may actually grow in a circle and interfere with chewing, in which case the animal may starve.

—*Biological Science*

I. Rodents (gnawing mammals)
   A. Outnumber all other mammals—2,000 out of 5,000 species
   B. Most small and live in burrows
      1. Squirrels—trees
      2. Muskrat & beaver—water
   C. All have two pairs of incisors (large chisel-like front teeth) for gnawing food
      1. Keep growing throughout animal's life
      2. If not used enough, may grow in circle & cause starvation

EXERCISE 1. Read and outline the following paragraph from a home economics textbook.

Classes of Wheat. Wheats may be classified on the basis of the time of planting or the growing season, on the color of the kernel, and on the "hardness" or "softness" of the kernel. Wheats that are planted in the spring and harvested in the fall are called *spring wheats*, whereas those that are planted in the fall and harvested the following summer are called *winter wheats*. Since these wheats remain in the ground all winter, they are grown in areas with relatively mild winters. Some wheat kernels have a reddish appearance and are called *red wheats*, whereas others are white. A hard wheat has a hard, vitreous kernel, whereas a soft wheat does not. Hard wheats are usually higher in protein than are soft wheats, and the protein has more baking strength when flour from this wheat is made into dough. Spring wheats include hard red varieties, hard white and soft white varieties, and durum wheats, which are used only for the production of macaroni products. Winter wheats may be hard, semihard, or soft. Hard winter wheats have a fairly strong quality of protein and are suitable for bread-making purposes.

—*Introductory Foods*

■ Mapping notes

For lectures and book passages that are not highly organized, you may find it helpful to take notes by the *mapping* method rather than by outlining. In this method a map, or diagram, is used to show the relationships between main ideas, supporting ideas or facts, and smaller details. To take mapping notes, follow these steps:

1. Write the main idea of the lecture or reading passage in the center of the page, and draw a circle around it.
2. Write important ideas or facts on lines connected to the circle.
3. Write subordinate details on lines connected to the first lines.

MAPPING FORM

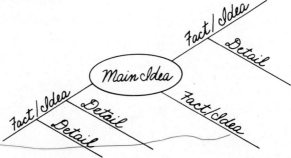

Read the following paragraphs from a world history textbook, and think about how you would take mapping notes on them. Then look at the sample map following the paragraphs.

EXAMPLE

How Did the Kingdom of Ghana Rise and Fall? Ghana is the name of the West African country located on the Gulf of Guinea. As a colony of Great Britain it was known for many years as the Gold Coast. When it became an independent nation, it changed its name to one that was used in its colorful past. The *ghana* was the title of the ruler of that older nation that once ruled a large part of West Africa; Ghana also was the name of the land he ruled.

By the eleventh century Ghana's power was near its peak. It had complete control over the trade routes between the salt mines in the Sahara and the gold mines on its southern boundaries. During the reign of Tenkamenin, Ghana had become a highly developed state, similar to the monarchies that ruled in Europe at a later time.

In 1076, ten years after William the Conqueror had crossed the English Channel to establish his rule in Britain, Tenkamenin's empire fell. The Almoravids, a fanatical Moslem group, invaded the kingdom, and while their power was short-lived, Ghana never recovered. Although Tenkamenin had been a powerful ruler, neither the lands he ruled nor the exact borders of his empire were ever clearly defined. Rival chiefs were eager to establish themselves as monarchs of a great land. Tribal warfare and petty jealousies interfered with the restoration of the kingdom. Ghana began to decline but did continue to exist until the thirteenth century.

—*The Pageant of World History*

Kingdom of Ghana

name of ruler + nation / W. Africa / decline / lasted til 13th c. / 1076-Almoravid invasion / unclear borders / tribal warfare / chiefs' rivalry

peak in 11th c. / control of salt + gold trade / reign of Tenkamenin

EXERCISE 2. Read and map the following passage from a biology textbook.

Structure of the Skin. Human skin consists of two distinct layers, the outer *epidermis* and the inner *dermis*. The epidermis is about the thickness of tissue paper. The dermis is about as thick as cardboard. It is the epidermis that peels off after a severe sunburn.

The top of the epidermis consists of dead cells that are continually being worn away. As they are removed from the body, other cells from a lower layer of the epidermis replace them.

The deeper layer of the skin, or dermis, contains many nerves and blood vessels. In it can also be found the sweat glands with their twisted ducts, or tubes, leading to the surface. The roots of the hair shafts, enclosed in the *hair follicles*, also lie in the dermis. Near the follicles are the *sebaceous glands*. The oily secretion of these glands keeps the hair and skin flexible. It also prevents excessive absorption or excretion of water over the surface of the body. At the base of the hair shafts are nerves and the muscles that cause the hairs to stand on end.

—*Biological Science*

STANDARDIZED TEST QUESTIONS

By this point in school, you have probably already taken several standardized tests. A standardized test is one that is designed to be given to large numbers of students in a school district, a state, or even the entire nation. It measures general knowledge and abilities in a subject area rather than the specific material you have covered in a particular course.

Two main kinds of questions are used on standardized tests: multiple-choice questions and essay questions. Multiple-choice questions require you to choose the correct answer from two or more possibilities. They test your knowledge and ability to recall facts. Essay questions, on the other hand, require you to write answers of several paragraphs or longer. They measure your ability to think clearly and to organize facts and knowledge in coherent language.

Many standardized tests that you will take in high school are designed to measure your reading and vocabulary skills. The following subsections discuss five common kinds of multiple-choice questions used on standardized reading and vocabulary tests: (1) synonym questions, (2) antonym questions, (3) analogy questions, (4) sentence-completion questions, and (5) reading-comprehension questions.

17.c SYNONYM QUESTIONS

A *synonym* is a word that has the same or almost the same meaning as another word. For example, *increase* is a synonym of *grow*. Many standardized tests use multiple-choice synonym questions to measure students' vocabulary. These questions usually ask you to choose the word that is closest in meaning to a given word. Follow these suggestions in answering synonym questions.

■ Strategies for synonym questions

1. Read *all* of the choices given. Do not stop at the first choice just because it seems to be a synonym of the given word. One of the later choices may be a closer synonym.

2. If none of the choices seems to be an exact synonym of the given word, decide which one is *closest* in meaning. Few words have exact synonyms.

3. Remember that many words have more than one meaning or can be used as more than one part of speech. If none of the choices seems related in meaning to the given word, think about whether it has another meaning. Also, be sure to consider meanings of the word as another part of speech—as a verb rather than a noun, for instance. The answer choices will give you clues about the part of speech for which

you are looking. Using the word in a sentence may also help you find the closest synonym.

■ Sample synonym question

Look at the following sample synonym question, and study the explanation that follows it.

ASTONISHMENT: (A) confusion   (B) interference
(C) amazement   (D) resentment   (E) dissension

This question illustrates the importance of reading all the choices given. Choice (A), *confusion*, is somewhat related to *astonishment*. If you think about the two words, however, you will realize that confusion is a result of astonishment rather than the same feeling. Choice (C), *amazement*, is *closest* in meaning to the given word.

EXERCISE 3. Choose the word or phrase that means the same or most nearly the same as the word in capital letters.

1. AMBLE: (A) leap   (B) stroll   (C) enjoy
   (D) hasten   (E) complete
2. GESTURE: (A) movement   (B) appearance
   (C) success   (D) merriment   (E) position
3. NEBULOUS: (A) unknown   (B) calm
   (C) wealthy   (D) dishonest   (E) vague
4. STIFLE: (A) evaluate   (B) distrust
   (C) suffocate   (D) harass   (E) encourage
5. FLIPPANT: (A) impertinent   (B) joyful
   (C) indecisive   (D) talkative   (E) ridiculous

17.d ANTONYM QUESTIONS

An *antonym* is a word that has the opposite meaning from another word. For example, *fail* is an antonym of *succeed*. Standardized tests often contain antonym questions that ask you to choose the word or phrase that is most nearly opposite in meaning to a given word. These questions are similar to the synonym questions discussed in 17.c, but they are generally more difficult.

■ Strategies for antonym questions

Use the same strategies suggested for synonym questions in 17.c, remembering that you are looking for the opposite rather than the same meaning.

■ Sample antonym question

Look at the following sample antonym question, and then study the explanation following it.

TENSION: (A) dullness   (B) laxness   (C) balance
(D) lack of strength   (E) lack of purpose

If you looked at this question quickly, you might decide that Choice (A), *dullness*, is the best answer because a tense situation is not dull. The two words are not really opposite in meaning, however, because a situation that is not dull is not necessarily tense. To answer this question, you must realize that *tension* can mean "the tightness of a stretched rope or string" as well as "nervous strain." Choice (B), *laxness*, which means "looseness," is best.

EXERCISE 4. Choose the word or phrase that means the opposite or most nearly the opposite to the word in capital letters.

1. STIFF: (A) limber   (B) melted   (C) succulent
   (D) twisted   (E) silky
2. MYSTIFY: (A) praise   (B) evaluate   (C) rearrange
   (D) make clear to   (E) be indifferent to
3. NEGLIGENCE: (A) ability   (B) carefulness
   (C) importance   (D) immunity   (E) consistency
4. EQUILIBRIUM: (A) opposition   (B) insignificance
   (C) lack of freedom   (D) lack of contact
   (E) lack of balance
5. INFERNAL: (A) exquisite   (B) frigid
   (C) ephemeral   (D) mortal   (E) celestial

17.e ANALOGY QUESTIONS

The word *analogy* refers to "a similarity in certain aspects between things that are otherwise unlike." Analogy questions are a form of vocabulary question that appears on many standardized tests. They require you to understand the relationship between a pair of words.

◼ Strategies for analogy questions

1. Think about the kind or quality of relationship that exists between the given pair of words. Is the relationship one of large to small? Cause to effect? Group to individual? Part to whole?
2. Pay careful attention to the order of the words in each pair. A pair of words with the relationship of large to small, for example, is not analogous to a pair with the relationship of small to large.
3. Make up a sentence expressing the relationship between the given pair of words. Then substitute each of the other pairs of words in your sentence to see which makes the best sense.

◼ Sample analogy question

SUBMISSIVE : LED : : (A) wealthy : employed
                              (B) intolerant : indulged
                              (C) humble : humiliated
                              (D) incorrigible : taught
                              (E) inconspicuous : overlooked

Read an analogy question in the following way: *Submissive* is to *led* as *wealthy* is to *employed* . . . as *intolerant* is to *indulged,* etc. Your first step is to figure out the relationship between the given pair of words. In this case the relationship could be expressed in this manner: "To be submissive is to be easily led." If you study all the choices carefully, you can see that only Choice (E) expresses the same relationship: "To be inconspicuous is to be easily overlooked."

EXERCISE 5. Choose the pair of words that expresses a relationship most similar to that expressed by the pair of words in capital letters.

1. CEDAR : WOOD : :
   (A) textile : silk
   (B) copper : metal
   (C) porcelain : dish
   (D) lace : dress
   (E) clay : brick

2. THIMBLE : FINGER : :
   (A) muzzle : snout
   (B) collar : neck
   (C) bracelet : wrist
   (D) helmet : head
   (E) yoke : shoulder

3. STRUT : PROUD : :
   (A) stroll : eager
   (B) saunter : humble
   (C) scurry : pompous
   (D) shuffle : graceful
   (E) slink : furtive

4. IMMENSE : LARGE : :
   (A) calm : clear
   (B) searing : quick
   (C) glaring : bright
   (D) piercing : mild
   (E) savage : cautious

5. AFFECTATION : GENUINE : :
   (A) accident : premeditated
   (B) praise : complimentary
   (C) declaration : corroborated
   (D) invention : creative
   (E) portrait : distorted

17.f SENTENCE-COMPLETION QUESTIONS

A sentence-completion question consists of a sentence that is missing one or two words. You are to select the appropriate missing words from five choices offered.

Your understanding of the incomplete sentence will help you to fill in the blanks. There are key words within the sentence that control the possible words that can be substituted for the blanks.

■ Strategies for sentence-completion questions

1. Be alert to the clues contained in the sentence. The given parts of the sentence will always give you the clues to the correct answer.

2. If the sentence has two blanks, try to understand how the missing words are related to each other. For example, are they similar in meaning? Are they opposite?

■ Sample sentence-completion questions

Look at the sample questions below, and then study the explanations that follow them.

SAMPLE QUESTION A

Even if culture is learned rather than inherited, isn't it possible that what is learned depends upon _____ characteristics?

(A) environmental   (B) interrelated
(C) social   (D) salient   (E) innate

Notice that this sentence is a question and that the implied answer to the question is yes. The sentence says, in effect, the following: "Even if culture is *x* (learned) not *y* (inherited), isn't it possible that *x* (what is learned) depends upon *y*?" The blank in the original sentence takes the position of the last *y*. The missing word must, therefore, have a meaning similar to *inherited*. The only word that means the same as *inherited* is (E), *innate*.

SAMPLE QUESTION B

Because many people find Wagner's operas too _____, some recent productions have been _____.

(A) old . . . outdated
(B) long . . . abridged
(C) loud . . .recorded
(D) strange . . . complicated
(E) lyrical . . . dramatized

The sentence suggests that in some recent productions the operas have been changed in some way to reduce a characteristic that many people considered excessive. The word that goes in the second blank, therefore, should suggest a reduction of the quality in the first blank. The first terms of several of the answer choices seem to fit into the first blank. Only Choice (B), however, has a second term that refers to a reduction of the quality in the first term. *Abridged* means "shortened," which is the logical change that would be made in long operas.

EXERCISE 6. Choose the word or words that best complete the meaning of the sentence.

1. All statements about the origin and evolution of family types must be classed as _____, for none of them is susceptible of scientific proof.
   (A) facts   (B) tenets   (C) corollaries
   (D) suppositions   (E) fundamentals

2. At that time the _____ of science was colossal; people believed that science could accomplish almost anything.
   (A) outcome   (B) obscurity   (C) prestige
   (D) demise   (E) imitation

3. Although its publicity has been _____, the film itself is intelligent, well-acted, handsomely produced, and altogether _____.
   (A) tasteless . . . respectable
   (B) extensive . . . moderate
   (C) sophisticated . . . amateur
   (D) risqué . . . crude
   (E) perfect . . . spectacular

4. Certain strong individuals believe that they have the right to _____ ordinary people, that they are _____ the moral responsibility that weighs upon the rest of us.
   (A) inveigh against . . . held by
   (B) trample over . . . exempt from
   (C) lead about . . . restrained by
   (D) argue with . . . confused by
   (E) infiltrate among . . . critical of

5. Prominent psychologists believe that people act violently because they have been _____ to do so, not because they were born _____.
   (A) forced . . . gregarious
   (B) forbidden . . . complacent
   (C) expected . . . innocent
   (D) taught . . . aggressive
   (E) inclined . . . belligerent

17.g READING-COMPREHENSION QUESTIONS

Many standardized tests include questions based on reading passages of varying length and difficulty. These questions are usually designed to test your comprehension of the passage in several specific ways. The questions will usually ask you to do the following:

1. Understand the main idea of the passage.
2. Recall or identify facts and ideas.
3. Make inferences, or conclusions, from the facts or ideas given.
4. Evaluate the author's purpose, tone, or attitude.

■ Strategies for reading-comprehension questions

1. Before you read the passage, glance over the questions at the end to get an idea of what you should be looking for when you read.
2. As you read the passage, concentrate on *what* is being said and *how* it is being said.

■ Sample reading-comprehension questions

Read the following passage carefully, and then try to answer the questions that accompany it before you read the discussions of each.

> The Mescalero Apache tribe is one of seven linguistically and culturally related peoples whose aboriginal territories stretched over large sections of present-day southwestern United States and northeastern Mexico. The Mescalero were characterized by an economic system that harmonized well with their challenging environment. In late historic times they attempted desultory farming along some watercourses, but the severe weather and short growing season of the mountains and the precarious water supply of the lowlands did not encourage cultivation of the soil. Thus the Mescalero were forced to depend on hunting and the gathering of wild harvests.

Such an economy required mobility; there had to be readiness to follow the food harvests when and where they matured and to move from one hunting area to another when the supply of game dwindled. A concentration of population was inappropriate to such techniques of food procurement. As a result, the population was thinly dispersed over the immense range.

Since most economic errands were carried out in small groups, there was little incentive for highly centralized leadership. It is probable that never in its history did the tribe have a single leader who was recognized and followed by all. Rather, the Mescalero leader, or "chief" (literally "he who speaks"), was, as his title suggests, a respected adviser drawn from the heads of the families who tended to camp and move together.

Since he had no coercive power, he had to understand what his followers were willing to do. Serious misjudgments or unpopular counsel might cost him his position or a portion of his followers. Theoretically, the office of the leader was not hereditary; in practice, there was a tendency for sons of leaders to succeed their fathers. This was informal, however, not absolute. Typical situations which required a leader's judgment included such problems as whether to move to another site because of poor luck in hunting, repeated deaths, epidemic disease, or the proximity of enemies; whether to sanction a raid or war party; whether to sponsor an important social or ritual event to which outsiders might be invited; and what to do about disruptive behavior such as the practice of witchcraft. The ability to lead successful raids and war parties, as well as to sanction them, was a great asset for a leader; such expeditions meant booty, and this made it possible to distribute favors widely. In a society where generosity was one of the cardinal virtues, such activity built and sustained the good will so important to a leader.

Evaluating the Author's Purpose

1. The primary purpose of the passage is to
   (A) raise a question   (B) draw a comparison
   (C) describe a group   (D) discuss an event
   (E) identify a cause

This question requires you to decide what kind of writing the passage represents. It should be obvious that the answer is (C), because the entire passage is a description of the Mescalero Apache tribe. It includes none of the kinds of writing mentioned in the other choices.

Recalling Facts

2. The author states that one of the personal qualities held to be of prime importance among the Mescalero Apache was
   (A) gratitude   (B) generosity   (C) honesty
   (D) cautiousness   (E) cleverness

For questions of factual detail, the answer is explicitly stated in the passage. In this case the correct answer is (B), because the author says that "generosity was one of the cardinal virtues" of the tribe.

Making the Right Inferences

3. It can be inferred that the political organization of the Mescalero Apache tribe most resembled which of the following?
   (A) A modified democracy
   (B) A fascist state
   (C) An institutional monarchy
   (D) A form of theocracy
   (E) A military dictatorship

This question requires you to analyze factual information and to reach a conclusion about the category or pattern into which the information fits. As you can see from the choices, you must have a general familiarity with the vocabulary of political organization to be able to answer the question. The passage states that the tribe probably never had a single leader who was acknowledged by everyone. The man who served as a leader when necessary was simply an adviser with no power of command. This information eliminates Choices (B), (C), and (E), all of which are characterized by strong central leadership. Choice (D), *A form of theocracy*, refers to government by religious leaders, but the passage does not suggest that the leader had a religious role. Choice (A), *A modified democracy*, is the best conclusion.

4. It can be inferred that leading war parties reinforced a leader's power primarily by enabling him to
   (A) ensure that his power would be passed on to his son
   (B) reinforce the self-respect of his warriors
   (C) extend the boundaries of the territory over which he held authority
   (D) divert the people's attention from such problems as disease or poor luck in hunting
   (E) secure the enemies' goods for dispensation to the members of his tribe

Notice that this question asks you to choose the *primary* way in which leading war parties reinforced the leader's power. All of the choices are plausible answers, but (E) is the only one mentioned by the author. Therefore, it is safe to conclude that it is the most important.

Understanding the Main Idea
5. The author is primarily concerned with discussing
   (A) some economic and political aspects of life among the Mescalero
   (B) the dispersion of seven Apache tribes in the United States and Mexico
   (C) some tribal rituals of the Mescalero
   (D) special qualifications of a leader of the Mescalero
   (E) some effects of the Mescalero economy on the tribal hierarchy

To answer this question, you must differentiate between the *main* idea of the passage and secondary ideas contained in it. Of the answer choices, (B), (D), and (E) are discussed in the passage. Choice (A), however, best describes the subject of the passage as a whole.

A SAMPLE STANDARDIZED TEST

The following pages contain questions similar to those that appear on the Preliminary Scholastic Aptitude Test (PSAT). On this test you will find the kinds of questions discussed in the preceding pages.

17.h THE PRELIMINARY SCHOLASTIC APTITUDE TEST (PSAT)

The Preliminary Scholastic Aptitude Test (PSAT) is also the qualifying test for the National Merit Scholarship competition. Therefore, it is also known as the PSAT/NMSQT. The PSAT is taken by students in October of their junior year. As its name implies, it is essentially a shorter version of the Scholastic Aptitude Test (SAT) that many students take for college admission.

The verbal portion of the PSAT contains the same kinds of questions as the SAT verbal test: antonym questions, analogy questions, sentence-completion questions, and reading-comprehension questions. Refer to 17.c–17.g for a review of those question types.

The following exercises contain antonym, analogy, and sentence-completion questions similar to those on the PSAT. Read the directions carefully, and then answer the questions.

EXERCISE 7: Antonym questions. Each question below consists of a word in capital letters, followed by five lettered words or phrases. Choose the lettered word or phrase that is most nearly *opposite* in meaning to the word in capital letters. Since some of the questions require you to distinguish fine shades of meaning, consider all the choices before deciding which is best.

1. AGILE: (A) humble   (B) clumsy   (C) useless
   (D) timid   (E) ugly
2. NULLIFY: (A) examine   (B) ascertain
   (C) slander   (D) react   (E) validate
3. INGENIOUS: (A) incredible   (B) unintentional
   (C) instinctive   (D) unimaginative   (E) innate
4. SHIFTLESS: (A) covert   (B) ubiquitous
   (C) industrious   (D) compelling
   (E) opinionated
5. LOQUACITY: (A) blasphemy   (B) boastfulness
   (C) reticence   (D) servility   (E) insolence

EXERCISE 8: Analogy questions. Each question below consists of a related pair of words or phrases, followed by five lettered pairs of words or phrases. Select the lettered pair that *best* expresses a relationship similar to that expressed in the original pair.

1. TROWEL : BRICKLAYER : :
   (A) bark : woodsman
   (B) hinge : locksmith
   (C) porcelain : potter
   (D) ceiling : plasterer
   (E) chisel : stonecutter

2. RIFT : UNITY : :
   (A) flaw : variety
   (B) snag : identity
   (C) blot : darkness
   (D) spark : brilliance
   (E) ripple : smoothness

3. WRITER : ROYALTY : :
   (A) donor : charity
   (B) shareholder : dividend
   (C) accountant : debit
   (D) banker : finance
   (E) tenant : rent

4. SOLITAIRE : GAME : :
   (A) monotone : spectrum
   (B) monologue : speech
   (C) employee : corporation
   (D) airplane : travel
   (E) chapter : book

5. ASTRAL : STAR : :
   (A) universal : galaxy
   (B) celestial : comet
   (C) stellar : moon
   (D) terrestrial : earth
   (E) planetary : sun

EXERCISE 9: Sentence-completion questions. Each sentence below has one or two blanks, each blank indicating that something has been omitted. Beneath the sentence are five lettered words or sets of words. Choose the word or set of words that *best* fits the meaning of the sentence as a whole.

1. If your garden plot is small, it will not pay to grow crops that require a large amount of ＿＿ in order to develop.
   (A) moisture   (B) rain   (C) fertilizer
   (D) space   (E) care

2. If we survey the development of dancing as an art in Europe, we recognize two streams of tradition which have sometimes ＿＿ and yet remain essentially ＿＿.
   (A) changed . . . modern   (B) divided . . . separate
   (C) abated . . . primitive   (D) merged . . . distinct
   (E) advanced . . . comparable

3. They argue that the author was determined to ＿＿ his own conclusion, so he ＿＿ any information that did not support it.
   (A) uphold . . . ignored   (B) revise . . . destroyed
   (C) advance . . . devised   (D) disprove . . . distorted
   (E) reverse . . . confiscated

4. Mr. Dillon is a skeptic, ＿＿ to believe that the accepted opinion of the majority is generally ＿＿.
   (A) prone . . . infallible   (B) afraid . . . misleading
   (C) inclined . . . justifiable   (D) quick . . . significant
   (E) disposed . . . erroneous

5. The excitement does not ＿＿ but ＿＿ his senses, giving him a keener perception of a thousand details.
   (A) slow . . . diverts   (B) blur . . . sharpens
   (C) overrule . . . constricts   (D) heighten . . . aggravates
   (E) forewarn. . . quickens

ADDITIONAL EXERCISES

Additional Exercises

1. Nouns

PART A: In each group below, identify all of the common nouns. Some may be compound nouns. (Review 1.a.1.)

1. camera, snapshot, Polaroid, darkroom, slide
2. keyboard, Steinway, piano, concert grand, Baldwin
3. museum, art gallery, statue, Georgia O'Keeffe, dry point
4. tape deck, record album, turntable, component, Janis Joplin
5. brass, trumpet, slide trombone, oboe, Fats Waller
6. theater, theatergoer, Broadway, curtain time, footlight
7. Hollywood, movie, close-up, zoom lens, Radio City Music Hall
8. soap opera, sportscast, television set, disc jockey, *The Waltons*
9. National Football League, baseball, hockey stick, touchdown, quarterback
10. hobby, handicraft, sideline, spectator sport

PART B: Now identify each proper noun in Part A. (Review 1.a.1.)

PART C: Look at the common nouns that you identified in Part A. List those that are compound nouns. Remember that a compound noun can be written as two words, as one word, or as a hyphenated word. (Review 1.a.2.)

PART D: Write the plural for each common noun that you identified in Part A. (Review 1.a.3.)

2. Verbs

PART A: Select the correct form of the verb in parentheses. (Review 1.b.6–1.b.20.)

1. The Experimental Aircraft Association (began/begun) in 1953.
2. All home-built aircraft (is/are) "experimental" to the Federal Aviation Administration, according to present regulations.
3. Every summer the EAA (holds/was holding) an eight-day convention in Oshkosh, Wisconsin.
4. Over 150,000 aviation buffs (have assembled/has assembled) for the convention in some years.
5. In one recent year hundreds came from abroad, including a Japanese who (weared/wore) a sign that read "Take me to Oshkosh, Wisconsin, U.S.A."
6. One young woman (restored/restore) a 1942 Stearman, in which she arrived from Illinois.
7. A California doctor landed in a small biplane that he and his family (had built/have built).
8. A replica of the Fokker D-1, which was copied by a man from Pittsburgh, Pennsylvania, (were present/was present).
9. The construction (took/taked) 35,000 hours of work and 17,137 pieces of wood to make.
10. A copy of the 1931 Ramsey Flying Bathtub also (flied/flew) into Oshkosh that year.
11. In recent years hang gliders (had become/have become) familiar sights at the Oshkosh convention.
12. In 1978 almost 1,500 of the 12,000 airplanes at the convention (was/were) homemade.
13. The 1978 EAA Award for outstanding new design (went/has gone) to Bert Routan of Mojave, California.
14. Instead of a horizontal tail his plane has an air foil in front that he (called/calling) a canard.
15. At a speed of 80 miles an hour, his plane (travel/travels) 104 miles on a gallon of gasoline.
16. His plane is so stable that it (do not go/does not go) into a spin under any conditions.

17. Another original design, the Hummer (has/have) an aluminum irrigation pipe for a fuselage.
18. The open-cockpit Hummer (dashs/dashes) along at thirty miles an hour.
19. On a typical convention day air traffic controllers (stay/stayed) busier than those at commercial airports.
20. About 9,000 takeoffs and landings (keep/keeps) them on the alert.

PART B: Reread the sentences in Part A. Now identify any other verbs or verb phrases that you find in each sentence. Not every sentence will have an additional verb.

PART C: Tell whether each verb or verb phrase from Part A and Part B is an action verb or a linking verb. (Review 1.b.1–1.b.5.)

3. Adjectives

PART A: Identify all of the adjectives in the following lines from Shakespeare's *Julius Caesar*. (Do not identify determiners as adjectives.)

1. When the most mighty gods by tokens send
   Such dreadful heralds to astonish us.
2. Nor stony towers, nor walls of brass,
   Nor airless dungeon, nor strong links of iron.
3. My ancestors did from these Roman streets
   The Tarquin drive, when he was called a king.
4. As Caesar loved me, I weep for him; as he was fortunate, I rejoice at it; as he was valiant, I honor him; as he was ambitious, I slew him.

PART B: Identify any proper adjectives among the adjectives you identified in Part A. (Review 1.c.6.)

PART C: For each adjective (except proper adjectives), indicate whether it is in the (a) basic form, (b) comparative form, or (c) superlative form. For those in the basic form, write out their comparative and superlative forms. (Review 1.c.3–1.c.4.)

4. Pronouns

PART A: Select the appropriate pronoun from the parentheses within each of the following sentences. (Review 1.d.)

1. Reference books are vital to my collaborator and (I/me) in our writing.
2. (Who/Whom) does the name of the *Guinness Book of World Records* honor?
3. The man (who/that) produced the first edition of this book was Benjamin Guinness, Earl of Iveagh.
4. The earl soon found (hisself/himself) with a best seller on his hands.
5. Peter Roget, (who/whom) gave his name to *Roget's International Thesaurus*, compiled the first edition in 1852.
6. When you and your friends are looking for synonyms, this book can help (you and they/you and them) to find these words.
7. It is useful for anyone who wants to find the right words for expressing (their/his or her) ideas.
8. Another rich source for (us/we) writers is *Bartlett's Familier Quotations*.
9. When he compiled his first 258-page collection in 1855, John Bartlett had a job of (which/what) he was very proud.
10. He was running a bookstore that had (its/it's) start in Cambridge, Massachusetts.
11. A recent editor of *Bartlett's*, Emily Morison Beck, chose people under thirty for (their/her) staff.
12. Emily Beck believed that (her/she) and her staff should drop some of the old quotations.
13. Dudley Fitts and Elena Levin were among the people (who/whom) Emily Beck turned to for help and advice.
14. Do your classmates use *Webster's New Collegiate Dictionary* for increasing (its/their) vocabularies?
15. My collaborator and (I/me) often use *Webster's* to check our spelling.
16. *Webster's* is widely used; (its/it's) been through several editions since the first edition appeared in 1898.

17. A relative newcomer among dictionaries, *The American Heritage Dictionary of the English Language* made (its/it's) first appearance in 1969.
18. (Whomever/Whoever) prefers proper nouns listed with other words in a dictionary should like this book.
19. *The Columbia Encyclopedia*, which has over 75,000 articles, includes all (them/those) articles in one volume.
20. Its five hundred line drawings and twenty maps add (they're/their) visual impact to the informative entries.

PART B: Reread the sentences in Part A. Now identify any other pronouns that you find in each sentence. Not every sentence will have additional pronouns. (Review 1.d.)

PART C: Now identify the antecedent of each personal, possessive, reflexive, and relative pronoun in Part A. (Review 1.d.1–3 and 1.d.6–7.)

5. Adverbs

PART A: Identify the adverbs in the following sentences. One of the sentences does not have an adverb. (Review 1.f.1.)

1. On August 24, 1724, two treasure-laden Spanish galleons suddenly met their doom off Samana Bay, Hispaniola.
2. The *Guadalupe* and the *Tolosa* were carrying hundreds of tons of mercury and hundreds of passengers to Mexico.
3. The mercury was urgently needed for refining gold.
4. When the hurricane hit, the *Tolosa* managed to anchor at the mouth of the bay and ride out the night safely.
5. At dawn the anchor line parted, and the galleon ricocheted helplessly from shoal to shoal.
6. When the *Tolosa* was disastrously shattered on a coral reef, fewer than forty of the six hundred people on the ship survived.
7. Towering seas and raging winds soon drove the *Guadalupe* onto a sandbar.
8. The 250 tons of mercury stowed below prevented the galleon from capsizing, and most of the people were saved.

9. Two and a half centuries later, in 1976, a salvage company finally located the two historic galleons.

10. Gold jewelry and coins, silver and pewter flatware, and four hundred engraved drinking glasses from the ships can now be seen on display in Santo Domingo.

PART B: Decide in which category each adverb belongs: (a) time, (b) place, (c) manner, or (d) degree. (Review 1.f.1.)

PART C: For each adverb in Part A, indicate the word or words that the adverb modifies. (Review 1.f.1.)

6. Prepositions and Conjunctions

PART A: Identify each of the underlined words and group of words in the following sentences as either a preposition or a conjunction. (Review 1.g and 1.h.)

1. Max Perkins was not only an editor of genius but also a friend of unswerving loyalty to his authors.

2. Among the many young writers Perkins helped were famous authors such as Thomas Wolfe and Marjorie Kinnan Rawlings.

3. Perkins was in his thirties when he became an editor for the publishing firm of Charles Scribner's Sons.

4. The first major author discovered by Perkins was F. Scott Fitzgerald; however, Scribner's was hesitant to publish *This Side of Paradise* at first.

5. Before he edited Fitzgerald's book, Perkins spent most of his time proofreading, although he never really liked the work.

6. After Fitzgerald's book was published, Perkins met Ring Lardner, a popular sportswriter and newspaper columnist.

7. Lardner's first book of stories was greatly improved because Max made him write an introduction to each story.

8. Because of Fitzgerald's admiration for Perkins, he suggested that Ernest Hemingway give Max the manuscript of *The Sun Also Rises*.

9. Reviewers hailed the new author both as a master of dialogue and as a great storyteller.

10. Before the book was selling well, Perkins insisted on a vigorous advertising campaign.

11. After the publication of his first novel, Hemingway spent four years in Europe.

12. In the fall of 1928, Perkins learned about a long manuscript written by a North Carolinian, Thomas Wolfe.

13. When Perkins received the manuscript, it was accompanied by a plea for help from the author.

14. Since Wolfe was traveling in Europe at the time, Perkins had some trouble getting word to him.

15. As soon as Wolfe and Perkins met, they started arguing about the necessity for cutting the manuscript.

16. Neither Wolfe nor Perkins realized how long it would take to get the book into shape.

17. *Look Homeward, Angel* came out in September 1929, and Hemingway's *A Farewell to Arms* followed shortly.

18. Working with three temperamental authors, Perkins also found time to put out Marjorie Kinnan Rawlings' prize-winning novel *The Yearling*.

19. Under the leadership of Max Perkins, Scribner's published seven big best sellers in 1943.

20. Max Perkins never retired; furthermore, he was working on two major works when he died.

PART B: Tell in which category each conjunction you found in Part A belongs: (1) coordinating conjunction, (2) correlative conjunction, (3) subordinating conjunction, (4) conjunctive adverb.

7. Verbals

Identify the verbal in each of the following sentences. Indicate whether it is a gerund, a participle, or an infinitive. One of the sentences has two verbals. (Review 1.j–1.o.)

1. Felisa Rincon was a grown woman when she first disobeyed her father.

2. The privilege of voting had just been given to Puerto Rican women.

3. To vote was Felisa's dream, even though her father forbade it.

4. When Don Enrique saw that his daughter's mind was made up, however, he encouraged her to vote.

5. Dona Felisa was a woman liberated rather late in life, but once she had started, there was no way of stopping her.

6. The suffering poor of San Juan, the capital of Puerto Rico, were her concern.

7. She went into politics because it would give her power to alleviate this condition.

8. Her chosen career was unconventional for a Puerto Rican woman.

9. Eventually, she ran for the office of mayor and was the winning candidate.

10. To govern San Juan became her job for the next twenty years.

8. Verbal Phrases

Identify each verbal phrase in the following sentences. Tell whether it is a gerund phrase, a participial phrase, or an infinitive phrase. Some sentences have more than one verbal phrase. (Review 1.j–1.o.)

1. Reading *Bumblebee Economics* by Bernard Heinrich is an educational experience.

2. Heinrich, a young biologist, advances theories based on his scientific discoveries.

3. He was surprised to discover that bumblebees have a more delicate temperature control system than humans.

4. The bumblebee can choose between letting the environment control its temperature or doing so itself.

5. Originating in the Arctic, the bumblebee has acquired the ability to forage among distant food sources.

6. Heinrich believes that bumblebees are individualists pursuing personal profits.

7. Heinrich feels that honeybee workers waste time in waiting for instructions.

8. Each bumblebee, on the other hand, learns the skills of gathering food by trial and error.

9. Heinrich learned that it takes only a few trips for a young bumblebee to become expert.

10. Studying bumblebees is a fresh way of looking at individual goal setting and the economics of energy control.

9. Complete Sentences vs. Sentence Fragments

PART A: Identify each of the following items as a complete sentence or a sentence fragment. (Review 2.a.)

1. A fool and his money.
2. There is nothing new except what is forgotten.
3. A good worker is known by the work.
4. Time is of the essence.
5. Gives the best polish.
6. That does nobody good.
7. Kilroy was here.
8. Is stranger than fiction.
9. You can't catch the wind in a net.
10. Has a silver lining.
11. Had it been a bear.
12. Enough is as good as a feast.
13. Silence gives.
14. Experience is the creator of wisdom.
15. All is not gold that.
16. When poverty comes in at the door.
17. Jumps over the lazy dog.
18. It never rains but.
19. An apple a day.
20. Proverbs are short sentences drawn from long experience.

PART B: Look again at each sentence fragment that you identified in Part A. Make each fragment into a complete sentence. You can complete each fragment by quoting the famous saying or by adding your own words. (Review 2.a.)

10. Subjects and Predicates; Subject-Verb Agreement

PART A: Identify the complete subject and simple subject in each of the following sentences. (Review 2.b.)

1. All children (loves/love) music.
2. Many cultures (uses/use) some music for story-telling.
3. Music (is/are) really a universal language.
4. The children of West Africa (enjoys/enjoy) music.
5. They (has/have) music instead of television.
6. Most of the children in the Dagomba tribe (learns/learn) social habits and personal discipline through music.
7. Among the Dagombas music-making (includes/include) the study of folklore and history.
8. Five hundred years of history (is/are) studied by the musicians.
9. The best Dagomba musicians (plays/play) the drums.
10. To learn drumming (require/requires) patience.
11. A young drummer's lessons (begins/begin) with the names of the tribe's leaders.
12. Each of these chiefs (has/have) his own song.
13. *Nanto Nimdi* (is/are) the name of one historical dance.
14. (There is/There are) several kinds of drums.
15. The most common kind (seems/seem) to be the "talking drum."
16. It (is/are) shaped like an hourglass.
17. Five-gallon oil drums and evaporated milk cans (makes/make) interesting drums.
18. A flute player or fiddler often (accompanies/accompany) the drummers.
19. Many a club (is/are) formed by Africans for dancing.
20. Every Dagomba child (grows/grow) up with music.

PART B: Select the appropriate form of the action verb, linking verb, or auxiliary from the parentheses in each of the preceding sentences. Your choice must agree in number with the subject of the sentence. (Review 1.b.1–1.b.10.)

11. Direct Objects, Indirect Objects, Predicate Nominatives, Predicate Adjectives

Identify the direct objects, indirect objects, predicate nominatives, and predicate adjectives in the following sentences. (Review 2.j–2.l.2.)

1. A stitch in time saves nine.
2. Brevity is the soul of wit.
3. Necessity is the mother of invention.
4. Slow and steady wins the race.
5. A word to the wise is sufficient.
6. You cannot teach an old dog new tricks.
7. Haste makes waste.
8. Great men are not always wise.
9. A friend in need is a friend indeed.
10. On the day of victory, no one is tired.

12. Direct Objects and Complements

All of the items below are incomplete sentences. They are missing a direct object of the verb or a complement (a predicate nominative or a predicate adjective). For each sentence select a word to complete the sentence. Then tell whether that word is (1) a direct object of the verb; or (2) a predicate nominative; or (3) a predicate adjective. (Review 2.j–2.l.2.)

1. Classical music is usually
2. The concert includes
3. The conductor requires
4. The violinist seems
5. The performers become
6. The instruments are
7. The symphony has
8. The audience demands
9. The music that you hear is
10. Many young people prefer

13. Subordinate Clauses and Main Clauses; Kinds of Sentences

PART A: Identify the main clauses and subordinate clauses in the following sentences. (Review 2.m–2.o.)

1. He was also carrying one red rose, which he handed to Charlotte without looking at her.—Joan Didion
2. As I turned, I caught a glimpse of a convulsed face and frantic eyes.—Sir Arthur Conan Doyle
3. She had not been swayed by all the evidence against him. —Theodore Dreiser
4. Whistler had not yet made his appearance in London, but the others did quite as well.—Henry Adams
5. Carpentier's training camp was near Great Neck, which was my home, and I got pretty well acquainted with him. —Ring Lardner
6. Daisy put her arm through his abruptly, but he seemed absorbed in what he had just said.—F. Scott Fitzgerald
7. When Aunt Fanny came up, he turned back to the hedge and raised his clipper again.—Shirley Jackson
8. In the farm-house ahead of him, a light was shining as he peered ahead, and his heart gave another painful movement.—Hamlin Garland
9. People drooped and shambled, but the girls carried themselves tall and walked a straight line, as befitted young heiresses on their afternoon promenade.—Dorothy Parker
10. The spring evening was chilly, and Waythorn invited his guest to draw up his chair to the fire.—Edith Wharton

PART B: Decide whether each of the preceding sentences is a simple sentence, a compound sentence, a complex sentence, or a compound-complex sentence. (Review 2.v.)

14. Subordinate Clauses

PART A: Identify each subordinate clause in the following sentences. (Review 2.o.)

1. The safety bicycle, which was different from the old high wheeler, was invented in the 1890s.
2. Because anyone could ride the safety bicycle, it quickly became very popular.
3. Another reason for its popularity was that traveling by horse was slow.
4. While the bicycle craze lasted, songs were written about bicycles.
5. Magazines that specialized in bicycles were widely read.
6. Articles by doctors explained why bicycle riding was healthful.
7. Bicycles were especially welcome to young people, who had few other amusements.
8. Schools for riding taught beginners how a bicycle could be ridden safely.
9. Since they were expensive, bicycles were prized by young children.
10. The great bicycle craze ended when automobiles were introduced.

PART B: Tell whether each subordinate clause in the preceding sentences is a noun clause, an adjective clause, or an adverb clause. (Review 2.o–2.t.)

15. Capitalization, Semicolons, Colons, Apostrophes, Quotation Marks, Italics, and Parentheses

Rewrite the following paragraphs, correcting all errors in capitalization and the use of semicolons, colons, apostrophes, quotation marks, italics, and parentheses. You should find twenty-five errors. (Review 7.a, 7.h, 7.i, and 7.k–7.n.)

1   The War of 1812 (1812–1814 is sometimes called the Great
2 Sea war because many of it's most famous battles were
3 naval battles. these battles were usually duels between two
4 ships. The United States relied on three frigates the *Consti-*
5 *tution*, the *President*, and the *United States*.

6   The *Constitution* was also known as "Old Ironsides be-
7 cause it's hull was especially strong. The ships bolts came
8 from Paul Reveres shop. In 1812 the *Constitution* defeated
9 the british ship *Guerrière* in a battle off halifax, a City in
10 Nova Scotia.
11   Another American frigate, the *United States*, captured
12 the British ship Macedonian. In 1815 the captain of the
13 *United States*, Stephen Decatur, fought another battle. He
14 escaped from three British ships, then he defeated a
15 fourth. Decatur did not know that the treaty of Ghent,
16 ending the war, had already been signed.
17   It was during the War of 1812 that commander Oliver
18 Hazard Perry sent this famous message "We have met the
19 enemy, and they are ours'." Dont give up the ship" is an-
20 other well-known quotation from the war. Even more fa-
21 mous is The Star-Spangled Banner. Our national anthem
22 was written by Francis Scott Key as he watched British
23 ships shell fort McHenry in Baltimore. (they were not able
24 to capture the fort.) These and other events of the Great
25 Sea war are related in the book Great Naval Battles, by
26 Oliver Warner.

16. Periods, Question Marks, Exclamation Points, Commas, Hyphens, Abbreviations, and Numbers and Numerals

Rewrite the following paragraphs, correcting all errors in the use of periods, question marks, exclamation points, commas, hyphens, abbreviations and numbers and numerals. You should find twenty-five errors. (Review 7.b–7.g and 7.j.)

1   Dr Richard Moriarty was on duty in the emergency room
2 of Children's Hospital in Pittsburgh, when three year old
3 Sarah was admitted. Before coming to Children's she had
4 been treated for poisoning at a smaller hospital, where the
5 drs. had given her syrup of ipecac Something went wrong
6 however. 3 days later Sarah was dead!
7   The pills, that Sarah had swallowed, were not even poi-
8 sonous. Moriarty wondered why the first doctors who had

9   treated her had not known this? What was wrong with
10   their poison control system. A little research on
11   Moriarty's part revealed that there was no such system in
12   any Pittsburgh hospital including his own.
13   Moriarty's life work began with this discovery although
14   he did not realize it at the time. He is the founder and
15   director of the National Poison Control Network which is a
16   well established association of poison control centers. Its
17   purpose is 2-fold: to treat poison cases and to educate the
18   public. Parents are advised for example to keep a closer eye
19   on small children right before mealtime as most poison-
20   ings occur when youngsters are hungry, or thirsty. Parents
21   should also identify poisonous houseplants, and label
22   them. If a child has swallowed a possibly poisonous sub-
23   stance the best course of action is, to call a poison control
24   center for advice.

INDEX

The boxed material in Sections 1, 2, 3, and 7 is indexed here under three heads: "Avoiding Errors," "Punctuation," and "Spelling."

AVOIDING ERRORS

PUNCTUATION

SPELLING

Direct questions, question marks
at the end of, 355
Direct quotations
  capitalization of, 331, 395
  interrupted, 396
  quotation marks for, 395–397
  See also Quotation marks
discover, invent, 414
Dividing words at the end of a
  line, 326, 385–386
do, doe, dough, 304
do, due, dew, 304
doesn't, don't, 414
done, 414
Double comparison, 49, 434
Double negative, 83, 432
dough, doe, do, 304
Dr., 615, 616
due, do, dew, 304

each other, one another, 414
Editing
  a composition, 549–550
  first draft of research reports,
    601–602
  paragraphs, 490
Editing chart, 429–439
Editing signals, 429–441
edition, addition, 303
ei or *ie*, spelling rules for, 289
either . . . or, 420
Either-or thinking, 568
Elliptical adverb clauses, 156–157
Encyclopedias, 582–583
English language
  new words in, 236–237
  origins of, 233–234
Envelopes for business letters,
  619–620
Epigraph, 587
Epilogue, 588
Errors, 427–445
  in case, 430–431
  in clarity and style, 436–439
  in completing and joining
    clauses, 435–436
  with the negative, 432
  with parts of speech, 432–433

in persuasive writing and
  speaking, 567–570
with pronouns, 431–432
in subject-verb agreement,
  429–430
See also "Avoiding Errors" list
  on page 665
Essay questions, 633–634
Essays. *See* Compositions
Essential (restrictive) clauses,
  160–161
  commas with, 214, 367
Etymology, 233–234, 322–323
Evidence, 558–563
Examples, developing topic
  sentences with, 466, 471
Exclamation points, 356
  with quotation marks, 399
Explanation of process
  in compositions, 543
  logical connectives in, 511–512,
    514
  model for, 511–512
  ordering steps in, 513–514
  paragraphs, 487–488
Expletives, 115
Exposition (expository writing),
  493, 505–514
  comparison/contrast in,
    505–509
  explanation of process in,
    511–514
Expository paragraphs, 483–488
Extra (nonessential) clauses,
  160–161, 214
  commas with, 367
Extra expressions, commas with,
  373–375

Facts
  authoritative statements and,
    561–562
  developing topic sentences
    with, 467–468, 471
  in introductions to
    compositions, 546
  opinion versus, 559–562
  sound opinions and, 560–561

in explanation of process,
511–512, 514
in narrative writing, 494–495,
497
as transitions between
paragraphs, 545
Logical reasoning process,
562–566
errors in, 567–570

Macmillan Dictionary, 316
Magazines, 580–581, 586–587
Main clauses, 146–149
commas with, 194, 364–366
in series, 363
in compound sentences,
148–149
semicolons between, 149, 365,
366, 380–381
Main entry, 576
Mapping notes, 631–632
Maps, 583
Measurements, figures
(numerals) for writing, 351
me, I, after linking verbs, 141
meat, meet, 305
Mechanics of writing, 329–407
See also Capitalization;
specific marks of
punctuation
Metaphors, 241
Microforms, 586–587
might of, could of, 413
Misplaced modifiers, 102, 225
Mispronunciation, misspelling
and, 281–282
Miss, 347
Misspelling. *See* Spelling
Modifiers
dangling, 102, 225, 436
misplaced, 102, 225
varying the position of,
192–193
See also Adjectives; Adverbs
Money, figures (numerals) for
writing, 351
moral, morale, 419

morning, mourning, 306
most, almost, 419
Mr., 347, 615, 616
Mrs., 347, 615, 616
Ms., 347, 616
Multiple-choice questions,
633–644
analogy questions, 637
antonym questions, 635–636
reading-comprehension
questions, 641–644
sentence-completion
questions, 638–640
synonym questions, 634–635
Multi-word verbs, 318

Names. *See* Proper nouns
Narration (narrative writing),
492–497
comparison/contrast writing
and, 505
in compositions, 543
logical connectives in,
494–495, 497
model for, 494–495
sequencing of events in, 496
Narrative paragraphs, 480–481
Negative words as adverbs, 79
See also Double negatives
neither . . . nor, 420
Newspapers, 580–581, 586–587
New words, 236–237
Nominative (subjective) case, 55,
430–431
predicate pronouns in, 141
Nonessential appositives,
commas with, 373
Nonessential (nonrestrictive or
extra) clauses, 160–161, 214
commas with, 367
nor, or, 420
See also Correlative
conjunctions
Notes
for compositions, 534, 535
methods for taking, 618–631
for research reports, 597–598

with other marks of
punctuation, 399
single, 396
for titles of short works, 398
Quotations
books of, 584
See also Direct quotations;
Indirect quotations

rain, reign, rein, 307
raise, rise, 420
*Readers' Guide to Periodical
Literature,* 580-581
Reading-comprehension
questions, 641-644
Reading skills, 627-628
Reasoning process, 562-570
errors in, 567-570
reason is because, 420
Red herring, 567-568
Reference materials, 580-586
almanacs, 583
atlases, 583
encyclopedias, 582-583
newspapers and periodicals,
580-581, 586-587
*Readers' Guide to Periodical
Literature,* 580-581
specialized books, 584-585
See also Dictionaries
Reflexive pronouns, 53, 62
regardless, irregardless, 417
Regular verbs, 19
rein, reign, rain, 307
Relative pronouns, 54, 66-68,
153
Research report, 590-612
beginning research for,
592-593
checklist for, 612
final draft of, 605
finding information for, 595
first draft for, 600-602
footnotes in, 602-604
formal outlines for, 599-600
sample, 605-612
taking notes for, 597-598
topic for, 591-592

working bibliography for, 596
working outline for, 593-594
respectfully, respectively, 420
Restrictive (essential) clauses,
160-161, 367
Revising
first drafts, 548-549
paragraphs, 489
right, rite, write, 307
rob, steal, 421
role, roll, 307
Roman numerals, 538
Roots, 243-245
Rough draft. *See* First draft
rout, route, 307
Run-on sentences, 91, 149, 199,
366, 435

Sagging subjects, 437
Salutations
of business letters, 616-617
commas after, 360
says, said, 422
Scholastic Aptitude Test (SAT),
645
Schwa sound, 287-288, 320
Scientific names, in dictionaries,
324
Scientific reference books, 585
seam, seem, 307
Secondary (light) stress, 320-321
Second-person pronouns, 56
See also cards, 577
See cards, 577
seeing as how, 422
seem, seam, 307
Semicolons, 380-382
in compound sentences, 149
with conjunctive adverbs, 198
between main clauses, 149,
365, 366, 380-381
purposes of, 380
with quotation marks, 399
for separating expressions
containing commas, 382
Sentence adverbs, 77
Sentence combining
with adjective clauses, 215-217

Sentence combining (*Continued*)
with adverb clauses that tell
"when," 203–205
with adverb clauses that tell
"where" or "how," 207–208
with adverb clauses that tell
"why," or state a condition,
210–211
with appositives, 218–219
with noun clauses, 220–222
with participial phrases,
225–226
Sentences completers. *See* Direct
objects; Indirect objects;
Subject complements
Sentence-completion questions,
638–640
Sentence fragments, 112, 153,
435
Sentences
capitalization of, 331
clauses distinguished from,
145
clauses of (*see* Clauses)
command (imperative), 111,
124, 354, 356, 357
complex (*see* Complex
sentences)
compound (*see* Compound
sentences)
compound-complex, 152, 169,
222–223
definition of, 110
diagraming (*see* Diagraming)
parts of (*see* Parts of a
sentence)
period at the end of, 354
predicate of (*see* Predicate)
question, 124–125
run-on (comma splice), 91,
149, 199, 366, 435
simple, 148, 168, 182–185
statement (declarative), 124
subject of (*see* Subjects)
topic (*see* Topic sentences)
serf, surf, 308
Series
commas with items in,
361–363

consistent use of prepositions
in, 90
Series entry, 577
set, sit, 422
Silent consonants, 285–286
Similes, 241
Simple predicate, 112
Simple sentences, 148, 168
expanding, 183–185
kinds of, 183
writing, 182–185
Simple subjects, 116–119
sit, set, 422
so, 91
Sound opinions, 560–561
Sounds (*see* Pronunciation)
Sources for research reports, 595
footnote information on, 602
See also Reference materials
Specifics, developing topic
sentences with, 463–472
Spelling, 279–314
adding prefixes, 290–291
adding suffixes, 291–292
-cede, -ceed, or *-sede*, 290
comparative and superlative
forms of adjectives, 47
dictionary information on,
325
frequently misspelled words,
310–314
homophones, 302–309
noun plurals, 297–299
plurals of numbers and
numerals, 535
possessives, 300–301
present-tense verbs, 26
pronunciation and, 281–288
suggestions for improving
your, 280–281
Split infinitives, 106
Sr., 347
Statement of purpose, 532–533,
536
Statement sentences, 124
stationary, stationery, 308
Statistics
developing topic sentences
with, 467–468, 471

in introductions to
compositions, 546
steal, rob, 421
steal, steel, 308
Stereotypes, 565–566
Stress marks, 320–321
Study skills, 626–631
Subject cards, 574–575
Subject complements, 139–143
predicate adjectives, 142
predicate adverbs, 143
predicate nominatives, 139–141
Subject Index, 575
Subjective (nominative) case, 55,
430–431
predicate pronouns in, 141
Subject labels, 327
Subjects
clear, 228, 437–438
in command sentences, 111
complete, 116–117
compound, 126–128, 377
definition of, 111
prepositional phrases in, 133
sagging, 437
simple, 116–119
See also Subject-verb
agreement
Subject-verb agreement, 117
in commands and questions,
124–125
with compound subjects,
127–128
errors in, 429–430
with indefinite pronouns, 69
with intervening expressions,
129–130
in sentences beginning with
there or adverbs of place, 121
with special subjects, 122–123
Subordinate clauses, 146–147,
150–151
adjective clauses, 159–161
adverb clauses, 155–157
in complex sentences (*see*
Complex sentences)
in compound-complex
sentences, 222–223
noun clauses, 163–164

who versus *whom* in, 166–167
See also Subordinators
Subordinating conjunctions,
95–96, 152, 201–202
Subordinators, 150–152
for adjective clauses, 159, 213
for adverb clauses, 155–156,
202, 205, 206, 208, 209
for noun clauses, 164, 220
See also Subordinating
conjunctions
Suffixes
derivational, 253–267
dividing words with, 385, 386
patterns of, 258–267
spelling words with, 291–292
Superlative adjectives, 44, 47,
434
Superlative adverbs, 79
surf, serf, 308
Syllabification, 326
Synonym questions, 634–635
Synonyms, 328, 634

Table of contents, 588
take, bring, 413
teach, learn, 419
Tenses of verbs. *See* Time and
tenses of verbs
Term papers. *See* Research
reports
Testimonial, 569–570
Test questions, 633–645
Textbooks, skills for reading,
627–628
than, case of pronouns after, 59,
431
that, with essential clauses,
160–161
that, which, as relative
pronouns, 67, 431
the, 72
their, there, they're, 308
theirselves, 62, 434
there
diagraming sentences
beginning with, 171

LIST OF REFERENCE KEYS

There are several ways for you to become familiar with the content of each section of this book. First, there is the Table of Contents. Second, there is the title page of each section, listing all the main divisions of the section. Third, there is the following list of reference keys.

Each main head within a section is marked by a reference key. Each subhead is marked by another key. The main keys are also used as tabs on the top of right-hand pages to help you locate material.

SAMPLE FROM SECTION 7, "CAPITALIZATION AND PUNCTUATION"

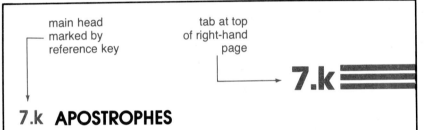

main head
marked by
reference key

tab at top
of right-hand
page

7.k

7.k APOSTROPHES

Apostrophes are used to form the possessive of nouns and indefinite pronouns; to form contractions; and to form the plural of letters, numbers, signs, and words used as words.

subhead marked
by another
reference key

7.k.1 Apostrophes for the possessive

Remember that *possessive* means "belonging to." The expression *Mary's book* means "the book that belongs to Mary." The apostrophe is often used in showing that something belongs to someone.

1. **nouns not ending in s**
Use the apostrophe and *s* to form the possessive of singular and plural nouns not ending in *s*. This rule applies to both common and proper nouns.

Keys

── PARTS OF SPEECH ──────

PARTS OF A SENTENCE

WRITING SENTENCES

VOCABULARY

SPELLING

THE DICTIONARY

CAPITALIZATION AND PUNCTUATION

GLOSSARY OF USAGE PROBLEMS

CATCHING, CLASSIFYING, AND CORRECTING ERRORS

THE PARAGRAPH

PATTERNS OF THINKING AND WRITING

THE COMPOSITION

CLEAR THINKING AND PERSUASION

LIBRARIES AND INFORMATION

EDITING SIGNALS AND REFERENCE KEYS

	Editing Signal	See Editing Chart
Editing for grammar and clarity		
Error in subject-verb agreement	*agree*	429–430
Error in case	*case*	430–431
Error with pronoun reference	*ref*	431–432
Error with the negative	*neg*	432
Error in noun plurals	*pl*	432
Error in possessive	*poss*	433
Error in verb tense	*tense*	433
Error in comparative, superlative	*adj*	434
Error in reflexive pronoun	*pro*	434
Error with *this* or *them*	*pro*	435
Error with *-ly* adverb	*adv*	435
Using commas instead of end marks	*run-on*	435
Incomplete sentences	*frag*	435
Misusing conjunctions	*conj*	436
Shift in voice	*voice*	436
Dangling elements	*dangling*	436
Misplaced elements	*misplaced*	436–437
Sagging sentences	*sag*	437–439
Wordiness	*wordy*	439

	Editing Signal	See Reference Key
Editing for spelling	*sp*	5.a–5.d
Editing for capitalization	*cap*	7.a.1–7.a.7
Editing for punctuation	*p*	7.b–7.n
Editing paragraphs and compositions		
Weak topic sentence	*t. s.*	10.c
Topic sentence poorly supported	*support*	10.d–10.i
Lack of unity	*unity*	10.j
Lack of coherence	*cohere*	10.k
New paragraph	*¶*	10.j
Weak introduction	*intro*	12.k
Weak sequencing of details	*seq*	11.c, 11.f, 11.i, 11.l
Weak transitions	*trans*	12.j
Weak conclusion	*conclusion*	12.l

Leroy

3069 Turner Dr

San Jose Calif

95148